D1596491

The Lonely Cold War of Pope Pius XII

The Lonely Cold War of Pope Pius XII

The Roman Catholic Church and the Division of Europe, 1943–1950

PETER C. KENT

McGill-Queen's University Press
Montreal & Kingston · London · Ithaca

© McGill-Queen's University Press 2002
ISBN 0-7735-2326-X

Legal deposit second quarter 2002
Bibliothèque nationale du Québec

Printed in Canada on acid-free paper that is 100%
ancient forest free (100% post-consumer recycled),
processed chlorine free, and printed with vegetable-
based, low VOC inks.

This book has been published with the help of grants
from the Humanities and Social Sciences Federation of
Canada, using funds provided by the Social Sciences and
Humanities Research Council of Canada, and the University of New Brunswick.

McGill-Queen's University Press acknowledges the
financial support of the Government of Canada through
the Book Publishing Industry Development Program
(BPIDP) for its publishing activities. It also acknowledges
the support of the Canada Council for the Arts for its
publishing program.

**National Library of Canada Cataloguing in Publication
Data**

Kent, Peter C., 1938–
 The lonely Cold War of Pope Pius XII : the Roman
 Catholic Church and the division of Europe, 1943–1950
 Includes bibliographical references and index.
 ISBN 0-7735-2326-X
 1. Christianity and politics—Catholic Church—History
 —20th century. 2. Communism and Christianity—
 Catholic Church. 3. Europe—Politics and govern-
 ment—1945– . 4. Papacy—History—1929–1945.
 5. Pius XII, Pope, 1876-1958. I. Title.

BX1378.K43 2002   327.456'34   C2001-902833-4

Typeset in 10/12 Sabon by True to Type

Contents

Preface

This study marks the culmination of a twenty-year period, during which my research and writing advanced in conjunction with teaching responsibilities and a career in university administration, first as chair of the Department of History and then as dean of the Faculty of Arts at the University of New Brunswick. I believe that the experience of administration has enhanced my ability to attend to tasks of research and writing just as, at the same time, it has reduced the time available for the completion of those tasks. I am satisfied that the completion of this project demonstrates the complementarity of research, teaching, and administration for those who choose to labour in the fields of academe.

I have been fortunate in having a supportive context for my research and writing. The Department of History of the University of New Brunswick is a model of collegiality and respect, where the work and the contributions of each member have been the concern and interest of all. I have also been supported by the enlightened policy of the University of New Brunswick which believes that its deans should also be scholars and has provided both the resources and the time, including sabbatical leaves at the conclusion of decanal terms, to support and encourage scholarship.

Funding for this project has been provided by the Social Science and Humanities Research Council of Canada and by the University of New Brunswick. Its publication has been made possible by a subsidy from the Aid to Publications Program of the Social Sciences and Humanities Federation of Canada.

In addition to my colleagues and students at the University of New Brunswick, I wish to thank the staffs of the Public Record Office in London, the archives of the Ministero degli Affari Esteri in Rome, the archives of the Ministère des Affaires Étrangères in Paris, the National Archives and Records Administration and the archives of the United States Catholic Conference in Washington, the archives of the Diocese of St Augustine in Jacksonville, Florida, the archives of the Diocese of Savannah, Georgia, and the National Archives of Canada in Ottawa. I also wish to thank Charles Gallagher and Richard Wiggers for providing me with copies of their unpublished manuscripts, James E. Miller for telling me of the existence of the archives of the National Catholic Welfare Conference, and the following scholars for their interest in and support for the project: John Conway, Frank Coppa, Gerald Fogarty, the late Peter Hebblethwaite, John Pollard, Andrea Riccardi, and Stewart Stehlin.

My wife, Wendy, and son, Darryl, have also lived with this project over the years and have not objected when it has been the occasion for sabbatical leaves in London, Paris, and Rome.

Peter C. Kent

Pope Pius XII in 1945 (AP/Wide World Photos)

Monsignor Domenico Tardini, Vatican undersecretary of state
(AP/Wide World Photos)

Monsignor Giovanni Battista Montini, Vatican undersecretary of state
(AP/Wide World Photos)

Myron C. Taylor, the American president's personal representative to the
pope (right, standing), speaks during a civic luncheon given by the City of
New York in honour of visiting Italian Prime Minister Alcide de Gasperi
(centre), while the Archbishop of New York, Francis Cardinal Spellman
(left), listens (AP/Wide World Photos)

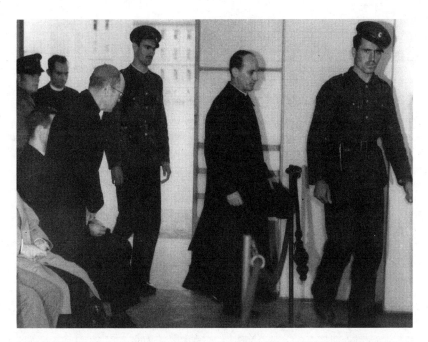

Bishop Joseph Hurley, the regent of the Apostolic Nunciature in Yugoslavia, bows as Monsignor Aloysius Stepinac, archbishop of Zagreb, is led into the courtroom for his 1946 trial. (Catholic News Service)

Joszef Cardinal Mindszenty, prince-primate of Hungary, in 1946
(AP/Wide World Photos)

Archbishop Josef Beran, primate of Czechoslovakia, converses with
Premier Klement Gottwald during the political crisis of February 1948
(AP/Wide World Photos)

PART ONE

The Church and the Challenge of Communism

Introduction

It was the election of the archbishop of Cracow, Karol Wojtyla, as Pope John Paul II in 1978 that instigated the public process leading to the end of the Cold War and the break-up of the Soviet Union. Working closely with President Ronald Reagan of the United States, the Holy See exerted sufficient pressure on the communist bloc to force a significant reevaluation of its continued effectiveness. When Mikhail Gorbachev became Soviet president, he recognized the need for substantial change as a result of the increasing social and economic paralysis within the Soviet bloc. Decisions were accordingly made to release the nations of eastern Europe from Soviet control and to terminate the hostility between the power blocs which had marked the latter half of the twentieth century. The pressure for change gathered its own momentum, fomenting revolutions in many parts of eastern Europe and culminating in the symbolic destruction of the Berlin Wall in 1989. The conclusion of a German peace treaty in 1990 and the reunification of that country effectively ended the division of Europe which had been the central feature and locus of conflict of the Cold War.[1]

As the Holy See was a major player in the events leading to the end of the Cold War, the question must be asked about its role in the initiation of that conflict. Did Pope Pius XII, who reigned from 1939 to 1958, play as central a role in determining the course of international events in the 1940s as his successor John Paul II played in the 1980s? Certainly, any cursory reading of the history of the Roman Catholic Church in the twentieth century would place that institution among the first ranks of the cold warriors. Fundamentally opposed to concepts of historical materialism from their early definition by Karl Marx in the nineteenth century, the church actively denounced the pernicious threat of atheistic Bolshevism following its seizure of power in Russia in 1917. Throughout the twentieth century, the Catholic Church provided both the rhetoric and the leadership for the anti-communist cause. Wherever communism and the radical left came to power, the church was usually its main target and its main victim. This was the case in Mexico in the 1920s, in Spain under the Second Republic in the 1930s, and it was the case in the Soviet Union and eastern Europe in the 1940s and 1950s. The church provided both the victims and the martyrs of the Cold War, most notably Cardinal Joszef Mindszenty of Hungary, locked up in a communist prison for seven years before being released to spend the next fourteen years hiding in the American embassy in Budapest. The culture of Catholic anti-communism facilitated Senator Joseph McCarthy's hunt for the "enemy within" in the 1950s, and gave support for the American war effort in Vietnam under the leadership of New York's Francis Cardinal Spellman and other prelates in the 1960s. As the first pope of the Cold War, Pius XII constantly warned about the threat of communism and worried about the future of his church in the event of the extension of communist power across the entire European continent.

If the Roman Catholic Church and Pope Pius XII were so adamantly opposed to communism, how much responsibility do they bear for the division of Europe and the world in the latter half of the 1940s? How close a collaboration existed between Rome and Washington after the Second World War and did the policy of containment as enunciated by President Harry Truman in 1947 accord with the goals of the Vatican? Was there a working alliance between the American government and the Holy See to resist the extension of communism and, if so, how effectively did it operate? Can the triumphal celebration of the Holy Year of 1950 also be read as a celebration of the anti-communist alliance of the West behind the leadership of the United States with the assistance of the Catholic Church? This study is designed to provide answers to these questions.

Initially, the study is complicated by a matter of definition. Just as the historic Soviet bloc has not been viewed for many years as a functioning monolith, so too must the internal complexity of the Roman Catholic Church be recognized in any discussion of its role in the Cold War. While the pope, as Bishop of Rome and the apostolic successor of St Peter, is leader of the church and, as such, infallible when speaking *ex cathedra* on matters of faith and morals, he is not the totality of the church. While he gives guidance and leadership to his flock and is advised by the bureaucracy of the Roman Curia, the real life of the church is found among the bishops, clergy, and laity of the various nations and cultures where the church is represented. In each national context, the church has a life of its own, shaped by the cultural ethos and the historic values of that community, which may accord to a greater or lesser degree with directives emanating from Rome. While conjoined by the 1870 Vatican Council to accept unquestioningly papal decisions on matters of faith and morals, the branches of the church are otherwise able to shape and develop their own destiny. This has meant the existence of a continuous tension between Roman directives and the needs of individual communities as interpreted by national hierarchies. It has led to attempts by national hierarchies to influence papal policy, just as it has seen moves by the pope to ensure the implementation of central policies by the appointment of sympathetic bishops. Any understanding and explanation of the role of the Roman Catholic Church during the Second World War and the early years of the Cold War must allow for the internal complexity of this institution. To analyse the role of the church in the development of the Cold War, this study will examine both the policy and the international stance of the papacy as well as the way in which it had an impact on or was influenced by the clergy and laity of individual countries. In this way, the study will attempt to assess the role of both the individual branches of the Catholic Church and the papacy in the formative years of the Cold War.

This study postulates that while the Roman Catholic Church provided some of the ideological rhetoric of the Cold War, the Holy See frequently promoted an agenda which ran counter to the goals of the European peoples and the American government. Consequently, the only time between 1945 and 1950 when there was a real concordance of policy between Washington and papal Rome was the period leading up to the Italian election of April 1948. The Holy See was not in sympathy with the policy of containment which separated Catholic Europeans of the West from Catholic Europeans of the East for forty years and resulted in extensive persecution of the church in eastern Europe. In 1948 and 1949, when Communist rulers initiated the restriction and persecution of the east European church, the Holy See found that it received no help and little sympathy from policy-makers in Washington. In fact, by 1949 Pius XII was induced to fight his own religious cold war, using excommunication, one of the few weapons available to him, in a desperate move to shore up the position of the church in eastern Europe. The image of the church triumphant in the Holy Year of 1950 belies the fact that, just as Pius XII stood alone at the head of his church, he also stood alone in pursuing his conception of the Cold War with scant sympathy or assistance from the government of the United States.

One of the limitations on the historian of the Holy See in the twentieth century is that, as late as the election of John Paul II in 1978, it was only possible to have access to materials in the Vatican Archives prior to the 1903 death of Pope Leo XIII. During the 1980s John Paul II opened the archives to 1922, at the end of the reign of Benedict XV, and that has remained the limit of archival access to the present day (2001).

The exception to this restriction is the authorized eleven-volume edition of documents drawn from the Vatican Archives for the period of the Second World War. Within five years of the death of Pius XII, that pope was represented on stage in Rolf Hochhuth's 1963 play, *Der Stellvertreter*, translated into English as *The Representative* or *The Deputy*. In contrast to the posthumous public adulation of the late pope, this play charged him with failure to protest the butchery of Hitler's Holocaust. It depicted Pius XII as a narrow bureaucrat, more concerned about the property and investments of the church than about the heinous crimes of the Nazis. In reaction to these accusations, the Holy See assigned four scholars the task of preparing an edited collection of Vatican documents on the activities of the Roman Catholic Church and the Vatican during the Second World War. Published between 1965 and 1981, the *Actes et Documents du Saint Siège Relatifs à la Seconde Guerre Mondiale* has had a major influence on writing the history of the pontificate of Pius XII.

The availability of this official Vatican documentation has meant that writing on Pius XII has been dominated by that pope's alleged sin of omission in not speaking out forcefully and specifically against the horrors of the Holocaust. On this matter, Pius has had both his critics and his defenders.[2] As a result of this concentration on the first six years of the Pacelli pontificate, however, there is relatively less scholarship on the remaining thirteen years of his nineteen-year reign, and no recent biography of the man and the pope. In many ways, the Polish scholar Oscar Halecki in his biography of 1951, *Eugenio Pacelli: Pope of Peace*, was able to present a balanced discussion of the life and career to that date, restricted as he was for his sources to papal pronouncements and documents already in the public domain.

Outside the period of the Second World War, the Vatican record is inaccessible. In their hunt for alternative sources on this pontificate, some historians have looked to domestic and ecclesiastical archives, especially within Italy, as evidenced by the work of Andrea Riccardi and of scholars in the collections edited by him.[3] Other scholars have turned to the diplomatic record. The opening of foreign ministry archives after a thirty-year period of closure has meant that, starting in 1975, the reports of diplomats accredited to the Holy See for the period after 1945 became accessible in the major archives of Europe and North America.

The diplomatic archives provide rich and varied materials for the study of Vatican history in the mid-twentieth century. Not only do these archives contain reports of negotiations and formal discussions between the accredited diplomats and the pope and representatives of the Vatican Secretariat of State, but they also include details of informal and unofficial conversations between these diplomats, Vatican officials, and diplomats of other nationalities accredited to the pope. Many of these conversations contain speculation about the course and direction of current Vatican policy. The diplomats also inform their home governments about important speeches, sermons, and pronouncements made by church leaders, frequently enclosing translations of these public documents. They also report on important articles in the Vatican newspaper, the *Osservatore Romano*, the Jesuit journal, *Civiltà Cattolica*, and other organs of the Catholic press, frequently including translations of these articles in their dispatches.

The diplomatic archives can be used to complement the Vatican record for the Second World War with other corroborative materials, as Italo Garzia has done in *Pio XII e L'Italia nella Seconda Guerra Mondiale* As a result of this documentation, scholars are now able to extend serious study of Pius XII beyond the period of the war. The useful collection of documents on Myron C. Taylor's mission to the pope, drawn from the American archives to be edited and translated into Italian by Ennio Di Nolfo,[4] has provided an important additional published source for the Pacelli pontificate. Making good use of the diplomatic record, Hanjakob Stehle and Andrea Riccardi have examined Vatican relations with the Soviet Union during the reign of Pius XII.[5] Anthony Rhodes, in turn, has used similar sources for his more general study of *The Vatican in the Age of the Cold War, 1945–1980*. The early sections of Peter Hebblethwaite's fine biographies of John XXIII and Paul VI have been based on an extensive use of archives from the pontificate of Pius XII.[6]

The present study is based primarily on the diplomatic record, consisting of the reports and perceptions of diplomats accredited to the Holy See who were in constant and regular contact with papal officials. It is also based on diplomatic reports on the position and role of the Catholic Church in various countries of Europe and North America. National archives in Rome, Paris, London, Washington, and

Ottawa have been consulted, along with such relevant ecclesiastical records as are available to scholars.

The central interpretive issue in the current scholarship is the degree to which Pope Pius XII was an active agent in shaping the destiny of the church during the Second World War and after. To what extent did he act on a predetermined political agenda? Hanjakob Stehle indicates that the reign of Pius XII, in contrast to that of his predecessor, was haunted by the indecision of the pontiff, who appeared incapable of making decisions unless he was in possession of all the relevant evidence. As a result, he frequently left decisions to those who had looked to him for leadership. In the case of eastern Europe after 1945, Stehle claims that Pius vacillated so much that he failed to explore opportunities for establishing a *modus vivendi* with any of the new Communist regimes in the east when those regimes were capable of providing guarantees to the church. By the time that he decided on a firm policy in 1949, Moscow was completely in the driver's seat in the satellites and the pope's firmness was, if anything, counter-productive to the welfare of the east European church.

A similar interpretation which casts the Church and the Vatican in passive roles is offered by Anthony Rhodes, whose book assumes that the Kremlin was set on a course to destroy the church behind the Iron Curtain and then relates the reaction of the pope and the church to various communist initiatives. He does not see, or at least he does not identify, any coherent Vatican strategy for coping with the postwar world other than resisting wherever possible communist incursions on the church's rights and freedoms. He assumes that those clergy who cooperated with the Communist regimes as "patriotic priests" or "peace priests" were weaklings and dupes. He makes no allowance for the fact that, by accepting administrative control by the state and direction in the area of faith and morals by the pope, these churchmen were attempting to resolve an impossible dilemma in order to continue to operate their churches.

The recent study by Jonathan Luxmoore and Jolanta Babiuch[7] contrasts the ineffectiveness, passivity, and traditionalism of Pius XII with the dynamic leadership provided by John Paul II in drawing on the popular strength of the church to challenge continuing communist domination of eastern Europe.

In contrast to Stehle, Rhodes, and Luxmoore and Babiuch, Carlo Falconi and John Cornwell contend that Pius XII had an active agenda as pope. In his essay on Pius XII in *The Popes in the Twentieth Century*, Falconi claims that Pius was driven by the anti-communism imprinted on him by his experiences in Munich during the 1919 Spartacist revolt. Consequently, during the Second World War Pius preached the importance of impartiality and did not criticize the atrocities of the Nazi regime. Yet, according to Falconi, this was a false impartiality, since the pope's silence really favoured Germany and was designed to facilitate a German victory over the Soviets. In addition to bringing about the destruction of communism, the papacy also sought an opportunity to send missionaries into Russia in the age-old Vatican quest to convert the Russian Orthodox adherents to Roman Catholicism. After the war the pope continued to be driven by his anti-communism and by a desire to preserve and protect the European community against communist incursion. In so doing, he was concerned to use diplomacy and his understanding of temporal power to bring about a centralized church over which he could rule to stand as a bulwark against the forces of twentieth-century secularism.

John Cornwell in his recent book refers to Pius XII as "Hitler's Pope," and at the same time predicates that this pope had a clear agenda. Eugenio Pacelli's career as pope, according to Cornwell, must be understood against the formative influences of his early career working with Cardinal Pietro Gasparri on the codification of canon law, working as nuncio to Bavaria and Germany, and serving as secretary of state to Pius XI, through all of which he worked consistently and in a variety of ways to enhance centralization within the church. The culmination of his life and career was when he became that all-powerful pope which he had helped to create who, with God's guidance, would preside over the fate of mankind.

With the exception of the published Vatican documents and such other materials as he found within the Vatican, Cornwell draws his interpretation from memoirs and secondary sources. Not having the sources for the later period, his book peters out in 1945 and he does not continue his study for the balance of the career of Pius XII. Yet he suggests that Pius XII carried a responsibility for playing the role of pope in a way that is worthy of a highly centralized church which, Cornwell contends, has been much admired by John Paul II.

Michael Phayer concurs with Cornwell's view of the power of Pius XII within the church and with the existence of his anti-communist agenda both during and after the Second World War. While the pope was prepared to provide strong and active leadership in the struggle against communism, Phayer indicates that Pius provided no such leadership where the Holocaust and Nazi genocidal policies were concerned, since these did not fit with his identification of significant priorities for papal action.[8]

Andrea Riccardi has opened yet a third approach to the subject. In his important study of the internal workings of the Vatican,

Il "Partito Romano" nel secondo dopoguerra (1945–1954), Riccardi examined the ecclesiastical and bureaucratic in-fighting over policy. In spite of his responsibility for the general direction of the church, Pius XII had to be responsive to the factions within his court who were promoting their own agendas in terms both of diplomacy and of theology.

The present study concurs with those who contend that Pius XII was indeed a pope with an agenda and that his agenda extended into the postwar period. Yet it was an agenda which ran counter to the policies of the great powers and occasionally to the demands of good sense. During the Second World War, Pius XII sought a compromise peace in the face of demands for unconditional surrender. At the end of the war he called for reconciliation and forgiveness for the peoples of Germany and Italy at a time when the victorious allies were coming to grips with the discoveries of the Nazi death camps. He favoured the reintegration of Europe when Harry Truman was calling for the containment of communism. And his advice to the churches and peoples of eastern Europe was to refuse all cooperation with their Communist overlords in spite of the fact that these Communists controlled all the power. Had he had less of a predetermined agenda, he might have responded to more of the responsible advice which he was receiving from his advisors within the Secretariat of State. He might also have provided more effective leadership to his church and given his east European bishops better support and assistance in coping with the impossible situation in which they found themselves between 1945 and 1950.

1 The First Cold Warriors

The rhetoric of the anti-communist position in the Cold War had been defined over a century earlier by the Roman Catholic Church in opposition to modern concepts of socialist materialism. In that sense, leaders of the church can be designated as the first "cold warriors."

The nineteenth and twentieth centuries had not been easy times for the papacy, beset as it was by the social, political, and theological challenges of liberal anti-clericalism and socialist atheism. The latter had been condemned as early as 1846, during the reign of Pope Pius IX (1846–1878), and the condemnations had continued throughout the nineteenth century. As socialist political parties were established at the end of the century to participate in elections with extended popular franchises, so the Catholic Church encouraged the development of competing political parties in an attempt to stop the spread of socialist values by the ballot box.

When the Bolshevik wing of the Russian Social Democrats seized power in Russia in November 1917, the Vatican was not initially perturbed. Socialism had already been identified as a danger and the Bolsheviks were merely a segment of a larger party in a country where Roman Catholics made up a minority of the population. Within Russia, the Roman Catholic Church had traditionally been the church of the minorities, associated with specific national groups, such as the Poles, the Ukrainians, the Belorussians, the Lithuanians, and the Latvians and, as such, closely associated with anti-Russian nationalistic movements. The Catholic Church had never acquired a nation-wide following nor an administrative structure which extended throughout

Russia. Anti-Catholicism was associated with the Russian Orthodox Church and was rooted in Russian culture.

Under these circumstances, the Bolshevik revolution was identified more as an opportunity than as a threat by the Vatican. Once established in power, the Bolsheviks turned their animosity against the Russian Orthodox Church. As a result, the new rulers of Russia were willing to negotiate with the Vatican who sought permission to send specially trained missionaries into Russia to secure converts from Orthodoxy. With the rise of Stalin in 1928, however, these negotiations ended and, having reduced the authority of the Orthodox Church, the Soviet dictator then turned his police apparatus against the remaining vestiges of the Catholic Church.[1] By 1939 the only Catholic churches still open in the Soviet Union were those in Moscow and Leningrad designed to cater to the diplomatic community. These churches had been kept open at the insistence of the Americans and the priests in both churches were American citizens.[2]

By 1930 the Vatican had recognized that communism was a more determined and militant variety of socialism. Not only did the Russian Bolsheviks seek to promote revolution throughout Europe and the rest of the world, but they had also, through the Comintern, coopted revolutionary socialists in every country to do their bidding. While the initial communist thrust of the 1920s had not been particularly successful, the onset of the Great Depression in 1929 brought widespread unemployment and reduced social benefits, and threatened to destabilize society in such a way that the Comintern could reap extensive rewards.

The social polarization caused by the Great Depression led Pope Pius XI (1922–1939) to warn Catholics against the attraction of communist radicalism in difficult times. Following a solemn expiatory mass for Russia and its persecuted Catholics in St Peter's Basilica on 19 March 1930, Pius XI turned the full scorn of Vatican disapproval on the communists with calls for prayers for those being persecuted in Russia and for the defeat of communism. In his 1932 encyclical *Caritate Christi*, Pius XI described for the faithful the present distress of the human race:

Profiting by so much economic distress and so much moral disorder the enemies of all social order, be they called Communists or by any other name, boldly set about breaking through every restraint. This is the most dreadful evil of our times, for they destroy every bond of law, human or divine; they engage openly and in secret in a relentless struggle against religion and against God Himself; they carry out the diabolical program of wresting from the hearts of all, even of children, all religious sentiment; for well they know that, when once belief in God has been taken from the heart of mankind, they will be entirely free to work out their will. Thus we see today, what was never before seen in history, the satanical banners of war against God and against religion brazenly unfurled to the winds in the midst of all peoples and in all parts of the earth.[3]

Anti-communism had been a basis of public support for the Italian Fascists, just as it was for the German National Socialists in the 1930s. Hostility towards communism had made Mussolini and Hitler acceptable negotiating partners for the Vatican, who concluded concordats with Italy in 1929 and Germany in 1933. The concordat with Hitler did not, however, offer the pope the same satisfaction as had the one with Mussolini. Hitler consistently violated the concordat, leading Pius XI to recognize that Hitler was as much of a threat to the welfare of the church as Stalin. The politics of the 1930s eventually reached such a degree of radicalism that many devout Catholics came to identify the Fascists and the Nazis as the only serious political alternatives to communism.

In addition to Stalin's persecution, the Catholic Church was also persecuted under the anti-clerical Mexican government in the 1920s and the left-wing governments of Spain in the 1930s. While the bishops could do no more than endure persecution with their flocks in the Soviet Union and Mexico, in Spain the bishops actively opposed the more radical aspects of the left-wing Second Republic of 1931, sponsoring both political movements and conspiratorial action. When General Francisco Franco staged a coup d'état in July 1936 which soon deteriorated into civil war, he did so with the blessing and support of the majority of the Spanish church, who appealed for and received international support for Franco's Nationalists from the Catholic community. In fact, in this case the Spanish bishops were far more enthusiastic about Franco than was the pope. While Pius XI often referred to his triangle of despair as a result of church persecutions in the Soviet Union, Mexico, and Spain, he withheld his initial recognition of Franco's government because of the Basque bishops and clergy who supported the Spanish government and also because he disapproved of Franco's close partnership with Hitler.

In refusing to sanction Hitler's anti-communist crusade against the Soviet-supported Spanish government, the pope was aware that the logic of his anti-communism had carried matters too far. Deploring the polarization of Spain and of Europe, the pope was not prepared to endorse nazism as an alternative to communism. Both deserved equal condemnation, which the pope delivered through a pair of encyclicals in 1937: *Mit Brennender Sorge* on 14 March against the Nazis, and

Divini Redemptoris on 19 March against the communists. While *Mit Brennender Sorge* was a call to German Catholics to resist the depradations and falsifications of the Nazi regime, it held out the hope of reconciliation should Hitler change his ways.[4] According to *Divini Redemptoris*, on the other hand, no reconciliation was possible with communism.

Divini Redemptoris consolidated all the previous teaching of the church on the subject of "Bolshevistic and Atheistic Communism." This encyclical was to remain, throughout the Cold War, as the authoritative Catholic position on communism. "Communism is by its nature anti-religious," argued Pius XI; "there is no room for the idea of an eternal God; there is no difference between matter and spirit, between soul and body; there is neither survival of the soul after death, nor any hope of a future life ... Communism, moreover, strips man of his liberty, which is the principle of his life as a rational being, robs the human person of all its dignity, and removes all the moral restraints that check the eruptions of blind impulse."

By rejecting all hierarchical and divinely constituted authority in society, starting from the basic institution of the family, communism ran counter to both reason and divine revelation. Pius XI explained that Communism had been successful because the liberals had de-Christianized the world in the nineteenth century and had left society in "religious and moral destitution." Communism took advantage of this destitution by offering to resolve the social and economic problems of the current economic depression and, in so doing, attracted the support of many well-meaning individuals, including many Christians, who had been blinded by the concern of communists for the welfare of the working classes. Communism was intrinsically wrong, and no one who would save Christian civilization should collaborate with it in any undertaking whatsoever. As communism removed concepts of morality from civil society, it created not a terrestrial paradise, but civil terrorism, as was currently being practised in Stalin's Russia.

In contrast to the communist, the Christian started from belief in the existence of God and the belief that man was "marvellously endowed by his Creator with gifts of body and mind," including "a spiritual and immortal soul." The Christian also believed that God had destined man for civil society: "Society is for men and not vice versa. This must not be understood in the sense of liberalistic individualism, which subordinates society to the selfish use of the individual; but only in the sense that by means of an organic union with society and by mutual collaboration the attainment of earthly happiness is placed within the reach of all." Morality did not reside in the social collectivity. "Only man, the human person, and not society in any form is endowed with reason and a morally free will." The main role of civil authority should involve the infusion of Christian love and social justice into the socio-economic order.

The pope concluded by offering guidance to Christians who wished to be "saved from the satanic scourge." They should actively practise the principles of the Gospel, especially, in this case, "detachment from earthly goods and the precept of charity." Christians must deny materialistic goals and accept the virtue of poverty, just as those with resources must practise charity to the less fortunate. Employers must always be aware of their responsibility to pay their workers a just wage. Clergy, laity, and constituted authorities must work together against communism.[5]

Through his denunciation of communism, the pope gave instruction to the Catholic faithful on the attitude they should adopt in dealing with the communist ideology and the Soviet regime. He was not so much taking a political position as offering spiritual guidance to his flock. In the 1930s it was possible to demonstrate political anti-communism by joining the fascist movements, which the pope did not wish to encourage. Communism was to be resisted, but it was to be resisted in the souls of the faithful, who must retain their trust and knowledge of God and their faith in the freedom of the human will to distinguish between good and evil.

At the same time, Pius XI did not see communism as posing any greater political threat to Christian civilization than did Hitler's Germany, with its aggrandizement of the state authority at the expense of individual liberties, its betrayal of signed agreements, and its aggressive militarism. The election of Eugenio Pacelli as Pope Pius XII in March 1939 changed this Vatican perspective.

Eugenio Pacelli had served as apostolic nuncio to Bavaria and to Germany between 1917 and 1930, at which time he had been named Vatican secretary of state. He had had personal experience of communism when he faced down a communist attack on his nunciature in Munich in 1919. While Pacelli styled himself Pius XII, the apparent continuity with his predecessor's regime concealed important differences. Pius XI had had a reputation for pugnacity, especially in his latter years, while Pius XII, true to his diplomatic vocation, was much more cautious in his dealings with the Nazi and Fascist dictators. Where Pius XI had seen little difference between Nazis and communists at the time of the Spanish civil war, Pius XII recognized in communism the much greater evil and threat to Christian civilization. Consequently, upon his election as pope, he stopped all criticism of Hitler's Germany and Mussolini's Italy and praised the victory of Franco's Nationalist forces in Spain.

In addressing the threat of communism, Pius XII was convinced that a new war would destabilize European society and leave it exposed to the depradations of Stalin and the Comintern. Peace was the best weapon against the communists and thus the pope sought to avoid the outbreak of war in 1939 by summoning a new European conference to examine German demands on Poland. The papal initiative was not well received at a time when the British and French had rejected appeasement and all the powers were turning to the Soviet Union to resolve the international impasse in their favour. The Nazi-Soviet Pact of August 1939 appeared to vindicate the fears of the Vatican since it allowed the German invasion of Poland in September and moved Soviet forces west to occupy Polish territory later in the same month.[6]

When seeking to understand this enigmatic pope, it is important to weigh his stated objectives against those personal idiosyncracies which influenced his performance in office. While born Italian, Pius XII had an affinity for all things German and believed that he had a unique understanding of the Germans, a people whom he loved dearly. "In a certain sense, indeed, his own temperament and his methodical punctilious habit of life could be said to have predisposed him towards the Germans and them to him."[7] His most significant foreign posting had been to Germany, and, as a result of this experience, he understood well the bitterness the Germans felt over their treatment following the First World War. The hierarchy of the German church at the time of the Second World War was largely Pacelli's creation since he had recommended most of the bishops for appointment during his terms as nuncio and secretary of state. When he became pope, many of his personal assistants and advisors were German. One of Pacelli's first concerns during the war was for the present and future welfare of the German church under the despotism of the Third Reich.

To his personal affinity for the Germans should be added the pope's stubborn refusal to compromise with evil, as represented by communism and the Soviet Union. In his vision of the papacy, Pius XII believed that his essential role was to act as teacher and spiritual mentor to Roman Catholics while defending the independence and organizational structure of the church. He could do this by enhancing the authority of the pope and the Roman Curia within the Church. It was his role to define and articulate teachings which he expected to be implemented by the faithful in the exercise of their free will as guided by the bishops and the clergy. An intellectual who grasped the many facets of any problem, Pius XII was always more comfortable in his role as teacher than he was as judge. Although he relished the opportunity to fashion his discourses on spiritual principle, when it came to judging the behaviour of people and nations, Pacelli had a difficult time resolving the many perspectives bearing on particular questions. His indecision in such matters was frequently remarked on by diplomats accredited to the Holy See, some of whom attributed it to weakness of character. On the other hand, those who worked most closely with him through the Vatican Secretariat of State, Monsignors Domenico Tardini and Giovanni Battista Montini,[8] testified that, although he was "by natural temperament, meek and rather timid" and lacked the temper of a fighter, he was nevertheless a strong individual who was capable of taking firm decisions and did not fear criticism or opposition.[9]

The papacy had been at its weakest in the eighteenth century, when national Gallican churches operated virtually independently of Rome. The nineteenth century, in contrast, saw a restoration of power to Rome when ultramontane loyalty to the papacy became a feature of European Catholicism. This was due to the weakening of the national branches of the church as a result of the revolutions of the late eighteenth century and to the determination of the papacy to stand firmly against the intellectual and ideological thrust of the modern age. The promulgation of the doctrine of papal infallibility by the Vatican Council in 1870 represented a culmination of this move to restore centralized authority in the church.

Operating in a world of continuing hostility since 1870, the papacy has been conscious of the need to augment the power of Rome within the church. For this reason, it had brought about a major codification and consolidation of canon law in 1917 which gave Rome control over all episcopal appointments. Immediately after the First World War there was a significant expansion of the papal diplomatic service as more and more countries established or re-established diplomatic relations with the Holy See. This expansion of papal diplomacy enabled the Holy See to deal directly with national governments in negotiating concordats designed to regulate the position of the church within individual states. The appointment of apostolic nuncios and apostolic delegates to more and more countries also gave the Holy See greater control and supervision over the national branches of the Church, since apostolic nuncios had a responsibility for relations with church hierarchies as well as with secular governments. The expansion of the papal diplomatic service and the codification of canon law have served both to diminish the role and independence of national church hierarchies in the twentieth century and to place ever more authority with the Curia in Rome.

In his recent study of Pope Pius XII, John Cornwell has identified Eugenio Pacelli as one of the great centralizers in the twentieth-century church. Pacelli worked to enhance the power of Rome over the national bishops, such centralization being seen as necessary for dealing with the hostile political environment of the early twentieth century. With his election as pope in March 1939, Pius XII took upon himself the mantle of the heavy responsibility which he had been defining for the papal office. Not only was he the earthly deputy of the Prince of Peace but his figure and his life represented the public image of the church militant. According to Cornwell, Pius "had a triumphant vision of the Church and papal authority" and an acceptance of the overwhelming responsibility which rested on his shoulders as God's representative on earth.[10] At the same time, it was his responsibility to give leadership to his flock in coping with the two major crises of the 1940s, the Second World War and the postwar threat of Soviet communism. In so doing, Pius XII was ever mindful of the need to retain the authority of Rome within the church, which meant retaining his authority over the bishops and their judgments on the best strategies for the church to follow.

PART TWO

The Roman Catholic Church in the Second World War

2 The Church and the Axis Powers

The Second World War rent the fabric of the European community in 1939, pitting European against European. As a transnational institution, the Roman Catholic Church found itself straddling the divide of the war, with Catholic fighting Catholic. More than any of the Protestant or Orthodox churches, the Roman Catholic Church had been one of the defining institutions of the concept of Europe and, through the development of western Christendom, of European culture and civilization. To the secular powers, the Second World War was a devastating international conflict; to the Catholic Church, it was a brutal European civil war.

Any civil war forces individuals to choose sides, allowing no one the luxury of neutrality. In the same way, the Catholic Church in Europe was forced to react to the divisions of the war and national churches, in particular, were expected to declare themselves and to define their loyalties. In civil wars, some people are placed in camps by circumstance while others choose sides for principle or advantage, and so it was with the Roman Catholic Church during the Second World War.

To understand the impact of the war on the church, it is necessary to understand the options open to each of its branches in Europe with the onset of war and, more particularly, with the occupation of their country by the Axis powers. Some branches of the church were fortunate and found that their position was respected and supported by their government and their society throughout the war. Such was the case in Hungary until the arrival of the Soviet Army in 1944; such, too, was the case with Roman Catholics in Romania and Bulgaria.

In the case of a hostile government or foreign occupation, the churches had to choose. They could endure the hostile government or the occupying power, protesting against abuses to individuals or groups, but never moving into opposition to the regime. This was the case with the churches in Nazi Germany, in Croatia under Ustase rule, in occupied Yugoslavia, and in territories occupied by the Soviet Union, where the Greek Catholic, or Uniate,[1] churches exercised particular caution. Some churches went further, however, seeking positive advantages from giving active support to a wartime regime or to a foreign occupation. This was the situation in Vichy France, in independent Slovakia, and in Italian-occupied Albania.

Conversely, rather than enduring and accepting the wartime regime, the church could oppose and resist. Some resistance could be passive where bishops and clergy remained at the side of their persecuted flocks throughout the war, providing what support and leadership they could. This was the case in Poland during the German and Soviet occupations; it was also the case in the Czech lands of Bohemia and Moravia, which were incorporated into the Third Reich in 1939. Alternatively, a church could move into active resistance and opposition and assist in preparing the political leadership of the future. Such was markedly the case only in Italy where, from the beginning of the war, Catholics, with support from the highest levels of their church, were preparing the Christian Democratic alternative to fascism.

An understanding of the complexity of the situation facing individual Roman Catholic churches in Europe during the Second World War, coupled with an appreciation of the perspective of the church in the United States, is essential to a comprehension of the role played by the papacy. With western Christendom in fragments, it was necessary to suspend judgment on individual behaviours and to accept the accommodations which churches had to make with the circumstances in which they found themselves. Above all, it was imperative to bring the war to an end in such a way that the spread of Soviet communism would be impeded and the European community and European culture restored and preserved. The unity of Christian Europe must not become the first casualty of this war.

The Holy See failed to achieve this goal, since the fragmentation of the Second World War was soon turned into new and more clearly defined divisions by the onset of the Cold War. Soviet-style communism became and remained a presence in eastern Europe for forty-five years. It was not, in fact, until 1989, with the end of the Cold War and the reunification of Germany that Christian and Catholic Europe was once again restored. The Holy See had participated in the first Conference on Security and Co-operation in Europe in Helsinki in the 1970s

and had looked towards "the spiritual unity of Europe" as it was proclaimed by Pope John Paul II at Gniezno, Poland, in 1979. The papacy
placed itself at the centre of the important developments of the late
1980s and the 1990s and was well prepared to play its role as the
patron of the re-emergence of Christian Europe.[2] John Paul II had been
effective in assisting a process which Pius XII had been powerless to
prevent. Only with the disintegration and decline of communism in a
new historical setting was it possible to achieve the aims which the
Vatican had sought in an earlier period.

The study of the role of the Roman Catholic Church in the origins
of the Cold War is a study of the way in which the European community, by indulging in war, lost control of its own destiny. It is also a
study of the way in which the church, as the transnational institution
with the greatest interest in a restored Europe, was incapable of influ-
encing the course of European and world history in the mid-twentieth
century.

The Roman Catholic Church was an important social and cultural
institution inside Germany and Italy during the years of Nazi and
Fascist rule. It was also important within those countries which voluntarily cooperated with the Axis, such as Hungary. While the Vatican
had concluded concordats with Italy and Germany to regulate the position of the church in 1929 and 1933 respectively, by the outbreak of
war in 1939, the church had become disillusioned with both regimes
and alienated from them. Hitler had persecuted the Catholic Church
during the 1930s and in Italy papal protests following racist legislation
in 1938 terminated the close working relationship between church and
regime which had existed throughout most of that decade. While the
church did not break with either the Nazi or the Fascist regimes,
church leaders in Germany during the war saw fit to criticize Nazi
euthanasia policies, while the Catholic community in Italy was an
active participant in the anti-fascist resistance with the tacit support
of the Vatican. The government of Hungary was comparatively less
ideological and, as a traditionally conservative regime, nurtured good
relations with the church throughout the Second World War.

THE CHURCH IN GERMANY

The Roman Catholic population of Germany was located in the south
and west of the country, notably in Bavaria and the Rhineland, with
the centre and east being predominantly Protestant. Prior to Hitler's
expansionism of 1938, which incorporated more Catholics into the
Third Reich, Roman Catholics made up 39 per cent of the German

population. The fall of the Hohenzollern dynasty in 1918 had resulted in a displacement of the influence of the Protestant Lutherans in favour of the Catholics under the Weimar Republic. The Catholic Centre Party, or Zentrum, had been one of the key political parties in the governing coalitions of the Weimar period.

Eugenio Pacelli had been named apostolic nuncio to Bavaria in 1917. When diplomatic relations were established between the Holy See and the German central government in 1920, Pacelli was also named nuncio to Germany while retaining his responsibilities in Munich and he served in that double capacity until his appointment as Vatican secretary of state in 1930. As papal nuncio, Pacelli was instrumental in negotiating concordats with Bavaria (1924), Prussia (1929) and Baden (1932). In this way, he laid the foundation for the conclusion of a concordat with the German government itself in July 1933. The accession of Hitler accelerated the final negotiations for this concordat when he accepted Vatican terms on condition that the Vatican not oppose the dissolution of the Catholic Zentrum. The bishops, however, disliked the National Socialist movement and had instructed Catholics not to support it politically. It was Pacelli who had put strong pressure on the bishops and the leadership of the Zentrum to cease their criticism of the Nazis and to accept the terms of the concordat.[3] Relations between church and state under the Nazis were constrained by the existence of the concordat which required the bishops to refrain from political involvement, in spite of continuous violation of the terms by Hitler's government.[4]

The concordat was designed to protect the Catholic Church in Germany, but the Nazis violated it even before the ink was dry. German Catholics, including the clergy and hierarchy, endured such persecution under the Nazis that, in March 1937, Pius XI denounced Nazi violation of signed agreements in the encyclical *Mit Brennender Sorge*. Yet upon the outbreak of war in 1939, pressure on the church eased somewhat, since Hitler needed the support of the churches for the war effort. The church gave its support to Germany's war effort and Catholics, along with other Germans, were euphoric about the quick German victory over Poland in 1939. In Germany, the Catholic Church was torn between pride in German military victories and disgust with the policies of the government. In the end, the bulk of the church elected to support the war effort.

While persuasion was used on the churches in Germany and western Europe, repression was the order of the day in the east. This was especially the case in those parts of Poland which were annexed to the Third Reich. West Prussia-Danzig and Posnania were joined to Germany and amalgamated into the Warthegau, where a program of

Germanization was instituted which sought to reorganize the area along lines of Nazi ideology once Poles and Jews had been expelled. The gauleiter of the Warthegau was Arthur Greiser, the former president of the Nazi-dominated Senate of Danzig, who exercised virtually unlimited power in his gau, or district. One of his goals, once the native Polish clergy had been either executed or expelled, was to eliminate churches as such from the area, and to reduce the remaining churches to the status of "religious associations." Historian John Conway believes that the persecution of the churches in the Warthegau foreshadowed what would have happened to the churches in Germany itself had Hitler won the war.[5]

The German bishops received moral support and collegial advice from Pius XII, who worked closely with them during the war, assisting them to "cope with the ordeal and the agony of the time," although he sometimes reprimanded those who were too willing to concede issues to the Nazis in the interest of the national war effort. In later years, he believed the experience of wartime Germany, where "a united hierarchy linked with the Pope could carry Catholics through a terrible ordeal," was worthy of emulation in countries coping with hostile communist governments.[6]

The bishops protested Nazi policies during the war. Bishop Galen of Munster spoke out against Hitler's euthanasia policy with some effect in 1941, and in August 1943 the bishops protested conditions in the Warthegau in a pastoral letter. At the same time, the Vatican expressed its concerns about the treatment of the church through Monsignor Cesare Orsenigo, the papal nuncio in Berlin. Orsenigo had been chosen by Pacelli as the person best able to maintain the concordat and German-Vatican relations, yet Orsenigo's requests were rejected and his protests largely ignored. From the summer of 1942 Hitler decreed that Orsenigo only had authority to speak about conditions in Germany proper and not about conditions in territories conquered by Germany. The Wilhelmstrasse refused to receive further protests about conditions in the Warthegau, including a strong letter from the Vatican secretary of state, Cardinal Luigi Maglione, in 1943.

German Catholics were recognized by Pius XII as being among the first victims of nazism – followed by the Austrians, Czechoslovaks, Poles, and so forth. While Nazi party membership tended to have been lowest in predominantly Roman Catholic areas, the question of the responsibility of German Catholics remained open in the rest of the world. Many outside observers believed that the Catholic Church, by concluding the concordat, by trying to cooperate with the Nazi government, and by supporting the German war effort, had been too willing to appease and support an obviously evil regime.[7]

THE CHURCH IN ITALY

The 1929 Lateran Agreements resolved the Roman Question of how to preserve the temporal authority of the pope within the Kingdom of Italy as it had been created in 1870. They also allowed Catholics to be accepted as good Italians. One of these agreements was a concordat between the papacy and the Italian government regulating the position of the Catholic Church in Italy, as a result of which the church established amicable working relationships with Mussolini's government in the early 1930s. Cooperation between church and regime reached its apogee in the active support of bishops and priests for the Italian war against Abyssinia in the winter of 1935–6. With the establishment of the Rome-Berlin Axis, however, the Vatican worried lest Mussolini's cooperation with Hitler would lead the Fascist dictator to adopt the anti-Catholic policies of the Nazi dictator. In denouncing Mussolini's racial legislation of 1938, Pius XI withdrew the Italian church from direct support of the Fascist regime, expecting it to assume a more neutral stance in relation to fascism in Italy.

As fascism lost popular support during the war, Catholic political alternatives were developed. One such alternative was Christian Democracy, linking former members of the Italian Popular Party (PPI), such as Alcide de Gasperi, who had spent the war years working in the Vatican library, with former members of the Federation of Catholic University Students (FUCI), the Catholic Action university student organization, such as Aldo Moro and Giulio Andreotti. The FUCI had been protected under the 1929 concordat. Direct linkage of this development to the Vatican was provided through the former national chaplain of FUCI and mentor to many of the future leaders of Christian Democracy, Monsignor Giovanni Battista Montini, who became Pope Paul VI in 1963.[8]

Another Catholic alternative emerged in 1941, when Gerardo Bruni, a librarian at the Vatican, brought together a left-wing group of Catholics with a concern for reconciling the labour movement with Catholicism. Bruni's initiative resulted in the creation of two other Catholic parties during the war: the Christian Social party, led by Bruni himself, and the Catholic Communist party. The latter was a party of young idealists with Fedele d'Amico, editor of the newspaper *Voce Operaia*, as leader. D'Amico admired the French Catholic left and believed that the Christian Democrats were too reactionary and too suspicious of the parties of the Italian left. The Catholic Communists intended to reach out and cooperate in the spirit of the anti-fascist resistance.[9]

While the war continued, Catholic leaders worked with other members of the anti-fascist resistance, including the Italian Communist party (PCI) and the Italian Socialist party (PSI). Many segments of Catholic youth, believing that the anti-communism of their elders was what had produced Catholic flirtation and compromise with fascism in the 1930s, joined one or other of these parties and actively sought cooperation with communists and other elements on the left.[10] Immediately following the liberation of Rome from German occupation in 1944, Catholics, in the spirit of the Resistance, signed the Pact of Rome with socialists and communists to create the Italian General Confederation of Labour (CGIL) as a non-partisan trade union.

The serious re-emergence of the Catholic movement also took place after the liberation of Rome. On 29 July 1944 the statutes of Christian Democracy were approved by a party congress meeting in Naples and Catholic Action, Pius XI's apostolate of the laity, resumed its full activity under the direction of the church hierarchy. Important developments within Catholic Action in 1944 included the resurrection of the Catholic Boy Scout and Girl Guide organizations, the creation of the Christian Workers' Association of Italy, and the opening of the Catholic Institution of Social Activity which ran libraries and other educational and charitable activities. At least eleven organizations were operating under the Catholic Action umbrella by the end of 1944.

The Vatican watched these developments with some apprehension, fearful lest the collaboration with the left in the Resistance might undermine the creation of a strong postwar Catholic movement and threaten the independence of the Holy See. Through the Lateran Agreements, only the Italian government had guaranteed the territorial integrity and the independence of the papacy. The treaty was put to the test during the Second World War when the Vatican continued to receive diplomats and visitors from Italy's enemies, but at no time was the integrity of the Vatican violated either by the Axis or by the Allies, with the exception of Allied bombs which hit the Vatican railway station. The pope's first concern was to sustain the temporal sovereignty of the Vatican City State and much depended on having a postwar government which would continue to respect the role of the Catholic Church in Italy. Pius XII feared the influence of the Italian Communist party in the Resistance, anticipating that a communist government would alter the contractual arrangements between Italy and the Vatican.

One of the ways in which the papacy had been able to reach agreement with the government in the 1920s had been by abandoning the PPI and negotiating directly with the Fascist regime. Catholic Action had been protected by the concordat and had enjoyed considerable popularity in the 1930s, much to the annoyance of the Fascists. With the imminent collapse of fascism during the war, Pius XII approved the formation of Christian Democracy which, it was believed, would be amenable to direction from the Vatican because of its Catholic Action links. At the same time, the Vatican opposed the rival Catholic political formations of the Christian Social and the Catholic Communist parties, which threatened to split the Catholic movement, were too enthusiastic about the Resistance coalition, and, if they came to power, would be outside Vatican control.

Within the Vatican, divergent views were vying for the attention and support of the pope. With the death in 1944 of the secretary of state, Cardinal Maglione, the pope kept decisions on Italian politics very much in his own hands as he tried to generate a synthesis between opposing points of view. In this, he was supported by Monsignor Domenico Tardini, the undersecretary for extraordinary ecclesiastical affairs, effectively the foreign minister of the Vatican, who believed that the church in Italy should be above politics and that Italian politics should be based on the middle classes. While the central concern of the pope was to protect Italy from Communism, he was prepared to adopt a variety of means to achieve this. Hence, Vatican policy lacked consistency as Pius XII first supported one internal group and then another.

There were two competing Vatican agendas. One was held by an ecclesiastical party which centred on the Substitute in the Secretariat of State, Giovanni Battista Montini, and his collaborators, including Count della Torre, the editor of the *Osservatore Romano*. Montini believed that there should be one autonomous Catholic party in Italy, in whose business neither the hierarchy nor the Catholic associations should interfere. Montini was opposed to encouraging any Catholic party other than the Christian Democrats which, he expected, would participate within the pluralistic process of Italian democratic politics. He encouraged the pope, for this reason, to condemn the Catholic Communist party.

Opposed to Montini and his patronage of the Christian Democrats was the Roman party. This internal Vatican pressure group was coordinated by Monsignor Roberto Ronca, director of the Roman Seminary, and had, as its most active member, Cardinal Alfredo Ottaviani, the assessor of the Holy Office. Cardinals Fumasoni-Biondi, Pizzardo, and Canali and a number of papal diplomats were united in their opposition to Montini and the Christian Democrats. Their mouthpiece was the Jesuit journal, *La Civiltà Cattolica*. This Roman party saw no reason to restrict Catholic participation in Italian politics to one political party and favoured more than one, including the Catholic Communists, so that the Vatican could exercise its choice by supporting whichever party was most willing to do its bidding. The ultimate goal of the Roman party was the creation of a Catholic state in Italy, through the elimination of communism and the integration of society around principles of Catholicism. Riccardi compares its goal to that existing in Franco Spain, where Catholicism was the only tolerated religion. In international affairs, Ottaviani was opposed to any compromise by Catholics with the communists.[11]

The pope accepted Montini's arguments that an outright condemnation of the Catholic communists was necessary to eliminate any doubt in Catholic minds about proper political behaviour. Two developments in the spring and summer of 1944 prompted the condemnation. The first was the return of Palmiro Togliatti, the leader of the Italian Communist party, from Moscow in April, who then expressed his willingness to support the royal government and see the Communist party cooperate with all parties in the liberation and future government of Italy. This "svolta di Salerno" put the Vatican very much on its guard, distrusting Togliatti's tactics, just as they questioned the sincerity of his church attendance in Naples.[12] According to Pius XII, Togliatti cultivated "that supremely well behaved political attitude and approach which one feels may be merely a cover to extreme cunning and stealth."[13] The Pope feared that the Catholic communists were particularly vulnerable to swallowing Togliatti's line.

The second critical development of 1944 was the founding in July of the Christian Democratic party. It was essential to prevent any fragmentation of the Catholic movement at this important meeting and it was therefore necessary to indicate that the Vatican only favoured one political direction for the movement by demonstrating the error of the approach taken by the Catholic Communists.

The condemnation arose in reaction to an article in the *New York Times* in July 1944 by Don Luigi Sturzo, the founder and former secretary of the PPI, who explained the need for cooperation between Catholics and communists to defeat the Axis and to free Italy. Sturzo took note of the Catholic Communist party and indicated that it was a natural outgrowth of this cooperation because "these Communist sympathizers are practicing Catholics who believe that it is possible to accept many of the economic principles of Communism and reject the old anti-religious policy of Moscow and the Marxist materialistic conception of life."[14]

The Vatican was not, however, prepared to tolerate this position and, one week after the appearance of Sturzo's article, the *Osservatore Romano* published an article by Father Mariano Cordovani, master of the Sacred Pontifical Palace, a close collaborator of Pius XII and an ally of Montini. His article declared that communism and the Catholic doctrine were incompatible. "I believe," wrote Father Cordovani, "that if [the Catholic Communists] do not correct their position they inevitably will jeopardize their catholicism. We Catholics, in every just cause ... must never be absent and must collaborate with everybody; but when we lean more on Marx than on the teaching of the Church we are not aware of what we embrace and what we abandon and (when) for the tyranny of one class there is substituted that of another then it cannot be said we are acting as Catholics."[15] The pope reiterated this condemnation on 24 July when he spoke of Catholics who had fallen into error and had shown themselves ignorant of the teachings of the church.[16]

In September 1944 the Catholic Communist party changed its name to the Party of the Christian Left in order to make itself more acceptable to Catholic opinion, and in November it attracted a large number of dissidents from Bruni's Christian Social party. Still the Vatican refused to recognize them as an official Catholic party; on 2 and 3 January 1945 an unsigned statement in the *Osservatore Romano* asserted that "the principles and tendencies of the so-called Christian Left-Wing do not conform to the teachings of the Church, and therefore the promoters of the movement have no right to speak as representatives of Christian thought and far less to claim that those Catholics who have the real welfare of the people at heart should support their movement."[17] In spite of the pope's denunciation, Catholic cooperation with socialists and communists was early established in the trade unions. The CGIL was directed jointly by representatives of the Christian Democrats and the Socialist and Communist parties. The Christian Workers' Association of Italy was an organization of Catholic workers who were members of the CGIL and had no independent existence in labour-management relations.[18]

At the annual congress of Catholic Action in April 1945, members were encouraged to participate actively in the political life of Italy in support of parties which would guarantee political liberty and enhance the moral and material welfare of the country. This emphasis on political participation was the brainchild of Montini, who sought to develop the necessary Catholic base for the Christian Democrats. So that there should be no doubt of the direction in which Catholic political activity was to develop, however, the pope, after speaking of the need to exercise control over the demands of the working classes lest they promote more dangerous demands, warned members of Catholic Action: "Hence no Catholic, above all any belonging to Catholic Action, is allowed to adhere to social theories and systems which the Church has repudiated or against which it has warned the faithful."

Similar warnings had been sent to the chaplains of Italian Catholic youth and, on the eve of victory in Europe, the *Osservatore Romano* repeated its January condemnation of the Party of the Christian Left, whose "principles and tendencies ... are not in conformity with the teachings of the Catholic Church."[19] Cardinal Lavitrano, the president of Catholic Action, had also let it be known that he was very much opposed to the youth workers movements and the worker-priest movements of France and Belgium. He conceived of Catholic Action as an institution for the integration of society, not one that would recognize divisions between social classes.[20]

The pope was extremely suspicious of the Resistance coalition within Italy, just as he was in other parts of Europe, and he was prepared to instruct the Catholic movement to have as little cooperation as possible with the parties of the left.

THE CHURCH IN HUNGARY

The Roman Catholic Church had been the mainstay of the Austro-Hungarian Empire and had continued as the dominant religion of post-1918 Hungary. Since nationalism was more important than religious commitment in the interwar years in Hungary, Catholics and Protestants cooperated without undue animosity. Initially many churchmen looked to the return of the Habsburg dynasty and certainly in the 1920s, Catholics were strong supporters of the Legitimist cause. Hungarian Catholicism was both conservative and traditionalist in a political culture which was itself conservative and traditionalist. The Catholic Church was also authoritarian, lax, and corrupt as befitted a complacent and established church.

The appointment of Justinian Serédi as prince-bishop of Esztergom and primate of Hungary in 1927 brought a much-needed reinvigoration of Catholic life. As a result of the work of Serédi, "by 1939 the Hungarian Catholics appeared to have awoken from their inactive conservatism and to be emerging with a more or less liberal programme of reform, hostile to State absolutism and racialism and demanding a wider and more equal distribution of property."[21]

The Vatican were very satisfied with the treatment of the church by the interwar governments of Hungary and saw no need to replace the concordat of 1855 which had been concluded with the Austrian Empire and remained operative in Hungary. Church privileges were respected and well protected and interwar Hungary manifested a healthy dislike of both communism and the Soviet Union, which also pleased the Holy See.

During the Second World War, while Hungary worked within the German orbit, it retained its ties with the Vatican. When Germany occupied Hungary in March 1944, the church was correct and, at the same time, worked to protect Hungarian Jews from German persecution. Right up to the end of the war, the Holy See enjoyed excellent relations with Hungary. The Hungarian clergy had heeded Cardinal Serédi's instructions to stay by their people during the war, and, as a result, when the war ended, the clergy were looked to as community leaders and spokesmen. Church attendance increased, as did the registration of children in church schools.

Hungary was invaded and occupied by the Red Army in 1944. Russian soldiers at first treated the Hungarians very badly, with reports of looting of church property and the shooting of the Archbishop of Györ. By the end of the war, however, the Soviet high command had ordered that church property be respected and that priests not be molested; Catholics and other Christians were allowed to exercise their religious functions without interference from the occupying power.[23]

The left-wing provisional government of Hungary instituted a hasty land reform program in January 1945 which was designed to redistribute the many large farms and estates of Hungary to landless peasants. By the end of June, 35 percent of the arable land of the country had been redistributed. The Communists took the lead in implementing this popular program, fully expecting that the peasant voters would show their gratitude when postwar elections were held. Since the Catholic Church was a major landowner, it was seriously affected by the reform, and in many cases lost one of its important sources of income. Although the government promised compensating subsidies, the final settlement was always postponed and no compensation was ever granted.[24]

In March 1945 the Catholic Church suffered two shocks in Hungary. First, the papal nuncio, Monsignor Angelo Rotta, and the Vatican diplomatic mission were expelled from Budapest by the Russians.[25] Then, at the end of that month, Cardinal Serédi died, leaving the primacy vacant at this critical moment. Thus, by the end of the war the Hungarian church was leaderless, with neither a nuncio nor a primate.

3 The Church under Nazi Occupation

The German occupation of other European countries during the Second World War elicited differing responses from the national branches of the Catholic Church. In Poland, following its defeat by the Germans in September 1939, the church was given no reason to support the occupation authorities and endured the German persecution alongside the Polish people. This was also the case in Bohemia and Moravia, incorporated into Germany in March 1939, where the church cast its lot with the anti-Nazi resistance from the beginning. In France, on the other hand, the church hierarchy saw advantage in supporting the conservative social values of Marshal Pétain's Vichy regime and in collaborating with the German occupation, while clerical supporters of de Gaulle's Free French tended to come from the lower clergy. In Slovakia, as in Vichy France, church leaders saw an opportunity to establish a Slovak clerical state through cooperation with Hitler in the destruction of Czechoslovakia. When such a state came into existence in 1939, it was headed by a priest and gave active and enthusiastic support to the Axis war effort.

THE CHURCH IN CZECHOSLOVAKIA

The Sudetenland was sacrificed to Germany in October 1938 as a result of the Munich conference. In March 1939 Hitler occupied what was left of Czechoslovakia, incorporating Bohemia and Moravia into the Reich and allowing Slovakia nominal independence under its own government. Apart from Austria, which had been incorporated into the

Third Reich one year earlier, Czechoslovakia was the first European nation to experience German occupation.

In 1918 the new state of Czechoslovakia amalgamated the former Austro-Hungarian provinces of Bohemia, Moravia, and Slovakia. Eighty percent of its population was Catholic, including all of the Czechs and most of the Slovaks and Germans. Non-Catholic Slovak Christians were predominantly Lutheran. In the pre-1918 Austro-Hungarian Monarchy, the Roman Catholic Church had been used as an agency of Germanization in Bohemia and Moravia and, to a lesser degree, as an agency of Magyarization in Slovakia. As a result, a wave of anti-Catholicism followed the First World War in Bohemia and Moravia, when religious statues were torn down and crucifixes were removed from classrooms. The Czech middle classes, who exercised most of the power in the interwar state, while Catholic, were also anti-clerical. Because most Slovaks were rural and more devout, they were suspected by the Czech middle classes of favouring the return of the Habsburgs. The most fervent supporters of Czechoslovakia in Slovakia were the Lutherans. Among the leaders of the new republic, President Thomas Masaryk played on the dissident Hussite religious tradition of Czechoslovakia, believing that, with the establishment of the republic, "theocracy" had been replaced by "democracy." Edouard Beneš, who succeeded Masaryk as president, was also a liberal and an anti-clerical.

Because Catholicism had not been identified with the national community of the 1918 republic, the Catholic community had divided along ethnic and regional lines. Church leaders, both clerical and lay, were initially willing to support the new state. Monsignor Jan Sramek, the leader of the Czech Peoples' party, and Father Andrej Hlinka, the leader of the Slovak Peoples' party, were initially prepared to coordinate their activities in the interest of developing a national Catholic position. Before long, however, Hlinka and his party reverted to their basic Slovak particularism when they saw that the Czech leaders of the republic did not intend to honour the pledges of Slovak regional autonomy in the 1918 Pittsburgh Agreement.

The Slovak Peoples' party used the Munich crisis to convert Czechoslovakia into a federal state and Father Josef Tiso, who succeeded Hlinka as leader of the party, became prime minister of Slovakia at the end of that year. It was Tiso who, under German pressure, invited Hitler to send troops to assist Slovakia separate from the Czech lands in March 1939. After Slovakia had become an independent state, Tiso was named its first president in October 1939. Czech and Slovak Catholics thus supported opposing sides in the Second World War. The Catholic Church in Bohemia and Moravia supported the government-in-exile and the Allies, while Slovakia became a one-party state based on Catholic social principles and Slovak nationalism and worked in close collaboration with the Axis.[1]

Czechoslovakia had established formal relations with the Holy See in 1923 but these relations had never been particularly close during the interwar years. The 1925 official commemoration of the death of religious reformer John Hus resulted in the withdrawal of the papal nuncio from Prague for two years. On his return in 1927, a modus vivendi was worked out between Prague and the Vatican which was not fully implemented for another ten years. In 1939, after the destruction of Czechoslovakia, the Vatican accorded full diplomatic recognition to the new Catholic state of Slovakia by moving the nuncio from Prague to Bratislava, the capital of Slovakia, and by accepting the appointment of a Slovakian minister to the Holy See.

Slovakia was an embarrassment for the Vatican. The Holy See had not been pleased when Father Tiso became head of state in 1939, since the church thereby stood in danger of being held responsible for the actions of that government. The Holy See became even less comfortable once the collaborationist nature of Tiso's regime became apparent. There had been a tradition of anti-semitism in Slovakia, and in 1939 Tiso introduced his Aryanization policy to reduce Jewish control of the Slovakian economy. In September 1941 the Slovak National Council approved the Jewish Codex which defined a Jew, made intermarriage a crime, and removed Jews from public office. The Slovak church protested that the Codex was contrary to Christian principle and the Vatican formally protested the ban on intermarriage to the Slovak government. In the spring of 1942 that government, on German orders, began to deport Slovakian Jews to Poland. The Vatican again made formal protest and put continuous pressure on Tiso to stop the deportations, finally succeeding by September 1942.[2] In June 1943 Vatican Radio broadcast the protest of the Slovak bishops against Bratislava's Jewish policy. The pope was prepared to assert his authority over Father Tiso to restrain the worst excesses of the Slovak government.[3]

THE CHURCH IN POLAND

Before 1939 approximately 65 percent of the population of Poland was Roman Catholic, with a tradition of active church attendance and support growing out of the historical role of the Catholic Church in defining Polish nationhood.[4] "The Roman Catholic Church in Poland has for centuries been a national institution. Embedded in the national fabric, Polish Catholicism represents not only a system of religious beliefs and sacramental acts but also the embodiment of Polish cultural values and traditions ... if the partitions [of Poland] weakened the authority of the State, they strengthened immeasurably that of the Church, which over the period of two hundred years had become the most important national institution."[5] Historically, Poland has represented the northern and eastern bastion of Latin Catholicism against Russian Orthodoxy and German Protestantism. The Uniate, or Greek Catholic, Church of Ukraine and eastern Poland represented an eastern missionary extension of Catholicism and a vehicle for facilitating conversion from the Russian Orthodox Church. Poland had traditionally provided the base for Catholic missionary effort in the east.

Poland was partitioned between Germany and the Soviet Union in the fall of 1939 and German-occupied Poland endured the terrible atrocities perpetrated by the Nazis on Slavs and Jews during the war. An extensive resistance movement was created around the Home Army, under the direction of the Polish government-in-exile in London. This army marshalled its resources until August 1944 when it rose against the German occupiers in Warsaw only to be brutally suppressed by the Germans while Soviet troops waited on the other side of the River Vistula. When they occupied Poland, the Russians murdered many officers of the Home Army. For Poles who had survived war and occupation, the future held few terrors and they faced the postwar period fortified by a shared experience of suffering.

In spite of the fact that the Catholic Church was the dominant institution in Poland, this had not ensured harmonious relations between the Polish government and the Holy See after the restoration of a Polish state in 1918. While Pius XI and Marshal Pilsudski had established friendly relations during the former's term as nuncio to Poland between 1918 and 1921, the bulk of the marshal's followers in the Polish government were anti-clericals. Hence, the Vatican disliked the Polish tradition of religious tolerance which entitled non-Catholics to instruction by their own religious leaders in state schools. A dispute over extensive church land holdings had been resolved when the church agreed to sell off land it held in excess of its real needs. Finally, there was what some Poles felt to be excessive Vatican concern for German minorities in Poland, especially when the German bishop of Osnabruck was assigned a role by the Vatican as the spiritual advisor to German minorities in eastern Europe. A concordat was eventually concluded between the Vatican and the Polish government in 1925 which regulated relations between church and state and reduced the independence of the Polish hierarchy, bringing them under closer control by the Vatican between 1925 and 1939.[6]

This control was curtailed at the beginning of the war, however, when the papal nuncio was expelled from Warsaw and all official contact was broken between the Polish church and Rome. Such information as the Vatican received about Poland during the war came from Monsignor Orsenigo in Berlin, or through smuggled reports from inside German-occupied Poland. Even Orsenigo was a problem for the Polish clergy, who saw him as a Nazi sympathizer and consequently disliked and distrusted him. As a result, the Polish church operated on its own initiative and under its own leadership during the war.

It was expected that the Vatican would re-establish its authority over the Polish church when the war was over. Yet the Poles were suspicious of the fact that Pius XII had not demonstrated great sensitivity for Polish suffering during the war. They recognized that Pacelli's German service had left him with an affection for Germany which had been little changed by the outbreak of war and they questioned whether the Vatican, with its worldwide priorities, would respond adequately to Polish issues. In order to demonstrate his neutrality and his availability as a mediator after the German invasion of Poland, Pius XII had not protested that invasion, nor had he spoken out explicitly or directly about the suffering of the Poles. In 1942 the German government asked the Vatican to assist their occupation of Poland by appointing a German as apostolic administrator for German-speaking Catholics in Poland. On the advice of Orsenigo, the Vatican had complied by appointing Father Hilary Brietinger, a German Franciscan, in spite of the fact that this was in clear violation of the terms of the Polish concordat.[7]

The Polish bishops, while aware of the Vatican's diplomatic protests in Berlin and recognizing the strategy of the pope in not openly criticizing Hitler, were concerned that the faithful within Poland might feel that the pope had little sympathy for their suffering. Accordingly, they put continuous pressure on the Holy See between 1940 and 1943 to express some public sympathy for the Poles. They succeeded in averting a serious crisis in the Polish church when Pius XII, in his name-day allocution of 2 June 1943, expressed compassion and affection for Poland and predicted the rebirth of that country. The Polish government-in-exile had protested to the Vatican Secretariat of State that the Brietinger appointment violated the concordat, as did the appointment of Bishop Splett of Danzig as apostolic administrator of the diocese of Chelmno-Pelplin inside Poland. In the latter years of the war, Polish suspicion was such that some Poles feared a Vatican deal with Stalin at their expense.[8] If the Vatican appeared to stand loyally by the London Poles in 1944, some Polish Catholics suspected that this had more to do with protecting Germany from communism than with preserving the integrity of Poland.

After Soviet troops crossed the Curzon Line in May 1944, the Soviet Union created the Polish Committee of National Liberation in Lublin which combined the Moscow-based Union of Polish Patriots with the underground Homeland National Council which was dominated by Polish Communist party leaders Boleslaw Bierut and Wladislaw Gomulka. This Lublin Committee was recognized by the Soviet Union in January 1945 as the provisional government of Poland in preference to the London Poles, and it sought to establish a base in liberated Poland during the winter of 1944-5. The communists recognized that they had little support among the Polish people, partly because they were allies of the hated Russians and partly because of the behaviour of prewar Polish communists who had been virulently anti-national. In 1944 the authority of the Lublin Committee rested on the Red Army but, by introducing a program of land reforms in October 1944, the committee sought to secure for themselves popular support among the peasantry.[9] Nevertheless, their hold on power was tenuous and some communist leaders wanted to broaden the base of the government by creating a national coalition of all anti-fascist parties. In this regard, the decision of the 1945 Yalta conference to expand the provisional government to include some members of the former London government-in-exile was not unwelcome to communist leaders.

Church leaders were prepared to cooperate with the government so long as it respected the rights and privileges of the church. In doing so, the church was confident that it could mount a serious and sustained resistance should the government attempt to restrict these rights and privileges. This did raise the question, however, of who was best placed for dealing with a Communist-dominated government in Warsaw: the Polish church leaders who understood the relative strength and influence of the various interest groups in Poland, or the Holy See which had a general impression of the threat to the church that was posed by the expansion of Soviet influence.

In assessing the situation in Poland, the Holy See was unhappy about the Communist-led government which had been put into office with the assistance of the Soviet Union. To formulate an appropriate approach to the Polish problem in 1945, the Vatican had to consider its own anti-communism, its support for German integrity, and a desire to lend support to the Catholic Church in Poland. The confusion of priorities for the Holy See in its dealings with Poland soon brought it into conflict with the Polish hierarchy who were prepared to work with the communists and supported the wisdom of creating new frontiers, along with the rest of the Polish people.

THE CHURCH IN FRANCE

The contributions of the clergy during the First World War in France had facilitated new church-state relationships in that country during the interwar period. In spite of the 1905 separation of church and state, the war effort of the church, coupled with the 1927 condemnation of the Action Française by Pius XI and his pressure on the French bishops to work within the Third Republic, had resulted in amicable relations by the mid-1930s, even under the Popular Front government of the socialist prime minister, Léon Blum.

With the defeat of France in 1940, however, the bishops and archbishops of the Roman Catholic Church supported the regime of Marshal Pétain as the legitimate state authority. The staunch anticommunism of Pétain's Vichy regime appealed to the church, as did the government's return of former ecclesiastical properties and in its provision of subsidies to church schools. The lower clergy, both secular and religious, while less enthusiastic than the hierarchy, nevertheless followed their lead in accepting the legitimacy of Vichy.

In 1940 the Vatican saw no reason to withdraw the apostolic nuncio, Monsignor Valerio Valeri, who had been accredited to France under the Third Republic. Valeri remained at his post and moved from Paris to Vichy with the Pétain government, yet the Vatican was sometimes embarrassed by the continuing and unquestioning support of the French bishops for this regime. While both the bishops and the papal nuncio protested the Vichy government's involvement in the persecution of the Jews,[10] the bishops maintained their silence over the wartime conscription of French workers for German factories. Moreover, even when requested to do so by the Vatican, the bishops refused to acknowledge the legitimacy of the Free French or to appoint chaplains to work with the fighting units of the Resistance.[11]

General Charles de Gaulle, the leader of the Free French, recognized the importance of restoring and stabilizing French society after the war. He intended to do this by re-establishing the traditional institutions of France, including the Roman Catholic Church. With assistance from the Vatican, de Gaulle helped the French church make the transition from support of the Axis to support of the Fourth Republic without suffering unnecessary persecution. For the Vatican, the respect shown to French Catholics stood as an example of what goodwill could achieve in healing the wounds of war and yet, even with a person as favourably disposed to the church as de Gaulle, the relationship between France and the Vatican was not always an easy one.

After Rome was liberated in June 1944, de Gaulle was one of the first visitors to the Vatican. He understood that, for the preservation of a Catholic France after the war, it was imperative that the church not be pilloried by the left-wing members of the Resistance as a collaborationist institution. Lacking sympathy from the French hierarchy, de Gaulle sought Vatican support to secure the loyalty of the Catholic community in France, knowing also that papal recognition of his government would be a signal that the French hierarchy would be bound to follow. He reassured the pope that the liberation of France would not result in a new wave of anti-clericalism and convinced Vatican officials of the importance of the early restoration of French power, arguing that French recovery "would be the condition of a new equilibrium" in Europe. The pope, in turn, spelled out his grand design, "that only the close union of those European states inspired by Catholicism – Germany, France, Italy, Spain, Belgium, Portugal – could build a dam against the [Communist] danger."[12]

The pope's reception of de Gaulle in June 1944 made a great impression on the French, who saw the papal audience as tantamount to Vatican recognition of the Free French movement.[13] At the beginning of July, Maurice Couve de Murville, the French delegate to the Allied Control Commission in Italy, asked if the Vatican would receive an offical representative from the French provisional government,   and on 9 August Hubert Guérin, formerly French minister in Helsinki, arrived in Rome as the delegate of the French Committee of National Liberation to the Holy See. The Vatican took pains to stress that, while Guérin was the "official agent of the Committee of Algiers," his reception by the Holy See did not constitute formal recognition of the Algiers government which would have to wait until peace was restored.[14] The opening of such a diplomatic channel with the provisional government before metropolitan France had been liberated represented a striking deviation from traditional Vatican practice which would not normally give official recognition to wartime changes of territory and government. It was also a strong vote of confidence in de Gaulle. After the Allied invasion of southern France on 15 August 1944, and the subsequent resignation of Léon Bérard, the Vichy ambassador to the Vatican, Monsignor Montini of the Secretariat of State hoped that the French provisional government would soon name a new ambassador to the Holy See.

The major domestic ecclesiastical problem facing the provisional government concerned the removal of those bishops who had opposed the Free French and had cooperated too closely with Vichy and the Germans. Initially, the provisional government wanted to deal with hostile bishops in the French empire where the authority of the government was stronger. Guérin was instructed to raise with Vatican officials the cases of the bishops of Rabat, Dakar, and St Pierre and Miquelon and the possibility of their removal from office at the first opportunity,[15] and he discussed the matter during his first audience with Pius XII on 25 August. The pope responded that he sought a full normalization of relations between France and the Holy See and told

Guérin that he intended to have Valerio Valeri move from Vichy to Paris so that he could continue his work as nuncio to France.[16]

The issue of Valeri's return to Paris soon developed into a major obstacle between the Holy See and the provisional government. The pope had given early recognition to the provisional government by accepting Guérin as de Gaulle's representative in August 1944 and intended to extend formal recognition by moving Valeri back to Paris to work with the provisional government. The pope reasoned that Valeri had been accredited to the government of France when he had presented his credentials during the Third Republic. During the war, he had worked with the Vichy regime as the established government and, in 1944, he would move back to Paris, thereby indicating that the pope now recognized the legitimacy of de Gaulle's government. Presumably, once the Vatican had made this gesture to Paris, the French could respond by naming a new ambassador to the Holy See. Montini told Guérin that it would be preferable to re-establish formal diplomatic relations before dealing with the difficult matter of the French bishops.[17]

The prospect of the transfer of Valeri from Vichy to Paris created difficulties at the Quai d'Orsay, however, and two objections were cited. The first was an objection on the principle that, by merely transferring its diplomatic representative from Vichy to Paris, the Vatican and conceivably other governments would not be required to recognize the new political reality of liberated France as they would if they had to renew their missions to the new government. The second objection was more specific: that Valeri himself had been involved in the fall of France and the establishment of the Vichy regime by acting as the go-between for French armistice negotiations in 1940.[18] Accordingly, the government decided that when Valeri returned to Paris, he would not be recognized in any official capacity and that the Vatican would be advised that Valeri would have to present new letters of credence before being recognized as the nuncio accredited to the provisional government.[19]

Pius XII was furious at this treatment of Valeri, especially since, in his view, he had made every concession to de Gaulle and had personally taken the decision to return Valeri to Paris. The pope was particularly offended at the suggestion that Valeri was unacceptable because he had served at Vichy and was in some way tainted by that regime. Moreover, the pope had no intention of having his hand forced over the issue of the French bishops.[20] When Cardinal Suhard, the archbishop of Paris, was, on de Gaulle's orders, refused access to his cathedral during the Te Deum to celebrate the liberation, as a gesture of confidence in Suhard, Archbishop Francis Spellman of New York was sent to Paris by the pope to stand at the cardinal's side while he celebrated mass in Notre Dame Cathedral.[21] To increase the pressure on Paris, the French were also told that Valeri was held in such high regard by Pius XII that he could be made a cardinal as early as 1945 and there was even a possibility that the pope would name him to succeed the late Cardinal Maglione as secretary of state.[22]

The Roman Curia had been divided over the appropriate Vatican policy to Vichy France. Some Vatican officials, including the former nuncio to Republican Spain, Monsignor Federico Tedeschini, had disapproved of the position that the Secretariat of State and Valeri had taken to relations with Vichy France. They felt that during the German occupation of France, the Vatican should have recalled the nuncio and left the nunciature under the direction of a chargé d'affaires. In this way, neither the Vatican nor Valeri would have been compromised. Others, including Pius XII and Cardinals Fumasoni-Biondi and Pizzardo, believed that Valeri had done his duty in difficult circumstances and that France was being unnecessarily arbitrary in refusing to recognize him.

On 21 October 1944 Great Britain, the United States, and Canada recognized de Gaulle's government. Immediately afterward, Valeri was informed that de Gaulle was no longer prepared to have him as nuncio even with new letters of credence because he was now determined that the dean of the diplomatic corps[23] could not be the individual who had served the Vichy regime in the same capacity.[24] When Montini asked Guérin what France really wanted, the latter said France wanted a new candidate for nuncio who should receive the approval of the French government; once given this, France would do whatever the Holy See wanted. Guérin also received the impression from Tardini that the Vatican feared the French demand for a new nuncio would establish a precedent which could be repeated by other countries at the end of the war.[25] The Vatican reply objected that the recall of Valeri would create a dangerous precedent and "in the present circumstances, would be regarded by the Holy See as an unfriendly act."[26]

It was the approaching end of the year that expedited matters. On 30 November Guérin advised Montini that the French government wanted a new nuncio in place by 1 January to present the official new year's greetings to de Gaulle on behalf of the diplomatic corps. An internal report of the Quai d'Orsay had indicated that the pope had little comprehension of the "spirit of the Resistance" and was still very annoyed with what he saw as French bad faith, but recommended that France be firm and make real concessions to the Vatican as soon as the pope acceded to French wishes over Valeri.[27]

The Vatican finally decided that it was unproductive to continue this dispute with such a good friend of the church as de Gaulle, and granted official recognition to the provisional government on 4 December, along with assurances that the Vatican would be prepared to discuss the matter of the collaborationist bishops. It was speculated that the pope's change of mind may have been influenced by de Gaulle's scheduled trip to Moscow in December and the possiblity that the French leader might be able to address the position of the Catholic Church during his meetings in the Soviet Union.[28]

On 14 December the name of Monsignor Angelo Roncalli, the apostolic delegate to Turkey, and the future Pope John XXIII, was submitted as nuncio to France. Paris gave its approval promptly on 19 December and Roncalli presented his credentials and the official new year's greetings to de Gaulle on 1 January 1945.[29] Roncalli's appointment was well received by the French church, since they knew him to be a friend of Montini and not to be close to Ottaviani and the Holy Office, who had doubts about many of the ecclesiastical experiments involving worker-priests being conducted under the patronage of Cardinal Suhard. Valeri was received by de Gaulle in a long and cordial farewell audience on 20 December 1944, at which time the outgoing nuncio was assured that the French government recognized the good that he had done for France. Valeri was honoured prior to his departure by the award of the Légion d'Honneur.

Since the pope had accommodated the French government on the matter of Valeri, de Gaulle made a gesture to restore good relations with the Vatican by appointing the eminent Catholic philosopher Jacques Maritain as the new French ambassador to the Holy See. Maritain had established his reputation as the foremost modern interpreter of the works of St Thomas Aquinas during the two decades following the First World War. Both a devout Catholic and a political humanist, he had protested Italian behaviour during the Ethiopian war, had refused to endorse the Spanish Nationalists in the Spanish civil war, and had condemned anti-semitism during the Second World War. When France fell in 1940, Maritain was in Toronto, teaching at the Pontifical Institute of Medieval Studies. He remained in Canada and the United States during the war, working in support of the Free French through his writings and radio broadcasts, and founding the Ecole Libre des Hautes Etudes, "known as the only Free French university during the war."[30] Maritain was at first reluctant to accept the Vatican embassy since this would necessitate the sacrifice of his scholarship, but his friend, Foreign Minister Georges Bidault, convinced him with the argument that he was being appointed "because of the symbolic value for French Catholicism and for the Holy See of the presence in Rome of a personality who represents as perfectly as you the tradition of Christian France and the movement which animates us today."[31]

Not all Vatican officials approved of this appointment. While Montini, as chaplain of FUCI, had introduced many future leaders of Italian Christian Democracy to the ideas of Maritain in the 1930s, other Curial officials, including Tardini, had serious reservations about Maritain's liberal Catholicism.[32] Although formal approval was granted, the Vatican did point out that they would have preferred an individual who had not been so implicated in public party controversies. When conveying Vatican approval to de Gaulle, Roncalli indicated that the Holy See was accepting Maritain in spite of its reservations about him.[33] Maritain presented his credentials to Pius XII on 10 May, three days after the end of the war in Europe.

As the Vatican and the provisional government were thus composing their differences, the French hierarchy met in conference on 28 February 1945, and, in a gesture designed to signal their acceptance of the new political reality, issued a statement of loyalty to de Gaulle as the head of the provisional government. France benefited from papal insecurity in early 1945 by appearing to be the only European power on whom the Vatican could rely. The Vatican had great faith in de Gaulle as a bulwark against the extension of communist influence and against a revival of French anti-clericalism. Guérin believed that France was in a good position to assist the Vatican in European affairs and in its relationship with Stalin, with whom de Gaulle was on good terms. He argued that France could provide an alternate partnership for the Vatican to that which was developing with the United States, although he felt that the animosity of many Italians in the Curia to France prevented greater Vatican use of French assistance.[34]

The pope's remaining concern with Paris had to do with the purging of the French bishops. Neither the Vatican nor the French church wanted to make any changes until the war was over and the domestic situation in France had been clarified. Guérin believed that France needed to mount a coordinated campaign by sending influential French Catholics to Rome to report to the pope and the Curia on the behaviour of the collaborationist bishops, so that there would be no doubt about the Vatican not having been informed of the evidence in these cases.[35] But, given the anxieties of the Holy See, the French did not raise the question of the bishops again before the end of the war.

4 The Church in the Balkans

Unlike the nations of central and western Europe with their predominantly Catholic populations, the nations of the Balkans represented a more complex religious mix. It was in the Balkans that the Catholic west faced the Orthodox east and it was also in the Balkans that the only European frontier between Islam and Christianity was to be found. Religious loyalties were often combined with national and ethnic identities to create a potent brew of hatred and conflict. The involvement of powers external to the area was often used to favour one faction, nation, or religion over others and such was the case with Italian and German intervention in the Balkans during the Second World War.

Since the Roman Catholic Church was one of the religions with a Balkan presence, it became implicated in the wartime hostilities and persecutions of the area. The church found itself under the protection of Italian occupation authorities in Albania and Yugoslavia and, in wartime Croatia, was the favoured institution of Ante Pavelic and his Ustase regime. The role of the Catholic Church in Bulgaria and Romania, predominantly Orthodox countries, was considerably more benign than in the western Balkans.

THE CHURCH IN ALBANIA

Centred around the city of Scutari, Roman Catholics had traditionally been an influential minority in northern Albania where, according to the 1945 census, they made up 10.1 percent of the Albanian population, compared to 72.8 percent Moslem and 17.1 percent Orthodox. Most of the Catholic priests in Albania were of Italian origin and, during the interwar years, had been used by the Italian Fascist regime as agents for the promotion of Italian culture and in support of Italian influence. After Italy annexed Albania in 1939, the clergy cooperated willingly with the occupation authorities and, as a result, the Catholic Church enjoyed a position of favour and influence throughout the Second World War. Certainly, the Catholics of northern Albania made no contribution to the anti-Italian resistance during the war and, when a Regency Council was established by the Germans to govern the country after the fall of Mussolini, it was a Catholic priest, Father Anton Harapi, who was named regent, and a Catholic, Maliq Bey Bushati, who was named prime minister.

Historian Peter R. Prifti claims that Albanians have never been a deeply religious people because the major religions of the country all represented cultural impositions by foreign powers: Islam from the Ottoman Turks, Orthodoxy from the Greeks and the Serbs, and Catholicism from the Italians. He claims that the awakening of Albanian nationalism in the nineteenth century did not have a religious base and "that the national movement ... assumed a nonreligious character and in fact prompted leaders of the Albanian national movement to downgrade religion in order to upgrade nationalism."[1]

During the Second World War, the resistance movement in Albania against first the Italians and then the Germans, was led by Enver Hoxha and dominated by the National Liberation Front which was itself controlled by the Communist party, who defeated their resistance rivals and then took up the banner of Albanian nationalism themselves. By the time the last Germans had withdrawn in November 1944, the Communists were in complete control of the country. Helped by the Yugoslav Partisans, the Communists assumed control of the government with broad popular support inside Albania and with the external blessing of the Grand Alliance. Significantly, the Communists had come to power in Albania with no direct assistance from either the Soviet Union or the Red Army.[2]

None of the religions of Albania had supported the partisans and Hoxha's government was consequently beholden to none of them, which fitted perfectly with marxist-leninist doctrine. In Albania more than in any other country, the Catholic Church had been an anti-national force in the service of the national enemy. After the war, the Catholic minority showed "no willingness, for ideological, material and political reasons, to cooperate with the government on any terms acceptable to the latter" and the Catholic population of the north continued to support a guerrilla war in the mountains against Hoxha's troops well into 1946.[3] There was no reason for the Hoxha government to treat the Catholic Church with consideration in the postwar period and the government set about immediately to neutralize religion and the religious bodies of the country.

THE CHURCH IN YUGOSLAVIA

From the founding of the Kingdom of the Serbs, Croats, and Slovenes in 1918, the country had been divided along religious lines, with the dominant Serbs subscribing to the Serb Orthodox Church while the Croats and Slovenes were Roman Catholic. There was also a significant Moslem population in Bosnia-Herzegovina. The Serbs dominated the political life of the kingdom and, in so doing, favoured the Orthodox Church over the other religions. The Croat political opposition sought a federal constitution and equal treatment for the Catholic Church. In 1929, with the failure of existing constitutional arrangements to overcome deep-seated ethnic and regional differences, King Alexander suspended the constitution and changed the name of the state to Yugoslavia which he sought to develop as a unitary nation.

The king sought to negotiate separate agreements to regulate the position and activities of the various religious communities. In the case of the Roman Catholics, a concordat with the Vatican would define and protect the rights of the Catholic Church. In this way, Alexander hoped to bring the Slovenes and the Croats to support the Yugoslav nation and its constitution. Because of the intense Croat particularism of many of the Catholic higher clergy, the king could not deal with them, and instead negotiated an agreement directly with the Vatican, hoping thereby to bind the Catholic community to support of the state. Alexander did not live to see his project through, however, and the concordat was not signed until 1935, a year after his assassination in Marseilles. Yet, while signed, this concordat was never ratified. The Serb Orthodox opposition was great because of generous concessions made to the Catholics that had not been offered to the Orthodox and also because the Catholics, with their headquarters in Rome, were seen by many Orthodox Serbs to be a pro-Italian fifth column. While the concordat passed the lower house of Parliament, it was never put before the upper house, with the result that it never came into effect. One of the reasons for the lack of determination of the government of the day was the disinterest and opposition of members of the Croat Catholic hierarchy to the concordat. They resented Vatican interference in their national affairs and correctly saw the concordat as a device for curtailing their Croatian nationalism and bringing them under closer control of the Curia.

After the defeat of Yugoslavia by German and Italian forces in April 1941, an Independent State of Croatia, the Nezavisna Drzava Hrvatska (NDH), was set up in Croatia and Bosnia-Herzegovina under Ante Pavelic and his Ustase movement, while the remainder of Yugoslavia was occupied by either German or Italian forces. The Ustase had been formed as a terrorist movement of Croat separatists following King Alexander's 1929 suspension of the constitution and had been heavily financed by the Italian government during the 1930s. Fiercely nationalistic, the Ustase was also fanatically Catholic. In the Yugoslav political context, it identified Catholicism with Croatian nationalism and, once established in power, set about persecuting and murdering non-Catholics and, eventually, in forcing conversions to Catholicism with death as the alternative.

The Catholic Church was seriously compromised by the NDH. Archbishop Aloysius Stepinac of Zagreb was a young, energetic, and devout churchman who was also a narrow-minded Croatian nationalist. In April 1941 he welcomed the creation of a separate Croat state in which the Catholic Church would have prominence. Within a month of the founding of that state, however, Stepinac was disillusioned by the behaviour of the Pavelic regime. When the Ustase began their forced conversions of the Orthodox to Catholicism, the archbishop interceded to make the point that under canon law only voluntary conversions were acceptable to the Church. In November 1941, along with the Croatian hierarchy, he protested this point to Pavelic. In 1942 and 1943 Stepinac went from private to public protests over the state's treatment of Serbs and Jews while, at the same time, giving private assistance to many of those being persecuted. From 1942 on, Stepinac also spoke out against the behaviour and policies of the Germans who had occupied Slovenia. Historian Michael Phayer credits Stepinac with being the most outspoken of the east European church leaders during the war: "No leader of a national church ever spoke about genocide as pointedly as Stepinac. His words were courageous and principled."[4]

Yet while he did his best to "mitigate the savagery of the Ustase toward Serbs and Jews and to provide for the refugees from Slovenia," at no time did the Catholic hierarchy voice open opposition to the government or to the German or Italian occupying powers. Stepinac never broke with the regime and continued to attend and preside over official state functions at the side of Pavelic, thus giving the impression that the regime continued with the blessing of the church.[5]

All Croatian Catholics did not share Stepinac's position. While most of the bishops and clergy stood with Stepinac in respectful distrust of the Pavelic government, there were some religious, most notably members of the Franciscan Order and Monsignor Saric, the archbishop of Sarajevo, who gave active and whole-hearted support to the policies of the Ustase government, including the forced conversions. As the war came to an end, other Catholics, including some members of the lower clergy, were disgusted by the behaviour of their church leadership, and moved in the opposite direction to support Tito's Partisan forces against the Ustase, the Germans, and the Italians.[6]

The Holy See traditionally did not recognize political changes which took place during a war. It therefore refused to recognize the NDH, and continued to maintain its nunciature in Belgrade and to deal with the Yugoslav minister to the Holy See in Rome, representing the exiled royal government. Whenever Pavelic visited Rome, the pope refused to accord him a public audience and only agreed to meet him as a private Catholic with no entourage and no publicity.[7] In order to maintain contact with the church in Croatia and to look after its interests there, the Vatican named the Benedictine abbot Ramiro Marcone as apostolic delegate to Zagreb for the duration of the war, at the same time refusing to accept any official representative from the Croatian government.[8] Where possible, the Vatican used its influence with the Italians to mitigate German treatment of the Slovenes and, through the father-general of the Franciscan Order and the Franciscan provincial from Zagreb, asked that the Franciscans cease their involvement in the punitive expeditions in Croatia.[9] From its experience of the 1930s, the Vatican was aware that, where Croatian nationalism was concerned, it could exercise little control over the Croatian clergy.

After the surrender of Italy in September 1943, the Allies directed their military aid in Yugoslavia to the Partisan forces led by Tito and the communists who were deemed to be more energetic than the non-communist Chetniks under Colonel Draza Mihailovic. Where the Chetniks had been based in Serbia and were led by former officers of the Royal Yugoslav Army, the Partisans had had their main base in Bosnia. The Partisans had attracted many non-communists to their support because they promised to create a federal Yugoslavia after the war. In November 1943 Tito became the leader of the Council of National Liberation which put itself forward as an alternate government; and in 1944 he entered into negotiations with the London government-in-exile to create one government for the country. This was finally achieved on 7 March 1945, when Tito formed a national government which included representatives of the government-in-exile and which was quickly recognized by the Allies as the government of Yugoslavia. While the Red Army had entered Yugoslavia in September

1944 and had been present when Tito's Partisans captured Belgrade on 20 October, they had moved on to Hungary shortly after. This meant that the Partisans bore the brunt of the fighting in 1945 and the end of the war found Tito and the Communists clearly in control of the government of Yugoslavia which they had secured by their own military and political efforts. Yugoslavia, in particular, became "the pride and the showcase of the world Communist movement" in the period from 1945 to 1948.[10]

While individual priests had aided the Partisans, the Catholic Church as a whole had given them little support and, if anything, had stood by the occupying forces. There was therefore no reason for the Partisans to respect the personnel or the institutions of the church. As the war came to an end, the Partisans were especially harsh on those clergy, such as the Franciscans, who had collaborated with the enemy or who were suspected of collaboration.[11] Unfortunately for the church, it was often easier in the heat of victory for the Partisans to consider all churchmen as collaborators than to take the time to differentiate guilt from innocence.

Tito was caught in the middle. Collaborators should, of course, be punished and he was unable or unwilling to control every excess of the Partisans. On the other hand, he wanted to govern a united Yugoslavia and, in order to gain the support of the Croats and Slovenes, would have to show respect for the Catholic Church. His need of continued British and American assistance also required a display of respect for religion. Tito's strategy was to pardon the Catholic Church as an institution while insisting that those clergy who had collaborated should be punished. At the end of September 1944 two Yugoslav officers representing Tito appeared at the Vatican to explain the shooting of some priests by Partisan forces and to give assurances of Tito's goodwill toward the Catholic Church.[12] In February 1945 Tito told the British ambassador that he would have to take drastic action against the Franciscans for their participation in massacres and atrocities, but that "he was as strongly opposed as ever to any form of religious persecution."[13] On 9 March 1945 the consolidated Tito government publicly guaranteed freedom of worship in postwar Yugoslavia.

THE CHURCH IN ROMANIA AND BULGARIA

The bulk of the population in Romania and Bulgaria belonged to the Orthodox Church and Roman Catholics were clearly in a minority. Catholics were divided between those who practised the Latin rite and Uniates who practised Eastern rites. Because Roman Catholics in each country had played significant historical roles and because they had posed no real threat to the majority religion in the past, good relations between Orthodox and Catholics had become a tradition in both these countries.

Romania

At the end of the First World War the only church in Romania was the Romanian Orthodox Church. When Romania annexed Transylvania from Hungary in 1919, it acquired a sizeable body of Roman Catholics; at the end of the Second World War there were three million Roman Catholics and fifteen million members of the Orthodox Church in Romania. In 1698 Romanian members of the Orthodox Church in lands acquired by the Austrian Empire had sworn allegiance to the pope and had been allowed to continue practising their liturgical rites as Uniates. These Romanian Uniates retained and promoted their language and culture within the Empire through their churches and through their confessional schools. For this reason, after their return to Romania in 1919, the Uniates enjoyed considerable prestige as purveyors of a superior brand of Romanian cultural nationalism. The Latin-rite Catholics, on the other hand, consisted of groups of Hungarians and Germans who lived in Transylvania and were not as well regarded by the Romanians.

Relations between Orthodox and Catholics were good throughout the interwar period. Because of the Latin origin of the Romanian language, educated Romanians prided themselves on their western origins and orientation. Moreover, the Romanian Orthodox Church, being jealous of its autonomy, found that it could maintain its independence within the Orthodox communion by retaining close ties with western churches, especially the Roman Catholics and the Anglicans. The prestige of the Uniates and the western orientation of the Romanians encouraged good relations between the Romanian government and the Holy See. A concordat, signed in 1927 and ratified in 1929, defined the role of the Roman Catholic Church, both Latin and Uniate, within the expanded Romanian state. The concordat provided for Catholic confessional schools in recognition of the significance of these schools as guardians of Romanian culture in the Austro-Hungarian Empire.

During the Second World War, when Stalin recognized the Russian Orthodox Church as one of the institutional pillars of the state, the Romanians, always wary of Russian imperialism, valued even more their close ties with the Vatican as a means of emphasizing their independence. There was even a rumour that King Michael was proposing that the Romanian Orthodox Church accept the authority of the pope and thereby protect itself from incorporation into the Russian Church.[14] In August 1944 Michael broke relations with Germany, arrested his prime minister, General Antonescu, and accepted an armistice with the Soviet Union, whereupon Romania was occupied by the Red Army. While the initial post-armistice governments were centrist coalitions headed by generals, in February 1945 the Soviet Union insisted that Michael install the left-wing National Democratic Front coalition, in which the Romanian Communists played the decisive role, as the government of Romania. Petru Groza, leader of the Ploughman's Front, became the prime minister. From this point on, the Communists were in a position to extend their control over the Romanian government.[15]

Under the Soviet occupation the Romanian Orthodox Church was put under pressure to move closer to the Russian Orthodox Church. Romanian Patriarch Nikodim attended the enthronement of Patriarch Alexei in Moscow in February 1945 and a delegation from the Russian church subsequently visited Romania for talks with Romanian church leaders. Suspicious that the Russians were aiming for union of the Russian and Romanian churches, the Romanians were cautious in their dealings with their ecclesiastical counterparts.

Bulgaria

At the end of the Second World War the Roman Catholic population of Bulgaria was reported to be fifty thousand, or an insignificant 0.7 per cent of the population of the country. Catholics were divided into three distinct groups.

The largest proportion, between thirty-two and thirty-seven thousand, practised Latin rites of Pauline origin. These Catholics traced their heritage to their ancestors' conversion to Catholicism by Bosnian missionaries at the beginning of the sixteenth century. Since that time, they had frequently been persecuted and had come to live by themselves in a number of farming communities where they had developed their own traditions and even their own dialect.

The second group consisted of Latin-rite Catholics of origins other than Pauline. In the twentieth century French, Italian and Croatian Catholics had opened schools and colleges in Bulgaria. As a result of this educational influence, a number of Bulgarians had converted to Catholicism from Orthodoxy. The fact that the Bulgarian monarchs were Catholic made such conversion respectable. This second group consisted of from seven to eight thousand persons in 1947.

The third and smallest group consisted of the Bulgarian Uniates. The Bulgarian Orthodox Church had separated from Rome in 1235 and had eventually come under the authority of the Ecumenical Patriarch in Constantinople. As part of the movement for Bulgarian independence from the Turkish empire in the nineteenth century, the Bulgarian bishops planned to separate from Constantinople and the Orthodox Church and submit to the authority of the pope. This Bulgarian Uniate Church was created in 1870 and immediately evoked a Turkish imperial rescript which granted autonomy to the Bulgarian Orthodox Church under its own exarch. An exarch was a lesser position than a patriarch and was offered out of respect for the sensibilities of the Ecumenical Patriarch. The creation of the exarchate stemmed the movement towards Rome and, upon the naming of the first exarch in 1872, the Bulgarian church declared its autonomy from the Patriarch, who in turn excommunicated that church. In spite of the creation of the exarchate, some Orthodox did accept the pope's authority and joined the Bulgarian Uniate Church. These Eastern-rite Catholics numbered six thousand in 1947 and still saw their mission as keeping alive the plan to lead the rest of the Orthodox into communion with Rome.

Bulgaria had traditionally been the most pro-Russian country in eastern Europe. During the Second World War, while fighting on the side of the Axis, it had refused to declare war on the Soviet Union. As the Red Army advanced in 1944, the Soviet Union declared war on Bulgaria three days before Soviet troops entered the country on 8 September. A ceasefire was immediately accepted by Bulgaria and on 9 September a Fatherland Front government, dominated by the Communists, was installed in Sofia.[16]

During the interwar years, the Church of England had helped the east European Orthodox churches to resist Roman Catholic proselytizing by bringing the leaders of the Bulgarian church together with the leaders of the Romanian and Serbian churches.[17] The situation changed radically with the wartime revival of the Russian Orthodox Church. On 6 April 1945 a delegation from the Russian Orthodox Church arrived in Sofia for discussions with the Synod of the Bulgarian church. The delegation carried a letter from Patriarch Alexei which stressed the importance of cohesion and unity between Orthodox churches in the face of the growing pretensions of the Catholic Church and their fascist allies. The Russian Church was prepared to offer its services as the protector of the Bulgarian church.[18]

The Bulgarians were wary, however. Bulgarian Catholics were insignificant in number and posed no threat; the Bulgarian Orthodox had enjoyed good relations with the Vatican in the past and expected to continue these relations in the future. Exarch Stephen I, described by the British minister as "a wily political fence-sitter,"[19] received the Russians graciously, but had no intention of depending solely on their patronage.

While Soviet troops and officials were not particularly friendly towards the Catholic Church after they had occupied Bulgaria, they did not interfere with the functioning of that church, save to requisition the Catholic school Pro Oriente from an Italian religious order to provide accommodation for Soviet troops. Beyond this, the communications of the apostolic delegate with the Vatican were not interfered with.[20]

5 The Church in the United States

The Roman Catholic Church in the United States had traditionally been the church of the European immigrants, whether from Ireland, Italy, Poland, Germany, or the nations of eastern Europe. As the off-spring of the original immigrants secured education, business success, and social status in the twentieth century, so the social and political status of the Catholic Church changed. The Roosevelt New Deal of the 1930s received strong support from Catholics and from immigrant groups who, almost for the first time, felt that the federal government was deliberately looking out for their interests. The political support which Catholics gave to Roosevelt was reciprocated as FDR extended himself to incorporate the Catholic community into mainstream American politics.

American Catholics were not initially of one mind over the war in Europe where Catholics were fighting Catholics. As a result, they tended to fall back on their traditional support for isolationism. The attack on Pearl Harbor brought American Catholics out of this isolationism, however, to give wholehearted support to the American war effort against Japan. The war in Europe continued to bother Catholics, where they were asked to fight alongside the British oppressors of Ireland and the atheistic Russians against their co-religionists in Germany and Italy. The Catholic community had particular difficulty seeing the United States work in close collaboration with the Soviet Union, a nation which had persecuted the Catholic Church and was the sworn enemy of religion. However, Catholics were also fighting for the protection and liberation of Catholic Poland, Austria,

Czechoslovakia, and Belgium, so the war effort in Europe was ultimately justified. By their eventual active and enthusiastic support of America's war effort, the Roman Catholic community established their Americanism, despite their varied ethnic origins.[1]

Having given their support to Franklin Roosevelt and his New Deal, the Catholic bishops felt that they had a duty to speak out where Catholic principles and American foreign policy came into conflict. Such was the case when Roosevelt sent lend-lease aid to the Soviet Union after the Nazi invasion of June 1941. The president was greatly relieved when the Vatican agreed in September 1941, that, while condemning communism, it would be willing to see aid provided to the Russian people. Monsignor Amleto Cicognani, the apostolic delegate in Washington, instructed the American bishops to issue a pastoral letter declaring that the 1937 encyclical, *Divini Redemptoris*, was "not to be applied to the present moment of armed conflict."[2] After the United States entered the war in December 1941, Cicognani personally visited those bishops who had been most outspoken in their anti-administration views and warned them that the Holy See would be displeased at public statements which would "lessen in any way popular support of the policies of the administration."[3]

While the bishops thereafter supported the national war effort, they remained wary of Roosevelt's dealings with Stalin. In 1944 a number of individuals and groups, including the apostolic delegate, advised the bishops that they should publicly oppose the way that Roosevelt was appeasing Stalin. In April 1944 William C. Bullitt, former American ambassador to Moscow and Paris, told a representative of the bishops that "the time had come to oppose the apparent intemperate pro-Russian attitudes on the part of our highest Government officials." Bullitt said that the president and his closest advisers "felt helpless in the face of [a] well organized pro-Russian bloc in the Government" and he "bore down heavily on the Hopkins' influence and the pitiful incompetence of much of the personnel of the State Department." Bullitt sought "to gain the publicity and leadership of the Catholic Church against the rising Russian menace." Later in the year he wrote a long article for *Life* magazine, in which he warned the American people about the coming struggle between Christianity and communism.[4] R.H. Hadow, secretary for Latin American Affairs at the British embassy in Washington, like Bullitt, warned the bishops "about the tremendous organization of Russian propaganda throughout the hemisphere."[5]

In September the Union of Slovenian Parishes of America warned of certain persecution of Roman Catholics in Slovenia should a Communist government come to power in Yugoslavia. In a letter to the bishops, the organization urged that the American government not support Tito and pleaded "that the United States, at the proper time, raise its voice in defense of the Catholics in Slovenia." In October the Coordinating Committee of American Polish Associations in the East wrote "that they hoped and prayed that the Catholic Bishops will join once more in a collective call of conscience for a return to the principles of the Atlantic Charter for which our country set out to fight."[6]

Unlike other countries with comparable Catholic populations, the American Catholic bishops were highly organized at the national level. Since the end of the First World War, the American hierarchy had held annual meetings as the National Catholic Welfare Conference (NCWC), an organization with an administrative board, a general secretary, and a secretariat to function between meetings and to prepare materials for consideration by the bishops.[7] The American bishops thus had a functioning infrastructure capable of providing them with informed advice on political and social issues and of disseminating their messages to the extensive Catholic newspaper and media outlets throughout the United States.[8]

In their mid-November annual meeting of 1944, the bishops gave close scrutiny to the the draft charter for a new international organization which had recently been prepared at a conference at Dumbarton Oaks in Washington, DC. Following the meeting, they issued a statement critical of the dominant role to be assigned to the great powers in the proposed United Nations organization. The postwar peace should be based not on power politics, argued the bishops, but on Christian principle, in which force would be subordinated to law. The international organization must be universal and democratic and must allow for treaty revision. National sovereignty should not be used to screen nations from their international obligations nor must the great powers dominate the new organization. This argument of the bishops was based on their view that one of the main roles of the United Nations should be to force the Soviet Union to respect the rights of individuals, the family, and religion.[9]

Upset by the appeasement of the Soviet Union at Yalta on 15 April 1945, the NCWC administrative board released a statement on world peace to coincide with the opening of the founding conference of the United Nations at San Francisco. The statement was a direct attack on the charter of the United Nations, claiming that "if in the name of realism an attempt is made to substitute for a juridical world institution what is in effect only an Alliance of the Great Powers, many nations will take refuge in isolationism." The bishops deplored the veto provision for the Security Council and the expansion of the powers of the Security Council at the expense of the General Assembly. They called for an international bill of rights because "dangers to world peace have come from the unjust treatment of minorities, the denial of civil and religious liberties and other infringements on the inborn rights of men."

Having forced Poland to surrender a significant part of her territory at Yalta, the great powers must now see that Polish liberties are preserved in "a free, independent, [and] democratic Poland." In spite of the Soviet absorption of the Baltic states, "we hope that when the final peace treaty is framed and approved, it will not be recorded that our country condoned the enslavement of these freedom-loving nations." The important issue of the postwar world would not be the resolution of the problems of fascism, but the great conflict between democracy and marxist totalitarianism. Democracy must gird itself to be constantly on guard against totalitarianism which "herds the masses under dictatorial leadership, insults their intelligence with its propaganda and controlled press, and tyrannically violates innate human rights."[10]

Before the Second World War had ended, the American bishops had defined the road that lay ahead. According to historian Earl Boyea, "This consistent attention to the evils of Communism could be said to have been one of the foundation stones of the Cold War."[11] Their declaration was relayed to Rome by the apostolic delegate and was published in the *Osservatore Romano* on 17 April 1945. The Italian Catholic press stressed that the declaration represented the views of the pope and the Vatican.[12]

NCWC REPORTS ON COMMUNISM

Following the November 1944 meeting, Monsignor Michael T. Ready, general secretary of the NCWC, commissioned two reports on the international and domestic impacts of communism to guide the bishops in their future deliberations. A report on the goals of the Soviet Union was commissioned from the young Jesuit, Robert Graham, a graduate of Georgetown and an editor with the Jesuit publication *America*. Graham's report assessed Stalin's current policy and the future directions that he was likely to take, and was delivered to the NCWC on 6 December 1944.[13]

The second report commissioned by Ready was a study of the domestic threat of communism in the United States. John F. Cronin, ss, a teacher at St Mary's Seminary in Baltimore and a disciple of Father John A. Ryan, "the pioneer of Catholic social thought," had long been involved in social causes and had served in the early 1940s as a CIO organizer with the dockside unions in Baltimore. On the waterfront, Cronin had learned of communist tactics in taking over union locals and had prepared reports on communist involvement in the labour movement for the FBI.[14]

Cronin had conveyed his concerns about communism to Archbishop Edward Mooney of Detroit, the chairman of the administrative board of the NCWC, in October 1942. As a result, it was Cronin who was commissioned in 1944 to conduct "a study of communism, its nature, extent, causes, and remedies." Temporarily attached to the Social Action Department of the NCWC, Cronin energetically set about his work, circulating a questionnaire to all bishops asking about communist strength and "the current state of public opinion in regard to communism" in their dioceses. A separate and shorter questionnaire was sent to two hundred selected priests across the country.[15]

By April 1945 Cronin had completed a tentative report based on the questionnaires, reports from independent investigators, the seven-volume report of the House Committee on Un-American Activities (which Cronin admitted had to be used with great care due to its simplistic investigative methods), and "inside information, obtained either by subpoena or by the use of spies or informants within the Party." Much of this last information came directly from the FBI through agent William Sullivan, whom Cronin had met during his years with the Baltimore unions. A restricted number of copies of Cronin's report were distributed to members of the administrative board, to NCWC staff members, and to the apostolic delegate.[16]

These two reports provided the American bishops with a basis for their future stance on communism, an ideology which threatened the future politics of Europe and which was present, if not well known, within the United States itself. The bishops were in a position to try to shape American foreign policy and to encourage cautionary moves in domestic politics. Since the reports were forwarded to the Vatican, one can assume that they also influenced thinking within the Curia. Because of their isolation from the moral complexities of European politics, the Americans could speak with clarity and precision on future directions in dealing with communism.

The Graham Report

Graham's report, entitled "Soviet Policy and Tactics in Europe," was based on a judicious assessment of the international situation and gave an accurate prediction of subsequent developments in postwar Europe. Describing Soviet designs in terms of three zones, Graham argued that

Stalin was not so much driven by long-range ideology as by practical politics.

His first zone included the "territories which are to be incorporated into the Soviet Union," including eastern Poland and the Baltic states. While Stalin was adamant on annexing these territories and there was nothing the West could do to stop him, Graham did feel that the West could put pressure on Stalin to allow a certain amount of religious liberty in this zone if he wanted to maintain the continued friendship of his allies. "There are signs," he wrote, "that the governing group in Moscow are conscious that world opinion will be mollified if some appearance of religious liberty is allowed." He recommended that the American bishops continue to express their concern about the fate of religion in eastern Europe in order to put pressure on the American government to in turn put pressure on Stalin.

The second zone included a ring of countries which were not to be incorporated into the Soviet Union, but "are to be under Soviet influence so completely that no anti-Soviet regime can possibly take its rise therein." In this zone, Graham grouped Poland, Yugoslavia, Bulgaria, Romania, and Hungary, while indicating that Czechoslavakia and Turkey were in separate categories because of their unique situations. Graham felt that Russia would resist outright annexation because of the reaction of world opinion and because of the obvious difficulty of administering these areas. Therefore, the Russians would be very careful to camouflage the new power of communism in those countries and, for the immediate future, the Catholic Church might be treated tolerably well, as it had been in Poland since the arrival of the Russians.

The third zone covered "territories more remote where Russia is anxious to gain not control, but at least a sizable measure of influence," in particular, in Italy, France and Belgium. In these countries, which Stalin could never control directly, the major concern was in preventing any anti-Soviet coalition from coming to power which could instigate an invasion of eastern Europe or of the Soviet Union. The Communist parties of western Europe would, therefore, denounce any potential anti-Soviet forces, such as the Catholic Church, as collaborators with the Axis powers.

The area where Graham expected the greatest conflict to arise between East and West was in Germany. He believed that Stalin wanted a Soviet Germany but, failing this, would look for major Soviet influence in that country. The great power agreement of 24 November 1944 for separate zones of occupation in postwar Germany was seen by Graham as being particularly ominous. He felt that the Soviet Union would "deport German labour to serve as construction battalions in the Soviet Union to restore German cities destroyed by the Nazis" and that there were "solid grounds for believing that under the mask of war reparations the greatest liquidation of the middle class that the Soviets have ever attempted may be carried out ... The wide interpretation given to the term 'war criminals', coupled to the control of Eastern Germany by the Red Army can lead to a legalized extermination of all conservative forces in that region of the conquered Reich ... It is clear that an ideological struggle for the mind and soul of Germany is on the horizon. In this battle the most formidable ideological power facing Communism will be the Catholic Church."

Graham saw the Soviets following a double policy with regard to the Roman Catholic Church: conciliation of Catholics under direct or indirect Soviet rule and "an attitude of resistance and opposition to the Vatican as such." Attacks on the pope served a twofold purpose: "They were aimed at undermining the authority of the Vatican in Europe. They also had the effect of putting Russia in the light of a defender of Orthodoxy. This would consolidate their influence with the Orthodox East."

Graham's conclusion was that the "conflict between Rome and Moscow will assume highest proportions in Germany" where the "Bolshevik peril" theme would no longer be serviceable for the church, since it had been discredited by the Nazis, and where communists and Catholics would have to compete instead in promoting social reforms. On the positive side, Graham noted that the prestige of the German bishops was high and that the Soviet zone of occupation would be in the least Catholic part of Germany.[17]

The Cronin Report

"In the judgment of this writer," wrote John Cronin setting out the theme of his draft report of April 1945 to the NCWC, "communism is a serious threat to the Catholic Church and to the welfare of the United States." While the immediate menace of communism lay in Europe and Asia, Americans could soon find themselves "surrounded by a powerful Communist empire, with its secret army in our midst." The main strength of the communists in the United States lay in the "field of labor, racial and religious minority groups." In the trade unions, communism was strongest in the CIO and "in industrial centres, especially where there is mass production and large groups of foreign workers or minority groups such as Negroes or Jews." Below the national level, many local branches and member unions of the CIO were completely controlled by the communists.

Cronin considered communist work with the "Negroes." Where blacks had suffered much injustice and discrimination, they had found that the Communist Political Association (CPA) was the only organization which was actively prepared to champion their rights. "The result has been the gaining of thousands of Negroes as CPA members," along with the support of Congressman Adam Clayton Powell and singer Paul Robeson who "still feel that the equality practised in the Soviet Union is the ideal."

"Communists try to influence youth from the cradle to maturity," Cronin wrote. "They promote factory nurseries which will break up the home; they favor amoral education, particularly the experimentalism which is associated with progressive education; and finally they attempt direct organization of youth groups and infiltration into existing movements."

Communists had also been infiltrating the federal government: "It is unquestionable that many communists have gotten on public payrolls, some of them in high positions. In part, this trend is explainable by the fact that groups discriminated against by private employers (Jews and Negroes) can obtain civil service employment. This very discrimination makes them ripe for communist propaganda, since their intelligence and education makes them keenly resentful of such injustice." Not only were there communists in high places, but they also had their defenders, such as "Mrs. Roosevelt, whose generosity and broadmindedness has been abused by Communists." The press, radio, motion pictures, magazines, and books provided other targets for the communists. "The list of Hollywood sympathizers and dupes includes many famous names," and those of Lillian Hellman, Charles Chaplin, and Orson Welles were cited.

Communists exploited the sensibilities of liberals, that group which "considers itself as opposed to the Catholic Church, which is labelled authoritarian and repressive, to say nothing of being reactionary and satisfied with the *status quo*" and yet was prepared to "swallow the stark totalitarianism of the Soviet state ... with its denial of basic human rights and complete denial of the individual freedom so lyrically extolled by the liberal mind." Communists did not attack religion openly, but they subtly encouraged Protestants to attack Catholics and they had conducted an active and successful campaign for the sympathy of Jews, with the result that "the percentage of Jews among Communists is high, probably as high as sixty-four percent ... In general, they attribute anti-Semitism to lying campaigns among Gentiles and hence are attracted to a new social order where equality will be practiced. It is extremely difficult to convince them that faults in their own group contribute to this phenomenon."

Cronin did not expect that the domestic activities of communists in the United States were likely to lead to a communist government. He believed, rather, that "their real menace today is in conjunction with Soviet political moves." To counter communism, Cronin recommended: "1) accurate information; 2) education and when necessary denunciation; 3) a positive program of justice; and 4) counter-organization." First, however, there had to be an adequate understanding of Catholic social principles among Catholics as well as agreement over their meaning and application. He concluded by asserting that "such a program would strengthen the American Church beyond the hopes of this generation. It would be more than a defense against Communism and anti-clericalism, it would win our own more firmly to the Church and attract millions from without ... When employers by the scores and workers by the thousands find the priest their friend and counsellor it seems logical to expect that, with God's grace, such friendly interest in the man will lead to inquiry into the principles which inspire him and thus to conversions ... We have the truth which the world needs so badly; this is an excellent opportunity to diffuse the truth."[18]

As the war came to an end, the Catholic Church in the United States had examined the issue of communism and saw its own role as that of playing an active role in politics and society to counter the threat of communism to the American people.

THE VATICAN AND THE AMERICAN CHURCH

With the advance of the Soviet Union into eastern Europe and the uncertain future of Italy and Germany, the Holy See came to rely more and more on the United States and its Catholic community. While American notions of political and religious liberty had not often sat easily with the Vatican and with European Catholics, the wealth of the United States and the material assistance provided by the American church were not to be ignored. The new domestic prominence of American Catholicism coincided with the international leadership of the United States at the end of the war and the determination of many American political and religious leaders that the United States should never again retreat into isolationism. The fact that the American hierarchy shared the same intense antipathy to communism as Pius XII facilitated closer collaboration between the Vatican and American Catholicism, as did the close personal friendship between the pope and Archbishop Spellman of New York.

From the 1930s the Vatican had given greater recognition to the international role which could be played by American Catholics. Most significant in this respect was the 1936 tour of the United States by Eugenio Pacelli in his capacity as secretary of state. The tour helped Roosevelt by controlling the utterances of the anti-Roosevelt priest, Father Charles Coughlin, and it recognized the importance of Catholic financial support. The main significance of the tour, however, was that it gave Pacelli an opportunity to propose the opening of diplomatic relations between the United States and the Vatican to the American President.[19] The Vatican could no longer depend solely on its European neighbours, who were then approaching the brink of a new war. It had to look farther afield and, as the Europeans appeared less attractive, the Americans became more important as partners for the Holy See.

The key figure in these developments was Francis J. Spellman. Spellman had worked with Pacelli in the Secretariat of State in the early 1930s when the two had become close friends and Spellman had become Pacelli's protégé. After his appointment as auxiliary bishop of Boston in 1932, Spellman continued to nurture his Roman contacts and it was he who made the arrangements for Pacelli's tour in 1936. In 1939 Pacelli was elected pope and, as his first appointment, he moved Spellman from Boston to become archbishop of the important diocese of New York.

Because of his intimacy with the pope, Spellman became "the Vatican's principal agent for dealing with the United States government" during the war. As archbishop of New York, Spellman was the military bishop of the United States, and in this capacity visited Rome several times during the war. This enabled him to maintain close contact with Pius XII and to carry out special missions for him, as well as for Roosevelt.[20] One of Spellman's tasks had been to look after Vatican monies that had been shipped out of Europe and deposited in American banks for the duration of the war. By the end of the war Spellman had proven his value to the pope as an effective financial manager, diplomat and administrator and as the only senior churchman whom the pope regarded as a personal friend.[21]

Sensitive to the importance of the Catholic community in the United States, Roosevelt had originally depended on the archbishop of Chicago, Cardinal George Mundelein, an early supporter of the New Deal, as his confidant within the American hierarchy. Important negotiations with the Vatican had been carried out through Mundelein[22] and, following his death in October 1939, Roosevelt decided to establish a direct link with the Vatican through the appointment of the Episcopalian industrialist Myron C. Taylor as his personal representative to the pope. Both Mundelein and Spellman had been instrumental in encouraging the president to take such an initiative.[23] Taylor's designation as personal representative was a subterfuge to avoid the necessity of Roosevelt's facing Protestant hostility by having to ask for Senate approval of this as an ambassadorial appointment.

As the war was coming to an end in 1944, the Vatican recognized the new power alignments in the world by inviting four American priests to join the staff of the Secretariat of State. Their task was to assist with the additional English-language correspondence made necessary by the growing importance of business dealings between the Holy See and the United States, especially in the area of relief programs where Washington and the Vatican cooperated closely.[24]

Cardinal Maglione, the Vatican Secretary of State, died in August 1944. The pope wanted to appoint Spellman as Maglione's successor and offered him the position at the end of September. Spellman asked to be allowed to defer his decision until the war was over, at which time he declined the offer, arguing that he could be more use to Pius XII as archbishop of New York than as secretary of state. Spellman's biographer John Cooney contends that Spellman did not accept the offer because he recognized that the pope rarely delegated authority and, in the past, had frequently circumvented Maglione. Spellman felt that he would have greater freedom and greater power by remaining in the United States than in working with the pope in Rome. Cooney also contends that Spellman ultimately did not accept the position because he believed that no non-Italian could ever be elected pope.[25] Nevertheless, such a sign of confidence from the pope at the end of the war meant that Spellman's influence would be considerable in the postwar reorganization of the Catholic world that lay ahead. "Spellman was destined to be the most powerful figure in the American hierarchy, not only because of his close personal friendship with Pius XII but also because of his role in negotiations with the United States government over the next two decades."[26]

Within the United States, Spellman helped American Catholics to challenge that anti-Catholic bigotry which had defeated Al Smith's bid for president in 1928. After 1945, Spellman never lost an opportunity to equate Catholicism with Americanism and, in his domestic anti-communist campaign, was able to demonstrate that Catholics were true Americans because they were the most anti-communist. By the 1950s, "the world view held for years by Spellman and Pacelli ... prevailed in America. The Cold War was on: the United States provided the cold steel, the Catholic Church the moral force." "The new American fear of Communism began to cancel out the old American prejudice against Catholicism."[27] In such ways Spellman helped to pave the way for the election of John Fitzgerald Kennedy in 1960 as the first Catholic president and for the full acceptance of Catholics in American political life.

6 The Soviet Union and the Catholic Church

Considering the hostile ideology of communism and the brutal treatment of the Roman Catholic Church inside the Soviet Union during the 1930s, Catholic churches which came under Soviet rule during the Second World War were treated relatively well. In fact, the war resulted not in attacks on Christianity in the Soviet Union, but in a restoration of the position of the Russian Orthodox Church as the official state church and its encouragement to mount a religious offensive against the pretensions of Roman Catholics and the Vatican. The Soviet Union thereby came to offer a double-threat to Catholicism as the traditional fount of materialist atheism on the one hand and as the new patron of the rival Russian Orthodox Church on the other.

WARTIME EXPANSION INTO EASTERN EUROPE

The occupation of eastern Poland by Soviet troops in September 1939 brought both the Latin Catholics and the Greek Catholics, or Uniates, of Galicia under Soviet rule. Galicia was considered to be a western province of Ukraine and the Uniates had traditionally been at the centre of movements for Ukrainian independence from Russian rule. "Dating from the Union of Brest of 1596, the Greek Catholic church has in modern times closely identified with the Ukrainian ethnic consciousness and the national-cultural revival in Galicia, supplying it with several generations of leaders, institutional protection, and moral and material support."[1] The venerated leader of the Galician Uniates was Metropolitan Klement Sheptyckyi, who had served as archbishop of Lvov since 1907.

In June 1940, when the Soviet army occupied the Baltic states of Lithuania, Latvia, and Estonia, the Soviet Union acquired a further contingent of Latin Catholics, particularly in Lithuania and, to a lesser degree, in Latvia. Soviet policy towards these Catholics during what came to be known as the "first occupation," was reasonably moderate. While the churches were restricted to devotional activities, the hierarchies continued to function. Moscow did not want to create difficulties for itself with the peoples of these border regions nor to give Hitler any reason to intervene.

The German invasion of the Soviet Union in June 1941 transferred most of these Catholics from Soviet to German control. Initially Catholics had expected to be able to use the opportunity of German military victories to send missionaries into occupied Russia behind the German troops. These Catholics were soon disabused, however, and found, in fact, that the church was treated worse by the Nazis than it had been by the Bolsheviks. Metropolitan Sheptyckyi so informed the Vatican in 1942: "Today the whole country is agreed that the German regime, perhaps to a higher degree than the Bolshevist, is evil, indeed even diabolical ... It is simply as if a band of madmen or rabid wolves were throwing themselves upon the poor nation ... It will take much freely sacrificed blood to atone for that shed as a result of these crimes."[2]

In 1944 Soviet troops once again occupied those areas which they intended to incorporate into the Soviet Union proper – namely, the Baltic states and Poland east of the Curzon Line. Yet, in re-entering these areas, the Soviets soon found that they had to contend with Lithuanian and Ukrainian nationalist partisan units which had earlier been fighting the German occupation. As the Germans were driven out, Ukrainian and Lithuanian nationalists attempted to prevent the return of the Soviets. It became important for the Soviets to come to terms with the Roman Catholic Church in Galicia and Lithuania where it was closely associated with these nationalist forces.[3] The initial approach taken by the Soviets in both areas was one of leniency, seeking to benefit from popular relief at being freed from the German occupation. Metropolitan Sheptyckyi was allowed to consecrate new bishops, including his designated successor, Jozef Slipyi, and when Sheptyckyi died in November 1944, he was given a state funeral, attended by Nikita Khrushchev, the party boss of Ukraine. When Metropolitan Slipyi sent a delegation to Moscow in December 1944 to seek recognition for the Uniates, the Soviet authorities were noncommittal but did ask that the church help them to control the Ukrainian nationalist partisans.

THE REVIVAL OF THE RUSSIAN ORTHODOX CHURCH

As a result of the Soviet victory at Stalingrad, Stalin promoted traditional Russian nationalism over communist revolution, designating the conflict as the Great Patriotic War. The revolutionary vehicle of the Comintern was dissolved in May 1943 in order to allay the fears and suspicions of Stalin's capitalist allies and, after twenty years of persecution, the Russian Orthodox Church was given official recognition.

Before the outbreak of the Second World War, the situation of the Russian Orthodox Church was desperate, since only four bishops remained out of prison and only a handful of churches remained open. Metropolitan Sergei, who had acted as patriarch since 1925, had realized that the only hope for his church lay in demonstrating its loyalty to the state, even through the dark Stalinist repression of the 1930s. Sergei persisted in the hope that some day permission would be granted for the election of a patriarch and the restoration of the church. With the German invasion of June 1941, Sergei called on the Russian people to support the Soviet war effort and gave such strong support to the government and military that the Soviet government felt it had to take the contribution of the church seriously and to grant more freedom and privileges to that body.

On 4 September 1943 Stalin met Sergei and authorized the calling of a Sobor, or church council, to elect a patriarch and a synod. The Sobor met on 8 September and formally elected Sergei as patriarch of Moscow and all Russia. A month later, the Council of People's Commissars created a State Council for Orthodox Church Affairs and named G.G. Karpov as its chairman, charging him to look after the interests of the Orthodox Church and to act as an intermediary between that church and the Soviet government. The election of a patriarch was significant since, under the tsarist government from the time of Peter the Great until that of Nicholas II, the Russian Orthodox Church had been governed by a synod, not by a patriarch, with power dispersed among the episcopate. After the revolution, the Bolsheviks authorized the election of a patriarch and, following the death of Patriarch Tikhon in 1924, Sergei had sought a restoration of the authority of the patriarchate to enable him to work with the Soviet government. The patriarch was to be advised by a representative synod of bishops.[4]

This new partnership of church and state was a marriage of convenience. It certainly did not involve any denial of the anti-religious commitment of marxism nor any decrease in atheistic campaigns in the Soviet Union. Recognition of the Russian Orthodox Church brought Stalin domestic advantages in terms of popular support for the regime's war effort. The revival of the church also served to bolster the Grand Alliance by giving evidence of Stalin's tolerance for religion and thereby helping to undermine western hesitations about fighting for "godless" Russia. Soviet patronage of the Russian Orthodox Church could counter Vatican opposition to the Grand Alliance and their attempt to weaken American support for the Russian war effort. Stalin also anticipated an eventual move of Soviet troops into eastern Europe, where religious bodies could prove useful in coping with potentially hostile elements in east European society.[5]

At the same time, the leaders of the Orthodox Church, virtually to a man, had been supporters of the tsarist regime which had been destroyed in 1917. Because these leaders had endured so many years of persecution, they had survived with a firm commitment to their faith and could accept the recognition of the state in terms of "rendering unto Caesar." Metropolitan Sergei had argued since 1927 that the church should confine its activities to the purely spiritual realm in return for recognition by the Soviet government. The church could accept the social goals of communism as an attempt to build a moral community. On the other hand, they disagreed with the materialism of marxism and reserved their right to challenge this aspect of official doctrine. In 1943 the Orthodox Church had a lack of trained clergy and a shortage of church buildings. A seminary was opened in Moscow and the applications for the priesthood soon exceeded the places available. The government also offered funds to build churches, but the church authorities refused the offer, preferring to rely on their own resources.

The church realized that its existence in the Soviet Union was still very restricted, but it recognized that it had little choice in the matter and believed that if the church could prove its value to the regime and to the Russian people, it might be able to expand its sphere of operation. The one area where it believed it could be of real assistance to the state was in the area of foreign policy and it was in this area that it sought to reach out to other Orthodox churches and other religious communities. It also hoped that extended influence abroad would help to preserve and improve its position at home. As Maurice Peterson of the British Foreign Office commented: "If only the Orthodox Church in the USSR can gain sufficient accretion of strength through the cynical and opportunist policy of the Soviet leaders it may never be worth their while to suppress it again. That, no doubt, is the Patriarch's hope; and, meanwhile, both he and the Politburo are playing a waiting game."[6]

The Russian Orthodox Church, with its long tradition of anti-Catholicism, was of particular help to the Moscow government in mounting Christian arguments against the pretensions of the Vatican; the Orthodox Church understood that this was one of the roles that Stalin had assigned to it. The Soviet dictator resented the way in which the Vatican appeared to have supported any anti-communist fascist leader in the 1930s. During the war the Soviet press sought to warn the West about the way in which the Vatican had supported the rise of Nazis and fascists, arguing that there would be no permanent peace in Europe unless the Vatican were deprived of all power when the war was over.[7] In the spring of 1944 Sergei reiterated this theme in his own attack on the pope and the Roman Catholic Church, demonstrating that church and state were of one mind where the Holy See was concerned.[8]

After the death of Sergei in May 1944, the Orthodox Church was allowed to summon another Sobor to elect his successor and to discuss church policy. This Sobor met in Moscow on 31 January 1945, on the eve of the Big Three meeting at Yalta. Alexei, metropolitan of Leningrad and Novgorod, was elected patriarch and was enthroned in Moscow Cathedral on 4 February. Karpov addressed the Sobor and pledged that the State Council "would not interfere in any way with the internal affairs of the Church" and that it would "also take all measures to remove obstacles to the exercise by citizens of their right to freedom of conscience in the Soviet Union." The Sobor reinforced the centralized power of the patriarch and his synod over the bishops of the church.[9]

The meeting was attended by a large number of high-ranking Orthodox churchmen from other countries. The Russian church sought to extend its international influence in two ways. In the first place, it sought to encourage branches of the church in other parts of the world to accept the sovereignty of the Moscow patriarchy once again and to attract other Orthodox into the Russian church. Before the February meeting, the Russian church had accepted the application of the Ruthenian Orthodox Church, Ruthenia having recently been incorporated into the Soviet Union, to submit itself to the Moscow patriarchate. The second approach involved inducing autonomous Orthodox churches in Europe and the Middle East to recognize the primacy of the Moscow patriarchate and thereby to challenge the pre-eminence of the Ecumenical Patriarch at Constantinople. The restoration of the Russian Orthodox Church gave it a dominant position after the war in its dealings with the Orthodox churches of Romania, Bulgaria, and Serbia, all of which were either occupied by the Red Army or under Communist control.[10] In May 1945 Alexei visited the leaders of the Slav churches, as well as the patriarchs of Antioch and Alexandria. The Canadian ambassador in Moscow commented that "it seems to be clear policy to build up Moscow, ecclesiastically speaking, as in a sense a second Rome."

At the end of the February council meeting, a message from the Orthodox prelates to Christians throughout the world called on them to support the "sacred task in which we are engaged ... to destroy fascism ... so that the vile teaching of fascism may be wiped from the face of the earth forever." The message also responded to the pope's 1944 Christmas address by condemning "those who call for mercy for the murderers of children and traitors. Such people cannot be called Christians and they become sharers of the guilt of the fascists. All Christians should oppose such perversion of Christ's teaching."[11]

While Archbishop Slipyi, following his December 1944 visit to Moscow, had made some gestures towards calling for the cooperation of the Ukrainian nationalist partisans with Soviet authorities, he was unable to do more and, by the spring of 1945, once the Yalta conference had confirmed Soviet control of Galicia, the Soviets decided that they would no longer tolerate the independent existence of the Galician Uniates. The Soviets saw the Uniate Church as the main institutional barrier to the sovietization and russification of the border areas and believed that control of the Uniates would facilitate the campaign against the nationalist partisans and cut the ties of local Catholics with the Vatican and its anti-Soviet propaganda. The forced reunion of the Uniates with the Russian Orthodox Church was a relatively humane solution since it would only sever the ties of the Uniates with the pope, but would not otherwise affect their practice of worship, since their liturgy was already the same as the Orthodox.[12]

On the other hand, the Italian ambassador in Moscow argued that the initiative for the reunion of the Uniates of western Ukraine with the Russian Orthodox Church came from the Orthodox patriarchy. The Orthodox were jealous of their position in relation to other religions, especially the Roman Catholics, and were particularly wary lest some agreement be reached between Moscow and the Vatican which could militate against the position of the Orthodox in Russia. It would, in fact, be most useful to the Orthodox if Soviet antagonism to Catholicism could be institutionalized. One way of doing this would be by encouraging the government to force the Uniates to reunite with the Russian Orthodox from whom they had separated 350 years before. This would have the double advantage of eliminating religious rivals for Stalin's attention as well as impeding any serious future negotiations with the Vatican. The Russian Orthodox were especially pleased that Vatican postwar hostility to the Soviet Union was based not on ideological anti-communism and anti-materialism with which the Orthodox would have had to agree, but on resistance to the expansion of Soviet influence in eastern Europe, with which the Orthodox could not agree.[13]

The attack on the Vatican at the end of the Russian Orthodox Congress and the program to convert the Uniates coincided with an anti-Vatican campaign in the Soviet press. The Soviet media had criticized the pope's 1944 Christmas message as an attempt to justify fascism by calling for mercy for the Nazis and Fascists while saying nothing about the war crimes that they had committed.[14] The Vatican was later accused of following a pro-Nazi policy before the war and now of working to prevent the establishment of democracy in Italy and Poland in favour of Catholic political regimes. "On the eve of the complete defeat of Hitlerite Germany, the Vatican is making attempts to save her from just retribution. In the light of these attempts, the slogan of the Vatican programme of post-war world organization sounds specially false."[15]

The Vatican, through the *Osservatore Romano*, was careful to answer every criticism of the Soviet press and radio and they were particularly upset by the criticisms that they had to endure from the leaders of the Russian Orthodox Church.[16] Nevertheless, as the war came to an end, Soviet expansion posed a double threat to the Vatican and to the European cultural community. Either the Soviets would eliminate all religion in central and western Europe, or they would support the conversion of European Christians to Russian Orthodoxy. The papacy during the First World War had feared a Russian conquest of Constantinople and the restoration of power to the Ecumenical Patriarch. Now it again appeared as if eastern Orthodoxy would challenge the Roman Catholic position in central and eastern Europe.

7 The Papacy and the Second World War

For Pius XII, there were two distinct phases to the Second World War. His initial concern was to end the war or to prevent it from spreading. Like Benedict XV in the First World War, he made himself available to both sides to serve as a mediator who could broker a peace or otherwise limit the war. For the latter part of the war the pope used all his influence to hamper the extension of communism in Europe.

THE PROSPECTS OF PAPAL MEDIATION

Pius XII feared the revolutionary destabilization of European society which could result from war. Once the conflict had started in September 1939, he recognized it as his duty to be ready to assist in fashioning a compromise peace. For this reason, he sought to give the impression of holding to a strictly neutral position between the belligerents by refusing to denounce the German invasion of Poland or to comment on the atrocities committed against Poland by the Germans and the Russians. Historian Hansjakob Stehle argues that the pope was troubled by the dilemma of how to respond to the Soviet Union and could not make up his mind about the situation in Poland and the Baltic states where the church was being treated tolerably well by Soviet authorities. Stehle attributes this to a reluctance to make "decisions in situations that did not seem to him to be easily or at all comprehensible," but this appears to be belied by the record of Pius XII later in the war who was anything but vacillating in his decisions where the Soviet Union was concerned.[1]

In reality, the pope's impartiality was a fiction, since the sympathies of the Vatican clearly lay with the liberal democracies from the beginning. With Germany and the Soviet Union working together under the Nazi-Soviet Pact between 1939 and 1941, it was easy for the Vatican to provide quiet assistance to the Anglo-French cause as the war progressed. The pope was genuinely pleased with the closer tie with the United States when Roosevelt named Myron Taylor as his personal representative in December 1939.[2] In 1940 the pope sought, in collaboration with Roosevelt, to deter Mussolini from dragging Italy into the war at Germany's side.[3] The German invasion of the Soviet Union in June 1941 posed a dilemma for the Vatican, however, since its two main antagonists were now on opposite sides of the conflict.

The Vatican response to the new shape of the war indicated further where its true sympathies lay, when the pope refused to endorse Hitler's invasion of the Soviet Union as an anti-Bolshevik crusade. Yet the Vatican was uncomfortable with the new western alliance with the Soviet Union. Following the 1941 German invasion, Roosevelt had extended lend-lease aid to Stalin, but had worried about a negative Catholic response to this action and was greatly relieved when the Vatican agreed in September 1941 that, while condemning communism, it would be willing to see aid provided to the Russian people. After the United States entered the war in December 1941, Cicognani, the apostolic delegate in Washington, personally visited those bishops who had been most outspoken in their anti-administration views and warned them that the Holy See would be displeased at public statements which would "lessen in any way popular support of the policies of the administration."[4] Vatican support of the Anglo-American alliance with the Soviet Union did have its limits, however, and the pope was unwilling to make any direct gestures to Moscow.[5]

When the Vatican provided assistance to the Anglo-Americans in the war, it did so in the expectation that it would be able to influence the shaping and definition of the postwar world. Roosevelt, however, was concerned only with defining processes for international collaboration after the war, and would not commit himself to any defined shape for a postwar Europe. The war aims of the Vatican, because they progressively came to be shared by members of the American Catholic community, could, nevertheless, not be ignored by the American president.

What is striking in the examination of Vatican war aims, however, is their static nature. The aims which Pius XII defined in 1939, shortly after the outbreak of war, he promulgated unchanged as the war was drawing to a close. Yet the world had changed utterly in those six years. Not only had the Soviet Union worked as an ally of the British and Americans for four years in defeating the Axis powers, but many

Germans and other Europeans had, at the same time, perpetrated unspeakable atrocities. None of this was acknowledged by the papacy, with the result that it was not in a position to play any significant role in healing the wounds of the war, either in assisting people to cope with the presence of Soviet troops and communist reform and revolution in central Europe or in dealing with the aftermath of the Holocaust. The issue of war aims serves to demonstrate both how detached the papacy was from the important issues of the war and, at the same time, to illustrate how that detachment was itself due to a blinkered and inflexible view of the world emerging from traditional European Catholic cultural values.

In October 1939 Pius XII defined his preferred outcome for the war in his inaugural encyclical, *Summi Pontificatus*. In it he deplored the violence of the war and identified "the denial and rejection of a universal norm of morality" based upon the laws of God as being at the root of the problems confronting mankind in the modern age. Peace could only be established on a permanent basis if mutual trust existed and this would only be possible if Divine Law were to guide the work of civil authorities. The first test for the establishment of a secure peace would come at the moment of victory which

is an hour of external triumph for the party to whom victory falls, but it is in equal measure the hour of temptation. In this hour the angel of justice strives with the demons of violence; the heart of the victor all too easily is hardened; moderation and far-seeing wisdom appear to him weakness; the excited passions of the people, often inflamed by the sacrifices and sufferings they have borne, obscure the vision even of responsible persons and make them inattentive to the warning voice of humanity and equity. There is danger lest settlements and decision born in such conditions be nothing else than injustice under the cloak of justice.[6]

Peace, therefore, must be built by the spirit, not by the sword, and must rest on a foundation of Christian morality. The themes identified in *Summi Pontificatus* were reiterated by Pius XII in subsequent messages during the course of the war, particularly in his Christmas radio broadcasts. A lasting peace would result from a peace of reconciliation which could reintegrate the European community.

The turning point in the war came with the German defeat at the battle of Stalingrad early in 1943. Thereafter, the Red Army began its advance towards the west. Meeting at Casablanca in January 1943, Roosevelt and Churchill sought to sustain the Russian offensive by assuring Stalin that they would fight until the unconditional surrender of the Axis powers. This declaration destroyed the wartime strategy of the pope. His entire position had been based on the prospect of a compromise peace brokered, he had hoped, with the assistance of the United States. In the fall of 1942 Myron Taylor had been working with the pope to devise some way to induce Italy to withdraw voluntarily from the war. Yet now the United States had declared that there could be no negotiation and that the war would be fought to the finish. In these circumstances, was there any wartime role for the representative of the Prince of Peace?[7]

Dismissing the Anglo-American declaration as "idiotissima!" the pope felt that the result of the war would now be a bitter victory, leading to the political, social, and economic destruction of Italy and Germany. Such destruction of the core of Europe would only benefit the communists.[8] The pope believed that unconditional surrender imposed collective guilt on the German and Italian people and did not encourage either the Germans or the Italians to rid themselves of their Nazi and Fascist rulers in order to secure a compromise peace. In his allocution to the Sacred College of Cardinals on 2 June 1944, the pope "deprecated the confrontation of the German people with a choice between complete victory or complete destruction, since the dilemma would serve to prolong the war."[9] The pope assumed that the insistence on unconditional surrender was a particular interest of the Russians who wanted to prepare the way for a communist takeover in Germany after the war. The leaders of German Catholicism, "the elements most necessary for the rebuilding of a Christian Germany," would be decimated, the Pope believed, once they had been identified as part of the collaborationist German bourgeoisie.[10] Given the impossibility now of a negotiated peace, the remaining option for the Holy See was to use its influence to hinder the advance of communism in Europe.

HOLDING BACK THE COMMUNIST ADVANCE

Papal concerns about the future of Germany and Italy were linked with more pressing concerns about the future of Poland once the victory at Stalingrad enabled the Russians to articulate their aims for eastern Europe. In the spring of 1943 the Russians announced that they expected to move the eastern frontier of the Soviet Union to the west when the war was over, thereby annexing the eastern part of prewar Poland to the Soviet Union. At the Big Three meeting in Tehran in 1943, Churchill and Roosevelt, again paying the price for the unity of the Grand Alliance, supported Stalin's request and agreed to compensate Poland for its loss with lands taken from Germany in the west. At that same conference, it was agreed that Britain and the United States would invade western Europe while the Soviet Union would liberate the east. Poland was to be left to the care of the Russians. Such an outcome would require some accommodation by the Poles, especially by the Polish government-in-exile in London which broke off relations with the Soviet Union following the discovery of the bodies of Polish officers murdered by the Russians in the Katyn Forest in the summer of 1943.

When Soviet troops entered prewar Polish territory in January 1944, the future of Poland became an issue of practical politics and the Holy See gave its support to the position of the London Poles. At the beginning of February, the Polish government-in-exile outlined to the Vatican the dangers that they perceived were facing Poland in the event that it should fall under the control of the Communists. They called on the Vatican to "take all possible steps in order to prevent the spread of Communism in Europe."[11]

Unlike the Vatican, American Catholics did not initially object to the prospect of unconditional surrender, since it was in conformity with their perception of the war as a moral crusade. Poland, however, was another matter, especially when the politics of the Big Three towards Poland challenged principles which had earlier been defined in the Atlantic Charter.

President Roosevelt anticipated Catholic hostility to what had to be done in Poland and he sought to neutralize a negative reaction at the Vatican and among American Catholics. In September 1943 he told Archbishop Spellman that Russia would control eastern Europe at the end of the war because it had too much power and deserved some reward for defeating the Nazi army.[12] On 5 February 1944 Roosevelt sent a direct warning to the pope to expect that sacrifices would have to be made to obtain Soviet support for a peaceful world after the war. Because the Soviet Union had made a major contribution to the fight against Germany, it had "earned the right to participate in arrangements for peace." The United States expected postwar cooperation with Russia to continue and was actively working to lay the basis for such cooperation. Russia must be included in the postwar peace.[13] The Americans argued that the recognition of the Russian Orthodox Church indicated Stalin's sympathy for religion and religious freedom but the pope was unimpressed so long as Catholics continued to be persecuted inside the Soviet Union.

Relations between the Vatican and the Americans had cooled since Allied bombing of Rome in 1943 and, in spite of Roosevelt's warning, the Holy See responded to the request of the London Poles with alacrity, becoming a key player in the Polish situation. On 27 February the apostolic delegates in London and Washington were instructed by

Cardinal Maglione to warn local Catholics and government officials of the danger inherent in a Communist occupation of eastern Europe. Maglione believed that Catholic opinion could have a real impact on government policy in Britain and the United States.[14]

The instructions to William Godfrey, the apostolic delegate in London, struck a favourable chord with Britain's Catholic community who remembered that the Second World War had started as a result of the 1939 invasion of Poland.[15] In the spring of 1945 Monsignor Bernard Griffin, the archbishop of Westminster, kept pressure on the government by making a speech on Poland, the object of which was "to hold the British Government to their promises to see that there should be a representative Government in Poland and that there shall be free elections."[16] American Catholics were similarly active on Poland's behalf, with the result that Roosevelt's foreign policy consensus started to come unravelled.

Like Roosevelt, Stalin was concerned about Vatican influence on the Polish situation; so in the spring of 1944 he sought to establish some contact with the Holy See.[17] The unusual intermediary selected by Stalin was Father Stanislas Orlemanski, a left-wing Polish-American priest and the pastor of Our Lady of the Rosary Church of Springfield, Massachusetts. Orlemanski was a supporter of Roosevelt's policy of friendship with the Soviet Union and disliked the London Poles, who, representing the traditional governing classes of Poland, were always instructing Polish-Americans on how to direct their prayers.

Since diplomatic relations had been broken between the London Poles and the Soviet government in the summer of 1943, it was necessary to fashion a Polish government that could be supported by the entire Grand Alliance. Consequently, in January 1944 Stalin proposed to the Americans that such a goverment might include representatives of the London Poles and the Poles in the Soviet Union along with three members of the Polish-American community, including Father Orlemanski. In April 1944 Orlemanski, with Roosevelt's support, accepted Stalin's invitation to visit the Soviet Union. At the end of his meeting with Orlemanski, Stalin signed a document confirming that the Soviet government would never carry out a policy of coercion and persecution of the Catholic Church and that he was willing to join Pius XII in the struggle against religious persecution.

Orlemanski returned to the United States to find that the Polish-American community and the American Catholic hierarchy were incensed at the gratuitous support which he had given to Stalin's policies. American government representatives, on the other hand, especially those closest to Roosevelt, were less critical. Joseph E. Davies, who had encouraged Stalin to make his peace with the pope in 1943, believed that the meeting was a "definite, if bizarre, Soviet overture to the Vatican."[18]

The Holy See was not impressed by the Orlemanski mission. They recognized that widespread public sympathy for the mission in the United States coupled with a division of opinion among American Catholics undermined the Vatican campaign to enlist American support for the London Poles.[19] Cardinal Maglione advised Cicognani that the Vatican had no intention of dealing with a discredited priest such as Orlemanski and that, if Stalin gave proof through his actions that he was serious about respecting religious liberty and then wished to open diplomatic relations with the Vatican, he should do so through normal channels. That was the end of it as far as the Vatican was concerned.[20]

While Stalin was dealing with Orlemanski, the Americans tried to get the Vatican and the Russians to agree to a statement on religious liberty. Roosevelt believed that he could avoid domestic difficulties with his Catholic supporters if he could lessen the tension between Moscow and Rome. In June 1944 Myron Taylor consulted with Ivan Maisky, the Soviet ambassador in London, and prepared a draft statement for Stalin wherein he would proclaim "complete freedom of religious teaching and freedom of worship in all Soviet territories." This draft was conveyed to Pius XII in an audience on 12 July, when Taylor stressed the importance of Soviet support for the new United Nations organization which was expected to incorporate a guarantee of religious freedom in its charter.[21] The pope refused, however, to make cosmetic gestures for short-term gains and would not cooperate. The Vatican wanted practical demonstrations of religious liberty before they would respond to any gesture by Stalin.[22]

The Vatican stood firmly with the London Poles and, on 28 July 1944 the pope held an audience for Polish forces who were fighting in Italy, for their commanding officers, for the Polish ambassador to the Holy See, and for the former nuncio to Poland. He called for the "resurrection" of Poland and for reconciliation between Poles and Germans on the basis of Christian charity, suggesting that a renewal of hatred would only leave Poland at the mercy of the Russians.[23] The rising of the Polish Home Army against the Nazis in Warsaw in August 1944 offered Stalin a different way of dealing with the anti-Russian Poles. The Red Army halted outside Warsaw and let the Nazis destroy the main forces of the Polish resistance. Nothing had come of Stalin's gestures to the Vatican, so, after the defeat of the Warsaw uprising, Stalin no longer sought Vatican support for the Soviet occupation of Poland.

COMPASSION AND
THE PROSPECT OF VICTORY

By the end of 1944 it was obvious that the war would soon be over. Pius XII used his annual Christmas message that year to offer warnings to the Allied powers as they stood on the verge of victory. He was worried about the resistance coalitions in France and Italy where well-meaning liberal democrats were working in close collaboration with communists; the pope did not accept the evidence of a changed communist attitude and believed their agenda still aimed at a seizure of power. In his message, he supported liberal democracy but warned against communist attempts in these radical and revolutionary times to subvert democratic impulses for their own totalitarian goals of mass rule. In an effective democracy, the pope argued, the citizen has a right to make his views known and the state has an obligation to listen. He castigated the so-called democracy which arose as a result of mob rule, contrasting it with true democracy which respected the rights of individuals as well as the rights of constituted authority derived from "the authority of God."

In his 1944 Christmas message, therefore, the pope pleaded for equitable treatment for defeated enemies and outlined the conditions for a just peace. He supported national self-determination and the establishment of an international organization "for the maintenance of peace and the timely repression of threatened aggression." The postwar settlement must be different from the punitive peace which followed the First World War. It should not "impose any perpetual burden" on governments or peoples, and, while governments and peoples to whom responsibility for the war could be attributed, must "for a time undergo ... security measures, they must be assured the promise of eventual association with the community of nations." The pope endorsed the punishment for war crimes of individuals "for whom supposed military necessity could at most have offered a pretext, but never a justification," but under no circumstances should communities be punished for such crimes rather than individuals. The pope repeated these arguments in his encyclical of April 1945 calling for prayers for a humane peace which would stress fairness and not vengeance.

By the end of 1944 Roosevelt was faced with opposition to his policies from the American hierarchy and from the Vatican. Since Catholic support was important to his foreign policy, he took pains to show concern for Catholic sensibilities. In October he sent the pope the draft proposal for the new United Nations organization which had been agreed upon at Dumbarton Oaks. Following the American hierarchy's

November 1944 support for Polish independence, Roosevelt hastened to assure the apostolic delegate that the United States would use its influence after the war for the reconstruction of a strong, free, independent, and democratic Poland. In spite of this assurance, Cicognani was instructed by Rome to keep reminding the American government of Vatican concern for Poland.[24]

The spring of 1945 was a difficult time for the Holy See. In spite of earlier assurances by Roosevelt, the decisions taken by the Big Three at Yalta ran directly counter to Vatican support of the London Poles and to Vatican war aims, with the result that the Holy See found itself progressively isolated among the powers. Roosevelt knew the importance of assisting the Vatican and the Catholic community to accept whatever decisions might have to be made by the Allied leaders when they met at Yalta. Accordingly, he sent Harry Hopkins to Rome at the end of January 1945 to learn of the pope's concerns. Pleased by this attention, the pope told Hopkins of his fear of the consequence of a complete Russian victory for European equilibrium. The Vatican was less pleased, however, when the outcome of the Yalta conference appeared to ignore the pope's fears. It appeared that the great powers were really turning eastern Europe over to Russian imperialism.

Roosevelt sought to elicit some gesture from the Kremlin to allay Catholic disappointment with the results of Yalta. This was the reason for his taking the New York Catholic Edward J. Flynn to Yalta with him. Ostensibly Flynn intended to find out how the Soviet government was treating the church in general and the Roman Catholic Church in particular "with a view to reassuring American Catholicism on this point on his return."[25] He was also investigating whether any possibility existed for a rapprochement between the Vatican and the Soviet Union. Flynn went from Yalta to Moscow, where he had difficult and unsuccessful meetings with Soviet officials. From Moscow, Flynn travelled to Rome to report to the pope who dismissed any prospect of serious negotiation with the Russians.[26]

The Yalta Conference posed a severe challenge to Vatican aims. Bolsheviks might be Bolsheviks but, in eastern Europe in 1945, the Red Army held all the power. Should the Vatican hold firm to its principled stance and its support for the London Poles and thereby lose whatever influence it might have had? Or alternatively should it seek to accommodate the Russians over the situation in eastern Europe and try to save what could be saved?[27]

The two most senior officials of the Vatican Secretariat of State were divided on the correct course to follow. Domenico Tardini, the undersecretary for extraordinary ecclesiastical affairs, favoured an uncompromising line in all dealings with the Soviet Union, while Giovanni

Battista Montini, the substitute, favoured compromise in order to be able to make contact with Catholics under Soviet rule. The issue was ultimately resolved by Pius xII, who supported Tardini's view, believing that any compromise with Russia would only make it more possible for the Russians to do what they wanted in Germany and make it less possible for the Vatican to protest.[28] In his inflexibility, the pope was influenced by immediate personal concerns arising out of the central European Catholic context which had shaped him. Being, one might say, Italian by birth and German by adoption, he was obsessed by worries about the future of Italy and Germany.

He was afraid that harsh Allied treatment in Italy might augment the power of the Italian Communist party within the Italian Resistance and threaten the continuation of the Lateran Agreements. He believed that popular misery at the end of the war could lead Italians to support parties offering radical social solutions. If Britain and the United States continued to treat the Italians as defeated enemies, rather than as the co-belligerents they had become in September 1943, they might turn for support to the Communists and their Russian allies. Vatican officials used their friends in the United States, such as Archbishop Spellman of New York,[29] to get better treatment for Italy and to limit the suffering of the Italians by securing food and medical supplies from the western democracies. The pope wanted the United States to keep its troops in Italy and to develop a plan for postwar Europe lest the lack of such a plan create "a most fertile field for Communistic activity throughout Europe."[30]

Similarly, he wanted to ensure that the governance of Germany should be turned over to those Germans who had been the victims, and therefore the opponents, of nazism, foremost among whom would be the leaders of German Catholicism. The pope wanted a peace settlement to permit Germany, under new leadership, to return to her rightful place among the family of nations. Only in this way would a genuine and just peace be established and none of it would be achieved by appeasing the Russians.[31]

As the war drew to a close in the spring of 1945, the Vatican and the Catholic Church increased their criticism of wartime diplomacy, completely ignoring the critical role of the Soviet Union and the attempts of the Americans and the British to contend with it. Roosevelt's foreign policy support was crumbling and barely three days after his death on 12 April, the NCWC administrative board in Washington released their public attack on the charter of the United Nations. The bishops' statement reflected the war aims of the Holy See and, in an encyclical at the same time as the NCWC statement, the pope renewed his call for a peace of reconciliation.

The aims of the Holy See had remained constant throughout the war, in spite of changing circumstances in Europe and the world. One might argue that, in calling for a peace based on Christian principles of love and reconciliation, the papacy was only citing eternal principles of Christianity. Yet this is belied by divisions of opinion between senior officials of the Vatican Secretariat of State in 1945 over the principled course to follow in eastern Europe. It is also belied by a recognition that Pius XII was obsessed by contingent concerns about the fate of Italy and Germany. Recent public debates about the Vatican's response to the Holocaust have indicated that there were alternative principled positions which could have been taken by the pope over that issue. By the same token, the aims defined in October 1939 need not have remained as constant as they did in the context of the changing circumstances and fortunes of the war.

The difficulty was that the Vatican made no gesture whatsoever to respond to the policy of the "extended hand" and continued to try to convince the Americans and the British to stand firm against Soviet expansion when they had neither the ability nor the desire to stop the movement of Soviet troops. The pope was displeased when the Red Army was welcomed by some Polish bishops and, in returning the Polish primate, Cardinal Hlond, to Poland at the end of the war, the Vatican did so in the belief that it could avoid dealing directly with the new masters of Poland. Above all, the Vatican had no intention of withdrawing its support from the London Poles.

Hansjakob Stehle claims that Pius XII assumed that the Communists would seize power in eastern Europe in a radical and revolutionary fashion and that a new war would be inevitable because any lasting peace between the Soviets and the West was impossible. The pope entirely neglected the extent to which Stalin's policy could be cautious, careful, and non-ideological, just as Vatican policy had been during the war in its attitude to Nazi Germany. Pius XII also made no allowance for the national and cultural contexts of the predominantly Catholic countries of eastern Europe where Stalin would never be able to treat the church in the same way that he had treated it in the Soviet Union proper.[32]

PART THREE

Il Dopoguerra:
Neither War nor Peace,
1945–1946

8 Papal Leadership after the War

Historian Modris Eksteins, with the advantage of hindsight, has referred to the year 1945 as "ground zero," the critical turning point of the twentieth century, the year of total destruction following which none of the structures, certainties or authorities of the past would ever be the same again. With the ending of the Second World War, Pope Pius XII, who was the source of authority and certainty at the pinnacle of the Roman Catholic Church, thought differently. He recognized the threats of the postwar situation to his beliefs, to his followers, and to his church and he entered the new historical period determined to provide activist leadership to Catholics in interpreting and responding to the challenges of the time. Above all, Pius sought to sustain the integrity of Europe and, in this sense, "he was one of the first and most consistent apostles of a United Europe."[1]

THE CHALLENGES OF COMMUNISM

Communism presented the Roman Catholic Church with a threefold challenge in 1945. The first challenge was posed by the role of the Soviet Union as one of the three major allies which had just defeated the Axis powers. The end of the war saw the liberation of the states of eastern and central Europe from Nazi tyranny by the Red Army, which finished the war as far west as Berlin. Under the control of Soviet troops and their communist supporters lay millions of Catholics in Poland, Czechoslovakia, Hungary, Yugoslavia, Albania, Lithuania, Latvia, Romania, Bulgaria, and Germany, all of whom were vulnerable to the power of Stalin's armed forces which, it was believed, could easily suppress and eliminate the Church in the east.

The second challenge was posed by the Communist parties of western and eastern Europe which had worked with non-communists in the various resistance coalitions against the Axis and thus had a claim to participation in the postwar governments of Europe. Since all Communist parties took direction from Moscow, this represented another way in which the Soviet Union could threaten the position of the church throughout Europe and especially in Italy, the home of the papacy. The Vatican knew that all communists were deceitful and committed to their materialist revolutionary goals whatever the cost and that they could not be trusted to cooperate with non-communists in good faith. To cooperate with them merely played into their hands.

The third challenge was that of the Russian Orthodox Church which had received the patronage of the Soviet government during the war and was now being used to assist in the extension of Soviet influence in the Balkans. The Russian Orthodox Church could, moreover, be used to draw east European Christians away from the Roman Catholic Church and into the Soviet sphere and thus posed a direct challenge to the integrity of the Catholic Church.

The Pope believed that the end of the war gave enormous power and potential influence to the Soviet Union and its Communist allies. It was also apparent that the continuation of the unity of the Grand Alliance meant that the British, and particularly the Americans, were going to concede to Russian demands in the postwar settlement and, in so doing, assist in the Communist domination of Europe to the detriment of the Roman Catholic Church.

TOWARDS RECONCILIATION WITH GERMANY

While Russia controlled eastern Europe directly in 1945, the critical question for the immediate postwar period was what the fate of the defeated Axis powers, Germany and Italy, was to be. It was obvious that the Soviet Union would be pushing hardest for a vindictive peace settlement and therefore the Holy See saw its first task to be that of making the case with the British and Americans for a peace of reconciliation with Germany and with Italy.

The first and only voice to be raised in defence of the Germans in 1945 was that of the pope. As the world was reeling from the discoveries of the evidence of the Holocaust, Pius XII, true to his stated war aims, called for reconciliation and understanding between peoples. In response to accusations in the Soviet press that the Vatican and the German Catholic Church had collaborated with the Nazis, Pius XII

denounced, for the first time, the "satanic spectre" of National Socialism in his annual name-day allocution on 2 June 1945. He accused the
Nazis of promoting "the cult of violence, the idolatry of race and
blood, [and] the overthrow of human liberty and dignity" but, at the
same time, he explicitly rejected the collective guilt of the German
people for the crimes of the Nazi era.[2] The pope explained that
German Catholics had been among the earliest anti-Nazis and, therefore, should not be punished but should be entrusted with the construction of a new Germany. The denunciations of the church by the
Nazis, argued the pope, were "the clearest and most honourable testi-
mony to the strong, incessant opposition maintained by the Church to
such disastrous doctrines and methods." Calling for a genuine peace
where the rights of men and of religion would be respected by all, the
pope warned against the alternative in "those mobs of dispossessed,
disillusioned, disappointed and hopeless men who are going to swell
the ranks of revolution and disorder, in the pay of a tyranny no less
despotic than those for whose overthrow men planned."[3]

Under these circumstances, it was not surprising that the Vatican
was distressed by the decisions taken by the Allies at the Potsdam Conference in July. Papal officials had grave reservations about making the
Oder-Neisse frontier the western border of Poland, which would
remove such essentially German cities as Königsberg and Breslau from
Germany. The Vatican also had serious concerns about the expulsion
of German populations from Polish and Czechoslovak territory, which
it claimed to be a blatant violation of the human rights of innocent
people who were being wrenched out of their traditional communities.
The Vatican suggested that these policies were reminiscent of the worst
policies of the defeated Nazis.

The Vatican appeal for a peace of justice continued throughout
1945. The *Osservatore Romano* took up the theme in August in reaction to the dropping of atomic bombs on Hiroshima and Nagasaki.
During his audience with Generals Eisenhower and Mark Clark on
September 13, the pope spoke of the need for charity in dealing with
defeated enemies and in his 1945 Christmas message he returned to the
theme, saying that Christian justice was the only guarantee of a continuing peace. "He who exacts the expiation of crime through the just
punishment of criminals should avoid doing what he denounces in
others as crimes and misdeeds."[5]

The Allied powers were concerned lest the Vatican overlook the war
crimes that had been committed by supposedly ordinary Germans. At
the end of the war the British government suggested that the Vatican
send a representative to see the concentration camps at first hand so
that the Catholic Church would have "fully authenticated evidence" of

Nazi crimes. The pope demonstrated that he had not been unaware of these matters by providing d'Arcy Osborne, the British minister to the Holy See, with copies of reports that had been received at the Vatican on the ill-treatment of Polish Catholics in Germany. Included was a report from Cardinal Bertram of Breslau on the concentration camps which, Osborne felt, " must have produced a considerable impression on the Vatican."[6]

TOWARDS STABILITY IN ITALY

The pope sought to stabilize postwar Italian politics by securing relief aid for Italy and by convincing the Allies not to punish Italy for her part in the war. In 1945 Pius XII was concerned that, "even in the Holy City of Rome, the red flag with the hammer and sickle is to be seen in the streets," and he expressed doubts about the quality of political wisdom and political leadership which would be found in postwar Italy.[7] He turned to the United States and to France in the hope that they could assist in the fashioning of a lenient peace settlement for Italy. Archbishop Spellman of New York calculated that Harry Truman would be sympathetic to Vatican and Italian concerns because of his need for Catholic votes in the 1948 presidential election.[8]

The Council of Foreign Ministers were scheduled to meet in London in September 1945 for initial discussions on the peace treaties with Italy and the lesser enemy powers. The Italian Foreign Ministry believed that a direct statement of support by the Vatican would carry additional weight at these meetings, especially since the US secretary of state, James Byrnes, was a Catholic who had converted to Protestantism and had always been concerned to retain his Catholic support. The Italian ambassador to the Holy See was assured that the pope took every opportunity to speak well of Italy with visiting North Americans.[9] The apostolic delegate in Washington was instructed to support the Italian position over Venezia Giulia in the United States[10] and, prior to the meeting of the NCWC in mid-November 1945, he was told by Monsignor Tardini to ask the bishops to give their support to the Italian case.[11] On 18 November, to the great satisfaction of Vatican officials, the American bishops deplored "the tragic indifference to the plight of the Italian people who threw off the chains of a Fascist regime, who fought side by side with us in ardent loyalty. For over two long years of agony the friends of democracy in that country have had to stand by in impotence while we have toyed with the vital problems of relief and rehabilitation and deferred the fulfillment of our own solemn promises. Our own national interest, as well as the cause of world peace, and the fate of Christian culture are at stake in Italy. Today it is an outpost of western civilization."[12]

While the Vatican promoted the Italian cause internationally, it also looked out for the interests of the Christian Democrats within Italy. Against the background of political cooperation between Catholics and Communists in the postwar Ferruccio Parri government and in the directorate of the CGIL, the church laid the foundation of a Catholic political culture to provide future electoral support for the Christian Democrats. The Vatican's staunch anti-communism was part of this strategy of dissuading Catholics from voting for the Communists or the parties of the left when Catholics were reminded by the *Civiltà Cattolica* that "when Communism is considered as an integral doctrine, it is absolutely incompatible with membership of the Church. No compromise is possible. The Church which would yield in such matters would – to state an absurdity – no longer be the true Church."[13]

One area of active Catholic outreach was towards the Italian working-classes when, in the summer of 1945, the church appointed a number of labour chaplains to go to factories and workshops to act as "spiritual guides and companions of workers." A seminary was opened in Bologna to train these chaplains who were to refrain from involvement in political or labour issues and to concentrate only on acquainting the workers with the "Christian and Catholic concept of labour" and through this, to strengthen the ties between the Church and labour.

The church also enlisted the women's vote since women's suffrage had only been granted as recently as March 1945 after a campaign strongly supported by Catholics. The first national convention of Italian Working Women was convened in Rome in mid-August and warned by the pope that the CGIL must be maintained as a non-partisan trade union and not be allowed to "be changed into an instrument of class warfare or party interest." On 21 October the pope spoke to the women's section of Catholic Action and advised them that, as electors, they should "use their influence for the safeguarding of the home and the family and should combat the political dangers of class warfare at home and imperialistic warfare abroad."[14]

The fall of the Parri government in December 1945 was the occasion for considerable discussion between the Italian court, now presided over by Prince Umberto as lieutenant-general, and the Vatican. The court, under pressure from the British, had approached the Vatican with a plan for the replacement of the National Liberation Committee-based Parri government with a government of the political right, possibly led by V.E. Orlando. Within the Vatican, Tardini and Montini found themselves confronted over this issue by the influence of the Roman party on the pope. Fearing the election prospects of the Communist and Socialist parties, Pius XII did not share Tardini's optimism that the Christian Democrats stood an excellent chance of winning the first postwar election. With the Vatican being attacked by the left for having been too close to fascism, Tardini and Montini both favoured moderation and convinced the pope that it was better for the Christian Democrats to be associated with the revival of Italian democracy than with right-wing reaction as was preferred by the Roman party. The pope, therefore, eventually refused to cooperate with the court's plan and insisted on maintaining a government based on the Resistance coalition.[15]

The invitation to Alcide de Gasperi, the leader of the Christian Democrats, to form his first government in December 1945 gave great satisfaction to the Vatican, linking the church and the Italian government for what turned out to be the next half-century. At the instigation of the Communist party, who wanted to work more closely with the Christian Democrats; the party of the Christian left dissolved itself and suspended publication of its newspaper, *Voce Operaia,* immediately after the appointment of the de Gasperi government. With a Christian Democratic government in Italy, the Vatican were in a position to argue much more persuasively with the British and the Americans in favour of relief aid for Italy.

Integral to the peace settlement with Italy was the future status of the Vatican City State and the question of the continuing validity of the Lateran Agreements. Given the potential danger of a hostile left-wing government in Italy, other possibilities for guaranteeing the Vatican's independence had been considered which did not depend entirely on the word of the Italian government. In 1945 there were seen to be two options for the Vatican in establishing its independence within Italy. One direction was to secure an international guarantee – possibly as part of the Italian peace treaty – whereby the great powers would guarantee the independence of the Vatican City and would be ready to protect that independence should the need arise. The other option involved internationalizing the senior personnel of the Curia, so that the Vatican would be less Italian in its make-up. In this way, it would become a truly international institution completely independent of Italian society and could expect assistance from the great powers without any prior written guarantee. The choice was between a formal, explicit guarantee of Vatican independence and an informal, implicit guarantee that the independence of that institution would be respected by its nearest neighbour.

The French government favoured a formal international guarantee, which, among other things, could restore France to a position as "Defender of the Faith." Curia officials on the other hand, most notably Monsignor Montini, were less interested in an international guarantee and preferred a change in the nationality of senior Vatican personnel to permit the Vatican to secure broad international sympathy and support. Non-Italians would have to be recruited to the Vatican bureaucracy and, at the next consistory, the College of Cardinals would have to have a significant infusion of non-Italian candidates. The moment, Montini believed, was propitious for such a development. France conjectured that internationalizing the personnel of the Curia would mean the Americanization of the Vatican, which it did. Since the French Foreign Office believed that American Catholicism lacked originality, they were apprehensive lest the Americans would be too content to adopt and to continue Italian styles and procedures.[16]

THE AMERICANIZATION OF THE VATICAN

Since the United States had emerged from the war as unquestionably the strongest power in the world, it became important in the Vatican's quest to influence American policy and opinion for it to forge closer links with the government and people of the United States and to make the papacy appear to be a less Euro-centred institution. This involved giving the Americans a higher profile in Rome as part of the general postwar internationalization of the Curia and also developing a closer working relationship with American church leaders.[17]

Immediately after the war the Holy See made extensive and deliberate use of its connections with the United States. When it proved impossible to appoint Spellman to be secretary of state, the pope allowed the business to be conducted by the two undersecretaries, Domenico Tardini and Giovanni Battista Montini, who reported directly to him. British minister d'Arcy Osborne believed that having no secretary of state was perfectly agreeable to Pius XII:

The trouble is ... that he is constitutionally reluctant to commit himself to a definite line of policy. He hates to cross or to burn a bridge. Consequently, the absence of a head of the government of the Vatican City State and of an official spokesman for the Holy See suits him down to the ground. There is no one to insist upon the adoption of a line of policy or action. There is no other voice ... than his own. And there is no possible deflection of the limelight from the occupant of the Throne of St. Peter.[18]

Harold Tittmann, Myron Taylor's assistant, felt similarly that "being his own Secretary of State is not distasteful to [the pope] and that he welcomes the opportunity personally to supervise even the minutest details of administration. Furthermore it is understood that by temperament important decisions do not come easy to Pius XII." Tittmann also thought that the pope might have been delaying until the international political situation had developed "to the stage where the appointment [of Spellman] would cause the minimum of dissent."[19]

In June 1945, there were new rumours that the pope was about to name Spellman as secretary of state. Osborne was not surprised, since he knew that the pope "could ... rely on Monsignor Spellman's complete deference and subservience so that in effect he could continue to be his own Secretary of State." Osborne saw the appointment as a compliment to the United States, which was "probably the most important source of Papal revenues"; moreover, Spellman was known to be an excellent administrator and Osborne felt that the Secretariat could stand "a dose of the stimulation of trans-Atlantic business methods."[20]

Monsignor Filippo Bernardini, nuncio to Switzerland and former apostolic delegate to the United States, assumed that the pope would make this appointment in "manifest gratitude for good will and friendliness of US toward Holy See." The appointment would be an attempt to facilitate the continuation of American diplomatic representation at the Holy See, which, among other things, served as a protection for the Vatican. It would "render Italy a service by appointing to key position in Rome national of great power well disposed toward this country [sic]," it would help to internationalize the Curia and, finally, it would give the pope a "close personal friend" with whom he could work. Bernardini underlined the fact that the pope had been eager to see that his pro-Americanism was advertised widely.[21]

Much depended on Spellman himself, who flew to Rome at the end of September for a meeting with the pope, during which he once again turned down the offer of appointment, indicating that he felt that he could be more useful to Pius by remaining in New York.[22] By the end of the year, the pope accepted that he could govern without a secretary of state, a move which effectively enhanced the centralization of power within the Vatican. With a great capacity for work, Pius XII "preferred a working system which allowed him direct, personal choice and supervision" over everything that happened in the church. His workload was, consequently, immense. Tardini remarked after the death of Pius that this pope worked alone, needing no "collaboratori," only "esecutori."[23]

If the pope was unable to appoint an American as secretary of state, he did appoint another American as minister-general of the Order of the Minor Franciscan Friars in July 1945. Father Valentine Schaef, a sixty-three-year-old native of Cincinnati, Ohio, became the first American minister-general of this order which was "considered the most important, the most active, and the most typical missionary organization of the Catholic Church," with a total of 24,500 members. The pope named Schaef primarily because he was an American; there were other more senior candidates, but Pius chose to name the minister-general personally, rather than convening a general chapter of the order to choose the new leader. The appointment allowed the pope "to express his appreciation of the generous donations extended for relief purposes to the Holy See by American Catholics and the Catholic hierarchy in the United States," as well as make a "gesture of appreciation and good-will to the Government and people of the United States."[24]

At the same time, the Curia chose to appoint American bishops to sensitive positions in the papal diplomatic service. Bishop Joseph Hurley of St Augustine, Florida, was named regent of the nunciature in Yugoslavia; Bishop Gerald O'Hara of Savannah, Georgia, was named regent of the nunciature in Romania; and Bishop Aloysius Muench of Fargo, North Dakota, would be named apostolic delegate to Germany. Other Americans were appointed to senior positions in the Curia in Rome.

The immediate postwar period was also noteworthy for the number of delegations of visiting Americans who were received in private audience by the pope and to whom Pius usually delivered an address that had been specially written for the occasion. The visitors included "Members of the United States Senate and the House of Representatives, ranking officers of [the] Army and Navy, UNRRA officials, business executives and newspaper correspondents." Between June and September 1945 the pope received such diverse individuals and groups as the National Commander of Veterans of American Foreign Wars and his party, the Motion Picture Executive Committee of Hollywood, and Congressman Luther Johnson and six other congressmen of the Foreign Affairs Committee.[25]

The pope used these audiences to try to influence the policy and outlook of the government and people of the United States. In June he warned the Veterans of American Foreign Wars about the danger of revolution if "a strong, even violent reaction should sweep through the masses in countries that have been so utterly devastated by a war that should never have been begun." In August he warned visiting congressmen against communism, arguing that, before true peace can be established, a victory must be won over "a self-sufficient materialistic philosophy, which would usher God out of His world and thus leave man without any basis on which to build an order of justice that will be something more than a hollow sham supported by mere force." In September, he spoke to the members of the House Foreign Affairs Committee about the need for charity in dealing with defeated enemies.[26]

The pope paid so much attention to visiting Americans because he was uncertain about his formal relationship with President Truman.

Myron Taylor's mission to the pope had been designated as a temporary one and President Roosevelt's sudden death in April 1945 had created consternation in Rome where the Holy See feared that, without Roosevelt, the partnership between the United States and the Vatican would be seriously damaged. Myron Taylor returned to Washington after Roosevelt's death, with the intention of briefing Truman on relations with the Vatican, but Truman, less interested in the Vatican connection, was in no hurry to see Taylor or to have him return to Rome. By August, Truman had not decided what future relations with the Vatican were to be.[27]

In November, Truman sent word to the pope through Colonel L. Curtis Tiernan, the senior chaplain with the United States army in Europe, that he desired "continued relations with the Vatican." According to Tiernan, the pope was "exceedingly delighted" to receive this news, but the news came with qualifications. As Tiernan explained to Montini, "political conditions might make it inexpedient to return Mr Myron Taylor," but Harold Tittmann, the chargé d'affaires in the Rome office, could "continue functioning without inviting criticism or opposition." Truman confirmed with Byrnes that the use of Tittmann in this way was exactly what they had been doing, what seemed to work, and what they would continue to do.[28] In spite of the enthusiasm of the pope and the Vatican for a close relationship with the United States, the presidential link with the pope was being downgraded by Washington after the war.

CATHOLIC UNITY IN EASTERN EUROPE

It was important to the Vatican to demonstrate to the Catholic clergy and laity of eastern Europe that Russians and communists could not be trusted and that the best defence of the church lay in resisting their blandishments and taking a principled and uncompromising stand in all dealings with them. The Holy See sought to encourage Catholic unity in the face of the communist challenge and members of the Church were advised to avoid factional splits which could weaken their resistance and benefit the communists.

The central question for Catholics living in eastern Europe was how they should respond to the Soviet occupation and to the activities of local communists. Political scientist Jan Gross contends that the period of the Second World War and the early Cold War in eastern Europe must be comprehended as a period of continuing social and political revolution. As a result first of the Axis, and then of the Soviet and Communist occupation, the traditional societies of eastern Europe were undergoing radical change, imposed from the outside, but much more a spontaneous internal development. The establishment of Communist regimes in the area offered to many the prospect of new and progressive opportunities while, to others, it presented a continuation of the totalitarian governments of the war.[29]

In some countries, such as Poland, Czechoslovakia, Yugoslavia, and Albania, the Communists had been welcomed as liberators, responsible for driving out and ending the Axis occupation. They worked with other parties to bring about needed reforms, especially in the redistribution of land, which were generally welcomed by the populations. In many countries, also, the Communists initially showed considerable deference and respect for the church. Many Catholics welcomed the end of the war and the programs of reform and were willing to co-operate with the new regimes. At the same time, they were wary of the hostility of communism to the church and of reforms which might affect the property of the church, just as they were wary of educational reforms which could reduce the teaching of religion in the state schools. Some Catholics, such as those in Albania, Croatia, or Slovakia, stood in much greater danger with the liberation, since they had actively collaborated with the Germans and Italians and expected to lose much with the liberation.

The most sensible response of the church in these times was to wait upon the course of events, since, in many countries, the church had extensive influence which could be used to good advantage in negotiations with new governments desperate to secure some measure of popular support. If the church were left alone, it could reciprocate in kind and give the government a modicum of support. If there had to be persecution, that would be dealt with as it arose and not necessarily anticipated in such a way that it became a self-fulfilling prophecy.

This, however, was where the Vatican insisted on directing the relationship of the church with the new occupying and governing forces. Waiting upon events was not acceptable and, while Pius XII was prepared to give the Germans and Italians the benefit of every doubt, he was not prepared to do the same for the Russians and the Communists. Postwar Poland was, in the pope's view, a creation by the Soviet Union to the detriment of the Germans and a major impediment to the pacification of Europe. For this reason, he could not recognize the government or the new borders of this nation and did not expect the church in Poland to either cooperate or negotiate with the new government. Similarly, postwar Yugoslavia, under Marshal Tito, sought to bring Catholic Slovenia and Croatia under the control of the central government of Belgrade after their relative independence during the war. The pope was sympathetic to the resistance which the Slovenes and the Croats presented to Tito's centralization and again encouraged non-cooperation with this Communist government.

Pius XII made his most direct statement in Hungary with his appointment of Archbishop Jozef Mindszenty to replace Cardinal Seredi as primate of Hungary in October 1945. Mindszenty was a Habsburg loyalist who was anti-republican, anti-democratic, and anti-communist and came into office with a reputation as a difficult and intransigent individual. With the appointment of Mindszenty, the first major church figure to be appointed in eastern Europe since the war, Pius XII indicated the kind of pugnacious church leader whom he admired and in whom he was prepared to place his full confidence.

The one government of eastern Europe with which the Vatican cooperated after the war was that of Czechoslovakia where President Edouard Beneš deliberately sought Vatican assistance to enable him to use the Roman Catholic Church as an institution to reintegrate the Czechs and the Slovaks into one national unit. Rome gave Beneš every possible assistance in dealing with this difficult situation.

The determination of the pope to direct the strategy of the church in eastern Europe created difficulties with bishops and clergy in that area who felt that, in many cases, they were better placed to understand how the church might best be served. Many of the more moderate churchmen were caught in the dilemma of choosing between doing what they believed to be right and advantageous as opposed to blindly following directives from Rome which they knew to be ill-conceived.[30] Many were distressed to see that it was the intransigence of Mindszenty of Hungary and Stepinac of Croatia which was most admired by Rome and that the pope showed very little empathy for the plight of the Church in more complex contexts such as that of Poland.

THE REDUCTION OF THE CATHOLIC PRESENCE IN THE SOVIET UNION

In dealing with communism, the Vatican could expect to find allies who would join it in the battle against atheism and materialism. In some ways, a more difficult antagonist for the Holy See was the Russian Orthodox Church, against whom the Catholic Church was essentially defenceless. At issue after the war were the Uniate churches of eastern Europe, especially those inside the Soviet Union. It was difficult for the Uniate Church to resist pressure for reunification with the Orthodox Church after the war, and it was especially difficult for Catholics to do a great deal to assist their co-religionists in territories which were directly governed by the Soviet Union. The situation inside the Soviet Union contributed to the postwar pessimism of the Vatican.

As the war came to an end, the Soviet Union began its campaign against its own Catholic community. The critique of the pope's 1944

Christmas message by the Russian Orthodox Council coincided with a move to induce the Galician Uniates to transfer their allegiance from the pope to the Russian Orthodox patriarch. In March 1945, Patriarch Alexei invited the Uniate clergy and laity to sever their ties with Rome and return to the Russian Orthodox Church and, on 11 April, Soviet authorities removed the Uniate hierarchy when Metropolitan Slipyi and the other Uniate bishops of Galicia were arrested and deported to eastern Ukraine. The administration of the Uniate Church was thereupon turned over to the "Initiative Group for the Reunification of the Greek-Catholic Church of Galicia with the Russian Orthodox Church," somewhat reluctantly led by Dr Gabriel Kostelnyk, "one of the best-known theologians of the Uniate church."[31] Kostelnyk was charged with encouraging the voluntary reunion of the Uniates with the Orthodox Church while the NKVD was charged with convincing those who were reluctant. On 28 May 1945, Kostelnyk issued his first appeal for reunion to members of the Uniate clergy and arrests of recalcitrant clergy began shortly thereafter. By November, fifty church buildings had been requisitioned by Soviet authorities and turned over to the Orthodox Church.[32] Dr Kostelnyk and his supporters, with help from the NKVD, had asked each member of the Uniate clergy whether they were prepared to accept reunion with the Orthodox Church. Those who were not so prepared were arrested, interrogated by the secret police, and deported to Siberia.

By the spring of 1946 over 50 percent of the clergy had agreed to the proposed change and Kostelnyk, accordingly, summoned a reunion Sobor. On 8 March 1946, this Sobor, meeting at Lvov, decreed the revocation of the 1596 Union of Brest and announced the return of the Galician Uniate Church to the body of the Russian Orthodox Church. By this vote, the Uniates of Galicia passed out of official existence. The fact that the remnants of the Uniate Church for many years thereafter operated underground as practising Orthodox who were secretly loyal to the pope indicated that many did not accept the union.[33]

The destruction of the Galician Uniates was paralleled by the treatment of other Catholics within the Soviet Union in the following years. In 1945 the region of Trans-Carpathia passed from Czechoslovakia to the Soviet Union by agreement, bringing another body of Uniates under Soviet control. In the case of Trans-Carpathia, the capable Bishop Rosma cooperated fully with the authorities, giving them no reason to turn against his church. After Rosma was killed in an alleged traffic accident in October 1947, Moscow was able to bring about the reunion of the Trans-Carpathian Uniates with Russian Orthodoxy.[34]

In the Baltic states the Catholic Church was reduced to an existence where it was not totally eliminated but it was "only provisionally tolerated." In Lithuania the Catholic Church was at the centre of the resistance movement against Soviet rule which gave Moscow difficulties from 1944 to 1952. Starting on 3 February 1946, the Soviets attacked the church hierarchy. The leading bishops, who had ignored a Soviet request to denounce the partisans, were arrested; by 1947 all except one elderly bishop were in prison, as were many members of the clergy. By 1947 religious ceremonies could take place only in church buildings and state functionaries were threatened with dismissal if they attended these services. Churches and religious institutions had to pay heavy taxes. A seminary for 150 students operated in Kaunas, although the rectors had been arrested. Pastoral letters and circulars were forbidden. By late 1947 earlier clerical opposition to the occupation had died away. In 1948 the Soviet authorities named their own Catholic bishops in Lithuania with the intention of setting up a Latin-rite Catholic Church independent of the Holy See, using "progressive clergy" who supported the regime as opposed to the "reactionary clergy" in jail who had opposed it.[35]

In Latvia about a third of the population was Catholic and had originally been divided into two dioceses under the ministrations of about two hundred priests. During the first Russian occupation in 1940, twelve priests had been deported to Russia. When the Germans retreated at the end of their occupation, they took thirty-one priests and two bishops with them, leaving only the aged archbishop behind. Many of the priests who left with the Germans did so voluntarily because the church had cooperated with the German occupation. After the war, there were only 140 Catholic clergy left in Latvia and a number of them were arrested on charges of collaboration. By late 1946 the clergy were allowed by the Soviet authorities to conduct religious services and to teach in church buildings, to prepare children for confession and communion, and to administer the sacraments in churches, homes and hospitals; the laity were allowed to attend church and to participate in pilgrimages. A theological seminary operated in Riga. On the other hand, the Catholic Church was not allowed to communicate with the Vatican or with Catholics in Lithuania.[36]

In Estonia the small Roman Catholic community had been virtually eliminated during the first Soviet occupation in 1940. The head of the church in Estonia, Monsignor Profittlich, had been deported to Russia and heard of no more. With the return of the Soviets at the end of the war, the Estonian Catholic community was completely eliminated by 1947.[37]

9 Early Persecution in the Balkans

From the perspective of the Holy See, the Balkan states of Albania, Yugoslavia, Bulgaria, and Romania had two common features after the Second World War: the Communists were firmly in control of the government when the war ended; and in none of these countries were Roman Catholics in a majority. Albania was predominantly Moslem, while the dominant religion of the other Balkan states was Eastern Orthodoxy. Yet in spite of these similarities, the initial treatment which the church received differed radically – from persecution in Albania and Yugoslavia, to benevolence in Romania and Bulgaria.

THE ALBANIAN PROLOGUE

While the Vatican were not surprised by the behaviour of the Soviets, the development of the situation in Albania came as an early indication of the treatment that awaited Catholics in other countries once communists had acquired political control. Coming into power at the end of the Second World War as a result of their own exertions, the Albanian Communist party exercised firm control over their nation from the beginning. Party Secretary Enver Hoxha had developed his own guerrilla movement and when he formed his postwar government, he did so with extensive popular support. While he had accepted aid from the Allies, his victory had not depended on outside influences such as the Red Army. Where many east European communist movements were weak and unpopular and had to depend on the Soviet presence to secure power, Hoxha's regime, like that of Tito in Yugoslavia, was in a strong position to implement its program of radical modernization immediately after the war.

The Roman Catholic Church was horrified to see Albania in the hands of Communists, especially since many of the bishops and clergy had supported and cooperated with the Italian and German forces of occupation and their Albanian allies. The church expected to pay for cooperating with the losing side in the war and to receive little sympathy from the victorious Communists, but the treatment it received in Albania confirmed its worst assumptions.

It was not long before the government began its campaign to eliminate Catholicism from Albania, a task which it effectively completed by the end of 1946. The anti-Catholic campaign was designed to undermine the basis of the guerrilla resistance in the north and to eradicate Italian influence from the country.[1] The apostolic delegate, Monsignor Leone Nigris, had left Albania for Rome in March 1945, only to find that, after the war, whenever he obtained permission from Albanian authorities in Italy to return to his post, he was turned around by partisan forces in Albania and sent back to Italy. This exclusion was also applied to Italian priests and missionaries who had left and tried to return to Albania after the war.

The government deprived the Catholic Church and the other religions of virtually all their property through its land reform decree of 29 August 1945.[2] At the beginning of October, the government ordered all Italian priests and missionaries to leave the country immediately. This was a severe blow to the Catholic Church, since there were insufficient Albanian priests left to fill the gap; the Albanian bishop of Pulti believed that it would take at least two years to train enough priests to minister to the needs of Albanian Catholics.[3]

In December the police raided Catholic institutions in Scutari, including the Jesuit seminary. The discovery of oppositional brochures in the seminary led to the arrest and interrogation of some of the seminarians who reputedly incriminated the directors. Consequently, on 30 December, Father Giovanni Fausti, the superior of the Jesuits, and Father Danjel Dajani, the rector of the seminary, were arrested along with two other senior priests, and in January 1946 a continuing anti-Jesuit campaign served as a cover for further arrests and for the confiscation of Catholic properties.

On 8 January 1946 Father Franco Gjini, an Albanian who, in the absence of the apostolic delegate, was acting as the regent of the apostolic delegation, sent a letter of protest to Enver Hoxha, but Hoxha refused to receive Gjini or to discuss his letter.[4] On 2 February 1946 thirty-six arrested Catholics, including twenty-one members of the clergy, were put on trial in Scutari amid a blaze of publicity. During the trial the anti-national activity of the Catholic Church "from before the Italian occupation to the present attitude of the Pope was reviewed." Five of the priests were condemned to death and executed during the first week of March. At the same time, Italian religious made haste to get out of Albania; the officer in charge of the British military mission reported that eighty-two priests and nuns had received permission to leave Albania on 26 February.[5]

By mid-March, all Catholic priests and nuns had been forced from their homes and required to live in their churches. Many churches had also been requisitioned by the government and put to other uses. One church at Devoli was turned into a lunatic asylum, while others were turned into prisons, meeting halls, and cinemas. Many clerics were in prison or concentration camp and government officials were kept busy in the spring of 1946 taking inventory of confiscated church property. A number of priests and religious were still allowed to say mass, but they were sleeping in their churches and cooking in their sacristies and were required to return any donations which they received.[6]

The Communists held the Catholic clergy responsible for the anti-government guerrilla bands of the north. When an attack on Scutari was defeated by government forces on 9 September 1946, leading members of the Catholic hierarchy, including the archbishop and metropolitan of Durazzo and the archbishop of Scutari, were arrested, tried, and executed. In December 1946 the authorities discovered a cache of German and Italian arms in the Franciscan convent in Scutari and, subsequently, arrested all the remaining Franciscans as well as Father Gjini. In early 1947 reports on the church in Albania described the humiliation of the remaining priests and nuns and the general terror meted out to Catholics.[7]

The Albanian church received little outside help or support during this period because it had indeed sullied its hands by collaborating with the Italian and German occupations. The church was being attacked when Albanian partisans were still being feted in the west as co-victors in the war; their action against the church was seen as a legitimate move against Balkan "Quislings."[8] The Italian church and the Vatican could exert no influence in the matter other than providing defence funds for the priests on trial. In February 1946 the Vatican asked the British government to take an interest in the Scutari trials, but the British were reluctant to become involved and suggested that the Vatican work through the Italian foreign ministry.[9] This lack of British interest meant that the Vatican had to look elsewhere for help to protect the church against communist depradations. Later efforts to interest the Americans were equally fruitless.

The Franciscans and Father Gjini were brought to trial and

sentenced to death at the beginning of 1948. In a last-ditch effort, the Vatican tried to get the French government to intervene in their favour, but it was too late as the priests by then had already been executed.[10] By 1948 the Roman Catholic Church was a devastated institution in Albania. It had suffered the worst possible outcome imagined by the Vatican at the hands of communist atheists. As other countries of eastern Europe came under tighter communist control, the example of the Albanian church stood as a warning to the Vatican of the lengths to which Communist regimes could be expected to go.

YUGOSLAV CATHOLICS AND TITO'S REPUBLIC

At the end of the war the Yugoslav Partisans, like their counterparts in Albania, attacked the Roman Catholic Church for its collaboration with the occupying Germans and Italians and with the wartime Ustase government of Ante Pavelic. Yet the treatment of the church differed in Yugoslavia where, unlike Albania, Roman Catholics made up a sizeable and important percentage of the population. While the Partisans believed that Catholic bishops and clergy had much to answer for, the new government of Yugoslavia under Marshal Tito exercised restraint in their treatment of the church. Like King Alexander before him, Tito wanted to create a Yugoslav political nationality and chose to do this through the creation of a federal state which would allow a degree of regional autonomy to its various national communities.

The position of the church in Yugoslavia was complicated in 1945. Although an independent Croatia had been discredited by the Pavelic dictatorship, many Catholics were not interested in a reunited Yugoslavia under Communist or any other auspices. On the other hand, the hierarchy owed their allegiance to the Holy See which, at the end of the war, was actively supporting a peace favourable to Italy. Since Italy and Yugoslavia were locked in dispute over the future status of Trieste and the Istrian peninsula and the Vatican did not want to see any more Catholics from the Venezia Giulia region of Italy handed over to Yugoslav Communist rule, support for the Holy See meant that the Catholics of Yugoslavia should work against the interests of the Belgrade government.

In spite of earlier church support for the Axis powers, Tito was prepared to ask the hierarchy of the Catholic Church to support the concept of a Yugoslav nation and to give national interests priority over those of Italy and the papacy. At a meeting on 2 June 1945 in Zagreb, Tito told representatives of the Catholic bishops and clergy that "our Church needs to be national, that it [needs to] be more responsive to the [Croatian] nation ... I do not want to undertake the right to condemn Rome ... and I will not. But I must say that I look at it critically, because [church policy] has always been attuned more to Italy than to our people. I would like to see that the Catholic Church in Croatia now ... have more independence." He went on to say: "We want to create a great community of South Slavs and in this community there would be both Orthodox and Catholic, who must be closely linked with all the other Slavs. The Orthodox are nearer to this than the Catholics, and the question of relations between the Orthodox Church and the Catholic Church must also be included in the great idea of the drawing together and close cooperation of the Slav people, who have suffered so much in their history from divisions." On 4 June Tito specifically asked Archbishop Stepinac of Zagreb to demonstrate independence of the Vatican by supporting Belgrade in its dispute with Italy over Istria and Trieste.[11]

While Croatian and Slovenian Catholics had generally been far from enthusiastic about the Axis occupation and about the Ustase state, they had adapted and had not opposed either of them. As a result, they were vulnerable to charges of collaboration. In the spring of 1945, after the Partisan press attacked Archbishop Stepinac for not denouncing wartime atrocities, he denied the validity of the argument and drew attention to the Red Terror, to the "irresponsible and evil-loving groups" which were "slaughtering priests, intellectuals and good Catholics on the pretext of punishing them as war criminals."[12]

Tito had shown the church leaders how they could redeem their position in the new Yugoslavia and he waited for a response from the church. Meanwhile, the arrest and execution of Catholic priests continued through the summer. The Communist government's program of radical reform created new difficulties for the church, as economic and educational changes restricted privileges which the church had traditionally enjoyed. The first major program of land reform, instituted in August 1945, resulted in the confiscation of many church properties.

Unlike the Polish hierarchy, who found themselves in an embarrassing dilemma over Vatican support of German interests to the detriment of Polish sensibilities, the Croat hierarchy showed little hesitation in siding with the Vatican and with Italy against the Belgrade government. Like the pope, they were unwilling to trust the Communists or to give them the benefit of any doubt. Believing that the best defence of past conduct was a good offence, the church had challenged the legitimacy of the new government of Yugoslavia from the early days of the peace.

The Catholic bishops had demonstrated their independence of Belgrade for too long to submit to the dictates of a Communist government which they opposed on ideological grounds. They were unwilling to support Tito's regime and sought, following the lead of Stepinac and the Vatican, to develop a case which would take the focus off charges of collaboration and give the hierarchy a different basis on which to argue with the regime. The Catholic bishops eventually replied to Tito's June request through a pastoral letter read in all churches in the country on 30 September 1945, which, according to historian Stella Alexander, was "a massive frontal attack, an all-out defiance of the government."[13]

In their pastoral, the bishops claimed that, in spite of the change of regime, the church had been prepared to give its support to the new government so long as its policies conformed to ethical principles. Now, however, the bishops felt that the government was violating those principles and they had to set forth their charges: they objected to the arrest, execution, and disappearance of so many priests, to the suspension of all Catholic publications, to the closing of most Catholic printing presses, to the confiscation of Catholic schools and seminaries and of much other church property, to the introduction of civil marriage, to the prevention of Catholic welfare work, and to "the spread of materialism and atheism throughout Yugoslavia – all of which resulted in a position differing only in name from a state of open persecution."

Mindful of the elections for a constituent assembly scheduled for 25 November 1945, Tito remained conciliatory in his public reply of 25 October when he asked why the Catholic bishops had not issued a similar pastoral against the crimes of the Ustase, and indicated that the sole purpose of the present pastoral was to sow hatred among the peoples of Yugoslavia. Tito held that the Yugoslav government was looking for a partnership with the church to build the new Yugoslavia and wanted to work out some kind of agreement on questions of property and education. Tito warned, however, "that laws existed which forbade sowing discord and treachery, and anyone who wished his country well must honour these laws."[14]

On the eve of the elections Stepinac wrote an open letter to Tito in which he pointed out the falsity of the government's charges that the bishops were only objecting because the planned agrarian reform would remove their property from them. The bishops were objecting, argued Stepinac, because the church was being persecuted, because the bishops were the trustees for the ecclesiastical property and were expected to defend the lands of the church and, above all, because the Communists had already decided that there was to be no real role for the Catholic Church in postwar Yugoslavia.[15]

King Alexander had found the Vatican useful for getting around uncooperative Croatian bishops. In the same way, Tito saw an advantage in opening a channel to the papacy, particularly after the September pastoral indicated that the hierarchy was reluctant to respond to his overtures. In 1945 Monsignor Nicolo Moscatello was still serving as the chargé d'affaires at the Yugoslav embassy to the Holy See to which he had been appointed by the prewar royal government. He convinced Tito of the wisdom of restoring full diplomatic relations and when, in early September, the Vatican proposed to send a representative to Belgrade, Tito accepted on condition that the representative not be an Italian. In October the Vatican and the Yugoslav government agreed to restore diplomatic relations.

The Vatican had been wary of Tito's Partisans throughout the war because of their communism. The apostolic delegate in London believed that the British had been mistaken to give such full support to the Partisans and the general feeling at the Vatican was that the Allies were naive about the communist danger in Yugoslavia.[16] Yugoslav postwar reprisals were seen as part of the Red Terror which the papacy expected to follow a communist victory and the Vatican reported to the Allies on the murder of priests and the confiscation of church property in those parts of Yugoslavia occupied by Tito's forces. In the opinion of the British ambassador in Belgrade, who was prepared to give Tito the benefit of the doubt, the Vatican was becoming hysterical and making accusations on ill-founded evidence of these massacres being part of a coordinated government policy.[17]

With Stepinac and the bishops standing on their rights and principles, no arrangement proved possible between church and state. Once Tito's hold on power was secured when the government slate received overwhelming approval in the election of 25 November, he abandoned his conciliatory policy towards the Catholics and his campaign against the church began in earnest. The Catholic Church as a whole, rather than individual members of the clergy, was now to be charged with complicity in the Ustase terror. On 16 December, Dr Vladimir Bakaric, the president of the Croatian federal government, accused the Catholic Church of protecting the continuing activities of the Ustase in the churches and church buildings. The tone of his attack prompted Stepinac to warn the clergy to be ready to defend themselves.[18] Dr Bakaric's charges formed part of a wider press campaign against the church from mid-December on. Many priests were prevented from serving mass at Christmas and further restrictions were placed on Catholic schools and the Catholic press. In January 1946 demonstrators in Zagreb called for Stepinac's arrest and trial before the People's

Court. Then on 31 January 1946 the government announced that they had found the evidence that they needed of Catholic complicity with the Ustase. Thirty-six wooden boxes containing valuables belonging to the Ustase, apparently including gold teeth, were discovered by the police in the Franciscan monastery adjoining Stepinac's archepiscopal palace. On the next day Tito announced his belief that Stepinac's complicity with the Pavelic government helped to explain the archbishop's consistent hostility to the new regime.[19]

COMMUNIST BENEVOLENCE IN ROMANIA AND BULGARIA

The treatment of the Catholic Church in Romania and Bulgaria was initially in stark contrast to its treatment in Albania and Yugoslavia. Both Romania and Bulgaria had sided with the Axis in the Second World War and, as a result, had been occupied by Soviet troops in the fall of 1944. With the assistance of Soviet authorities, left-wing coalition governments dominated by the Communists were quickly brought into power in both countries. While Allied Control Commissions existed for Romania and Bulgaria on which the great powers were represented, the British and Americans accepted that these countries were the primary responsibility of the Soviet Union.

The Communist parties of Romania and Bulgaria found themselves in office with limited popular support and, in the process of consolidating their power, needed to expand this support in some fashion. The Soviet strategy in both these countries was to use the Orthodox Church as a vehicle for extending Russian – and thus communist – cultural influence. In the postwar period Stalin encouraged the Russian Orthodox Church to reach out to the Balkan churches and to indicate the line that they should follow in return for receiving favours from the Communist regimes. Where the Orthodox churches had traditionally recognized the supremacy of the Ecumenical Patriarch of Constantinople, Russian Patriarch Alexei, with Stalin's support, sought to supplant the primacy of Constantinople in dealing with the churches of eastern Europe.

One aspect of Russian strategy was to drive a wedge between Orthodox and Catholic in order to restrict and eliminate the Catholics once the Orthodox had been brought into line with Soviet policy. It would be beneficial for the Soviets to have the Orthodox Church in the Balkans taking direction from the church of Moscow and to eliminate the influence of the Roman Catholic Church, whose leader was so clearly in the anti-Communist camp. Yet since the relationship with the Orthodox churches was the first priority for Communist religious policy, Catholics were only of secondary interest, and they were allowed considerable freedom until the independence of the Orthodox had been constrained.

Romania

Russian troops did not interfere with the functioning of the Romanian churches during the occupation period and both Orthodox and Catholic churches found that their personnel, property, and practices were respected by the new government of Petru Groza during its first three years of power. The Uniates enjoyed enormous prestige in Romania and Groza himself came from a Uniate family. In fact the minister of religion was a Uniate, as were most of the members of his department. In 1946 the prime minister went out of his way to thank the Uniate Church for help in securing the government's success in elections, which prompted the belief that he was deliberately sheltering the church from Russian attack.[20]

During the Soviet occupation, the Romanian Orthodox Church was under pressure to move closer to the Russian Orthodox Church. Romanian Patriarch Nikodim was invited to attend the enthronement of Alexei in Moscow in February 1945 and a delegation from the Russian church subsequently visited Romania for talks with Romanian church leaders. Suspicious that the Russians were aiming for union of the Russian and Romanian churches, the Romanians were cautious in their dealings with their ecclesiastical counterparts. Nikodim was accused by the Russians of being too close to the Roman Catholics and played a cautious game to preserve the independence of his church. In 1946 he deferred a visit to Moscow for talks as long as he possibly could, only acceding to the Russian invitation at the end of October. It was clear that no closer affiliation with the Russian Orthodox Church would take place as long as Nikodim was patriarch.[21]

The Russians wanted to isolate the Catholics by interfering with the relationship between Romania and the Holy See. The papal nuncio, Monsignor Cassulo, who had served in Romania for ten years and had enjoyed excellent relations with prewar government officials, found that, during the first year of Soviet occupation, he was unable to continue his dealings with the government or to communicate with the Vatican. At first the Russians asked the Romanians to break diplomatic relations with the Vatican. Then, the Romanian government resisted, the Russians put pressure on them to expel the nuncio.

The Romanians were reluctant to move against Monsignor Cassulo, for whom they had considerable respect; instead, they tried to get him to leave voluntarily. In March 1946 General Antonescu, the fascist head of government until 1944, was put on trial together with his foreign minister. As part of the proceedings, the government intended to release the transcripts of their wartime conversations with the nuncio. Cassulo was advised that it might be best for him to leave the country for the duration of the trial. He claimed, however, that he had nothing to hide and that his departure during the trial could be taken as an admission of guilt. The government, therefore, was left with no alternative but to ask the Holy See for Cassulo's recall.[22]

The Vatican were willing to replace Cassulo, realizing that his association with the former regime would create difficulties with the new government. The question then arose of whether the replacement should be a nuncio who would also be dean of the diplomatic corps, an arrangement which the Soviet Union was known to oppose. To circumvent this problem, the Vatican decided to appoint a regent for the apostolic nunciature in Bucharest as they had done in Belgrade.

As regent, the Vatican chose another American, Monsignor Gerald O'Hara, the bishop of Savannah, Georgia. There were a number of advantages in appointing an American citizen to the post in Romania: he could speak with some authority when dealing with the Romanian and Russian authorities; he could get useful assistance from the American and British representatives in Bucharest; and, perhaps most importantly, he could report with authority to the North American public on the situation of the church in Romania. O'Hara had never been part of the papal diplomatic corps, although he had worked in Rome for a time and was well thought of there. In 1945 he had been chosen to go to Albania as apostolic visitor, but his appointment had never been agreeable to the Albanian government. To secure O'Hara's appointment, the Vatican made Cassulo's departure conditional on the approval of the appointment by both the Romanian government and the Allied Control Commission, including the Russians.[23]

The Russians balked at accepting a replacement for Cassulo and preferred a complete rupture with the Vatican. Only at the end of December 1946 did the Russian representative on the control commission reluctantly give his approval for O'Hara. Possibly this belated Russian approval was due to the failure of the Russians to secure Patriarch Nikodim's cooperation for a scheme to force the Romanian Uniates to unite with the Romanian Orthodox Church as it had with the Galician Uniates. The Russians needed more time and acceded to the continuation of the nunciature. The regent began his mission in Bucharest at the beginning of 1947 and for the first year encountered few problems from the Romanian government, which continued to treat the churches with respect. O'Hara was judged by the Italian minister in Bucharest to be a most effective and popular diplomatic representative.[24]

Bulgaria

The real test of Soviet and Bulgarian intentions came in January 1946 when the apostolic delegate, Monsignor Giuseppe Mazzoli, died in office. To avoid difficulties with the Russians, who might have balked at a permanent appointment, the Vatican appointed Father Francesco Galloni, an Italian who had served in Sofia for twenty years, as regent of the apostolic delegation. Galloni's appointment received immediate approval of the Bulgarian government, and the Pro Oriente buildings were returned to the church when the Russians had finished with them. The Italian minister believed that the government had moved swiftly to establish its independence from Russia by indicating that it would have diplomatic relations with whom it wished to have diplomatic relations, even the Holy See.[25] It seems more likely, however, given the potential for a Russian veto on the Bulgarian Control Commission, that the Russians did not intend to interfere with the operation of the Catholic Church in Bulgaria. At the end of 1945 the Communist members of the Bulgarian cabinet dropped their earlier opposition to the continuation of official relations with the Vatican.

Orthodox Exarch Stephen took the initiative to heal the "Bulgarian schism" at the end of 1945 by making a conciliatory visit to the Ecumenical patriarch. Following this rapprochement, Stephen offered his services as an intermediary between the patriarchs of Moscow and Constantinople, a role he was able to fulfil for at least the first two postwar years. He intended to protect his autonomy by not being too precise about his relations with other churches and by maintaining his contacts with Patriarch Alexei, the archbishop of Canterbury, and the pope.[26]

10 The Catholic Majorities of East Central Europe

By the end of 1945 Communist parties exercised the greatest political control in those east European countries where a minority of the population belonged to the Roman Catholic Church. In Hungary, Poland, and Czechoslovakia, on the other hand, which all had majority Catholic populations, Communists shared power to varying degrees with other parties that had worked in the anti-fascist resistance. In these countries the church could count on the allegiance of the bulk of the population and possessed extensive social and cultural power and influence. As the Communists desperately needed popular support, they sought to achieve some accommodation with the church. An examination of the history of Hungary and Poland in this period indicates the differing strategies used by the church in dealing with its new circumstances.

MINDSZENTY OF HUNGARY: THE PAPAL SURROGATE

Post-1918 Hungary had continued the tradition of the Austro-Hungarian monarchy with the appointment of Admiral Nicholas Horthy to reign as regent until the Habsburg dynasty could reclaim the throne of St Stephen. The Habsburgs never assumed power, however, and 1945 found Hungary once again on the losing side of a major war. On 21 December 1944 a Soviet-sponsored provisional assembly had met in Debrecen to choose a provisional government for Hungary which could bring that country into the war on the allied side, institute a reform program, and prepare for national elections when the war was over. Marshal Voroshilov, the Russian chairman of the Allied Control Commission for Hungary, allocated the seats in the assembly proportionately to the various anti-fascist parties – the Smallholders', the National Peasant party, the Social Democrat, and the Communist parties – with the Communist party receiving the largest number. This was in spite of the fact that the lack of any sizeable Hungarian resistance movement meant the Communists had little popular following within the country.[1] The provisional government, along with the Soviet Union, Great Britain, and the United States, was determined to see Hungary established as both a political democracy and a republic and to have the Habsburg monarchy formally brought to an end.

To replace Cardinal Seredi, the pope named József Mindszenty, the bishop of Vesprem, to the prince-primacy on 8 September 1945. Mindszenty's appointment was controversial since, although he had been imprisoned by the pro-Nazi Arrow Cross government of Hungary in 1944, he was known to be against the creation of a democratic republican government. He was an outspoken Hungarian nationalist who had not been popular in his previous ministries, where his reputation had been "that of a very unbending and inhuman, but very zealous, exponent of the antique virtues." Cardinal Seredi had expressed doubts about Mindszenty in a 1943 letter to the pope, citing his lack of university education and his vehement temperament, and members of the Curia had also had concerns about Mindszenty's suitability for such a sensitive position. Before his enthronement in Esztergom, he issued a pastoral letter condemning dancing in his diocese and in his enthronement speech inveighed heavily against the sinfulness of the Hungarian people.[2]

During the interwar years, Mindszenty, along with many other Catholics, had supported the Legitimist cause, which believed in a restoration of the Hapsburg monarchy in Hungary, if not also in Austria, and in the principles of state autocracy that went with it. He strongly opposed a republican Hungary and had a profound distrust of political democracy. His view was that republicanism, democracy, and communism could all be attributed to the subversive influence of the Russian presence in postwar Hungary. In the absence of emperor and regent, Mindszenty believed that the stewardship of the Hungarian people devolved constitutionally upon the archbishop of Esztergom as prince-primate. Esztergom, which had been the capital of medieval Hungary, "had also been the symbol of the medieval Christian concept of the state, in which *sacerdotium* and *imperium*, pope and emperor, collaborated." He considered "the dignity, the rights and the duties of the primate had remained intact in the new constitution that was drawn up after the end of the First World War" and these had been unchanged by the Debrecen provisional assembly in 1945. On his appointment, in keeping with these beliefs Mindszenty sent a telegram to the provisional government: "The highest constitutional authority of the country stands ready to serve his native land."³

In his enthronement address, Mindszenty spoke of the role which he saw for himself in his country's future: "Many a constitutional bastion lies still in ruins but the Primate is here, ready to step into the footsteps of his predecessors. When the tide of misfortune is ebbing and sobriety will reign over the whirling waters I as your Pontifex, as the first constitutional factor in this country in the 900 years, as your Archbishop and Primate shall take my place in the reconstruction and promotion of our constitutional life." He deplored the occupation of his country by Russian troops and saw Hungarian communists as both foreign agents and radical reformers at the same time. He saw serious difficulties ahead: "Today a wild and halting abyss opens before us. Our bleeding country is floundering in the greatest economic, constitutional, moral whirlpools of history. Our psalter is the De Profundis, our prayer is the Miserere, our prophet is Jeremiah and our world is the world of the Apocalypse. We are sitting by the waters of Babylon and they want us to learn songs foreign to us to the sounds of an unstrung lute." The archbishop disagreed with the assertion that Hungary must break with the past and renew itself; rather, he claimed, Hungary must continue in the traditions of her "illustrious ancestors."⁴

The Roman Catholic Church in Hungary was, however, divided between those who, like Mindszenty, retained a loyalty to the Habsburg monarchy and those who were prepared to support the parliamentary republic. Mindszenty charged those Hungarians, even Hungarian Catholics, who supported the republic or the democratic government with being disloyal and having sold out to the Soviet Union. He was blessed with boundless energy, an aggressive personality, complete confidence in his own rectitude, and a rigid concept of ecclesiastical authority. He was often more concerned with establishing his authority over Hungarian Catholics than in organizing an effective Catholic response to the threat of communism.

The interesting question is why Pius XII chose Mindszenty for such a sensitive appointment. One would assume that the pope had been advised on suitable candidates and that he was aware that there were others whom he could have chosen who would have taken a more conciliatory approach to the postwar political regime. The fact that the pope chose Mindszenty stands as a clear statement of how Pius XII felt the church should respond to the challenge of communism in postwar Europe. The appointment of Mindszenty was, after all, to the only primatial see that Pius XII had to fill in eastern Europe at the end of the war and, therefore, the only one where he had a direct opportunity to demonstrate his belief that martyrdom awaited the church under communism.

The absence of a papal nuncio since Rotta's expulsion in the spring of 1945 served to augment the authority of the prince-primate, since he was the sole interpreter of the wishes of the Vatican in Hungary and also the sole channel of information to the Holy See about the condition of the church. The subtleties of the situation in Hungary were not conveyed to Pius XII who, in addition to having great sympathy for the defeated nations, had a great admiration for Mindszenty's principled refusal to compromise with evil. Mindszenty acted with the knowledge that he spoke with the full authority of the pope.

The diplomats and politicians were not impressed by the new prince-primate. The Soviet counsellor expressed his displeasure to the Hungarian foreign minister and the British representative, while commenting that the primate was a man of courage, energy, and conviction, allowed that he was "not perhaps always as tactful as he might be."[5] The reaction of the Hungarian press to the enthronement speech indicated clearly that Mindszenty "and the present Hungarian leaders were out of sympathy with each other."[6]

Mindszenty lost no time in pointing out alleged Russian violations of religious liberty to the British and American representatives on the Allied Control Commission. No sooner had he been appointed than he spent two hours describing to Gascoigne, the British representative, "the Russian-Hungarian Communist terror existing at present in this country." He subsequently protested to the Allied authorities that the Russian commander in his diocese had interfered with the free exercise of religion by confiscating the pastoral letter against dancing. "I do not interfere in the way the commander deals with his soldiers," wrote Mindszenty, "and I therefore do not permit that the commander should interfere with the affairs of the Church. If the Hungarians do not dance, the interests of the United Nations are in no way affected."[7]

Elections for the National Assembly were scheduled for 4 November 1945. Three days before the election a pastoral letter was read in all the churches of Hungary, throwing the full support of the Roman Catholic Church behind the anti-communist and pro-Catholic Smallholders' party. This intervention was significant since it represented a bid by the church to replace the former political leadership of Hungary in giving the Hungarian people, who had not been involved in anti-government resistance during the war, a political direction for the future. The pastoral helped to focus their voting and the outcome of the elections gave the Smallholders' party 57 percent of the popular vote and 245 seats in the 409-seat assembly. The Communist party, to its great surprise and disappointment, received only 17 percent of the popular vote and seventy seats. Zoltan Tildy, one of the republican leaders on the left wing of the Smallholders' party, became the prime minister of a coalition which included Socialists and Communists. The Russians insisted that the government remain a coalition and that the Ministry of the Interior be given to a communist. In spite of his clear majority, Tildy was unable to challenge these pressures because Hungary was still under foreign occupation as a defeated enemy country.[8]

Shortly after the election Tildy acknowledged the electoral support which his Smallholders' party had received from the church and asked Mindszenty to convey to Rome a request for the resumption of diplomatic relations between Hungary and the Holy See. Mindszenty, however, was not enthusiastic about having a papal nuncio return to Budapest, knowing that such an official would serve as an alternate centre for negotiations with the government and an alternate channel to the Vatican. Believing that Tildy was trying to limit his authority, Mindszenty, in turn, sought Tildy's promise not to change the monarchical constitution of Hungary for a republican one, inferring that such would be the preference of the Holy See.[9] By the beginning of December both the Hungarian government and the Allied Control Commission, including the Soviet representative, had given their blessings to the resumption of diplomatic relations with the Vatican. With this approval, the Vatican planned to send the nuncio back to Budapest before the end of the year.

The ease with which the return of a nuncio was approved confirmed Mindszenty's suspicions. The Hungarian government hoped that a nuncio might give Mindszenty some "diplomatic sense." The British diplomats felt that a nuncio would be able to provide the primate's energy with some wise direction and fully expected the Russians to see that "the Holy See's experienced guidance to the Prince Primate would be considerable and would be a useful 'brake' to the latter's excessive zeal."[10]

On 30 November Mindszenty took the matter to Rome for discussion with the pope. During the three weeks that the prince-primate was out of the country, Tildy seized the opportunity to announce his intention of turning Hungary into a republic. According to his memoirs, Mindszenty believed that Tildy had betrayed him and, for that reason, he dissuaded the pope from returning the nuncio to Budapest: "We ... agreed that after my return I would first inform the country about my visit to Rome and the possibility of eventual resumption of diplomatic relations. Then I would wait to observe the effects of such an announcement."[11] What seems more likely is that Mindszenty deliberately went to Rome to prevent the return of the nuncio.

To Mindszenty, the Hungarian government was doubly suspect, both because it was democratic and because it had Communist membership. On his return to Budapest, rather than supporting Tildy and his Smallholder colleagues in their difficult situation, Mindszenty sought to galvanize public pressure to force them to oppose their Communist partners in the government. On the last day of 1945, the primate made a radio broadcast to the Hungarian people, claiming that the Tildy government had done nothing to "lessen the restriction of liberty, to enhance the freedom of the press, freedom of speech and individual liberty, [or] to carry into effect the dictates of the Ten Commandments."

In addition to rallying Hungarian opinion against the Tildy government, Mindszenty sought to warn the Allied powers about developments in Hungary. In the first week of January he met the head of the British political mission to expound on the "evils of the present political situation in Hungary," pointing out how, in his view, Tildy was "giving way all along the line to the Communists" and that it was only a matter of time before the Communists, with Russian help, would stage a coup d'état in Budapest. Under these circumstances, Mindszenty asked, would Great Britain "be prepared to permit Hungary to fall altogether into the hands of the Communists?" Gascoigne, the head of the British mission, did not share Mindszenty's concern and, instead, saw this as an opportunity to provide the primate with wise counsel "to be patient and not to indulge in public criticisms of the present régime until such time as we had, at any rate, had a chance to assess the worth of the Tildy administration. I told him that I thought that tirades against the present government might only result in playing into the hands of the extremists, and that I felt very strongly that if I were in his shoes I would... reserve my ammunition and husband my strength until such time as it might be really opportune to use it."

Mindszenty's reaction to this lecture is not recorded, although Gascoigne urged on his government the importance of getting a nuncio appointed "lest Cardinal Mindszenty may, in the absence of the wise counsel which he will undoubtedly receive from Monsignor Rotta, overstep the mark and place himself in a serious situation vis-à-vis the present Hungarian Government."[12]

With the proclamation of the Hungarian Republic on 1 February 1946, Mindszenty's beloved Habsburg monarchy was brought to an end. Given the primate's attitude towards the new republic and his outspoken criticism of the Communists, the Russian occupation authorities were reluctant to do anything that would increase the influence of the church – and presumably of Mindszenty – such as allow the appointment of a papal nuncio. The Soviet military commander and the Soviet government had been infuriated by Mindszenty's pre-election pastoral letters and since the election had "displayed a mistrust of Hungarian Catholicism" to such a degree that they regarded "with suspicion every action undertaken by the clergy or by Catholic associations." The Russians were now "against the whole idea" of a nuncio.[13] Without a return of the nuncio, Mindszenty remained the only ecclesiastical channel between Rome and Budapest.[14]

It was not only the diplomats and the Hungarian political leadership who felt that Mindszenty's criticism of the government had been unreasonable. A large number of Hungarian Catholics had welcomed the institution of a republic and did not feel that the church had been badly treated by it. They pointed to the relative freedom of operation of the church and the lack of anything that could be described as religious persecution. Religious education was still being given in the schools and the Catholic press, while subject to certain constraints, was still relatively free to print what it chose. Even the Russians, after their initial brutalities, had left the church alone. It was true that church lands had been forfeit as part of the general land reform program, but even in this the church had been treated fairly and had lost no more than other landowners. Banned Catholic associations were even able to continue operation under different names. Many Catholics welcomed Hungarian democracy and supported the new government.

The leader of these Catholics was Mindszenty's successor as bishop of Veszprem, Ladislav Banass. Bishop Banass, described in Mindszenty's *Memoirs* as "a man who liked to push to the forefront,"[15] made no secret of his opposition to the primate. Banass called on Hungarians to reassess their country's future as a potential bridge between East and West, since the Russians obviously bore them no ill will. Banass's views stimulated a new publication at the beginning of 1947, designed to promote "progressive and democratic" views to Catholics.

Fearful that Mindszenty would exacerbate inter-allied relations over Hungary, and with scant hope for the appointment of a nuncio, the British sought to control and limit the prince-primate through his superiors in the Vatican. At the end of February 1946 Osborne sent a "private and confidential" letter to Monsignor Tardini, suggesting that he "urge Cardinal Mindszenty to be a little less violent and provocative in his utterances and attitude. It seems to me that he is going too far in exposing himself to the charge of bringing the Church into politics. As it now seems unlikely that there will in the discernible future be any Nuncio in Budapest to urge moderation upon him, it might perhaps be well for the Vatican to do so."[16]

Conflict between Soviet authorities and the Catholic Church continued into the summer of 1946, when the Russians, as a result of anti-Soviet demonstrations, ordered the Hungarian government to ban a number of specified Catholic associations, including those for university students, village young men, village girls, Catholic workers, and

Boy Scouts, and to bring charges against priests who were held to be responsible for the incidents.

In response, Mindszenty sent a blistering letter to the Hungarian foreign minister, accusing the government of endorsing these "grave charges" against the Catholic Church. Prime Minister Ferenc Nagy, who had replaced Tildy in February 1946 when the latter had been elected first president of the Hungarian republic, replied that the primate's own behaviour had been responsible for Soviet distrust of the Catholic Church, reminding the cardinal that Hungary had not yet received a return of her sovereignty and was still under the armistice terms of occupation.[17]

The Hungarian government worried that further demonstrations against the occupying forces could invite retaliation from the Russians at the peace conference. Since the primate was uncooperative, the government turned to the clergy and, on 2 August, made a public appeal to the clergy of all denominations to tell the people that the Red Army had helped to establish democratic government in Hungary and were prepared to respect the position of the churches. In return, the government promised that it was prepared "to guarantee the rights of the Churches and to support them in the fulfilment of their religious duties." These government promises and assurances served to settle matters between church and state for the duration of the peace conference.

In the latter half of 1946 the Hungarian government sought to respond to the wishes of those Catholics who supported the republican constitution. On 20 August the government sent official representatives to attend the massive celebration of St Stephen's Day in the cathedral in Budapest. In early October, just as the Paris peace conference was in its final stages, the government charged Professor Joseph Janosi, a Jesuit, with a new mission to Rome to discuss the opening of diplomatic relations with the Vatican. In going to Rome, Janosi was not optimistic, since he felt that Mindszenty's intransigent attitude, "which has been interpreted by the Russians at least as approved by the Vatican," was the major stumbling block to such relations. The government intended to prepare the way for the opening of relations once the peace treaty had been signed and the Russians had withdrawn their troops.[18]

Yet any dealings with the Vatican had to take Mindszenty into account. Osborne, believing Mindszenty to be "a fanatic, both as a patriot and Churchman," suggested to Tardini that a warning from the Vatican could prevent the cardinal from doing further harm to his church and his country, and Tardini appeared "to be only too well aware of the intemperance and provocation of the Cardinal's conduct and speech" but did not feel that he was able to control him.[19] Mindszenty would only respond to the pope and it was noticed that, following his visit to Rome early in 1947, Mindszenty became much more moderate in his behaviour. While agreeing with the cardinal's basic ends, the pope asked Mindszenty to change his methods and see how the situation developed in Hungary once the Allied occupation was brought to an end. If it should develop to the advantage of the church, all well and good; if not, then the cardinal would have to speak out once again. By August 1947 the Vatican indicated that they were satisfied that Mindszenty was "behaving well."[20]

THE VATICAN, THE POLISH HIERARCHY, AND THE LIBERATION OF POLAND

When the Communist-dominated Lublin Committee was expanded in July 1945 by the addition of five members of the Polish government-in-exile, Britain and the United States gave it formal recognition as the government of Poland and simultaneously withdrew their recognition from the London Poles. It fell to the new government to assist the Poles to recover from the years of German tyranny and to reorganize the country, since the borders and the populations of Poland had been radically changed as a result of the westward shift of Poland to the frontier on the Oder and Niesse rivers. Because of its left-leaning orientation, the government also intended to implement what it felt were much-needed social and economic reforms. The government was welcomed by the Poles as representative of the forces of liberation from Nazi tyranny although, at the same time, many Poles were unhappy about the preponderant influence of the Communist party in the provisional government.

Because of its lack of a popular following in Poland and also because some of the Communist leaders, such as Wladyslaw Gomulka, general secretary of the Polish Communist party, wanted to reduce their dependence on Soviet support, the Lublin Committee did not want to antagonize the church, which had the potential to become their most formidable opponent.[21] Within the new frontiers, the Catholic share of the Polish population had now increased from 65 to over 90 percent. The Poles of the Russian Orthodox tradition had been returned to the Soviet Union, Protestant Germans had been expelled to Germany, and the large prewar Jewish population had been practically eliminated by the Nazis during the war. Not only was there an increase in the proportion of Polish Catholics, but, unlike much of the political leadership of postwar Poland, most of the Catholic bishops and clergy had seen the war through in Poland with their people. "The patriotic stance and suffering of the vast bulk of the clergy during the German occupation and the transformation of Poland from a state populated not only by Roman Catholics, but also by Greek Catholics, Orthodox, Jewish and Protestant communities into a homogenous Catholic one, led in the later 1940s to a certain renaissance of the Church in Poland."[22]

Knowing the strength of the Catholic Church in Poland and their own weakness, the Communists hoped that by showing respect for the church they would obtain the acquiescence of the church hierarchy in their programs. Before the war had come to an end, the Catholic University of Lublin had been reopened, while services had been resumed at the famed Jasnagora Monastery in Czestochowa. Priests were especially happy to be allowed to use Polish again in their religious services and the authorities honoured Monsignor Adam Sapieha, the archbishop of Cracow, the most senior churchman to remain in Poland throughout the war, holding him up as "a model Pole who had shown outstanding qualities in resisting the German invaders." Moreover, church lands were deliberately exempted from the government's 1944 land reform program. Nor was there any interference with the teaching of Catholic principles in the schools.

Catholics were pleased and surprised at the good treatment that they received from the provisional government. In March 1945, the bishop of Poznan had declared in a radio broadcast that "with liberation, the enslavement of the Church has also ended. The fetters which bound the Church are broken." Judging from the number of priests and bishops who were willing to testify to the new government's respect for religious freedom, it was being successful in its attempt to conciliate the Catholics. Since the liberation, the churches had been "crowded to overflowing."[23]

The church in Poland had been without formal leadership during the war, a situation which continued into the summer of 1945. The last papal nuncio had been ejected by Hitler in 1939 and Cardinal Augustus Hlond, the primate, had left Poland in 1939 and spent most of the war in exile in France. In February 1944 Hlond had been arrested by the Gestapo and imprisoned, first in France and then in Germany, where he refused to issue a pro-German proclamation to the Polish people. As the war was coming to an end, the cardinal also refused to rally the Poles to stand with the Germans against the Russians in defence of western civilization. At the end of the war he had found his way to Rome. While Hlond had shown courage in resisting German demands, questions remained about his departure from Poland at the beginning of the war and about his failure to make contact with the London Poles or to offer assistance to the Polish resistance when he was living in France.[24]

De facto leadership of the church within Poland had been provided by Archbishop Sapieha of Cracow, its most respected figure after the war. He understood the common suffering of the Poles regardless of political affiliation, and was prepared to work with the new government so long as it respected the rights and privileges of the church. Catholic intellectuals had gravitated to his see of Cracow, where they expressed this view in the weekly newspaper *Tygodnik Powszechny*, which had received government permission to begin publication in April 1945.[25] Under these circumstances, Catholics, who along with the rest of the Poles, supported the Oder-Niesse frontier, felt that they could cooperate with the provisional government, being confident that they could mount a serious and sustained resistance should the government attempt to restrict their rights and privileges.

The first issue to arise in the postwar was the question of Vatican recognition of the government of Poland. While Polish Catholics accepted the situation within Poland as the best they could hope for in 1945, such was not the case with the Vatican. Pius XII liked nothing about the new Poland. He was unhappy about the Communist-led government, which had been put into office with the assistance of the Soviet Union. He also disliked the new Polish frontiers, which had been inflicted on Germany as a punishment. The western territories had been taken from Germany, the Germans living in those territories had been uprooted and expelled, and the land had been given to Poland in compensation for land in the east which had been seized by the Soviet Union. The new Poland stood as the symbol of the vindictive peace which the Soviets wanted to force on Germany.

The Holy See had not been a party to the Yalta agreements, nor did it agree with them. The result was that it followed its traditional policy of not recognizing postwar political changes until the conclusion of a peace treaty. While the great powers gave recognition to the new Polish government in July 1945, the Holy See continued to recognize the London Poles as the representatives of the prewar government. Casimir Papée, the ambassador of the Polish government-in-exile to the Holy See, continued to be accorded recognition by Vatican authorities. In addition, the Holy See was not prepared to recognize the Oder-Niesse Line as the western frontier of Poland. The transfer of German territory to Poland and the uprooting of the German population of that area led the *Osservatore Romano* to comment that the issue of religious freedom in eastern Europe was inadequately dealt with at Potsdam. The pope himself, in an August 1945 conversation with D'Arcy Osborne, was not prepared to credit British reports of religious freedom in Poland and claimed that "conditions in general and in particular the situation of the Catholic Church could hardly be worse."[26] The Polish church soon found itself in a difficult dilemma, having to choose between cooperation with the Polish provisional government and loyalty to the larger goals of the Holy See.

To re-establish communication between Rome and the Polish church, the pope sent Cardinal Hlond back to Poland in August 1945. During that month Hlond toured Poland, examining the condition of the church under the new regime. In doing so, he deliberately avoided contact with government representatives. His studious neutrality was not appreciated by the government, who resented the fact that the Vatican was unwilling to give them formal recognition in spite of the fact that they were treating the church well.[27]

By the beginning of September the government was exasperated by the attitude of the Vatican. Polish government officials indicated to the British ambassador that the favoured treatment of the Catholic Church in Poland could not last indefinitely without some formal recognition from the Vatican.[28] The Polish government had made overtures to the church and, while the clergy in Poland had responded, such had not been the case with either Cardinal Hlond or the Holy See. A more deliberate shock was needed and this was provided on 14 September by the Polish government's abrogation of the 1925 Polish concordat. The government claimed that the Vatican had violated the concordat when, in spite of a clause which held that no part of Poland could be governed by a bishop from outside Poland, the Holy See had turned over the administration of the Polish diocese of Chelm to the German bishop of Danzig during the war. The Vatican had also appointed a German administrator for the diocese of Gniezno. Since the Vatican had not recognized the Polish provisional government, the government would, in turn, not recognize the ecclesiastical appointments which had been made by the Vatican in August.[29]

The abrogation of the concordat, in fact, worked to the advantage of the Polish hierarchy. The absence of a concordat prevented decisions about the future of the Polish church being made between the Holy See and the Polish government with little reference to the church. It also gave church leaders considerable independence in their dealings with the government. In the same way, the non-recognition of the government by the Vatican prevented the return of a papal nuncio to Warsaw and allowed the hierarchy to deal directly with the Vatican rather than through a papal diplomatic representative.

The Vatican received little sympathy from the Polish bishops who believed that the Vatican had brought this abrogation on themselves. Archbishop Sapieha felt that the failure to recognize the Warsaw government and the failure of Hlond to make any contact had hurt the church, as had the decision by the Vatican to keep the bishop of Danzig in office until he was arrested by Polish authorities in August 1945. According to Sapieha, the bishop had acted "in a very German manner" and the Poles had been right to arrest him. Nevertheless, Sapieha did not believe that the abrogation of the concordat would make much practical difference. The state did not give much money to the church because it was adequately financed by its parishioners and it did not own that much property which needed to be protected.[30]

Monsignor Adamski, the bishop of Katowice, a popular bishop who had endured the German occupation with his flock and was on good terms with members of the government, felt that the anti-fascism of the government gave it wide popularity with the Polish people. Adamski believed that the abrogation of the concordat was fully justified, as the Vatican had indeed violated it during the war; moreover, he said that Catholic Poles supported the abrogation and he agreed with Sapieha that the consequences would not harm the church.[31]

In its defence, the Vatican claimed that the bishop of Danzig had been appointed to Chelm because there had been no other way to provide for the needs of that diocese and a German apostolic administrator had been named in Poland because the German authorities had insisted on separating Polish Catholics from German. Beyond this, the Vatican claimed that it had resisted all German pressure to name German prelates in Poland. Taking the offensive, the Vatican countered that the Polish government had also violated the concordat by not allowing the Vatican to communicate with its clergy in Poland.[32]

The tactic of the Polish government during the winter of 1945–6, as it sought to establish a popular and organizational base for its continuance in power, was to treat the Polish church and the Vatican differently, favouring the former while attacking the latter, and attempting to drive a wedge between them.[33] The trial of Monsignor Splett, the German bishop of Danzig and wartime administrator of Chelm, in late January 1946, provided the Polish government with a suitable opportunity to criticize the Vatican. Bishop Splett was accused of assisting the German persecution of the Poles by not allowing the Polish language to be used in his diocese during the war and by refusing to let Polish priests return after they had been released from concentration camps. His defence was that he was not a Nazi and that he had only been following the orders of the Gestapo, to which the prosecution responded that he could equally well have invoked the higher orders of the pope. The Polish press, which attacked the Vatican for its pro-German and anti-Polish attitude during the war, called Splett, who was sentenced to eight years' imprisonment, a "Gestapo collaborator imposed on a Polish diocese." The Italian ambassador believed that Polish Catholics approved of the trial of Bishop Splett and the anti-Vatican press campaign.[34]

By the spring of 1946 complete deadlock had been reached in relations between the Polish government and the Vatican, with neither side willing to take the initiative for the opening of negotiations.[35] This conflict had been bearable for the Polish church as long as the government was working to cultivate the support of the church. By the summer of 1946, however, when the church refused to demonstrate its gratitude by organizing political support for the government, the domestic relationship between the church and the government began to sour. Bishops and clergy then found themselves cast adrift with little sympathy from either the Polish government or the pope as they were forced to navigate the shoals of Polish politics on their own. At the same time, alleged church support of anti-semitism in Poland alienated what sympathy that church had in the west, especially in the United States. The Polish church appeared to be cut off from any possible support and, as during the war, it had to look once again to its own resources.

The Polish government delayed holding the free elections mandated by the Yalta agreements as long as possible, wanting to present one multi-party government slate for the elections and thereby to ensure continued Communist dominance of the government. The Peasant party of Stanislaw Mikolajczyk, however, and the Party of Labour, consisting of Catholics, young intellectuals and university and professional groups, had provided non-Communist members of the government coalition and were reluctant to be part of such a government electoral bloc. Mikolajczyk believed that his party had sufficient popular support to win the elections and to replace the Communists as the dominant political force in the country.[36]

Unable to secure their electoral bloc, the government decided to forestall the Yalta powers and hold a public consultation through a referendum on 30 June 1946. The referendum was to consist of three questions:

1) Are you for abolition of the Senate?
2) Are you for making permanent, through the future constitution, the economic system instituted by land reform and nationalization of basic industries, with maintenance of the rights of private initiative?
3) Are you for the Polish western frontiers as fixed on the Baltic and on the Oder and the Niesse?[37]

Ideally, the government hoped that all the government parties would stand behind the referendum campaign slogan, "Three times Yes." Mikolajczyk and the Peasant party, as well as the Party of Labour, decided instead to test their electoral strength by calling for a negative answer to question one on the abolition of the Senate. The land reforms and the Oder-Niesse frontier were known to be very popular in Poland, so there was to be no challenge on questions two and three. The government sought assistance from the church hierarchy in neutralizing the Party of Labour; so between March and May, the communist leadership held out the possibility of a new concordat or at least a modus vivendi between church and state if the church would encourage Catholics to support an electoral bloc of all parties for the referendum campaign.[38]

At the same time, the government was in the process of creating a new Catholic party to be a member of the governing coalition and draw off Catholic support from the opposition parties. Urban Catholics and young intellectuals could be enticed away from the Party of Labour, just as Catholic peasants could be drawn away from the Peasant party. To lead this new party, the government chose Boleslaw Piasecki, a Catholic with a checkered political history. Before the war, Piasecki had been the leader of Falanga, the Polish fascist movement, a reactionary, anti-Bolshevik, and anti-semitic organization. During the war he had fought in the anti-German resistance, was arrested by the Russians in 1944, and freed by Gomulka in the autumn of 1945. In 1946 he founded a new weekly newspaper, *Dzis i Jutro (Today and Tomorrow)*, to proclaim his political conversion to the new regime and to organize a political movement seeking support from Catholics.[39]

The Catholic Church was not prepared to give the government the electoral support it sought, since government success in the referendum would help to consolidate the control of the Communist party and its attendant police state over Poland.[40] Hlond believed that the only role of the church in the referendum campaign should be to ensure that the campaign was carried out peacefully, since unnecessary disturbances could become an excuse for intervention by Soviet troops. It was Hlond's belief that there would be no benefit to the church from negotiations with a government which, pending the outcome of the elections, could well only be temporary.[41]

Polish Catholics, therefore, were reminded that active support of a marxist government was not in their long-term interest. A communiqué from a meeting of the Polish hierarchy was read in all churches of Poland on Sunday, 10 June, expressing concern about the unrest and violence in the country, calling on the Polish secret police to stop their atrocities, and insisting that all religious requirements of the church must be met in Poland. The communiqué elicited an immediate protest from the government, who called it a "declaration of war," but Cardinal Hlond was still invited to a meeting with President Bierut. Before this meeting could be held, however, a letter which Pius XII had sent to the Polish bishops in January, "making veiled attacks on the Communist system," was read in Polish churches on 29 June, the day before the referendum. While Hlond claimed that the coincidence was fortuitous since the decision to read the letter had been made before the referendum had been announced, the government took offence at what they interpreted as a political gesture and cancelled the planned meeting between Hlond and Bierut.[42] According to observers, the voting in the referendum was orderly and no violations of electoral procedure were seen. However, the counting of the ballots had not taken place in the voting districts and the count had not been watched by disinterested parties. Consequently, the reported results of the voting indicated a strong "Yes" vote for all the questions, even though it was well known that a large number of Peasant party supporters had voted "No" on question one.[43]

On 1 July 1946, the day following the referendum, an ugly incident took place in Kielce, when twenty-six Jews were murdered by armed gangs that staged "the worst anti-Jewish pogrom since Poland was liberated."[44] The attacks in Kielce inaugurated a wave of anti-semitic violence throughout Poland in succeeding days, forcing Jews to barricade their communities throughout the country. In the countryside armed gangs boarded trains and forced Jews to disembark, took them away, stripped them, and shot them. The Kielce pogrom and its aftermath was indicative of the growing distrust between the church and the government.

Hostility between Poles and Jews had not stopped in Poland with the end of the war and the defeat of the Nazis. Much mutual suspicion remained in the country and resulted in a continuing series of attacks on Jews during 1945 and 1946. A number of Polish Jews in flight from Nazi persecution had spent the war years in the Soviet Union. In 1946 Stalin gave them until the end of June to choose between becoming Soviet citizens or returning to their countries of origin. Many returned to Poland and their return served to augment the anti-semitic fever in the country. Attacks, carried out in some places by anti-semitic gangs and rural police officials, were successful in inducing many of the remaining Jews to leave Poland.[45]

The anti-semitic outbreaks appeared to have been spontaneous, although the government attributed them to the right-wing underground, to the Peasant party, and to the church. Government officials reported that only one member of the clergy in Kielce actually tried to do anything to stop the pogrom and the government press laid the blame on the church for its extent.[46]

At the same time, there was an aspect of the anti-semitism which represented a popular reaction against the government. According to a pro-memoria prepared by the American embassy in Warsaw in October 1946, many of the senior officials of the Polish government and civil service were Jewish, as was the Soviet ambassador to Poland and as were "ninety percent of the employees of the central office" of the Polish secret police.[47] Anti-semitism served as an expression of anti-communism and, no doubt, had been an aspect of the anti-government stance in the referendum campaign.

In January 1946 Cardinal Hlond had condemned anti-semitism to a representative of the Jewish Religious Alliance "as a Catholic and as a Pole." Yet at the May meeting of bishops at Czestochowa, a petition from a Jewish organization calling on the bishops to issue a statement in opposition to anti-semitism had been denied by the bishops on the ground that there had been insufficient cause for issuing such a proclamation.[48]

The Kielce pogrom and its aftermath did not show the Polish church in a good light to its foreign friends. Newspaper reports of the pogrom created a major sensation in the United States, leading Bliss Lane, the American ambassador, to insist that Cardinal Hlond hold a press conference to explain the position of the church. In the conference on 11 July, Hlond did not handle himself well, condemning the recent murders, but attributing them not to racial causes but to a rumour concerning the Jewish killing of children. The cardinal was satisfied that the Catholic clergy of Kielce had done their duty but he made the unfortunate assertion that, while Jews and Catholics had cooperated during the German occupation, these good relations had deteriorated in recent months because "the Jews occupying leading positions in Poland in state life ... are to a great extent responsible for [the] deterioration of these good relations." The Italian ambassador found Hlond to be cold and almost cynical over the event and did not feel that he deplored the pogrom with the vigour that one might have expected for such an ugly occurrence. Sapieha echoed Hlond and was reported to have said that the Jews brought it on themselves, a position also taken by the rural clergy.[49]

Making the disinterest of the church in the fate of the Jews appear to be even worse, Moscow Radio reported on 21 July that the pope had interceded with the Polish government on behalf of Arthur Grieser, the notorious Nazi gauleiter of the Warthegau in western Poland, who had been sentenced to death by Polish authorities on 8 July. The Vatican replied that the pope had interceded as would any Christian who prayed for his persecutors. Karol Modzelewski, the Polish vice-minister of foreign affairs, retorted that it was striking that the pope would not intervene with Franco on behalf of Spanish Republicans or with Hitler about the atrocities inflicted on the Poles, but he was quite willing to defend Grieser, an accomplice of the murderers. Modzelewski argued that the reaction of Hlond and others to the Kielce pogrom encouraged anti-semitism.[50]

When the bishops met again at Czestochowa in September 1946, with the experience of the Kielce pogrom behind them, they were less interested in issuing a statement against anti-semitism than they were in mounting a campaign against alcoholism. In disgust, the British ambassador, Victor Cavendish-Bentinck, commented: "Trying to persuade Polish Bishops not to be violently anti-Semitic is similar to the task of making a silk purse out of a sow's ear!"[51] The Polish church was very much alone.

11 Catholics and European Reconstruction

In spite of the difficulties of the church in most of eastern Europe and the Balkans, there were other countries where, in the early postwar years, Catholics were an inherent part of the reconstruction process. In Czechoslovakia, in France, and in Italy, Catholics had a significant role to play in rebuilding society and restoring the political culture. In these countries, rather than being part of the problem, they were part of the solution to the times of dislocation.

BENEŠ AND THE REINTEGRATION OF CZECHOSLOVAKIA

President Edouard Beneš, leader of the Czechoslovakian government-in-exile, recognized that the restoration of Czechoslovakia at the end of the war would require the support of all the Allies. For this reason, he concluded a treaty with the Soviet Union in 1943 which led Stalin to instruct the Czech and Slovak Communist parties to cooperate with Beneš. In March 1945 anti-fascist Czechs and Slovaks met in Moscow to organize a coalition government for postwar Czechoslovakia, with Beneš as president, and to formulate a reform program.[1]

After liberation, Slovak autonomy was recognized through the creation of a Slovak National Council, from which Catholics were excluded because of their association with the collaborationist Tiso regime. The council was controlled by the Slovak Communists and the Lutheran community. Hatreds were running high in Slovakia and the council, after arresting collaborating priests and bishops, prevented the reopening of Catholic parochial schools and forbade the operation of Catholic youth organizations or the Catholic press.[2] At war's end it appeared as if the Catholic Church of Slovakia, compromised and discredited, would have to suffer for its sins.

In seeking to rebuild his nation, Beneš realized that reconciliation between Czechs and Slovaks was essential to his goal. Such reconciliation required that Slovak autonomy be recognized, that a veil be drawn over the past activities of the Slovak nationalists, and that ways be found to reintegrate Czechs and Slovaks into one nation. Beneš sought to bring about this reconciliation through the mediation of the Catholic Church. He hoped that the church would re-emphasize the common bonds in such a way that the hatreds of the war years could be forgotten. Moreover, favourable treatment of the church by the national government would be a gesture of reconciliation to Slovak Catholics. Beneš also recognized that, with Czechoslovakia in the Soviet sphere of influence, he would need to build up the anti-communist forces of the country to resist any move by Stalin for the imposition of communism. The Catholic Church, with its long tradition of antipathy to communism, could serve as an effective counterweight to the Communist party. While the Communist party did not believe in Slovak autonomy and favoured instead a strongly centralized government in Prague, it was prepared to make tactical concessions to the Catholic Church, recognizing both its strength in the country and the importance that President Beneš accorded to it.

To work closely with the church, Beneš needed the support and assistance of the Vatican. Accordingly, on 18 July 1945 he asked the Holy See to return Monsignor Xavier Ritter to his post as papal nuncio. Ritter had served as nuncio to Czechoslovakia before 1939 and as nuncio to Slovakia until he was withdrawn at the insistence of the Germans in 1940. The Soviet Union, however, was not in such a rush to see relations restored with the Vatican and forced Beneš to amend his original request. Instead of a nuncio, Beneš asked if a chargé d'affaires could be sent temporarily, indicating that Czechoslovakia would not be sending a diplomat to the Vatican for some time.

The Vatican willingly complied and Monsignor Raphael Forni, a Swiss national, went to Prague as chargé d'affaires on 6 August. Czechoslovakia was the one nation of eastern Europe where the Holy See was prepared to cooperate in an attempt to restore a workable relationship between church and state. The presence of such a major statesman as Edouard Beneš in the presidency gave confidence to the Vatican that the church would receive fair treatment in spite of the presence of the Red Army and local communists.

Forni's first tasks were organizational. He had to deal with nominations to vacant sees and to leadership of religious orders, to devise new diocesan boundaries, and to assist in the "nationalization" of the church after the government had expelled German and Hungarian clergy from the country. Order had to be restored to a generally chaotic situation before questions of the future relationship between Czechoslovakia and the Holy See could be considered.

Forni found that the support of the Czech Catholic clergy for the resistance and the willingness of the Vatican to leave sees unfilled and ecclesiastical boundaries unchanged in Czechoslovak territory during the Nazi occupation gave the church a standing with the Czechoslavak government which overshadowed the wartime collaboration of the church in Slovakia. Ecclesiastical property which had been seized at the time of the liberation was returned to the church because the government recognized that canon law assigned the property of religious orders to the Vatican. The reconstruction began well, and in November 1945 Beneš addressed a meeting of clergy, praised the patriotism of the Czech clergy, and emphasized the importance of religious liberty in the state. By the end of the year, Foreign Minister Jan Masaryk indicated that the government intended to send a chargé d'affaires to the Vatican in the near future.[3]

THE CHURCH AND FRENCH POLITICS

During the first year after the war, the church in France overcame its affiliation with the Vichy regime and played an important role in the development of the Fourth Republic. This came about for two reasons: the sensitivity of the Vatican and the papal nuncio, Angelo Roncalli, to concerns about the role of the church during the war; and the affiliation of the church with the emergence of the Mouvement Républicaine Populaire (MRP), the new left-leaning Christian democratic party of France.

The matter of removing compromised bishops had been taken up by the French ambassador, Jacques Maritain, in negotiation with Tardini in the Secretariat of State. Initially the provisional government, under pressure from Resistance leaders in various parts of France, had requested the removal of thirty bishops accused of collaboration. By the summer of 1945, however, the government had reduced its request to ten and the Vatican had promised to ask at least seven of them to resign voluntarily. Negotiations continued into the fall and, by November, the government had reduced their demand to the removal of five bishops, whose resignations were secured by the Vatican. Accordingly, on 29 November 1945 the resignations were accepted of three bishops from the French empire – Dakar, Rabat, and St Pierre and Miquelon – and two bishops of metropolitan France, those of Arras and Mende.[4]

The government were also interested in the future appointment of bishops, wanting those clergy who had supported the Resistance to be promoted. While the Vatican was reluctant to discriminate against the rest of the French clergy in this way, the government nevertheless persisted in indicating acceptable and unacceptable clergy to the papal nuncio, feeling that it had to make its views clear to avoid scandalous appointments being made by Rome.[5] Potential curial appointments also posed difficulties for the government. The suggestion in 1947 that, in a reform of the Curia, Monsignor Gillet, the archbishop of Nicée, might become the prefect of a new Congregation of Seminaries and Universities and provide France with a second curial position of some influence was troublesome for the government because of Gillet's earlier support of the Vichy regime. On the other hand, the French were reluctant to lose the position by presuming to suggest a more suitable candidate to the pope and decided that the safest route was neither to support nor to oppose Gillet's nomination.[6]

It was expected that the pope would appoint a large number of new cardinals at the first postwar consistory and the French government sought to give the Vatican some guidance about those clergy who would make acceptable cardinals and those who would not. On 24 November 1945 Maritain was instructed to tell the Vatican that France expected more than one new cardinal and that parity with the United States in the number of new appointments would be agreeable. Those bishops who had supported the Resistance should also be looked on more favourably than those who had supported Vichy. In specific terms, the government would not accept red hats going to Bishops Feltin of Bordeaux or Marmottin of Reims or to Monsignor Piguet, while they insisted on the elevation of Bishop Saliège of Toulouse to the Sacred College. Saliège had been the leading bishop to support the Resistance and was viewed as a symbol of the Christian Resistance. Roncalli had argued that Saliège was not well enough to travel to Rome, but the government claimed his exclusion would be viewed "in the worst manner" and that no other person should be honoured before Saliège.[7]

Maritain was somewhat taken aback by these blatant demands of his government. While relaying them to Montini, he commented in his report that this was as far as one could legitimately go since, had Pius XI been on the throne, he would have automatically rejected all such demands to preserve the principle of papal independence. He cautioned that Roncalli, when being told of the French government's position in the matter, should not be given evidence of the government's insistence lest such information make the pope stubborn in making his appointments. On 23 December 1945 thirty-two new cardinals were announced by the Vatican along with the date of 18 February 1946 for the consistory. The French démarche had been successful, as the three new French cardinals were Saliège who, because of his health, would be given his red hat in Toulouse rather than Rome, Petit de Julleville of Rouen, and Rogues of Rennes, all of whom had been requested by the French government.[8]

Other ecclesiastical matters were sorted out to the satisfaction of the French government in the winter of 1945–6. Although it was felt in some Catholic circles that the purge of the hierarchy had not gone far enough, it was noted that Cardinal Suhard of Paris was given an auxiliary bishop to deflect some of the attacks on him for his pro-Vichy attitude. Roncalli was delighted when the chaplaincy service was restored in the French military and a chaplain-general was appointed. The relationship between France and the Holy See was improving steadily.

During the interwar years, French Catholics had left their traditional right-wing politics and had shown a willingness to support more diverse political perspectives, including the Christian democracy represented by the Parti Démocrate Populaire from 1924, which was inspired by social Catholic teachings. While never a strong presence in French politics during the period, nevertheless, Christian democracy was influential through the Catholic press of the 1930s and the vitality of social Catholicism as practised by various groups in Catholic Action. During the war Christian democrats often supported the Resistance, drawing strength from the Christian trade unions and from other specialized groups in Catholic Action. These elements came together in November 1944 to establish the Mouvement Républicaine Populaire (MRP) as a new political party committed to the spirit of the Resistance and to the French traditions of social Catholicism. Georges Bidault, the leader of the party, worked closely with de Gaulle as foreign minister in the new government and the party worked diligently to establish its importance as a body sufficiently anti-communist to be worthy of clerical support. In October 1945 the first postwar elections were held for a constituent assembly. The Communist party won 26.1 percent of the seats in the Assembly but the MRP, having secured the full support of the church, ran second with 25.6 percent. Part of the concern of the government, and especially of Bidault and the MRP, about the replacement of collaborationist bishops and the appointment of the right French cardinals had to do with a need to demonstrate that the Vatican was sympathetic to the ideals of the Resistance and was prepared to recognize the dignity and importance of liberated France.

The tripartite Resistance coalition led by de Gaulle had placed the Catholic MRP in the same camp and government as the Socialist and Communist parties. The Vatican followed French politics with interest and concern, being especially wary of any support the French government might provide to the Soviet Union or the communist cause. In the summer of 1945 the Vatican was upset by the decision of the government to discontinue Vichy's subsidy to the church schools and was reported to dislike de Gaulle's policy of playing Russian interests off against those of the British and Americans.[9] The Vatican believed that France should be more concerned about the problems of Italy and should help the Italians to avoid a punitive peace treaty, but in the summer of 1945 de Gaulle was too close to Moscow to be able to be of any help to Italy in this matter.[10]

Like the clergy and the hierarchy, some elements of the Catholic press had been compromised by the occupation. The Catholic newspaper *La Croix* had traditionally been the official voice of the church in France. It had continued publication during the war and supported the Pétain regime. Yet the position of the editor, Father Merklen, and the publisher, Alfred Michelin, was decidedly ambivalent, since they were both Christian democratic in outlook and very much opposed to the right-wing Catholics around Charles Maurras and the *Action Française*.[11] *La Croix* resumed publication in February 1945; during the spring and summer it urged its readers to exercise care in dealing with the communists who, while having made a worthy contribution to the Resistance, were nonetheless atheists and a threat to religion[12]. By the winter of 1945–6 *La Croix*, especially editorial writer Jean Caret, was concerned about the growing division between East and West and was calling on the French to show a sympathetic comprehension of the real international fears of the Soviet Union which were leading it to be particularly difficult and impeding mutual trust and understanding.[13].

On 20 January 1946 Charles de Gaulle resigned as president of the council because the political parties were unsympathetic to his belief in the necessity of a strong executive for the Fourth Republic. By 1946 the church had been effectively rehabilitated in France, particularly through its connection with the MRP, and it demonstrated its integration into the community by playing an active part in the politics of constitution-making. In April the draft constitution of the Fourth Republic was presented to the electorate and a referendum was scheduled for 5 May. The church joined the MRP in opposing the new constitution, believing that the proposed unicameral legislature would benefit the parties of the left who would be able to secure large majorities there. Cardinals Suhard and Liénart issued statements against the constitution in Paris and Lille and parish priests throughout France warned their congregations against an affirmative vote. During the campaign the pope alluded to the referendum when he spoke to a party of French journalists, saying that France was spiritually strong but must beware the "forces of destruction, the enemies of all true grandeur, of all beauty, of all enlightenment" that were trying to seduce and destroy it. The outcome of the referendum on 5 May was the rejection of the draft constitution which "must to a large extent be attributed to the influence of the Church."[14]

Duff Cooper, the British ambassador in Paris, was troubled by this political resurgence of the church. While he felt that it was appropriate for the church to cooperate with the MRP, "a truly democratic and progressive party," he feared that the church, once it had re-emerged as a political force, would not stop there, but would shift its influence to the political right. There were a few indications in the subsequent campaign for the election of a new constituent assembly on 2 June, that the church, out of its fear of communism, was transferring its sympathy from the MRP, which was prepared to cooperate with the Communist party, to the more right-wing parties. If this should happen, noted Duff Cooper, "the Church may commit a fatal error and relapse into the unhelpful intransigence of the past."[15]

The election returned a constituent assembly in which the MRP was the largest party, having won 28.2 percent of the seats while the Communist party had held its own with 26.4 percent. Electoral losses were suffered by the Socialists and by the smaller parties. It has been claimed by historian Jean-Pierre Rioux that this election marked "a watershed in the political history of the post-war period, one whose significance exceeded that of the constitutional issue which had provoked it" because, for the first time since the war, the "Socialist-Communist Left no longer had the majority in France."[16]

The Vatican watched the elections of June 1946 in both France and in Italy with great interest, since in both countries Christian democratic parties challenged the Socialist and Communist parties at the polls. The MRP victory was duly noted by the *Osservatore Romano* on June 7 when it commented on the French elections that "the people gave an unmistakable indication of their determination to stand by their traditional moral principles; those Christian values which are the indispensable guarantee of a democratic community."

By 1946 the church in France appeared to have returned to a position where it could influence the country's future direction.

THE CHURCH AND THE ITALIAN ELECTION

While the papacy was an interested observer of the 1946 French election, it was an active participant, as was the Italian church, in the Italian elections. Italian political activity had revived in March 1946 with the setting of the date of 2 June for national elections to choose the members of a constituent assembly and to pronounce on the future of the monarchy. On 17 March, the first Sunday of Lent, the pope addressed the priests of the diocese of Rome and insisted that the clergy had an "essential duty" to instruct their congregations on the principles to be followed in casting their votes. Jacques Maritain commented that the speech demonstrated that Pius XII was unable to detach himself from the national politics of Italy to which the temporal interests of the Vatican were so closely tied.[17]

Both the Communists and the Christian Democrats assumed moderate and respectful positions in the election campaign. If Christian Democrats were moderate, however, the Vatican was less so. In his public speeches during the campaign, the pope warned his listeners of the attacks traditionally mounted on the Christian church by the enemies of Christian culture. When speaking to the leaders of Italian Catholic Action on Easter Saturday, the pope said that it was "essential that Catholic Action, together with all other religious organizations of the lay apostolate, should exert themselves to the fullest extent and should make use of their utmost efforts and energies ... to defend and clearly to proclaim before men the doctrine of the Church, and to recall the indifferent to the practice of religion."[18]

De Gasperi picked up on this theme when he discussed the role of the church in Italy at the Christian Democratic congress in Rome on 20 April and concluded that "the Italian people should send to the Constituent Assembly, which would establish the fundamental principles for future centuries, men who were convinced and practising Christians." In May the pope spoke again on "the duty of the Catholic Italian elector to give his vote to Party lists of candidates, 'who offer, not ambiguous promises, but reliable guarantees that they will respect the rights of God and Religion.'" Finally, on the eve of the election the pope made a "passionate appeal to the world, and especially to the populations of Italy and France, ... to defend Christian civilisation against 'subversive and atheistic elements.'" He reminded his hearers that, on the following day, "the citizens of two great Latin nations would go to the polling booths to decide whether they would continue to rest on the firm rock of Christianity ... or whether, instead, they would entrust their lot for the future to the unfeeling omnipotence of a materialistic State. The victors at the polls would come to be either the champions or the wreckers of Christian civilisation."[19]

On the other hand, the church kept its own counsel on the institutional question. The pope was sympathetic to the monarchy, as were many of the bishops, but realized that many of the lower clergy were not and that the wisest course would be to say nothing on this question and to live with whatever was decided.

While working directly on the religious principles of the Italian electorate, the pope also feared that external factors, such as the food shortage, and the 25 April meeting of the Council of Foreign Ministers to consider the Italian peace treaty, might influence the vote. With the concurrence of the British and American governments, Pius XII broadcast an appeal on 4 April for self-sacrifice on the part of those nations with adequate food supplies and assured the Italian ambassador to Washington immediately afterwards that "it was his intention to do all in his power to help in the solution of the Italian food problem." The pope was assisted in this campaign by the leaders of the American church.[20]

On 2 June, the Italian voters brought the era of the Resistance coalition to an end when they reduced the ruling parties of Italy from five to three: the Christian Democrats, the Socialists and the Communists, with the most seats in the assembly going to de Gasperi's Christian Democrats. After the election de Gasperi fashioned a new tripartite government with support from the Socialists and the Communists. The pope and Vatican officials were delighted with the election outcome. With the Christian Democrats being the largest party in the assembly, the Vatican could resign itself to the necessary political compromises that would have to be made in the new government of 1946. Osborne found the pope in June 1946 to be "much more confident and self-assured than during the war years."[21]

12 The Catholic Church and the Occupation of Germany

As one of the few German institutions to survive the war intact, the Roman Catholic Church took upon itself the task of representing the German people in their dealings with the postwar occupation authorities. As they acted on behalf of the new Germany, the German bishops spoke with the authority and support of the papacy and were frequently critical of the occupying powers.

THE ISSUE OF WAR GUILT

The German hierarchy was unsympathetic to the Allied four-power occupation of Germany. They echoed the pope in rejecting the concept of the collective guilt and responsibility of the German people for the crimes of the Nazi regime to which the occupying powers subscribed. In his pastoral letter of 8 May 1945 Archbishop Konrad Gröber of Freiburg condemned the evil of the Nazi regime but, at the same time, circumscribed the guilty by pointing out that many, even within the Nazi movement, were exempt from blame for the crimes conceived and carried out by "certain conscienceless circles." It was difficult to resist the Nazis because "every resistance broke on the merciless use of power unhampered by conscience."[1] Gröber did, however, ask in his pastoral of 31 May 1945 whether Catholics should not make "vicarious atonement" for Nazi crimes: "There were men of alien races who without any guilt ... were ... murdered in their thousands ... Is it not our vicarious duty to atone for these crimes against foreign blood?"

The Bavarian bishops ignored the issue of "vicarious atonement," but followed Gröber's other themes in their pastoral of 28 June when they claimed that "the German people ... were unaware of the inhuman atrocities perpetrated in the concentration camps." The bishops thanked the pope who "found a good and just word for the German people and ... refused ... to make the entire people responsible for the crimes of the guilty."

The bishops held their first postwar conference in August and issued a pastoral letter in which they acknowledged "terrible things perpetrated ... before the war in Germany and during the war by Germans in the occupied territories." They added that "many abetted crimes by their attitude, many became criminals themselves. A grave responsibility rests upon those who because of their position could have known what was going on in our midst; who because of their influence even made them possible, thereby manifesting their solidarity with the criminals." Although the bishops accepted that individual Germans had committed many errors, they still rejected any collective responsibility for these errors.[2]

When the council of the Evangelical Church at their Stuttgart meeting in October 1945 accepted collective responsibility for German sins of omission, Archbishop Gröber responding for the Catholics, attempted to demonstrate that "all the pernicious theories of National Socialism (denial of the existence of God and of the immortality of the soul, Darwinism, anti-semitism, racialism, sexual immorality) were imported from outside Germany and were alien to the German character."[3]

Cardinal Michael Faulhaber of Munich continued this theme in a pastoral on 17 March 1946, somehow forgetting the support of the church for the German war effort: "The Holy Father has never talked of the 'collective guilt' of the Germans. A nation is a passive community in distress: that means that the distress consequent upon a lost war must be borne by the whole nation. Our nation, however, was not an active community in the fight; that means that the crimes which brought the present stress upon our people were committed by individuals and not by the whole people."

The closest to an admission of collective responsibility by the Catholic bishops came in the pastoral of Dr Johannes Sproll, the bishop of Rothenburg, on 16 February 1947. A noted anti-Nazi, Sproll had been ejected from his diocese by the Nazis in 1938 and had only been restored in 1945. Sproll remembered the church support for the war, when he said:

I know well that everyone wishes to be innocent (of the concentration camps). ... Everyone wishes to push the guilt upwards, to attribute it to the Führer alone, and believes that he is thus exonerated. If National Socialism had conquered, and if its adherents had returned home in triumph, would it not have turned out that the great mass of its adherents would have met it with jubilation and that each would have proclaimed his particular share in the victory? My Christians! By so much as you committed yourself to victory, by so much at least you must feel yourself guilty of everything evil which this time has brought forth.[4]

THE BISHOPS AND THE OCCUPATION

The reputation of the Catholic Church within Germany was high at the end of the war, since the church had demonstrated a degree of independence of the National Socialist regime. Believing that they were among the original anti-Nazis, the bishops felt that they should have a major say in the reconstruction of Germany, while the occupying powers had no intention of giving them this power. The bishops felt that it was their responsibility to speak on behalf of the German people who had been deprived of any government or spokesperson, while the occupying powers did not feel that any Germans had a right to express themselves after the horrors of the war. The bishops believed that all Catholic clergy and laity had been seriously opposed to National Socialism while the occupying powers expected that the bishops would participate actively in carrying out a denazification program among their clergy and laity.[5] The bishops were thus set on a collision course with the occupation authorities from the beginning.

Cardinal Faulhaber was the senior member of the German hierarchy. In February 1946 the pope raised three other German bishops to membership in the Sacred College: Archbishop Joseph Frings of Cologne, Archbishop Konrad von Preysing of Berlin, and Bishop Clemens von Galen of Münster. Von Galen, who died shortly after receiving his red hat, was elevated in recognition of his opposition to the Nazi regime. Because of his age, Faulhaber surrendered the acting primacy of Germany to Cardinal Frings in 1946, with the result that it was Frings who thereafter chaired the annual meetings of the bishops at Fulda.

In addition to the issue of German collective responsibility, on which the bishops spoke extensively, they were also exercised about the loss of the eastern territories to Poland. Von Galen, who had criticized the policies of the Nazis, was equally prepared to speak against the victorious allies: "We must protest to the World against the evacuation of Germans from the Eastern territories, especially Polish-occupied territories ... For centuries they have been German. The manner in which these wretched folk are forced to abandon their homes and all their possessions, often with less than an hour's notice, is ghastly ... I know similar crimes have been committed by Germans all over Europe, but I was not silent then."[6]

Another issue which upset the bishops was their feeling that the occupation authorities were not treating them with the respect to which they were entitled. For the consistory of February 1946 the Americans flew Faulhaber from Munich to Rome, but the British authorities only offered to drive Frings and von Galen to Rome in regular military transport. The trip was not well organized and there were a number of accidents en route which meant that the cardinals were very uncomfortable. Once they reached Rome, Frings and von Galen protested loudly about their treatment, with the result that Cardinal Spellman flew them back to Germany after the consistory in his private plane. The British authorities were upset by the unpleasantness of the incident, but not all British officials believed that the cardinals warranted better treatment. "I do not see," minuted Burrows of the Foreign Office, "why we should compete with the Americans in sucking up to enemy cardinals." Nevertheless, the indignation continued in German Catholic circles toward the British authorities for their treatment of "high church dignitaries who certainly were no Nazis."[7]

Finally, the bishops refused to cooperate with the denazification process. When the British authorities ordered all churches in the British zone to set up denazification panels to review the role of the clergy in their relationship with the Nazi regime, the Evangelical Church complied but the Roman Catholics refused to do so for some time.[8]

At Easter 1946 the German hierarchy decided that it was time to make their position clear for the benefit of both the Catholic faithful and the occupation authorities. In a pastoral letter, the bishops issued a devastating critique of the Allied occupation. The National Socialist regime, argued the bishops, had "contributed the most to the moral collapse of the people in that it systematically trampled down the sense of right." While they expected to see severe punishment meted out to those responsible for the crimes of the Nazis at the end of the war, the bishops also hoped "that the new authorities in power would do everything to found anew the consciousness of right in the German people." This had not happened, however, and the bishops admitted that they had been "deeply deceived by the continued existence of a great uncertainty of right, which gives fresh wounds to the consciousness of right."

Specifically, they criticized the forced expulsion of whole German populations from Silesia and the Sudetenland, "without any examination being held as to whether they are personally guilty or not." Almost a year after the end of the war, millions of German prisoners of war were still in detention, when "the only thing that one can reproach them with is that they were soldiers." The denazification program and its disregard for considerations of law and justice was another example of the way in which the occupying authorities disregarded the German people's consciousness of right. The concept of collective guilt was a further manifestation of the poor example being set by the victorious powers, as was the uncompensated expropriation of landed property in the Soviet zone. The bishops concluded their pastoral with the exhortation: "May conquerors and conquered remember this! May each one in his sphere guard himself against every violation of right and contribute his share thereto that above all the young generation may be freed from the ruinous error that might goes before right. May it gain new respect for the majesty of right founded by God, even if it is on the side of the weaker. Only when this respect once again comes to its own, can better and truly peaceful times arrive."[9] The pastoral clarified the role of the bishops as the leaders of German resistance to the occupying powers.

VATICAN POLICY IN OCCUPIED GERMANY

Pius XII obtained his information about conditions in occupied Germany from the German bishops with whom the Holy See had re-established communication by the fall of 1945. The pope also received advice on German policy from the German prelates in the Vatican, in particular from Ludwig Kaas. It was the pope's plan to define general policy guidelines for Germany and to leave their implementation in the hands of the German bishops in whom he had the greatest confidence. Maritain sensed that Vatican officials were not unanimous in their support of Germany, however. While the germanophile pope and Monsignor Kaas were opposed to any kind of punishment being inflicted on Germany, Monsignor Montini and other officials in the Secretariat of State wanted to keep all options open until the German situation was better clarified.

Vatican policy towards postwar Germany was designed to re-Christianize the German people by ensuring that the institutional structure of the Catholic Church remained strong and the church was able to operate freely. The Vatican wanted to involve the laity through a renewed Catholic Action to provide a defensive barrier against communism. Unlike Pius XI who had favoured developing Catholic Action as a mass organization, Pius XII intended to use the organization on a more limited basis to develop a lay Catholic elite in Germany. Politically, the Vatican wanted the restoration of a united Germany rather than a divided one because it was the view of the pope that a series of small states would put German Catholics in a dangerous minority position in some of them, especially in eastern Germany. His constitutional preference was for a federal union with a strong central government but with many powers decentralized to the Länder (or states).

In mid-November 1945 the pope sent a letter to the German bishops in which he outlined specific guidelines for church policy in Germany. He indicated that the Vatican would ideally like to see an educational system based on confessional schools but, if this were not feasible, it would settle for a system with state schools where confessional schools were permitted and supported financially by the state. The Vatican was prepared to support a Christian trade union which would be assisted by the religious associations. Parish- or diocesan-based youth organizations were preferred to those organized nationally. The Vatican was opposed to a revival of the Catholic Centre party or any other specifically Catholic political party; instead, it was prepared to see Catholics vote for the party of their choice so long as that party respected religion and the church. Catholics were to be encouraged to cooperate politically with Protestants over questions of education, religious rights, and divorce.[10]

Policy recommendations on religious affairs in Germany were issued by the Coordinating Committee of the Allied Control Authority on 15 April 1946, and demonstrated that the occupation authorities were prepared to cooperate with the churches. The document recommended that the churches should be free to develop their own internal constitutions, that freedom of religious belief should be permitted and protected, that church property should be protected and that seized property should be returned as soon as practicable, that facilities should be made available for printing religious newspapers and other publications, that the collection of voluntary church taxes should be permitted, that religious organizations should be encouraged to carry out works of charity, and that religious organizations should be allowed to work with the youth of Germany.[11]

The most important issue between the Holy See and the occupying powers was whether the 1933 concordat should remain in effect. Before the occupation began, the Allies had agreed that "the Concordat ... will be regarded as continuing in force. Allied C.-in-Cs will, however, ... be entitled to ensure that the application of the terms of the Concordat does not conflict with the terms of any proclamation, order, ordinance or instruction issued under their authority." In meetings of the Religious Affairs Committee of the Allied Control Authority, however, the Soviet delegate was reluctant to accept the permanent continuation of the concordat. The Russians claimed that it had been an instrument to subject the Catholic Church to Nazi policy and was, therefore, an expression of Nazi ideology. The committee had not resolved this issue by the end of 1947.[12]

DIPLOMATIC REPRESENTATION

The question of Vatican diplomatic representation in Germany created problems between the Holy See and the occupation authorities. At the end of the war Monsignor Orsenigo, the long-serving nuncio to

Germany, was still in the country, and the Vatican decided to keep him there in his official capacity, in spite of the fact that there was no longer any German government to which he could be accredited. At least, the Vatican reasoned, he could maintain contact with the German hierarchy, serve "as a 'clearing house' for postal and telegraphic communications between the Bishops and the Vatican and *vice versa*," and even, possibly, maintain contact with the occupation authorities.

Concerned about the problem of food supplies in Germany and Austria, the Vatican organized a Pontifical Aid Mission to those countries in the fall of 1945 under the direction of Father Zeiger, a German Jesuit. It was hoped that Father Zeiger might also serve in a quasi-diplomatic role.

In discussions at the consistory of February 1946, the German cardinals confirmed that Monsignor Orsenigo was too old and infirm to continue his work as nuncio, so the Vatican announced its intention to replace him with an apostolic delegate. The candidate for the new post was Monsignor Aloysius Muench, a German-American who had considerable European experience. It was calculated by the Holy See that an American bishop would have more influence with the occupying powers than would a European. Since an apostolic delegate was only accredited to the church in a given country, formal governmental approval was not required. The Vatican did, however, approach the British, American, and French governments with the request that Monsignor Muench be allowed to travel freely through their zones and to establish contact with the Catholic bishops there. The western powers were also asked to support a similar Vatican request to the Soviet Union.[13]

The Allies were sympathetic to the Vatican request and the Americans were even prepared to suggest that Muench be allowed to circulate in the western zones if the Soviets created difficulties in the east. The matter became urgent when Orsenigo died in April 1946 leaving no official Vatican representative in Germany. When the German bishops criticized the occupation authorities in their Easter pastoral of 1946, Montini suggested to representatives of the occupying powers that the Vatican could better control the utterances of the German hierarchy if its apostolic delegate were approved as soon as possible. Montini realized that the German bishops always spoke with the approval of the pope, but believed that an agent of the Secretariat of State could prevent their statements giving the offence that they did.[14]

The Soviet Union opposed an apostolic delegate for Germany, though it did not make its formal rejection known until the end of September 1946. By this time the Vatican had given up on the idea of an apostolic delegate in favour of naming Muench apostolic visitor to

Germany, a designation which only signified that he was an observer on behalf of the pope. Muench had been sent to Germany in this capacity in June 1946, well before any final decision on the apostolic delegate had been made known. In addition to his assignment as apostolic visitor, he was made responsible for Father Zeiger and the Pontifical Relief Mission. From the beginning of 1947 he also became the administrator of the Vatican mission for refugees, expellees, and displaced persons in Germany.[15] While the western occupying powers accepted Muench's designation as apostolic visitor, the Soviets did not and prevented him from entering the Soviet zone.[16]

The Americans placed much faith in Muench and gave him specifically American tasks to perform in addition to his Vatican assignments. He was commissioned by the American government to report on German educational problems and the us War Department asked him to serve as liaison between the us military government in Germany and the Catholic bishops. He also acted as Catholic chaplain-general to us troops in Germany.[17]

While the Americans thought highly of the apostolic visitor, the other occupation powers were not so impressed. In November 1946 he visited the French zone and made an ill-advised speech critical of French occupation policies. Muench called for the liberation of all German prisoners of war and blessed all the German people, thus acknowledging the idea of one Germany which the French themselves had not accepted. Even more galling, the apostolic visitor offered no recognition of the way in which French occupation policies had favoured the interests of the Catholic Church. The French were unsure whether Muench was another badly informed American who was being led astray by the Germans or whether he sincerely believed in righting the wrongs as he saw them.[18]

Maritain met Muench in Rome early in 1947 and offered the assessment that "with his narrow spirit and surety of judgment, he seemed to share the outlook of United States Catholics on Europe and Germany in overlooking the complexity of the problems of the Old Continent." Maritain felt that Muench was looking for a quick solution to the German problem and gave no consideration to its profound roots which did not lend themselves to easy solution. Like the Vatican and the German bishops, the main concern of Muench in his conversation with Maritain had been to exonerate German Catholics who had only been, he claimed, victims of Nazism. Muench had no difficulty with the nationalism of the German clergy, which he interpreted as legitimate patriotism. Father Zeiger, described by Maritain as a German patriot, also spoke harshly of the behaviour of the French occupation authorities.[19]

THE REVIVAL OF GERMAN POLITICS

Political life began to revive in Germany as early as the summer of 1945. While the church remained in the background, Catholics took the lead in establishing new political parties, it being decided not to revive the old Catholic Centre party, in favour of collaboration between the Christian denominations, deliberately building on the wartime cooperation of Catholics and Protestants. Following the example of the Christian Democrats in Italy and the MRP in France, Christian democratic parties began taking shape in Germany. The Christian Democratic Union emerged from the Rhineland, and linked with the Christian Social Union from Bavaria, to provide a political party based on Christian principles but not affiliated directly with any particular church. The party was anti-communist, centre-left in orientation, and reached out to voters of all political and religious persuasions. While not directly involved in the party, Catholic clergy gave it their support. Cardinal Frings of Cologne issued a pastoral on the eve of the October 1946 municipal elections, calling on Catholics to be aware of their moral duties to support those who were "prepared to stand for Christian principles ... and a social order in accordance with natural rights and Christian revelation."[20] Other Catholics were wary of a political party that would identify the church too closely with any particular political ideology and were more interested in working for serious social reform in the Socialist Party or even the Communist Party; yet others explored the possibility of a left-wing Catholic party. The church had taken a strong lead in establishing its position in postwar Germany, so it had no need of an official political voice.

THE CHURCH AND
THE OCCUPYING POWERS

The Americans

The American zone of occupation was located in the south of Germany and included all of Bavaria where the population was 70 per cent Catholic. Otherwise, the population in the American zone was almost equally divided between Protestant and Catholic, with the Catholics having a slight lead. The Vatican were initially very pleased with the attitude of the United States to its occupation responsibilities. The Americans had allowed the German bishops to resume their regular conferences at Fulda in the summer of 1945 and in September of that year Generals Eisenhower and Mark Clark confirmed to the pope the American desire to base their policy in Germany on close cooperation with the Catholic Church. The Vatican had every reason to be confident that the Americans would give Catholics a major role in the reconstruction of Germany.[21] The Holy See also knew that the Americans had the wherewithal to provide material support for German relief. The naming of an American citizen as apostolic visitor to Germany demonstrated how the pope intended to rely on American support for the implementation of Catholic policy in Germany. Early in 1947 German-American-Vatican ties were further secured when Cardinal von Preysing of Berlin made a visit to the United States. By the end of the year Father John Cronin at the National Catholic Welfare Conference was investigating the possibility of fund-raising in the United States in order to launch an anti-communist campaign in Germany.[22]

While the Vatican enjoyed a close relationship with the American government in the development of its German policy, such was not always the case in the relationship between American occupation authorities and the German Catholic hierarchy. German Catholics were pleased with some of the initiatives of the Americans, such as free correspondence with the Vatican, the restoration of church property, the revival of religious orders and religious organizations, and the incorporation of denominational schools in the new Bavarian constitution. At the same time, relations between the church and the American occupation were occasionally strained. The Americans had given the Catholic bishops permission to continue their regular meetings at Fulda as long as allied observers attended. However, it was these same American authorities who censored the pastoral letter issued after the first postwar Fulda meeting in 1945. In spite of the intervention of Cardinal Spellman, the American authorities also forbade the reading of the 1946 Easter pastoral in the American zone.[23]

American enthusiasm for initiating the denazification program in their zone upset the German Catholics. Of all the occupying powers, the Americans were the only ones who really believed it was possible to denazify the German people and, through education, to turn Germany into a democracy like that of the United States. Alone of the occupying powers, the Americans did not hate or distrust the Germans and did not worry about the revival of a strong Germany. While the Americans approached the task of denazification as idealistic "liberators," they soon found that the Germans, including the church leaders, did not view them in this way. As the denazification program, by its very slowness, was causing untold hardships and annoyances in the American zone, the Americans eventually turned the program over to the Germans themselves, which caused even greater problems. The Americans also found that it was all very well to dismiss former Nazis from important jobs, but frequently there was no one to replace them. By 1948 the United States was looking for a way out of the program.[24]

In May 1946 the Vatican responded to the concerns of the German Catholics and passed along a note of complaint to the American government through Myron Taylor. The note consisted of "information reaching the Holy See from informed persons, among whom was a person of American nationality, in Germany." The "informed persons" can only have been the German bishops, while the "person of American nationality" must have been Muench. The note expanded on the themes of the Easter pastoral and was an inaccurate and blatant defence of the German position in 1946. That the Vatican would pass on such a note in an unquestioning fashion indicated the extent to which the pope's support for German Catholics was unconditional.

The note said that "the really fine element of the German people" have lost their faith in the Americans because they have managed to squander "the entire fund of confidence and goodwill which had been theirs from the German people." The major sources of complaint included the American policy of non-fraternization with the Germans, to the point that "the Americans would not return the greeting which they had received from even the highest and most respected among the German people" – including a Catholic bishop. The denazification policy was mentioned because it was claimed that it did not take into account the fact that many innocent Germans, such as school teachers, had been forced to join the Nazi party in order to keep their jobs and, once there, had "openly sabotaged the Nazi doctrine in the classroom, at the risk of the direst punishment." American troops had made German prisoners of war suffer hunger and discomfort and "the anxiety of the people at home was further aggravated by the misconduct of American soldiers, particularly toward the German women and especially when the soldiers had been drinking to excess." The Nuremberg trials were being used by the Americans to blacken the reputation of the whole German population which was unfair as "the common man knew nothing about these crimes or, if he did know, he was unable to do anything about them by reason of the cruel and cunning system of terror which was everywhere in effect." The overall concern of the note was that all Germans were being made to suffer for the crimes of a few.

"Objective criticism of occupation policies is welcomed by the American occupation authorities," wrote Robert Murphy, the United States political advisor for Germany, but "the tone and inaccuracy of the memorandum under reference makes it difficult to consider it as objective criticism."[25] This memorandum, in fact, showed just how far the Vatican, or perhaps Pius XII, was prepared to go in supporting the position and outlook of the German hierarchy.[26]

On 20 August 1946 the Vatican provided the American government with yet another report on the religious situation in Germany. This report was more balanced, although it still reflected the German perspective. When discussing the zones of occupation of Germany, the report referred to five such zones instead of the usual four, presumably all considered to be temporary: American, Soviet, British, French, and Polish, and pointed out the hardships being inflicted on the German population, including their priests, who were being expelled from the Polish "zone of occupation." While information was scarce from the Soviet zone, it appeared as if the church was functioning reasonably well there, as it was in the other three zones of occupation.[27] When forced to choose between his old friends the Germans, and his new friends the Americans, the pope preferred the perspective of the German Catholics.

The British

The British zone, which was located in the northwest of Germany, contained a Catholic western section and a Protestant eastern section. The zone was about 60 per cent Protestant. While the British attempted to administer their zone fairly as far as the churches were concerned, they did not display great sympathy with the position of the Catholic Church and its bishops, as was illustrated by the incident over transporting the cardinals to the consistory. The 1945 Fulda pastoral as well as the 1946 Easter pastoral were read in full in the British zone but the British officials felt that the bishops, in their Easter pastoral, were "displaying arrogance and impertinence" and it was suggested by one official that the bishops should be advised that their attitude was not well calculated "to encourage the British public to give them more food." The British took a practical and rather cynical approach to the matter of denazification, using it to remove obviously committed Nazis from important positions, but, beyond that, not pursuing the matter further.[28]

By 1947, relations between the British authorities and the Catholic Church were strained. Part of the problem stemmed from the willingness of the British to leave relations with the churches in the hands of local German politicians and, where those politicians were not themselves sympathetic to Catholic rights as guaranteed in the concordat, the British did not insist that the concordat be followed. As a result, the return of church property was slow and piecemeal, and denominational schools were not reintroduced where there was a mixed Catholic and Protestant population. Part of the problem also stemmed from the British insistence on continuing to censor mail between clergy inside Germany as well as between the German clergy and the Holy See. The unhelpful attitude of Cardinal von Galen before his death in 1946 did not encourage British authorities to be more cooperative.

The French

The French zone of occupation was in the south-western part of the country and was the most Catholic of all, with 63 percent of the population belonging to the Roman Catholic Church. The French were the most sympathetic of all the occupying powers to the considerations of the Catholic Church in their zone. Education was based on denominational schools from the beginning, with the churches being recognized as chiefly responsible for education. A new Catholic university was opened in Mainz, Catholic organizations and religious orders were encouraged and assisted, and church property was promptly returned and restored. The French realized that it was the Protestants rather than the Catholics who had worked closely with the Nazis, and the denazification requirements, especially among the Catholics, were applied with the greatest leniency, with each case being considered on its own merits. Like the British, the French did not pursue the matter of denazification beyond removing former Nazis from office, believing that the problem was traditional German militarism and nationalism, not just nazism, and therefore any attempt to wipe out nazism and thereby create "good" Germans would be a waste of time.[29]

While relations were generally good, the only difficulty in the zone came from the bishops, especially Archbishop Gröber of Freibourg, who was outspoken in defence of the innocence of German Catholics and particularly critical of the French. The French authorities had banned the 1946 Easter pastoral and also a pastoral by Gröber in the autumn of 1946. In June 1947 Gröber issued a further pastoral in which he criticized the Allies, and particularly the French, for the shortage of food, saying that German misfortunes were due not so much to responsibility for having started the war as to the fact that they had lost it and the victors were taking their revenge. This was not calculated to encourage Catholic cooperation with the French occupation.[30]

Maritain was concerned about the attitude of the German hierarchy towards the issue of collective guilt. In the spring of 1946 he took issue with the pope and Montini, arguing that, if the Germans were to take their place in the international order once again, they must first recognize their responsibility for the crimes of the war and accept the necessary sanctions. Only in this way would the air be cleared, as the international community expected some recognition of collective guilt by the German national community. The ambassador told the pope that the attitude of the German hierarchy must change, since they were still more concerned about the national success of their country and about a sense of ethnic superiority than with Christian principle in their outlook. At present the hierarchy was contributing to a nationalistic revival which could only serve to undo all Vatican efforts at fostering spiritual unity in the world. Maritain criticized the statements of Gröber and his attitude to the Russians and the Soviet occupation authorities in the eastern zone, which could only serve to pit eastern Germany against western. The pope and Montini received Maritain's views in stony silence, only indicating that the Vatican could better control the utterances of the bishops if the Allies would approve the assignment by the Vatican of an apostolic delegate to Germany. In support of this, Montini later indicated a degree of sympathy with the French ambassador's position, but claimed that the German bishops were acting without any specific directions from the pope.[31]

The Russians

The Soviet zone of occupation was in complete contrast to that of the French. Before the war, eastern Germany had been 95 per cent Protestant. This meant that the Soviet zone of occupation had the lowest percentage of Catholics and that Russian dealings were largely with the Protestant churches. The expulsion of Germans from Poland and Czechoslovakia, however, increased the Catholic proportion of the population to 16 percent, since the majority of those expelled were Catholic and most of them settled in the Soviet zone. Nevertheless, the main concern of Soviet authorities was with the Protestant clergy, many of whom had supported the Nazi regime.

The Soviet Union was at first especially hard on former Nazis and applied the denazification program with vigour. But the Soviets did not have their heart in this program either, because of their belief that nazism was an extreme manifestation of capitalism and that true denazification involved the destruction of German capitalism. Therefore the Soviets soon dropped formal denazification before any serious ill-will had been engendered. Some non-communists suggested that it was also dropped because so many former Nazis were flocking to join the German Communist party.[32]

One of the problems faced by Catholics in the Soviet zone was that the diocesan boundaries of eastern Germany had not been altered since 1938, with the result that bishops were presiding over dioceses which were divided between different secular administrations. This posed problems when the bishop lived in one of the western zones of occupation and the Soviet authorities would not allow him to visit that part of his diocese in the Soviet zone. Apostolic administrators had been named for those parts of German dioceses that found themselves in Poland.

Generally speaking, the Soviet authorities were conciliatory in their religious policy and were willing to accommodate the Catholic Church and the other churches and to allow the clergy to carry out their religious duties without interference. The confessional schools, which had been closed by the Nazis, were not allowed to reopen, however, nor was religious education allowed in the state schools. Cardinal von Preysing protested that this was in violation of the concordat, but to no avail. The concordat was not applied in the Soviet zone because of the reluctance of German politicians in the zone, either left-wing or Protestant, to give special privileges to the Catholics. While the youth organization in the zone had a strong communist bias, it was noted that chaplains were able to function and to work with the youth through this organization. The Catholics were not allowed to publish their own newspapers.[33]

Catholics in the Soviet zone had other difficulties because the church in eastern Germany had traditionally been poor, with all the wealth in the area being held by the Protestants. Consequently, eastern Catholics had traditionally been supported by the wealthier Catholics of western and southern Germany. Now this source of funds was no longer available. Yet the great influx of Catholics from Poland and Czechoslovakia meant that funds were urgently needed, as were church buildings and priests. There was also no seminary in the eastern zone, with the result that it was very difficult to provide priests for the growing congregations. The Soviet authorities were not inclined to help the Catholic Church out of these difficulties.

The problem of the Catholic refugees in the eastern zone was a difficult one for the church hierarchy. Tactically, the bishops, because of these refugees, had to be very careful about their anti-communist utterances and leave all ideological criticism to the Vatican itself. The bishops did, however, criticize the Poles for their treatment of the refugees. In his pastoral of March 1946 Gröber spoke of an "inhuman Asiatic bestiality," called the Poles "incendiaries, robbers and murderers," and spoke of "these Hitlerite methods at the hands of the Allies." He then went on to ask the Poles to surrender voluntarily "the thoroughly German territories west of the Oder." Late in the fall of 1946 the pope named Bishop Maximilian Kaller of Ermland in the former East Prussia as "Bishop for German Refugees." This appointment served to defuse the issue somewhat, as Bishop Keller's approach was conciliatory and low-key and he set about his work with a genuine concern for the Catholic refugees. The example set by Keller was thereafter followed by the rest of the hierarchy.

PART FOUR

The Cold War Begins

13 The Martyrdom of Archbishop Stepinac

In order to secure a conciliatory peace settlement for Italy and Germany, the Holy See understood that the postwar credibility of the Soviet Union had to be undermined with the western allies. This was necessary because the Soviet Union had a vested interest in a punitive peace for Germany to assist with the reconstruction of the USSR and also because Stalin's ally, Tito of Yugoslavia, sought his own advantage from the peace settlement with Italy. The difficulty was that the Vatican had little cause for complaint with the behaviour of the Soviet Union and its supporters immediately after the war. The Catholic Church was shown considerable respect in those areas occupied by the Red Army: Poland, Czechoslovakia, Hungary, Bulgaria, Romania, and the Soviet zone of Germany. Only in Albania, Yugoslavia, and the Soviet Union itself, where it came under direct Communist rule, was the church experiencing rough treatment. In Albania the church was being made to pay for its support of the Italian occupation. In Yugoslavia individual clergy who had supported the Axis occupation or the Ustase regime were punished while Tito had held out an olive branch to the hierarchy of the Catholic Church if they would support the Yugoslav case over the Italian in the peace discussions. The hierarchy's rejection of Tito's offer raised expectations in the Vatican that persecution of the church in Yugoslavia would begin in earnest in 1946. Yet by the end of 1945 there was little evidence of unprovoked communist persecution of religion and western public opinion still placed considerable trust in Soviet intentions.

If Italy were not to receive harsh treatment at the meetings of the peace conference scheduled to begin in 1946, the Holy See believed it important to establish with the British, French, and Americans that Tito's Yugoslavia, although on the winning side in the war, was an untrustworthy partner in the postwar period, driven as its actions were by ideological atheism. The Catholic Church was about to be put on trial for collaboration with the enemy, and accordingly, the Holy See took the offensive in 1946 to spearhead a campaign to reinterpret these trials of Yugoslav bishops and clergy as exercises in religious persecution.

In this initiative, the Vatican was highly successful in depicting the Soviet Union and its allies as atheists who would stop at nothing to persecute and torment those whose only crime was a belief in God. The public image of Archbishop Stepinac of Zagreb was overnight converted from a sometime collaborator of Ante Pavelic to the first martyr to communist expansionism. While not of great help to the Italian cause, this Vatican public relations exercise was nevertheless a significant factor in bringing western opinion to see the Soviet Union in less benevolent terms and in creating a ready audience for President Truman's declaration of the policy of containment in the spring of 1947.

In 1945 the Vatican had been continuously attacked in the Soviet and communist press for its pro-fascist sympathies. It had responded through articles in the *Osservatore Romano* and other Catholic journals which were not, however, deemed to have been very effective. When Montini complained to Osborne in the summer of 1945 that press agencies like United Press and Reuters were only carrying the Soviet attacks and not Vatican rebuttals, Osborne pointed out that articles in the *Osservatore Romano* did not lend themselves to reporting as news because "they were too long, too involved and too ironical."[1] The Vatican needed a more effective publicity campaign to counteract the charges of pro-fascist sympathies. The treatment of the church in eastern Europe provided the Holy See with new strategies and new opportunities.

In November 1945 the American bishops took the initiative and launched their postwar campaign to reverse the foreign policy of the United States. Following their annual meeting, the bishops attacked Soviet disregard for human rights and the rule of law in eastern Europe and deplored the return to power politics in the world. Coming only six months after the victory of the Allies in Europe and three months after the victory over Japan, this frontal attack on the Soviet Union called for a radical change of direction in American policy. Four months before Winston Churchill's "Iron Curtain" speech, the Catholic bishops of the United States denounced Stalin's evil intentions for the postwar world. The American government, argued the bishops, must stand by its Yalta pledge to the Polish people and should speak out against religious persecution in Slovakia, Croatia, Slovenia, and elsewhere in eastern Europe. The United States should prepare itself for the new conflict by quickly healing the wounds of the last one with Italy and Germany.[2]

In his 1945 Christmas message, the pope followed the lead of the bishops with an attack on the totalitarianism of the Soviet Union. Totalitarianism, he argued, is a threat because it promotes the interests of the state above those of the individual and does not represent the "true measure of progress," which is "the progressive creation of ever more ample and better conditions in public life to ensure that the family can evolve as an economic, juridical, moral and religious unit." The response to state totalitarianism, which is incompatible with "a true and healthy democracy," is to return the world to a Christian order, since true peace was to be found "in the internationalism of Christian democracy and not in the internationalism of atheistic communism."[3]

THE CONSISTORY OF 1946

The first postwar consistory was convened in Rome in February 1946 in order to create thirty-two new cardinals. This consistory was significant for a number of reasons. It was, first of all, an opportunity to bring together the College of Cardinals to celebrate the universalism of the Roman Catholic Church. This was contrasted with totalitarian imperialisms by Pius XII in his charge to the consistory, when he claimed that the duty of the church "is to form, model and perfect man, and thereby to prepare a secure basis for human society. Modern imperialism on the other hand, subordinates the individual to material elements and forces, and thereby endangers the foundations of human intercourse."[4]

The pope's speech was interpreted as a gesture towards the creation of a Catholic "international," bringing together the Italian Christian Democrats, the French MRP, and other Catholic parties to challenge the Communist international. Lord Halifax, British ambassador in Washington, wrote of the consistory: "There is no doubt that the prestige of the church outside her own walls stands high at the moment – certainly higher than it did at the corresponding period after the last war, and that the lengthening shadow of the Soviet Union is leading to an increase in the influence of its most inveterate antagonist.."[5]

The consistory allowed the pope to make the Holy See less of an Italian institution and by his appointments to give a public manifestation of the universalism of the church. Of the thirty-two new cardinals, only four were Italian, meaning that, after February 1946, a majority of the College of Cardinals were non-Italian, as opposed to only 45 percent non-Italian in 1937. In his address to the new cardinals, the pope emphasized that, with the College of Cardinals becoming more international, the church was truly a "supranational" institution; narrow nationalism was a prime enemy of the Church.[6] The internationalization of the Curia, which distanced the Vatican from Italy and Italian interests, was itself a guarantee, beyond the continuation of the Lateran Agreements, of the independence of the Vatican City State.

The consistory was also an opportunity to draw attention to the prominence of Americans within the church. Red hats were presented to Archbishops John Glennon of St Louis, Edward Mooney of Detroit, Samuel Stritch of Chicago, and Francis Spellman of New York, who joined Cardinal Denis Dougherty of Philadelphia as the American representatives in the College of Cardinals. Halifax felt the five American cardinals were "an indication that the Vatican recognized America's pre-eminent position as a world power" and commented that "the greater voice which she will now have in church affairs is regarded as only proper."[7]

Of the cardinals, the most newsworthy was Spellman, and the rumours of his possible appointment as secretary of state surfaced once again in the European press, coupled with speculation that he might become the first American pope.[8] Spellman and the German von Galen were reported by Osborne as being "the most conspicuous and spot-lit figures of the Consistory." Like von Galen, famous for his resistance to the Nazis, Spellman's appearance was greeted by "ripples of applause in the course of the public Consistories ... but he brought so many friends and relations with him, and the American press had invaded Rome in such strength that it was natural to doubt the disinterestedness of the applause."

In fact, Osborne reacted against the media interest in Vatican affairs, suspecting that "perhaps Cardinal Spellman and the American pressmen were partly responsible for a slightly Hollywood atmosphere about the ceremonies," including arc lights in St Peter's and press and motion picture photographers everywhere, registering every scene "in hundreds of yards of film and from every possible viewpoint."[9]

Finally, the consistory was significant for the strategy for coping with the communist threat which appears to have been developed behind closed doors between the pope, Curial officials, and the American cardinals, possibly also with those from Great Britain, Canada, and some other countries. What emerged from the consistory was a well-articulated plan to publicize the persecution of the church in Yugoslavia and to try to generate pressure on governments for action against the Tito regime, particularly by favouring Italian interests at the peace conference. The Secretariat of State would provide information on the persecution of the church in eastern Europe to the press office of the National Catholic Welfare Conference which would, in turn, ensure that the American press was well informed about the treatment of Catholics in Yugoslavia and elsewhere and would secure statements urging government action from influential Catholic politicians.

THE ANTI-YUGOSLAV CAMPAIGN

At the beginning of February 1946, and with the agreement of the Yugoslav government, a regent took charge of the papal nunciature in Belgrade. A regent was a temporary appointment who, unlike a nuncio, would not expect to be recognized as the dean of the diplomatic corps. The Vatican now had an opportunity to obtain first-hand information on developments within Yugoslavia. As regent, the pope nominated the American Monsignor Joseph P. Hurley, the bishop of St Augustine, Florida. Hurley was a veteran papal diplomat who had worked in the Secretariat of State from 1934 to 1940. Tito was willing to accept Hurley, who had a reputation as an anti-Nazi and would have the great advantage of being outside the traditional quarrels of the Balkans.[10] The appointment of Hurley offered a double advantage to the Holy See: because he was not a European, he was less likely to be suspect to the government of Yugoslavia; because he was an American, he was in a position to influence the United States to take an interest in the treatment of the church in Yugoslavia.

The American cardinals had barely returned home from the consistory when the Vatican Secretariat of State sent the first of a series of confidential reports on the situation in Yugoslavia to apostolic delegate Amleto Cicognani. Cicognani, in turn, passed the report along to the Reverend Paul Tanner at the National Catholic Welfare Conference, advising him that the report was "for whatever use you may find fitting and calculated to be effective" and cautioning him to use it "with the utmost prudence and caution."[11] Subsequent reports were forwarded to Tanner and to Bishop Howard J. Carroll at the NCWC by Cicognani at regular intervals throughout the spring and summer of 1946. On 14 March he asked that the source of the information should be "considered as confidential."

On 13 April the apostolic delegate forwarded a copy of a report "submitted to the Secretariat of State of His Holiness on the condition of the Church in Jugoslavia" and asked that copies of the report be "made available for Their Eminences, Cardinals Stritch, Mooney and

Spellman, for whatever use may be deemed prudently advisable." The report dealt with the difficulties facing the Catholic Church and the general persecution of faithful Catholics in the diocese of Ljubljana. This was followed on 18 April by a further two reports containing information which Cicognani felt "should be brought to the attention of the general public in the most effective way possible" and suggesting that "in addition to the Catholic press you can find an outlet for it through the secular press or widely read columnists." Two days later he sent information on the trial of four Daughters of Charity in Yugoslavia, three of whom were sentenced to death and one to twenty-one years in prison. The trial had reportedly been carried out "in contradiction with every rule of justice and principles of equity [sic]." Cicognani hoped that Bishop Carroll would "be able to find the proper channel for publicizing this sad story." In June and again in August, Cicognani forwarded further information on religious persecution in Slovenia, Croatia, and Bosnia.[12]

On receipt of this information, the NCWC prepared news releases for the Catholic and secular press detailing the evidence of persecution of Catholics in Yugoslavia, "partly revealed in documents that have become available here." The impact of these releases was demonstrated when Congressman John W. McCormack of Massachusetts, the majority leader in the House of Representatives, "spontaneously interested himself in the case" of the nuns who had been sentenced to death, contacted the State Department about the matter and, apparently as a result, managed to have the sentences of two of the nuns commuted to twenty years' imprisonment, the death sentence of the third having been carried out the week before.[13]

The greatest early public success of the NCWC campaign was a speech in the House of Representatives by McCormack on 27 July, when he outlined the "present situation in Yugoslavia under Tito." The timing of the speech was critical because it was delivered on the eve of the 29 July opening of the Paris peace conference, which was intended to deal with the Italian peace treaty, including the boundary issue between Italy and Yugoslavia. McCormack's speech sought to inform the American public and to convince State Department negotiators to be sympathetic to the Italian side. He referred to a story in the *New York Times* of 24 July – no doubt from one of the NCWC press releases – under the headline "Murder of 230 priests reported in Yugoslav antichurch terror," and said that Tito and his associates, who had been "imposed upon the Yugoslavs by a small minority," were carrying out a program of religious persecution against the Catholic Church and the Catholic faithful in Yugoslavia. He argued that "we, as a nation, must be firm, through our all powerful State Department, in our dealings

with national governments who would make a plaything of religion or
a foible of Christianity ... The present religious terrorism in Yugoslavia
calls for dynamic defense by dynamic leadership throughout the decent
world, both church and state ... The people of the United States cannot
slumber while such conditions exist in any nation."[14] Cardinal Spellman was delighted with the speech and saw to it that copies were distributed to every Catholic bishop in the United States.

The Vatican also made direct diplomatic approaches to the American government. Recognizing that there were too many close links
between Great Britain and Tito's Yugoslavia[15], the Vatican sought to
interest Washington in the fate of the Yugoslav church immediately
after the war. At the end of September 1945 the pope sent a memorandum to the American government, reporting on the impossibility
for Catholics in Yugoslavia to communicate with the Holy See. and
giving evidence that the general situation of religion in Yugoslavia "has
in no way evidenced an improvement." Details were provided from
Croatia, Slovenia, and Venezia Giulia on the arrest of bishops and
clergy for opposing the Communist regime, of the confiscation of religious property, and of the interference with religious education and
with church schools. At the end of March 1946 Pius XII talked to
Harold Tittmann about the "virtual reign of terror" in Yugoslavia,
"where the situation of Catholics could not be worse," and said that
the Allies should do something about it immediately. When Tittmann
asked what should be done, the pope suggested "perhaps a show of
force."[16]

Myron Taylor finally returned to Rome in May 1946. During one of
his audiences with the pope, Taylor was told of terrible conditions in
Yugoslavia and Pius asked him to visit Yugoslavia, Romania, and
Vienna to learn about conditions at first hand. On the same day Taylor
met the bishop of Trieste, who warned of the political, humane, and
religious dangers which could befall his diocese if Yugoslav control
were extended there. The United States must defend Italian claims at
the peace conference. Harry Truman was too clever a politician to be
trapped by the Vatican, however, and when Taylor sought permission
to visit Yugoslavia, Truman replied that the situation was much too
tense in that country for him to visit at the present time.[17]

The Catholic propaganda campaign in the United States had been
extremely successful by the summer of 1946 in whitewashing the
Yugoslav church. In the question period following McCormack's
House speech, not one voice had been raised to suggest that Tito might
have had a reason for punishing priests and nuns apart from an ideological hatred of Christianity. On an even more official level, a Vatican
memorandum on the political and religious situation in Yugoslavia,

prepared for the State Department on 1 August 1946, omitted all reference to the role of the Ustase during the war, pointing out that the Catholic Church had been in conflict with the Serb Orthodox before the war, that Catholics had been persecuted by the Germans during their occupation, and that "after the occupation of Yugoslavia by Tito's troops the Catholic religious situation became ever worse."[18]

YUGOSLAV CATHOLICS ON TRIAL

The anti-Catholic campaign in Yugoslavia operated in several arenas in 1946. In the judicial arena, many members of the clergy were condemned to death on charges of collaboration and war crimes. In the legislative arena, the official separation of church and state, which had been provided in the federal constitution of 31 January 1946, resulted in the removal of privileges and resources from the church. In the public arena, press attacks continued against the clergy and the Vatican. Strategically, Tito wanted to undermine the authority of the church hierarchy by encouraging the lower clergy and the laity to think of themselves as Yugoslavs first and Catholics second and to agitate for internal church democracy.[19]

In 1946 a new sense of urgency influenced the government's need to bring the Catholic Church into line. The planned reconstruction of Yugoslavia as a modern industrial state required tight central direction and the elimination of potential opposition to the Communist regime. One such opponent in Serbia was Colonel Mihailovic, the leader of the wartime Chetniks, who was captured by Yugoslav authorities in March 1946, put on public trial on 10 June, found guilty of collaboration, and executed on 17 July. In Croatia, Stepinac and the Catholic Church had been the leading opponents of the regime and expected that their turn would be next. According to the British Foreign Office, Stepinac "is now almost the only man of whom the authorities are afraid. His popularity, always great, has grown as the people have become more disillusioned with the regime. He represents, moreover, the one great opposing force to Communism, the Catholic Church, which has always wielded great influence in Croatia, and which is now regarded as the only possible source of organised opposition to the regime."[20]

Tito was reluctant to confront Stepinac and initially tried to get Regent Hurley to have the Vatican recall the archbishop to Rome. The Vatican left the decision to Stepinac who decided that it was his duty to remain with his flock. With the failure of this request, Tito realized that he would have to call the archbishop to account.[21] The opening of the Paris peace conference in June precipitated a series of moves which culminated in Stepinac's arrest. The Vatican and the Catholic hierarchies were actively espousing and promoting Italian claims to Trieste and Venezia Giulia at the expense of the Yugoslavs. In order to refute the charges of unreasoning ideological hatred of religion which had been laid against his government, Tito sought to demonstrate to the world that the Catholic bishops and clergy had cooperated actively and willingly with the butchery of the Yugoslav people during the war.[22]

Tito made a series of speeches in various parts of Yugoslavia in July and August, in which he demonstrated the lack of cooperation of the Catholic Church with the people and government of Yugoslavia. At Bled on 22 August he said that "the Yugoslav Government were fighting to get what was theirs by all possible means and were defending Yugoslavia's rights with the utmost energy. On whose side, however, was the Pope? He was not defending the Yugoslav cause, but the Italian cause, and that was understandable. The Pope was an Italian and would remain an Italian ...Why then must the Catholic clergy just listen to him?... They should not obey a foreign country and they should not obey those who were Yugoslavia's declared enemies ... The priests must serve their people and not the people's age-old enemy, Italian reaction." His conclusion was that "the Yugoslav Government wanted to have a national priesthood which loved its people."[23]

Vatican reaction to Tito's speech was prompt. The *Osservatore Romano* denied that the pope was taking Italy's side against Yugoslavia and argued that Tito was only echoing the Moscow line in calling for a national Catholicism. The Yugoslav hierarchy responded in a pastoral letter on 8 September, which rejected all of Tito's claims and declared "the indissoluble links of the Church in Yugoslavia with Rome, and then list[ed] the various acts of injustice and persecution committed by the State against the Church, the greatest of which concern[ed] the education of youth."[24]

As far as Tito was concerned, the church had had its last chance. The hierarchy had to be broken if the Catholic Church was to be given a definite Yugoslav orientation. On 21 August the Slovene Bishop Rozman of Ljubljana had been charged with war crimes and been tried *in absentia* together with two of his assistants. The bishop was sentenced to eighteen years in prison and one of his assistants was condemned to death. More significantly, the evidence brought out at this trial linked Bishop Rozman's activities to the Catholic Church generally and rumours in Belgrade held that the Rozman trial was only the first step.[25]

In mid-September eighteen individuals were accused of Ustase membership, including twelve priests and friars, and were put on trial in Belgrade. The most prominent of the accused was the secretary to the archbishop of Zagreb. The indictment in the case was clearly directed against Stepinac and the Catholic Church. Once the trial had started, a communiqué named Stepinac as the leader of those who had been indicted. On 18 September he was arrested and charged with support of the Pavelic government, with supporting the forced conversions of the Orthodox, and of treasonable conduct after the liberation in encouraging Ustase resistance. On 11 October, having been found guilty, Stepinac was sentenced to a prison term of sixteen years. Of his fellow accused, one was sentenced to death while the rest received long prison sentences.[26]

After Stepinac's conviction, Charles Peake, the British minister in Belgrade, claimed that the Stepinac trial was not only an attack on the Catholic Church but was also an indirect attack on Croatian nationalism, because "since the liberation ... Dr Stepinac has been the leader of the Croatian people and the most-loved and respected person in Croatia ... For this reason alone it is obvious also that the régime would be unlikely to tolerate his continued liberty, for in this country Allah has only one prophet and he happens not to be Dr Stepinac."[27]

Jean Payart, the French ambassador, believed that, because Stepinac had not been condemned to death, the regime still saw some room for negotiation with the Vatican. Historian Stella Alexander, on the other hand, claims that "the trial became the symbolic act which determined the nature of the relations between the Catholic Church and the state and between the Vatican and Yugoslavia for the next fifteen years."[28]

MAKING PEACE WITH ITALY

At the same time as it was blackening the reputation of the Yugoslav government, the Catholic Church attempted to give direct assistance to Italy in the peace negotiations, although with considerably less successs. The new American cardinals had witnessed Italian poverty and dislocation for themselves at the February consistory and had sensed directly the fears of the pope and Curial officials over future developments in Italy. Led by Cardinal Stritch, the cardinals sought to assist in securing a conciliatory peace settlement for Italy. Before the Council of Foreign Ministers gathered in Paris for peace talks on 25 April, Stritch met President Truman to impress on him the importance of a peace settlement which would recognize the Italian contribution to the war effort by allowing Italy to keep the South Tyrol, part of the Istrian peninsula and at least her pre-fascist colonies.[29]

Although Secretary of State Byrnes had spoken against punishing Italy in March, the meeting in April 1946 demonstrated that the Americans were prepared to sacrifice Italian concerns for compromises with the Russians. After the Council of Foreign Ministers sessions in April, the Italians turned to the Vatican for help and, in turn, Montini agreed to inform Cardinal Stritch that a satisfactory resolution in Paris would help the internal pacification of Italy at a most delicate moment. The encouragement had its effect, because in May Stritch reiterated his arguments to Truman, and warned Hannigan, the postmaster-general and the president of the executive committee of the Democratic party, that Catholic voters would be disappointed if the American government did not support Italy in Paris.[30] Monsignor Cody, the diocesan chancellor of St Louis, addressed a letter to both the president and the secretary of state, spelling out the case in favour of supporting Italy. Specifically, Cody was concerned about American acceptance of the Russian proposal to divide the Italian fleet, about the Russian demand for reparations from Italy, and about American opposition to letting Italy retain a trusteeship over her colonies. Most important was the issue of Trieste and Venezia Giulia. Having originally opposed Russian proposals to give all of Venezia Giulia to Yugoslavia, the Americans now appeared willing to compromise and to turn over part of that territory to Tito, including "more than half a million Catholic Italians." Cody also brought up the problem of the proposed American loan to Italy being stalled by the chairman of the House Appropriations Committee on the grounds that Italy was an enemy country. Unless the United States were prepared to be more sympathetic, the continuation of a democratic Italy could not be ensured.[31]

Yet the victory of the Christian Democrats in the June Italian elections undermined the arguments which the church had made to the Americans that failure to treat the Italians well in the peace negotiations would result in a popular swing to the left. The treatment of the Italians by the Council of Foreign Ministers in April appeared to have had little influence on the outcome of the June elections. With the full peace conference scheduled to begin in late July, there seemed to be little expectation that Italy would be better treated then. Nevertheless, the Vatican continued to campaign actively on Italy's behalf and encouraged others, such as the French MRP and the American hierarchy, to do the same.

After June 1946 the papacy supported the Italian government in order to reaffirm the Lateran Agreements in the new Italian constitution. In return for Vatican recognition of the Italian Republic, Montini advised the Italian ambassador that the pope wanted the Italian government to recognize the Lateran Agreements as the basis for church-state relations under the republic. The Italian concordat and the Lateran Treaty were indissoluble as far as the Vatican was concerned and the Vatican wanted them to be reconfirmed by the new government. Should such a reconfirmation not be possible, the Vatican threatened to consider other arrangements, such as a move of the Holy See out of Italy or an international guarantee of the Vatican City State.[32]

On 29 July 1946 all the countries which had been at war with Italy, Austria, Hungary, Romania, and Bulgaria met in Paris to approve the draft treaties of peace with those defeated nations. The Italian treaty was harsh and, when de Gasperi, the anti-fascist prime minister, arrived at the conference, he was treated by the conference delegates as a defeated enemy. Only Byrnes shook his hand.[33] The question of Trieste remained open but there was little hope for a settlement in Italy's favour. During the conference the Vatican was disturbed not only that the Americans were not more pro-Italian, but that the French MRP were not giving better support to their fellow Christian Democrats in Italy.

The behaviour of the French government at the peace conference was a disappointment to the Holy See. After the June elections Bidault had sought Vatican support for enhancing cooperation between French and Italian Christian Democrats in opposition to the existing collaboration between French and Italian Communists. In the peace talks, however, France had demanded that Italy return the towns of Brigue and Tende to France. The Vatican and the Italian Catholic press supported the Italian position and went so far as to compare French behaviour at the peace conference with the Italian invasion of France in 1940. De Gasperi was embarrassed by this check to his policy of rapprochement with France and Montini advised the French chargé d'affaires that the French were destroying any possibility for a Catholic European and Latin American bloc between the Russians and the Anglo-Saxons.[34] The Vatican was already distressed by French cooperation with the Soviet Union in the approach being taken to the defeated enemy nations and especially by French hostility to Germany. If the MRP wanted close cooperation with Italian and German Christian Democrats, it would have to support Italian and German positions in the peace negotiations.

It was while the peace conference was in session that Monsignor Stepinac was arrested – an obvious sign that Catholics who had collaborated with fascism deserved little consideration at the peace conference. To the Catholic Church, the arrest and trial of Stepinac only confirmed Catholic arguments against the cession of Venezia Giulia. By October the Italian peace treaty was complete. Italy was to lose all her colonies, had to pay reparations and saw Trieste become a free territory under international supervision. The pope was distressed with the treaty and, after its signature on 10 February 1947, contemplated ways in which Italy could be helped to secure its revision. The *Osservatore Romano* joined the rest of the Italian press in protesting the terms of the treaty.

THE UNEASY RELATIONSHIP WITH THE UNITED STATES

The outcome of the Paris peace conference demonstrated that the Vatican relationship with the American government in 1946 was anything but close. The Vatican was particularly concerned about Myron Taylor's continuation as the president's personal representative to the pope. Truman had not sent Taylor back to Rome in 1945, although he had assured the pope that he wanted to maintain the relationship. Taylor's absence from the February consistory was particularly noted, since the pope, by naming four new American cardinals, had paid a great tribute to the United States. On their return from the consistory, Cardinals Spellman and Stritch met Truman to convince him of the importance of re-establishing the Taylor mission.

At the same time Tittmann, the chargé d'affaires at the Holy See, had sent a long letter to Byrnes, in which he also put the case for the continuation of American representation at the Vatican. Tittmann argued that the United States and the Vatican shared the same goals in promoting world peace, that the Vatican offered good sources of information for the Americans, that formal relations with the Vatican helped relations with Latin America, and that the Catholic Church could be a useful vehicle for re-educating Germans and Austrians to democracy.[35]

As a result of these entreaties, Truman reversed his position, renewed Taylor's mission, and sent him back to Rome in May 1946. In a personal letter, Truman explained to the pope that he intended to ask Taylor to return to Rome from time to time to confer with the Pope on problems of peace in the world. The pope was delighted and shared with Taylor his "very grave concern" about the imminent election and referendum in Italy.[36] Osborne believed that Taylor's appointment was designed to show American approval of the pope's anti-communist position, while Maritain believed that the move signified a radical change in the outlook of the Truman administration on the significance of the Vatican. He believed that the growing rift between the United States and Russia on general issues resulted in the United States wanting to collect all the forces of morality on its side.[37] Taylor remained in Italy from 5 May until 10 August and, when he left, took with him a series of reports prepared by the Vatican offering their perspective on the political and religious situations in Romania, Hungary, Poland, Russia, Yugoslavia, Czechoslovakia, Austria, and Germany for consideration by the American government. These reports all stressed the unreasoning persecution of the church by east European governments.[38]

Taylor was aware that he had only returned to Rome in May on the sufferance of the president and had to make an argument to convince Truman that the office should be continued. After the June election victory of the Catholic parties in Italy and France, Taylor reported that the pope and the Catholic Church were the bulwarks of democracy in continental Europe and that the hostility of Christians to communism was vitally important for the future. In August he pointed out to Truman that the Christian democratic movement was emerging in a number of European countries as the main instrument for opposing communism. "The importance of the Church and thus of His Holiness the Pope is therefore worthy of serious consideration," concluded Taylor.[39]

By the end of 1946 Truman appeared to be losing interest in the Vatican office. The disastrous results of the November elections, when the Republican party had gained control of Congress, showed that Catholics had been either unwilling or unable to deliver Democratic votes. The president did, however, send Taylor back to Rome at the end of November. Because of Protestant objection to close cooperation between Washington and the Vatican, Truman tried to diminish the importance of this contact by stressing that Taylor's return would be for a period not exceeding thirty days and that, in addition to consulting with the pope about "matters of importance," Taylor would also continue his work with the Italian Red Cross and his chairmanship of American relief for Italy. In a secret audience that Taylor had with the pope on 3 December, Pius XII once again lobbied on Italy's behalf and presented the argument that it was necessary to continue American representation at the Vatican because of the open communist campaign in Rome against the Holy See.[40]

INTERNATIONAL REACTION TO THE TRIAL OF ARCHBISHOP STEPINAC

If there was little sign of an anti-communist alliance between Washington and the Vatican at the end of 1946, the aftermath of the trial and conviction of Archbishop Stepinac created a public anti-communist furore which politicians could ill afford to ignore. The Stepinac trial was one of the key events contributing to the public perception of an ideological split between East and West in 1946, especially in the Anglo-Saxon democracies and the countries of Latin America. Occurring between Winston Churchill's Iron Curtain speech of March 1946 and the enunciation of the Truman Doctrine in March 1947, the Stepinac trial played an important role in conditioning western opinion to the concept of a cold war. With the Stepinac trial, Tito had delivered his challenge to the Catholic Church and the Vatican only to find that the Vatican and the Catholic world had prepared themselves for this test of wills. International reaction to the Stepinac imprisonment was both hostile and ideological.

The Vatican immediately excommunicated those who had been responsible for the arrest and conviction of Stepinac.[41] The *Osservatore Romano* paid tribute to Stepinac as a great pastor, a defender of the faith and of Christian civilization and on 11 October 1946 claimed that the condemnation of Stepinac was "a tactical moment in a war of vaster proportions whose operations are not directed from Belgrade and in which are competing the two civilizations which are vying for control of the world." Vatican protests went no further than this, however, since more serious protest would have entailed withdrawing Bishop Hurley from Yugoslavia and the Vatican was not prepared to surrender its important listening post in that country. The *Osservatore Romano* published the many letters of sympathy and protest that poured in from around the world which had a greater impact on the governments and peoples of the West than formal Vatican protests could ever have had.

Regent Hurley anticipated an active press campaign in the United States and surreptitiously advised Carroll of the NCWC to get more personal information about Stepinac into the American papers and magazines, especially about his "magnificent" defence at the trial. Writing from Belgrade, Hurley warned Carroll that "this fight is vital – it can be won only by you folks outside the country." Hurley interpreted the campaign against the Yugoslav church as part of a long-range campaign: "I can see nothing ahead under the Communist regime but a progressively worse persecution. And when they have liquidated or 'nationalized' us they will go to work on Poland. The pace is quickening with the recent Communist victories in France and Italy; the party livers [*sic*] here are jubilant; they see an early domination of the continent."[42]

Catholics around the world reacted strongly to Stepinac's trial and sentence. In Great Britain, Cardinal Bernard Griffin, the archbishop of Westminster, wrote to Foreign Secretary Ernest Bevin within a week of Stepinac's arrest to urge the British government to leave no stone unturned to secure his immediate release.[43] On 29 September a special mass for Stepinac was held in Westminster Cathedral. One aspect of this pressure was a request from 250 members of Parliament to Prime Minister Clement Attlee to intervene on Stepinac's behalf.

Like the hierarchy of Britain and Wales, the American hierarchy also lost no time in speaking out. On 29 September Cardinal Stritch, in his capacity as chairman of the administrative board of the National Catholic Welfare Conference, issued a statement on behalf of Stepinac. Stritch claimed that "the people of Croatia had but one champion who stood fearlessly in defense of human rights against Nazi and Fascist oppression, as he has stood against the tyranny of those now in control" and that "the protagonists of the rights of racial and religious minorities, Jew and Gentile alike, when they were bitterly persecuted by barbarous tyrants, found in him a friend and a valiant defender." Stritch hoped that "our Government will voice its protest and use its influence in behalf of Archbishop Stepinac and those with him [who] are victims of this persecution."[44]

On 6 October Cardinal Spellman addressed a world peace rally in New York, claiming that Stepinac's "only crime was fidelity to God and country." Elsewhere, Spellman said that Stepinac was "but one of thousands of martyrs of every faith whom corrupt, ruthless dictators daily betray and befoul as they wield poisoned power and force to achieve their goal of godless government throughout the world." On this occasion, Spellman launched a fundraising drive to build a new high school in New York to be named after Archbishop Stepinac; the drive secured double its objective in two years.

These statements by the hierarchy were echoed by other Catholic organizations. On 4 October John Randall, the managing editor of the *Catholic Courier Journal* of Rochester, NY, wrote to all members of the Catholic Press Association, saying that "public opinion in America must be aroused" and that "Catholics ... must lead the way." Randall forwarded a petition to be circulated by the Catholic press and eventually presented to Truman, urging him "to join with us in a moral protest against the current violations of human rights in Yugoslavia."[45] At the 13 October meeting of the Ohio Holy Name Society, it was decided that a letter should be sent to President Truman, expressing sympathy "because of the difficult task of dealing with the Red, Fascist, atheistic, brutal and barbarous government of Yugoslavia, as now constituted under the domination of godless Soviet Russia," claiming that "the slavery of Communism in Yugoslavia is an outrage upon a Christian people and a blot on civilization" and asking Truman and the State Department "to take whatever measures can be appropriately taken to secure freedom for the Apostle of Freedom – Archbishop Stepinac." On 16 October, the National Council of Catholic Women forwarded a telegram to Secretary of State Byrnes, expressing "indignation at the arrest of the saintly Archbishop Aloysius Stepinac" and asking the government "to intercede with the government of

Yugoslavia in the Archbishop's behalf." On 11 January 1947 Truman was presented with a petition signed by forty thousand Catholics from Omaha, Nebraska, requesting that "the United States Government protest by diplomatic means against both the trial and sentence of Archbishop Stepinac of Zagreb."[46]

A number of exiled Croatians offered to help give the American campaign greater direction. Father Stephen Lackovic, a former secretary to Stepinac who was living in Ohio, wrote to Stritch, suggesting the creation of an "Archbishop Stepinac's Fund" to provide financial assistance to Croatian refugees in Italy, Austria and elsewhere. At the end of November the NCWC received a suggestion that Bishop Rozman of Ljubljana, Ambassador Krek, and Minister-Plenipotentiary Vosnjak, all of whom had been tried and sentenced *in absentia* by courts in Yugoslavia and Austria "on account of [their] fight for civil liberties in Yugoslav lands," would be willing to undertake a speaking tour of the United States to talk about religious persecution in Tito's Yugoslavia. The officials of the NCWC concluded, however, that "it is not advisable for us to encourage prelates and priests to come to us in their distress." As Archbishop McNicholas wrote to Bishop Carroll, "if some organized protest is to be made in a large scale, I think we should do it in our own way, according to the genius and spirit of the Church of the United States."[47] The Americans did not need the help of the exiles.

The groundswell of protest moved politicians such as Senator Robert Wagner of New York, who urged on 17 October "that proper steps be taken by our State Department in protesting the great injustice perpetuated in the case of Archbishop Stepinac," and claimed that the United States "must exercise [its] moral leadership in this vital instance of religious persecution." The State Department was not, however, prepared to be pushed into action. Acting Secretary of State Dean Acheson was reluctant to comment on the matter at all in October 1946, and, in the spring of 1947, he replied to Senator Wagner that "it [was] not possible ... for this Government to intervene effectively in a matter ... regarded by the Yugoslav Government as an internal affair," since Stepinac was "a Yugoslav citizen who [had] been convicted by the Yugoslav authorities for violation of their laws."[48]

In spite of Acheson's reluctance to become involved in Yugoslav internal affairs, the attitude of the American people was changing towards the Soviet Union and the Communist nations. In the previous spring, the American people had been shocked by the hostility towards the Soviet Union demonstrated by Churchill's "Iron Curtain" speech. By the fall, thanks in part to the campaign carried on by the Catholic Church, the public had been made aware of the way in which the Communists treated religion in eastern Europe, especially in Yugoslavia.

The Republicans were the first to respond to this by using anti-communism as an issue in the congressional elections of 1946. Their successful campaign was reinforced by a speech to the American Legion on 27 October 1946 by FBI director J. Edgar Hoover, who spoke of insidious communist control of trade unions, the press, radio and films within the United States. Truman and the Democrats only took up the anti-communist issue on the eve of the election, as a result of which they lost control of Congress. By the beginning of 1947 anti-communism was prominent in the American public mind, being an issue in the trade unions, in the press and on the radio, as well as in the churches.

Stepinac's trial also elicited statements of concern from Canadian Catholics. From the end of September 1946 until the first week of February 1947, the Department of External Affairs in Ottawa received a total of eighty-eight letters or telegrams regarding the trial of the archbishop of Zagreb, all in one way or another calling on the Canadian government to intervene. What is striking is that, of these eighty-eight pieces of correspondence, two were from Croatian immigrant groups, seven were from English Catholic bodies and the remaining seventy-nine appeals came from French-Canadian Catholic organizations in Quebec.[49] The threat to the church in eastern Europe struck a responsive note only in French Canada, possibly because the archbishop of Quebec had been the only representative from Canada to attend the 1946 consistory. Other protests arose in Latin America, from Chile and from Argentina, from the hierarchy of Australia, and from Ireland, where the Dáil adopted a motion calling on all nations to work for the principle of religious liberty as an inalienable human right.

While Communist parties were not serious contenders for political power in these countries, they were serious players in Europe where, interestingly, far less attention was paid to the Stepinac trial. The trial did not generate much interest outside Catholic circles in Italy, which only republished the protests from the United States and Britain.[50] Nor did it receive more than cursory attention in the French press. Both the French government and the French church, for whom the issue of collaborating clergy was too close and too uncomfortable, kept silent over the Stepinac affair. *La Croix* did not report the Stepinac arrest until one week after it had occurred and, at first, did not report the trial directly or comment on it. Its initial reports on the trial consisted of repeating what the *New York Herald Tribune*, *Quotidiano*, Vatican Radio, or the *Osservatore Romano* had said about it. It was, in fact, only with the sentencing of Stepinac in mid-October that *La Croix* made the story their own and, in a front page report, indicated that the Stepinac trial had "profoundly moved Anglo-Saxon opinion and, in France itself, had opened the most skeptical eyes to the designs and the methods of Communism."[51] During the following ten days, *La Croix* carried a series of reports on the international reaction to the condemnation of Stepinac. While American, British, Brazilian, Peruvian, and Vatican reactions were listed and described, any statement of French reaction was notable only for its absence.

THE UNNOTICED TRIAL OF FATHER TISO IN CZECHOSLOVAKIA

Where the Vatican was interested in encouraging international reaction to the trial of Archbishop Stepinac, such was not the case when Father Josef Tiso, the wartime president of Slovakia, was brought to trial three months after Stepinac, in December 1946. This trial represented an attempt by Communist politicians to embarrass the Catholic Church and to interfere with President Beneš's attempts to effect a reconciliation between Czechs and Slovaks. Consequently, the church, who accepted Tiso's guilt, sought to play down the importance of the trial both within Czechoslovakia and throughout the rest of the world.

By the spring of 1946 the Vatican wanted Monsignor Ritter to return to his position as nuncio to Czechoslovakia. Ritter understood Czechoslovakia and had considerable influence with many government officials, including Beneš with whom he had worked before the war. The nomination of candidates for appointment to important episcopal vacancies, such as the primatial see of Prague which had been left unfilled following the death of Cardinal Karel Kaspar in 1941, required the authority of a nuncio. The presence of a nuncio could also be important during the forthcoming trial of Tiso. Because of the importance of getting Ritter to Prague, the Vatican proposed to appoint him as an internuncio, which did not require that he be recognized as dean of the diplomatic corps. This arrangement being acceptable to both the Czechoslovak government and the Russians, Ritter presented his credentials to Beneš on 19 June 1946.[52] The Czechoslovak government reciprocated by appointing M. Maixner as ambassador to the Holy See in early August of that year. The appointment was ideal, since he had worked in the Czechoslovak foreign ministry in 1935 and had been instrumental in implementing the *modus vivendi* between the Prague government and the Vatican before the war. Pius XII was delighted with the appointment which represented the Vatican's first success in re-establishing diplomatic relations with one of the countries under Soviet control.[53]

Ritter's first task was the appointment of a new archbishop of Prague who would also serve as the primate of Czechoslovakia. In December 1946 Monsignor Josef Beran was named to the post. This was a popular and effective appointment since Beran had a good wartime record of opposition to the Nazis, and had spent much of the war in a Nazi concentration camp. Also, unlike previous archbishops of Prague who had usually been Austro-German, Beran was himself a Czech. In the spring of 1947 he was cautiously optimistic about the future of the church in Czechoslovakia. He knew that he had the support of Beneš and the government and he intended to work to establish better relations with the Slovak clergy and hierarchy.[54] In January 1947 the British minister to the Holy See commented in his annual report that "generally speaking, the Catholic Church had less to complain of in Czechoslovakia than under any other Communist regime."[55]

The first postwar elections in Czechoslovakia had been held on 26 May 1946. Each party mounted its own slate of candidates and the elections were conducted fairly. After the war the Slovak Peoples' party had been banned because of its association with the Tiso regime, leaving the Slovakian Communist party (KSS) and the Slovak Democrats, initially based in the Lutheran community, as the only specifically Slovakian parties. By the time of the elections, the Slovak Catholic community and the former members of the Peoples' party had found new political homes. Some had been recruited by the KSS, thereby inserting the issue of Slovak nationalism into Communist party deliberations. The bulk of the Catholics, however, had entered the Slovak Democratic party when that party opened its ranks to Catholic laity and clergy in March 1946. The potency of this Catholic community and Catholic vote was demonstrated in the election when the Slovak Democrats won 62 percent of the Slovak vote against 30.3 percent for the Slovak Communists. The combined vote for the Czech and Slovak Communists was 37.9 percent, however, which made them the largest single party in the national coalition. After the election, Klement Gottwald, the leader of the Communist party, was appointed prime minister.

Gottwald had been shocked by the active Catholic support given to the Slovak Democrats. After he became prime minister he sought to restrict Slovak autonomy and to remind the Czechs and Slovaks of the collaborationist role of the Catholic Church. For this reason, he planned to stage a public trial for Father Tiso in the latter part of 1946. Prime Minister Gottwald sought to isolate the Slovak Catholics, while President Beneš, Internuncio Ritter, and Archbishop Beran sought their reconciliation. This reconciliation was directly threatened by the trial of Tiso, which culminated in his conviction and death on the gallows in April 1947. One scholar referred to the Tiso trial as the trial of "Slovak independence."[56]

In line with their support for the aspirations of Beneš, Vatican officials let it be known well in advance of the Tiso trial that they had little sympathy for the former priest-president. In November 1945 Tardini informed an American diplomat that Tiso had accepted the presidency of Slovakia without consulting the Holy See and that he had carried out Jewish persecutions on Nazi orders in spite of the "vehement protests" of the Vatican. The best that Tardini was prepared to ask for him was a fair trial.[57]

While the Czechoslovak Communists expected that the evidence of Tiso's collaboration would discredit the Catholic Church, President Beneš and the leadership of the church hoped that this sorry tale would be quickly told and soon forgotten. There was little justification for the collaboration of the Tiso regime. What none of them expected was that the Slovak emigration in North America would take up Tiso's case and defend his actions just as the Croats were doing for Archbishop Stepinac. From the time of the First World War, the Czech and Slovak communities in the United States had participated in the founding and the sustenance of the Czechoslovak republic. They had been instrumental in the 1918 Pittsburgh agreement and in the interwar years had sent financial assistance to their home communities. In 1938 Father Tiso had visited the United States to secure the support of American Slovak groups for Slovak autonomy.

In the summer of 1945, on the suggestion of Archbishop Spellman, the Slovak Catholic Federation of America sponsored the creation of the American Slovak Catholic Religious Relief Association, designed to provide financial and moral support for Slovakian Catholics in the postwar turmoil. It sought to raise funds and to secure the support of the American Catholic hierarchy for the cause. A delegation of Americans of Slovak extraction visited Slovakia from September to November 1946 to see for themselves the condition of the Slovaks.[58]

As Tiso's trial approached, Monsignor Carroll of the National Catholic Welfare Conference told his press office to prepare for the trial. By late 1946 he was well aware of the interest and protests generated in Catholic circles by the trial of Stepinac and he wanted to be ready in the event that Tiso's trial generated similar interest. The press office knew that, while the Vatican had not looked upon Tiso's career with enthusiasm, he was venerated by American Slovaks as a national hero who had achieved that Slovak autonomy which many nationalists felt should have been rightfully theirs after 1918.[59] Slovak nationalists in the United States sought a press campaign in defence of Tiso which would argue that "his only sin is that he loves his God, his Church and his people," which "is treason behind the Iron Curtain in Slovakia."[60]

The planned press campaign on Tiso's behalf was never started, however, because the Vatican itself took preventive action to nip it in the bud. Three days after the beginning of Tiso's trial, apostolic delegate Cicognani informed Carroll, and through him the bishops of the United States, that "in the event that the circumstances of the trial make it necessary to inform the public, it should be kept in mind that the Holy See never welcomed the fact that this priest assumed the powers of government in Slovakia, and showed this attitude by a position of constant reserve in his regard. Moreover on the occasion of the anti-semitic persecutions the Holy See protested and intervened repeatedly. These efforts on the part of the Holy See were rewarded with a measure of success." Cardinal Stritch advised Carroll that the Slovaks could be expected to protest vigorously when the trial took place in earnest. "If we could only get to our Catholic Press a right word," commented the cardinal, "it would save us from being put in a very embarrassing position."[61]

The Vatican was concerned about the effect of Tiso's trial on Beneš's attempts to bring Czechs and Slovaks together. As the trial neared its conclusion, the Vatican hoped that Tiso, if convicted, would not be executed, since this would only embitter the Slovaks and the expatriate Slovak lobby. Since the bulk of the Slovak lobby was in the United States, the American bishops were once again summoned into action. On 17 April 1947 Cicognani sent Carroll a report from the Secretariat of State "regarding the situation in Slovakia and the effects of the activities of various Slovak Leagues in the United States." He asked Carroll to pass the report along to those bishops in whose dioceses these leagues were active and suggested that "the Bishops may find it possible to discreetly direct the dependable leaders of these groups." Cardinal Stritch agreed to comply but felt that any effective restraint would have to wait for emotions associated with the execution of Tiso to die down.[62]

14 Vatican Resistance to the Division of Europe

In spite of the Italian peace treaty, the Vatican were well satisfied with political developments in Italy in the spring of 1947. The relationship between the Lateran Agreements and the new constitution had been placed before the Italian Constituent Assembly in 1946 and assigned to a sub-commission for study. The Christian Democrats wanted the Lateran Treaty and the concordat both written into the constitution, while the Communists, although willing to be conciliatory, were only prepared to write in the concordat. On 18 December 1946 the sub-commission had accepted a formula on the Lateran Agreements:

The State and the Catholic Church are independent and sovereign, each in its own sphere.

Their relations are governed by the Lateran Pacts.

Any modification of these relations, which may be bilaterally accepted, will not require the procedure of constitutional revision, but will be submitted to the normal procedure of ratification.

On the sub-commission, the Italian Communist party had supported the first paragraph and the third, but had opposed the second because they wanted only the concordat to be mentioned; the Christian Democrats had opposed the third paragraph. The result was that only the first paragraph had been approved by the sub-commission when the matter was referred back to the Constituent Assembly.

On 20 February 1947 Togliatti made a conciliatory speech in the assembly, in which he said that the Communist party could cooperate with the Christian Democrats over the Lateran Agreements, although he had trouble with the fact that the original pacts had been signed by the Fascists. He suggested that the pacts be reworked and signed anew by the Republican government. The Catholic press responded that the insertion of the Lateran Agreements into the constitution would be a republican reaffirmation of their validity. In early March, Togliatti said that he considered the relationship between church and state to be substantially solved, and that the party did not intend to reopen this debate.[1]

The vote on the Lateran pacts was taken on 25 March when substantially the same statement as had been prepared by the sub-commission was adopted as article 5 of the Italian constitution. In the voting, the Christian Democrats, the Communist party, and Uomo Qualunque party supported the inclusion while the Socialists and the Social Democrats opposed it. Both the Christian Democrats and the Vatican were delighted with the outcome in spite of the fact that the Catholic Church was uncomfortable at finding itself in the debt of the Communist party.[2] The incorporation of the Lateran Agreements into the new Italian constitution assured the Vatican of the political and territorial security which it had been seeking since the end of the war.

BETRAYAL BY WASHINGTON

The international success of the Vatican's campaign in favour of Archbishop Stepinac had been coupled in the winter of 1946–7 with evidence that the American government was becoming more outspoken about the danger of communism and less willing to trust the Soviets. Certainly, Secretary of State James Byrnes had changed his position. In 1945 Byrnes had tried to continue Roosevelt's policy of appeasing the Russians, but by September 1946 he realized that this policy was achieving few results. In a speech at Stuttgart, he had committed himself to the necessity of taking a hard line with Moscow. The Holy See had good reason to believe that once negotiations resumed for a German peace treaty in 1947, the United States would reject Soviet demands for harsh treatment of the Germans.

One important factor in changing Byrnes's outlook had been the difficulty of dealing with the Soviet foreign minister, Vyacheslav Molotov at the Paris peace conference. At the end of that conference, Monsignor Howard Carroll, the national secretary of the National Catholic Welfare Conference, met Byrnes in Paris. The latter wanted Carroll to assure the pope that the United States "has now come to the conclusion that an ever stronger stand must be taken against Soviet efforts at international dictatorship and aggression." "Very much concerned and extremely annoyed about the arrest and trial of Archbishop Stepinac," Byrnes believed "that Jugoslavia is being used by the Soviet merely as a testing-ground for Soviet policy in occupied countries." He wanted Carroll to tell the Vatican that the American government accepted the wisdom of the warnings which the Vatican and American Catholics had been issuing since the end of the war. [3]

The central international issue for the Catholic Church was now the German peace treaty. At their November 1946 annual meeting, the American bishops expressed their concern for the fate of the German people, calling for respect for the rights of prisoners of war and of displaced peoples, particularly those millions of Germans who had been uprooted from eastern Europe "by agreement among the victors" and were "forced from their homes, without resources, into the heart of Germany." [4]

Apart from the favourable outcome in Italy, the year 1947 did not unfold as the Holy See had anticipated. The harsh winter of 1946–7 threatened the economic collapse of western Europe, and in February Great Britain asked the United States to take over its responsibilities in the Greek civil war. The active return of the United States to European affairs was heralded by President Truman's offer of support for Greece and Turkey and his call for the containment of communism in the Truman Doctrine of March 1947. Being most concerned about the economic survival of western Europe, the United States realized that only the full restoration of the industry of the western zones of Germany and its integration with the economy of the other nations of western Europe and North America would ensure the necessary economic turnabout. At the Council of Foreign Ministers meeting in Moscow in May 1947, the United States had to choose between securing an acceptable peace treaty with Germany by compromising with the Soviet desire for a Germany which would remain economically weak, or breaking off the negotiations for a German treaty in order to rebuild the industry of the western zones. By choosing the latter course in Moscow, the United States ensured the continued division of Germany and of Europe for the forseeable future and the deferral of a German peace treaty for over forty years. In June 1947 the Marshall Plan outlined the nature of American assistance for the economic revival of the European continent.

The Vatican was stunned by these developments. Roman Catholicism, as the dominant religion of Europe, was an essential component of European culture. This division of Europe forced half the Catholics of Europe to live under permanent Soviet or Communist rule. The hostility which communism had already shown to Catholicism ensured that the sufferings of the church in eastern Europe, once it had been abandoned to the Soviets, were only at a beginning. The initial response of the Holy See in the summer of 1947 was a cry of anguish and an attempt to counteract the intended division of Europe by seeing opportunities for cooperation between East and West where it had previously seen none. The Holy See began to argue that it was possible to cooperate in Europe in spite of the existence of Communist governments in the East and that Europeans were indeed capable of looking after their own affairs.

The pope's frustration was expressed in his name-day address of 2 June 1947, in which he deplored the conflict that had marked the first six months of the year and was particularly bitter about Allied policy towards Germany. Allied concern about security was denying to Germany the possibility of a return of prosperity and liberty. The Allies were, in fact, using the same methods as the Nazis in their treatment of Germany. The pope was upset by the ruins, the deportations, and the population transfers of the Germans and outlined his belief "that the deepening crisis in Europe has reached the state where, if public order within states and normal relations between states are not soon established, there may be no further opportunity to establish world security." He called for the urgent reconstruction of Europe rather than its division.[5]

George Marshall's speech of 5 June, announcing the European recovery program, was better received at the Vatican. At the same time there was a sense in the Vatican that the policy of containment may have resulted from its own anti-communism being misunderstood. Consequently, to rectify the situation the Vatican sought to clarify its own position. The goal of the papacy was to secure respect for the position and role of the Roman Catholic Church. If the Polish government and other governments of eastern Europe accorded humane treatment to the church, they could be recognized as members of the European family and this would undermine the centrifugal forces that were in operation. Moreover, if the Holy See were to promote East-West harmony and cooperation, the incipient division of Europe as a secular manifestation of the spiritual Cold War might be stillborn.

The crisis of 1947 elicited divergent responses within the Roman Curia. The pope was concerned about the welfare of Italy and Germany while Monsignor Tardini believed that it was most important to oppose the extension of Russian influence and Communist power in eastern and western Europe. Tardini was quoted as saying that today, "it is the invasion of Greece by the Slavs, tomorrow it will be the turn of Italy."[6] The conservative Tardini was inclined to sympathize with the anti-communist political right. Monsignor Montini, on the other hand, sympathized with the Catholic political left, as represented by the French MRP and the Italian Christian Democrats, both parties having been willing to cooperate with communism for the reconstuction of Europe. Montini believed that it was possible to cooperate with communists politically while opposing them spiritually.

Between these two approaches, much depended on the position of Pius XII. In 1945 and 1946 the pope had been strongly anti-communist, by drawing attention wherever possible to the threat of communism and the brutalities that it was perpetrating in eastern Europe. The political cooperation within the tripartite governments of France and Italy during this period reflected more the interests and inclinations of Montini than of either Tardini or the pope. Yet when it became apparent in the spring of 1947 that American policy was working against the reunification of Germany, the pope was prepared to give Montini his head to direct Vatican policy in such a way that it would underwrite the reintegration of Europe, which was inherent in the original Marshall Plan proposal. The Vatican came out in the summer of 1947 against political and territorial polarization and in favour of international cooperation for peace and development.

Montini's reorientation of Vatican policy away from a dogmatic anti-communism was supported and encouraged by France. Like the Vatican, the French also had been taken aback by the American decision to incorporate western Germany into western Europe. Georges Bidault recognized that the unity and importance of Europe would be sacrificed to East-West polarization should the Americans pursue their course of action toward permanent division of Germany. Maritain, who had great theological and political influence with Montini, supported the undersecretary in his endeavours in the summer of 1947.

The redefinition of Vatican policy was developed through a series of four articles in the *Osservatore Romano* in June, written by its editor, Count della Torre. These articles created a sensation because della Torre warned against the polarization of Europe and the mind-set that could lead to the outbreak of a third world war. The Vatican had always opposed the atheistic materialism of communism on the spiritual plane but it had never advocated that this opposition be continued in the realm of practical politics; it had certainly not suggested in any way that the conflict should be settled by war. It was quite possible to oppose communism spiritually and at the same time, argued della Torre, to cooperate with the Soviet Union for the pacification of Europe.

While many observers perceived this to be a dramatic change in policy, the Vatican strenuously denied that it was.[7] Bidault believed that the articles were designed to demonstrate to the Soviet Union that the Vatican was not tied irrevocably to the American point of view.

The Vatican had recognized the military potential of the Soviet Union and, in particular, the way in which its armies could overrun Europe before the United States could react. With greater hostility between the two power blocs, the Vatican was positioning itself to be able to mediate and to avoid war in Europe. Bidault believed that the symptoms of a conflict were becoming more and more ominous.[8]

Della Torre had worked in cooperation with Montini and had the approval of the pope. Montini spoke warmly of della Torre's articles and reacted strongly against those who attacked the Vatican for advocating the conciliation of communism. At the same time, those who subscribed to other views, such as Papée, the continuing Polish ambassador to the Holy See, were resentful of della Torre's position, which they feared would have a disastrous effect on American Catholics and would disconcert their strong anti-Soviet views. Maritain supported della Torre in a speech on 14 July, when he argued that the pope was indeed being consistent since, during the war, he had refused to participate in Hitler's planned anti-Bolshevik crusade against the Soviet Union. Maritain's speech was extensively quoted in subsequent articles in the *Osservatore Romano*, where the Marshall Plan was praised as an important vehicle for the assurance of European peace.[9] In opposing the division of Europe, the Vatican had staked out a position of neutrality between communism and anti-communism in the developing Cold War. Yet this neutrality was to be of short duration, lasting only through the summer and fall of 1947.

One factor in the 1947 distress of the Vatican was the indication that President Truman intended to terminate Myron Taylor's mission. In what was part of an earlier American plan to withdraw from European affairs after the war, the Truman administration had decided to scale down its diplomatic relations with the Holy See and, once the Italian peace treaty had been signed, to eliminate the position of personal representative to the pope and the American office to the Vatican. Foreign service officer Graham Parsons would be assigned to the American embassy to Italy with responsibility for relations with the Vatican and, once Taylor stopped going to Rome, Parsons would continue to maintain American contact with the Vatican. Catholic leaders were upset when they learned of this plan, especially Cardinal Spellman, who threatened Myron Taylor with Catholic displeasure should the plan be implemented.[10]

On 4 April, Truman announced that Taylor would not be returning to the Vatican for some time. At the Holy See, Osborne thought the decision was a mistake and that the anti-Vatican campaign by the American Protestants was "the more to be deplored since it plays the game of the Moscow propagandists in their attacks on the Vatican, which include the charge that Myron Taylor has acted as the liaison between the Vatican reactionaries and the American capitalists and imperialists."[11]

Taylor informed the pope that, although assigned to the United States embassy to Italy, Parsons would be designated as Taylor's assistant with responsibility for Vatican affairs. This arrangement was totally unacceptable to the Vatican. Tardini produced a telegram on 7 May containing Truman's assurances to Spellman that such a double assignment would never happen.[12] Truman, on the other hand, denied that he had ever given Spellman such assurances. Since the president intended to designate 30 June 1947 as the date for the final ending of the war, he felt that the position of personal representative to the pope should expire at that time, since it had been initiated as a wartime measure. In this way, the elimination of the Vatican office could be explained as part of the legal exercise of winding up the war and, in that sense, would cause less offence to American Catholics.[13] The Vatican thus felt that it had been doubly betrayed by the United States in the summer of 1947.

INCREASING POLARIZATION IN FRANCE

The increased polarization of Europe in 1947 was reflected in domestic polarization within France and marked by the ending of the postwar tripartite governments and the re-emergence of Charles de Gaulle as a force on the French right. In fact, it was the domestic situation within France which encouraged Bidault and Maritain to support Vatican opposition to the forces which were splitting Europe in the summer of 1947.

Relations between France and the Vatican had been cool during the winter of 1946–7. The close relationship between France and the Soviet Union had concerned the Vatican, which was worried about the French position in the event of a conflict between Russia and the United States. At the same time, the domestic fortunes of the Communist party had improved while those of the Catholic MRP had declined. The constitution of the Fourth Republic was approved by referendum in October 1946, following which elections were held on 10 November for a new national assembly. In spite of support from the church hierarchy, the MRP slipped in the polls and the Communists gained slightly to become the largest party in the legislature. The tripartite coalition nevertheless continued.

Following the election, *La Croix* began to comment more openly and ideologically on the French domestic scene. It warned against being deceived by the "embourgeoisement" of the Communists, who would create a totalitarian bureaucracy if they had sole power. It chastised Catholics for not voting against the forces of materialism in the recent elections and hoped that they would heed the pope's warning about the great wave of materialism that was sweeping across Europe. By December, *La Croix* was commenting on the polarization between a left-wing Communist bloc and an anti-Communist bloc supported by the capitalists, suggesting that Catholics should avoid active support of either side. Catholics should instead "work on the national and international level to install a new order 'on a human scale' and on a Christian scale."[14]

The international situation had an impact on French domestic politics when the enunciation of the Truman Doctrine was followed by the political re-emergence of de Gaulle. On 7 April de Gaulle rejected the regime of the political parties and founded a new anti-parliamentary political movement, the Rassemblement du Peuple Français (RPF). In de Gaulle's view, the regime of the parties and, especially tripartite governments, left the door open to the extension of communist influence in France.

The return of de Gaulle and the founding of the RPF presented the leaders of the MRP with a dilemma. The MRP had emerged from the "Spiritual Resistance" during the war and, in the immediate postwar, had been prepared to open and develop a Christian-Marxian dialogue through cooperation with the French Communist party. The MRP opposed the atheism of the party but shared its suspicions of French capitalism. Through cooperation with the left, the MRP had increased its influence with the peasantry, the petit bourgeoisie, and the workers. It was therefore unlikely to break willingly with the Communist party. The founding of the Rassemblement and the climate of East-West confrontation in the spring of 1947 placed tripartite cooperation under severe challenge.

De Gaulle's movement attracted the French right, including many Catholics who had formerly supported Pétain. There was, in fact, a threat that the Rassemblement might replace the MRP as the Catholic party of France. Much depended on the nature of the anti-communism of the RPF and the degree to which the MRP would be branded with "red collaboration." The concern of the MRP was such that they asked the pope not to recommend that French Catholics support the RPF. The MRP was caught between the obvious popularity and prestige of de Gaulle, which meant that they could not attack him or his movement directly, and the apparent shift of support of the Vatican and the French hierarchy away from them. The Vatican was losing patience with the MRP, which had cooperated with French communism and had been unwilling to follow the Vatican line in ameliorating the position of Italy and Germany in the peace negotiations. Now that there was the prospect of a new movement led by such a devout Catholic as de Gaulle and one which would not appease the Communists, the Vatican and the French hierarchy could be expected to shift their support away from the MRP towards the political right. The concern of Bidault and Maritain to encourage the Vatican to oppose European polarization in the summer of 1947 therefore had associated domestic implications for France.

The editorial writers of *La Croix*, echoing the *Osservatore Romano*, deplored the way that Russian hostility and the Truman Doctrine had frozen the peacemaking process before a final settlement with Germany had been reached. *La Croix* lamented that the failure of the Moscow foreign ministers' meeting in the spring of 1947 would only enhance the polarization and bring closer the danger of war. Once again, in June 1947, *La Croix* argued against polarization, suggesting there were not two but three poles of attraction:

There is not an inhuman and materialist front on one side and a human and spiritual front on the other. In reality, there are three groups of forces. There are those forces animated by Marxist materialism. There are those forces animated by liberal materialism in its social, economic and political forms. There are sane forces animated by a true humanism which wishes for legitimate and disinterested motives to oppose Communist atheism. This third force takes great care to avoid close solidarity with those forces that are only interested in advancing their profits.[15]

On 5 May the Socialist prime minister Paul Ramadier, noting Communist support for the spring strikes in France and aware of the changed American policies, removed the Communist ministers from his government. The era of tripartism in France had come to an end, with the Communist party in opposition on the left and the Rassemblement in opposition on the right. The MRP and the Socialists now devoted their attempts to shoring up the political centre.

TURNABOUT IN POLAND

Perhaps the most significant change in the Vatican position in 1947 occurred in relation to Poland. As the Holy See had waited for German peace negotiations in 1946, it had expected that one of the terms of these negotiations, if the Allied ties with the Soviet Union could be broken, would involve the restoration of territory to Germany, particularly East Prussia and the territories which had been ceded to Poland. Since an acceptable German treaty would have to be made at the expense of Poland, the Holy See had been reluctant to commit itself to recognizing the Polish government or to working out a modus vivendi with it. In fact, the Holy See believed that the German peace settlement would necessitate a new government in Poland with which the Vatican could more easily deal. Poland should expect to make the sacrifice for the future good of Europe. Yet with the failure of German peace negotiations and the division of Europe, the Holy See changed its position towards the Polish government and demonstrated a willingness to accept the legitimacy of that government as a partner for negotiation.

Polish parliamentary elections were scheduled for 19 January 1947. While seeking to enhance its control over Polish politics, the Communist party (PPR), resigned itself to the impossiblity of convincing Mikolajczyk and the Peasant party (PSL) to join the government bloc for the elections. Consequently, the PPR sought to destroy the PSL as an effective force before the elections took place. From October 1946 to January 1947, leaders of the popular Peasant party were subjected to assassination, harassment, and arrest.[16] At the same time the government made a determined effort to open talks with either the Polish hierarchy or the Vatican in order to secure the Catholic vote in these elections. As part of this process, it was important to wean the Catholic vote away from the Peasant party.

The government sought to capitalize on its lenient treatment of the church to secure electoral support. Wladyslaw Wolski, the minister for repatriation, approached Cardinal Hlond, who referred him to the auxiliary bishop of Warsaw, Monsignor Choromanski, for discussions. These talks were broken off, however, as a result of the 20 October pastoral from the Polish hierarchy in which Catholics were instructed not to vote for or represent a party or a bloc opposed to Christian doctrine whose programs or methods were contrary to the good of the nation, of Christian morals, or of the Catholic outlook.[17]

President Bierut made a conciliatory gesture in a newspaper interview in November, stressing government respect for the church and his hope that a durable agreement could be reached with that institution. Following the interview, a group of young Catholics, close to Piasecki and the newspaper Dzis i Jutro issued a statement calling for a rapprochement between church and state. These Catholics identified themselves as the "Catholic Group" and stated that they intended to put forward Catholic lists in the election, with the avowed purpose of showing "the Kremlin that the Communists are not the only people in Poland with whom it is possible for the Soviet Union to collaborate." The bishops were horrified by this division in Catholic ranks and refused to recognize that the new Catholic Group spoke for Catholic interests, even when three of its members were elected to the new parliament in January.[18]

Cardinal Hlond went to Rome in November to consult Pius XII about how the Polish church should respond to these overtures. The cardinal believed that the government was serious about wanting to reach an agreement, but was being constrained, either by the Russians or by the hostile atmosphere which existed between the Holy See and the Slav world.[19] Vatican officials felt negotiations with the Polish government at this time would be premature, since they expected Moscow to agree to a change of regime in Poland at the forthcoming foreign ministers' conference in order to obtain concessions in other areas. Hlond returned from Rome less disposed to reach accommodation, believing that the government might only be in office temporarily and therefore that the Church should maintain its independence from the government.

The January elections resulted in a triumphant victory for the Communist-dominated government bloc which secured over 80 percent of the official vote. The victory had been brought about partly by the use of the state security apparatus to limit the electoral influence of the Peasant party and partly because the Communists retained control of the electoral commissions which counted the ballots. The Peasant party and the other opposition parties were spent forces after January 1947 and, from that time on, state power was clearly in the hands of the Communists and their Socialist allies. After the elections the Roman Catholic Church was the only remaining internal opposition to the Communist government.

Since the end of the war the Holy See had prevented the Polish hierarchy from taking up serious discussions with the Warsaw government. As it became clear in 1947, however, that there was not likely to be a German peace treaty for some time, the Vatican changed its position and was itself willing to open negotiations with Warsaw. Yet in so doing, it failed to consult the hierarchy who once again found that the concrete needs of Poland were being ignored in the interests of broader European policy. In its new outlook, the Vatican met strong resistance from the leaders of the Polish church, demonstrating how little sympathy really existed in Rome for Polish sensibilities.

Before the January elections the Polish ambassador to Italy had approached the papal nuncio in Rome and asked him to convey to the Vatican the willingness of the Polish government to send a negotiator to Rome. The Vatican had agreed to receive a negotiator but it was not until after the elections that the government sent Ksawery Pruszynski, a left-wing Catholic journalist, to Rome where he obtained assistance from Jacques Maritain in making contact with Vatican officials. Pruszynski met Tardini and offered guarantees of liberty for the church and freedom of education but was advised that no further discussions would be possible unless the Polish government changed its attitude towards the role of Pius XII during the Second World War.[20] As a result, in March *Polonia d'Oggi*, the information bulletin of the Polish embassy in Rome, recognized the patriotic role of the Polish clergy during the German occupation and hoped for a call by the pope for a rallying of Catholics to the Polish government similar to the call of Leo XIII to the Third French Republic in the 1890s. Shortly after Pruszyn-ski's return to Warsaw, Bierut claimed to have been enlightened by him of ways in which Pius XII had helped Poland during the war. This public recognition by the Polish president resulted in an article in *Il Quotidiano*, the mouthpiece of the Secretariat of State, which sup-ported the new western frontier of Poland and the Polish annexation of Silesia. By June 1947 a cautious improvement was noted in relations between Poland and the Vatican.[21]

This change in Vatican policy had materialized without consultation with Polish church leaders and alarmed the Polish hierarchy. Cardinal Sapieha, more sympathetic to the Polish government than Hlond, went to Rome in May 1947 to outline for Pius XII what the hierarchy con-sidered the minimum conditions for any agreement with Warsaw. Sapieha learned that the Vatican genuinely wanted an agreement with Poland and cautioned that the liberties enjoyed by Polish Catholics were limited on the religious plane and did not extend to politics. While the government did not attack religious education directly, it sought to limit it wherever possible. The recent nationalization of Catholic printers and the rationing of paper for the Catholic press had the effect of restricting Catholic activity.[22] The pope assured Sapieha that he would never accept a concordat with Poland which had been extracted by threats to the Polish church and informed him that the Vatican had placed such conditions on Poland through the Pruszynski negotiations that it was not expected there would be any real agree-ment for some time. The Vatican were even prepared to allow the Polish episcopate to determine the most appropriate moment for reach-ing an agreement.[23]

In spite of these assurances, negotiations between Poland and the Holy See continued without any representative of the Polish hierarchy being present. In May, Hlond indicated that he was not impressed by the Catholic credentials of Pruszynski, and suspected that the Vatican might sacrifice the interests of the Polish church for an agreement with the Polish government. On 5 June he issued a pastoral letter, in which he warned the faithful to resist the threat of paganism and atheism and to protect the traditions of Polish Catholics. He offered this warning in spite of the fact that Pruszynski had returned to Rome and negotiations were reportedly progressing well at the Secretariat of State.[24]

Della Torre's June articles in the *Osservatore Romano* were not well received by members of the Polish emigration such as Papée, the continuing ambassador to the Holy See. Although the Polish hierarchy claimed that the Vatican was still as opposed to communism as ever, observers noted considerable unease among the higher clergy who asserted that the della Torre articles did not represent a strategic change of policy on the part of the Vatican. Rather, they represented a tactical move to enable the Vatican to be in a position to mediate should there be danger of war.[25]

At the same time as the Polish hierarchy felt slighted by the Vatican in the summer of 1947, there was clear evidence of the church's continuing popularity and influence in Poland. Catholics were providing generous financial support to their church, important when the government provided so little. Church attendance was up and there were many new recruits for the priesthood. Support for the church was the one remaining way for Poles to demonstrate their dislike of the government. Polish religious life had blossomed in the territories recovered from Germany, with new recruits to the priesthood and funds provided by the faithful for the reconstruction of churches and the opening of seminaries. This religious enthusiasm was only restrained by Vatican reluctance to develop new dioceses in the "recovered territories" lest, by so doing, they formally recognize the new Polish frontiers.

Because of the strong position of the church inside Poland, the hierarchy became more assertive in its dealings with the government and with the Vatican. On 24 August, *Tygodnik Warszawski*, the recognized newspaper of the episcopate, stated that there must be no official relations between the Vatican and the government "over the heads of the Polish Catholic hierarchy." Following their September meeting at Czestochowa, the bishops issued a pastoral letter which set out their concerns about the actions of the government and managed to interrupt the ongoing negotiations between Warsaw and the Vatican. In the pastoral, which was read in the churches of Poland on 28 September, the bishops enumerated their grievances:

a) that an anti-religious campaign was being carried on by the principal newspapers;
b) that the religious unity of the country was being threatened by the government-subsidized spread of Protestantism;
c) that private and confessional education was being discouraged;
d) that religious education was being hampered in the schools and that new schools were being set up with no religious education at all;
e) that the religious character of Sundays and feast days was being undermined by the call for voluntary work on those days to rebuild the country;

f) that there was pressure on Catholics to support anti-religious political parties; and

g) that the censorship of the Catholic press put Catholics in a position of inferiority in relation to the Protestant and atheist press.

What offended the government was the tone of the pastoral, which compared the "voluntary work" on Sundays and holidays to the forced labour of the Nazi occupation and which called for a re-establishment of the Polish resistance to meet the threat of the present government.[26] Many Catholics were embarrassed by the letter, since there really had been very little persecution of the church and many of the pastoral's complaints sought to protect Catholic privileges rather than to identify cases of persecution.

Government officials did not know how to react initially, since they wanted an agreement with the church and wanted to avoid a major confrontation.[27] Prime Minister Cyrankiewicz responded to the bishops on 29 October that "the government ... would not change its attitude of tolerance towards the Church but at the same time would not allow it to interfere in politics or to destroy the unity of the nation." The government then took two moves against the church: it restricted supplies of paper to five diocesan newspapers; and, in a potentially more serious move, it amended the Law of Association of 1935. Instead of allowing Catholic organizations to be created on the authority of the bishops and to have their executive committees nominated by the bishops, now new Catholic associations had to have their statutes approved by the government and the executive committees had to be elected. Under these circumstances, the church was reluctant to create any new organizations and even considered abolishing existing ones, from fear that their executive committees might "fall into the hands of Government stooges."[28]

Lack of communication between the Vatican and the Polish hierarchy over relations with the Warsaw government meant that the Polish hierarchy had had to resort to a public pastoral to disrupt talks between Warsaw and Rome in order to signify to the Curia that it expected to be included in any future talks.

15 The Impossibility of Vatican Neutrality

The Vatican deplored the division of Europe which resulted from American policy and Soviet reaction in the summer of 1947. Initially, the Vatican sought neutrality, not committing itself to one bloc or the other, until it was eventually forced to confront the reality of the developing Cold War. Because the situation in Italy was always of paramount importance to the Holy See, the call for elections in April 1948 and the Communist strength in that country precluded the possibility of the Vatican being politically neutral there. The Communist takeover of Czechoslovakia in February 1948 gave added urgency to using anti-Communist political organization to avoid a similar coup in Italy. By the summer of 1948, and largely as a result of the Italian election, Pope Pius XII had moved the Vatican into the forefront of the political as well as the spiritual anti-communist forces.

RENEWED TIES WITH THE UNITED STATES

The Marshall Plan salvaged the relationship between Washington and the Vatican. Truman's need to sell the Marshall Plan to the American people and Congress put the American relationship with the Vatican in a new light, since the pope's moral support of the Marshall Plan could help to secure this public approval. Early in July 1947 Truman sent the pope the draft text of a letter which he intended to transmit formally, arguing that any genuine peace must be based on Christian ideals and stating that the United States wanted to cooperate with the Holy See in building such a peace. In August, as a public demonstration of a renewed Washington-Vatican relationship, Truman sent Myron Taylor back to Rome to deliver his letter to the pope and to discuss problems of the peace. It was noteworthy that Truman, in his announcement of Taylor's visit, did not put any time limit on it as he had done in November 1946.[1]

When he received Taylor on 26 August, the pope praised the charity which was being demonstrated by the United States with Marshall Plan aid and discussed ways in which Rome and Washington might cooperate in demonstrating "to those who are hopeless in many places both within the Russian orbit and outside it such assurances that their misfortunes have not been forgotten in the stress of other controversies in states in closer proximity to the western powers and particularly to the United States."[2]

In his letter of reply, the pope rejected appeasement, declaring that the Vatican would now "compromise no principle in the face of Communism. Protection for the Catholic populations would have to be found through resistance, such as is being offered by the Bishops in Poland, rather than by attempted compromises."

The exchange of letters between president and pope was released to the press with maximum publicity. The pope and the Curia were obviously pleased that Truman was finally taking them seriously. The letters were reprinted in six different western languages by the Secretariat of State and distributed throughout Europe. Now the Vatican and the United States were formally aligned on the basis of Christian principle against the spread of communism.

Vatican observers saw the exchange of letters as the equivalent of a religious Marshall Plan, feeling that "Mr Taylor's return to Rome raised the curtain on an effort to mobilize Western Europe on a spiritual plane comparable to an earlier effort on a politico-economic plane (Marshall Plan). The tangible evidence of his trip, the Exchange of Letters, is regarded as an impressive achievement on the part of the United States."[3] Jacques Maritain felt that Taylor's trip had been a complete success in tying the Vatican into support of American foreign policy. According to Maritain, the Vatican had had real problems dealing with Soviet persecution of religion and were only too willing to be asked to support the American containment of communism. It was like plucking ripe fruit.[4]

Once Truman had asked the pope for help, Pius XII made a point of receiving all prominent Americans who requested an audience, especially if they happened to be members of Congress. On 12 November he received Senator George W. Malone, an opponent of the European Recovery Program, and, in a longer audience than expected, discussed the senator's opposition to the program.[5] At Thanksgiving in 1947 the pope addressed a special message to the American people, praising their help for the devastated of Europe by advising them that:

Another Winter is approaching, heartless and relentless, which promises to cut a wide swath through the ruined, ineffectual tenements of hundreds of cities in Europe and the East, opening the way for grim death to follow fast on cold and famine and stark exposure unimpeded. But, no! There stands Christian charity, rising to the full stature of its nobility, to block the path ... Under the tireless leadership of a large-hearted, devoted Hierarchy you, beloved sons and daughters of America, are in the vanguard of that army of Christian charity."[6]

NEUTRALITY BETWEEN EAST AND WEST

In spite of this moral alliance with Washington and in the face of developing East-West hostility, the Holy See still sustained its neutrality between the two halves of divided Europe through the fall and winter of 1947–8. It did not wish to be seen to be supporting either side.

In response to the doctrine of containment and the initiative of the Marshall Plan, representatives of the Communist parties of the Soviet Union, Bulgaria, Czechoslovakia, Hungary, Poland, Romania, Yugoslavia, France, and Italy met at Szklarska Poreba in Poland in September 1947 for the founding meeting of the Communist Information Bureau, also known as the Cominform. Subsequent to this meeting, which tightened Stalin's control over the national Communist parties, Communists throughout Europe became more aggressive and less willing to cooperate with non-Communists. Yet in October the French foreign ministry noted that the Vatican were displaying their tolerance for the Soviet Union together with their intolerance for communism and had recently emphasized their neutrality between East and West by promoting a native of Switzerland to be the new head of the Benedictine Order in preference to a strong American candidate. At the end of the year, the Vatican Secretariat of State sent special instructions to the papal nuncios, affirming that "the Holy See is not for one bloc or the other ... no one must be able to accuse the Holy See of having the intention to undertake a crusade on a single front ... the Vatican is firmly decided to continue all its efforts to safeguard Europe and the world against a new conflict ... the reaction against communists is moral and religious rather than political ... materialist and Marxist communism is the capital enemy of Christian civilization."[7]

In January 1948 the British foreign secretary, Ernest Bevin, made a proposal for strengthening the ties between the nations of western Europe, which resulted in the conclusion of the Brussels Pact of 17 March and the creation of the Western European Union between

Britain, France, and the Benelux countries. The Vatican reacted negatively in January when an article in the *Osservatore Romano* commented that Bevin's proposal meant "the inevitable if regrettable division of Europe into two *blocs*." The newspaper had welcomed the Benelux customs union of 1 January as "the first step towards a wider European union" and had felt that from this union and from the Marshall Plan, "a mighty movement might emerge, which would hasten the rebirth of Western Europe." There were, however, still reservations: "Unluckily ... only one part of Europe seemed to be in question ... while a Western defence system might be under construction, these treaties indicated that there still existed a European system whose vitality was unimpaired ... In terms of peace, there was no East and West; peace was indivisible."

Spurred by the February coup in Czechoslovakia, the American Senate approved funds for the European Recovery Plan in March 1948. Vatican support was not without regrets: "the first reaction of the Vatican to each step which the Western European countries, or the U.S.A., take to restore a sound economy to Western Europe and to protect it from Communist expansion, is to lament the effect which these steps have of solidifying Europe into two *blocs*, even though it follows up its laments by admitting that these steps are inevitable, and even desirable, in the present circumstances."[8]

THE MOBILIZATION OF ITALY IN THE SPIRIT OF JESUS

Neutrality in Europe was an intellectual possibility for the Holy See, but neutrality in Italian politics was a practical impossibility. The Vatican had too much at stake and the situation in Italy helped to move the Holy See away from its neutral position in Europe. The Vatican had been pleased when the Communists and the Socialists were dropped from Italy's tripartite government in May 1947, leaving the Christian Democrats in control. Its pleasure was mixed with concern, however, that the dropping of the left-wing parties was done at the external instigation of the United States as a result of the Truman Doctrine. Vatican officials feared that the move may have been premature and that the Christian Democrats might be too weak politically to control events should the Communists take to the streets.[9]

The initial meeting of the Cominform in September 1947 had resulted in an upsurge of strikes, demonstrations, and public disturbances organized and encouraged by the Communists, in an attempt to destabilize de Gasperi's minority government. The culminating event was a Communist-organized general strike in Rome on 11 and 12

December which prompted de Gasperi to reorganize his government and bring the Republicans and Social Democrats into power with the Christian Democrats.

As the Italian Communist party passed into active parliamentary and extra-parliamentary opposition, the Vatican could not remain neutral. If the Communists and their allies intended to mobilize the working classes and the peasants against the elected parliamentary authorities, then it was important that the Catholic community be mobilized in support of those authorities and of the parliamentary system. With the new republican constitution almost completed, Catholic society must be prepared to prevent the Communists from coming to power either legally or illegally under the new constitution. The mobilization intended by the Vatican was not so much in favour of the Christian Democrats as it was against the threat of a Communist takeover in Italy.

On 7 September, in an address to the faithful in Rome's St Peter's Square, the pope claimed that "the opposing fronts in the religious and moral fields are becoming ever more clearly defined." The tactic of the church was to help define the polarization of Italian society by indicating that no Catholic could be a marxist-socialist and still expect to receive the sacraments. Cardinal Schuster conveyed this message to the faithful of Milan in October. He challenged Togliatti's position that a good Catholic can also be a communist by saying that any Catholic who is also a communist is creating a grave sin and may not receive the sacraments. On 20 November, Schuster followed with a sermon in which he pointed out that "the Church does not demand less of her faithful than that they shall behave in such a fashion that the country may be provided with a Government corresponding to the Catholic sentiments of the nation." He also warned that "these successive strikes, these riotous meetings, these wreckings of premises and factories, these bombs thrown all over the place by unidentifiable people, all this violence forms part of a long-prepared campaign of which the purpose is well-known to everyone: to paralyse the Government so as to provoke a general rising in Italy which would permit the Communists to seize power. Italy would thus become, in her turn, just one more satellite of the dazzling sun of Moscow."[10]

The pope continued this theme in his speeches at the end of 1947, including his year-end Christmas message, in which he "stigmatised as a 'deserter or traitor' ... any Christian who gave his 'material support, services, talent or vote' to parties which deny God, substitute might for right and threats and terrorism for liberty, and make external or internal peace impossible."

At the same time, Pius XII made a deliberate effort to demonstrate that the church and the papacy shared interests with the average

Italian. In a well-publicized audience in November, he received Italy's most prominent cycling stars, Gino Bartali and Fausto Coppi – described by an American as the Italian equivalents of Ted Williams and Joe di Maggio – along with officials of the Italian Sports Centre. He later received a football team and, on another occasion, the Neapolitan comic actor Eduardo de Filippo. All of these audiences received extensive publicity.[11] However, the pope was concerned as to whether the Christian Democrats were doing enough to address issues of social reform so that this area was not left entirely to the parties of the left. Towards the end of 1947 observers noted an increasing insistence of church spokesmen on the need for social justice in Italy.

These clerical statements and activities were highlighted in a call by Father Riccardo Lombardi, the Jesuit editor of *Civiltà Cattolica*, for a general mobilization of all Catholics, laity as well as clergy, "for the revival of the country in the spirit of Jesus." Father Lombardi's exhortation was presented in a series of articles at the end of 1947 which in many ways paralleled the activity of Catholic Action to "stimulate the faithful to the observance of their Catholic and Christian duties."[12]

THE ITALIAN ELECTION OF 1948

On 22 December 1947 the Constituent Assembly approved the new Italian constitution to come into effect on 1 January 1948. Under the constitution, it was necessary to hold elections for a new Chamber of Deputies, scheduled for 18 April. To fight the elections, the Communist and the Socialist parties combined forces with the intention of mounting a single slate as a consolidation of the left against the Christian Democrats; at the same time, the left-wing bloc realized that their main domestic antagonists would be the Vatican and the Catholic Church.

The Vatican mobilized its resources for the campaign. The pope was concerned that the clergy be constitutionally correct in not supporting any political party by name, but at the same time he insisted on the right of the clergy to instruct their flock on the moral issues manifest in the election and to make it clear that the real contest was between communism and anti-communism. Cardinal Schuster gave the Catholic message to the clergy of Milan in February: "It is the grave duty of every Christian to exercise his vote, which should be free and according to conscience. It is a serious offense for the faithful to give their vote to a candidate or a list of candidates that are manifestly contrary to the Church or to the application of religious principles and Christian morality in public life."[13] Later that month, Cardinals Fossati of Turin and Ruffino of Palermo expressed themselves in similar terms. To ensure that all the clergy and members of religious orders cast their vote in the election, the Consistorial Congregation and the Sacred Congregation of the Affairs of the Religious gave instructions that everyone, even cloistered nuns, must vote on 18 April.[14]

One organization which could carry this message to the people was Italian Catholic Action, which was given so much attention by the pope during the winter of 1947-48, that one observer noted that "while in ordinary times Catholic Action is a social and Christian movement, in these extraordinary times its political action and significance is steadily increasing."[15] In late February the central executive of the Union of Catholic Men urged all its members to "campaign actively among their friends and fellow-workers emphasizing that it is the duty of every citizen to vote, to wake up and convince the indifferent and encourage the timid."

The spiritual mobilization of Italian Catholics had to be augmented by political mobilization to ensure success in the election campaign. Inspired by Father Lombardi, civic committees were formed in every parish and diocese of Italy. The committees were a separate creation from Catholic Action, being designed to encourage and assist Catholics to exercise their franchise and to campaign against the marxist parties. Three hundred diocesan and more than eighteen thousand parish committees were created in 1948. On the recommendation of the pope, Luigi Gedda, the president of the men's branch of Catholic Action, was appointed president of the national committee. Gedda had first come to the pope's attention as the organizer of a national Catholic Action rally in September 1947, and in 1948 the American ambassador commented that "many believe that he is the best Catholic organizer in Italy ... in outward appearance he is urgent, serious and tense with conviction as he expresses his point of view." Under Gedda's energetic leadership, the committees were given strong central direction and managed to enlist the support of many national and local notables in their anti-marxist campaign.

The emergence of Lombardi and Gedda represented the creation of a third interest group within the Vatican, distinct from both Montini's group and from the Roman party. They were the pope's men, who enhanced his anti-communist plans and, as such, were to find themselves at times in opposition to both Montini and to the Roman party.[16]

The work of the committees included preparing posters, handbills, films, and newspapers for the campaign and devising transportation systems which would not be dependent on the cooperation of left-wing trade unions. One of the main tasks of all the committees was fundraising, and Gedda also sought funds abroad. Irish Catholics sent funds, as did American Catholics. Funds were also raised from the American government through the Central Intelligence Agency. It was apparently Gedda who convinced the Vatican to encourage American Catholics to write their relatives in Italy to ask them to vote against the marxists. Gedda created an effective political organization which boded well for the church.[17]

The American government and American Catholics shared the concerns of the Vatican about the outcome of the Italian elections. A campaign through the church was devised and Carroll sent a letter to the bishops of the nineteen dioceses with the largest concentrations of Italian-Americans on 11 February. McNicholas had written an editorial on the importance of saving Italy from communism for the February edition of the Cincinatti *Catholic Telegraph-Register* and Carroll saw to it that the Catholic press of the country was informed of this editorial and encouraged to emulate it. The bishops took up the letter-writing campaign with enthusiasm and were also active in organizing crusades of prayer for the outcome of the Italian election.[18]

The Catholic campaign generated a good deal of interest throughout the United States, with plans being developed by various Catholic and non-Catholic groups to help influence the Italian vote. One of these groups felt that the appropriate way to protect Italy was for Truman to apply his doctrine to Italy in the same way that he had applied it to Greece, giving "an explicit guarantee that if Italy is attacked, either directly or indirectly, America will help to defend her." On learning of the development of this campaign, Cicognani, the apostolic delegate in Washington, was well pleased that "the idea already seems to have been well grasped throughout the nation." After the victory of the Christian Democrats in April, Cicognani relayed to Carroll the "deep gratitude" of the Secretariat of State "for the very active and efficient part taken by the NCWC in this campaign and its promotion."[19]

As a result of Communist activism in Italy in the fall of 1947, the United States had issued a warning to the Communist bloc prior to the opening of the election campaign. On 13 December 1947 Truman stated that the United States would not be indifferent to threats to the independence of Italy. During the campaign, the Vatican sought further active American intervention and Graham Parsons, Myron Taylor's assistant in Rome, passed the request along to Washington with the comment that "Vatican suggestions ... merit consideration."[20] Statements by Truman and Marshall in March that American aid to Italy would cease in the event of a Communist party election victory, indicated that these Vatican suggestions had indeed been acted upon. At the beginning of April Truman sent Myron Taylor to Rome to lend his presence to the course of the campaign as well as to maintain relations with the pope during the election campaign and during the possible difficult period to follow.

The Vatican was delighted with the statements by Truman and Marshall which senior officials believed had helped to reverse the defeatist trend among the Italian public resulting from the February coup in Czechoslovakia. Buoyed by these developments, the pope delivered a major address to four hundred thousand people in St Peter's Square on Easter Sunday. In the address the pope reiterated his themes strongly, indicating that "the great hour of the Christian conscience has struck," that "you, beloved sons and daughters, know full well what the alternative signifies and involves for Rome, Italy and the world."[21]

By April the Vatican had abandoned its neutrality between East and West. On 2 April, Count della Torre editorialized in the *Osservatore Romano* on the American Senate's approval of the European Recovery Program. He wrote that it was unfortunate that all states had not accepted the offer to join the plan and that, where the Marshall Plan had originally been a move to restore all of Europe, it now stood as a symbol of the division of that continent. The East, della Torre commented, had rejected the plan on political grounds, not economic. The Vatican now accepted the existence of the two blocs and had real hope for the beneficial development of the West: "Thus ... on the economic plane a fruitful basis of political developments is being constructed, a first seed of the United States of Europe, so the way to clearer political horizons will be opened and the harmonious vision of European collaboration will glitter in the light of peace."

The change in approach was noted inside Italy as well, particularly by Maritain, who was apprehensive about its implications. In a despatch to the Quai d'Orsay, Maritain indicated that Pius XII seemed to have burned his bridges with those Catholics who supported the Communist and Socialist parties and to have taken a crusading stance from which there would be no turning back. The most influential papal advisors during the election had been Gedda and Monsignor Ronca, who had organized the civic committees and were talking early in April of organizing a new super-party which would combine the Christian Democrats with the institutions of Catholic Action. Maritain believed that the Christian Democratic party would be in trouble within the Catholic community should it lose on 18 April.[22] He felt that the Vatican could also find itself in trouble because of the demonstration of recent weaknesses in internal administration[23] and because of the way in which the pope had overplayed his position politically. Maritain reported, presumably from an excellent source, that the pope and Montini were in disagreement on the future head of Catholic Action, with the pope favouring the energetic and political Gedda while

Montini favoured the non-political Veronese. The elections could have major ramifications for Italian Catholicism.

To the pope's great relief, the elections produced a striking victory for the Christian Democrats and excluded the left from participation in the national government. De Gasperi had insisted on retaining the independence of Christian Democracy from clerical control and, for this reason, Montini, his most sympathetic Vatican supporter, had not had any direct contact with the party's electoral strategy. After the election, the pope saw that he could influence and control the voting behaviour of Italians through the continuing use of the civic committee and through the agency of Catholic Action. Such political control could ensure the continued governance by Christian Democracy or at least the exclusion of the marxist parties. Accordingly, it was decided to keep the committees in existence indefinitely "as a permanent anti-Communist public opinion moulding body" for use in future electoral campaigns. After the elections, many members of Catholic Action called for the appointment of Gedda as the national president of that organization in place of the incumbent Veronese, but the pope preferred to retain Gedda as the committees' national president. Gedda, in fact, was looking forward to an international Catholic Action conference scheduled for Lourdes in September 1948 when he intended to explain the program of the civic committee movement in the expectation that it could be adopted in other Catholic countries. He spoke to American officials of the creation of a Catholic Action International.

These developments were not unanimously supported either within Italian Catholicism or within the Vatican itself. The left wing of the Christian Democrats, along with Montini, felt that the elections had placed de Gasperi in a strong position to effect significant social reforms, which in themselves could ensure the continued electoral success of Christian Democracy. On the contrary, many of the supporters of the civic committees were opposed to reform and believed that political organization rather than programs of reform was the way to keep the Communists out of power. There was also the concern within the Christian Democratic party that, because they owed their election to the committees, they would be expected by those groups to fulfil all their election promises. Certainly Gedda felt that the committees should feel free to criticize the Christian Democrats whenever they felt these promises were not being acted upon, lest the committees themselves appear to lose credibility with the voters.[24]

If the fortunes of Montini, de Gasperi, Gedda, and Lombardi were on the rise as a result of the electoral success, the Roman party saw its fortunes fall when Monsignor Ronca was sent to Pompeii as bishop and the party was left without its most active organizer.[25]

In his birthday address in June, the pope praised the work of the civic committees and expounded on the need for Christians to stand firm against their moral opponents, saying that politics and religion must be mixed together by the church as the "politics of the moral order." Integrism had returned to Vatican politics, as the pope seemed intent on attacking the duplicity of liberals and socialists who claimed to be good Catholics yet lent support to the enemies of the church. In this sense, the pope had adopted the ideas of Father Lombardi in rallying the Catholic community to a crusade in defence of their faith. While the pope favoured social reform, he did so rather hesitantly, arguing as much for cooperation in increasing productivity as for fairness in the distribution of the national income. Finally, as an indication of his confidence in the political stability of Italy and in order to encourage this confidence in others, Pius XII announced that plans would now go forward for the celebration of 1950 as a Holy Year.

CATHOLICS AND DE GAULLE'S RASSEMBLEMENT DU PEUPLE FRANÇAIS

At the end of June 1948 a minute of the French Foreign Ministry identified the new Vatican direction as one wherein the Vatican intended to renounce dependence on Catholic political parties in favour of dependence on all anti-communist political forces in a given state. The Vatican would now try to galvanize an alliance of anti-marxist forces in defence of western civilization. It had given up its dependence on Christian Democracy in Italian politics in favour of the organization of the civic committees, just as it was in the process of abandoning the Mouvement Républicaine Populaire (MRP) in French politics and, in line with many French Catholics, was looking to the anti-communism of de Gaulle's Rassemblement du Peuple Français (RPF) to protect the social order.[26]

The political situation in France had also contributed to this changed policy. In June 1947 the MRP had been one of the mainstays of the French government. Yet in the October municipal elections, de Gaulle's RPF won 38 percent of the vote, with particular strength in the large urban centres. The victories of the RPF were largely at the expense of the MRP and indicated that the Catholic vote had shifted to the right. "These elections in fact marked the start of the MRP's decline and the end of its ambitions to become a great popular party."[27] By the end of 1947 a new national governing coalition had been forged, known as the Third Force, bringing together a series of centrist governments uniting the MRP, the Socialist and the Radical parties, and excluding the Communists on the left and the RPF on the right. Third Force governments were largely defensive and, because of the challenge from left and right, held to an innocuous centrist position.

With the rallying of the political right and the fear of communism associated with the wave of strikes in France in November and December, French cardinals and archbishops wrote to the president of the republic on 23 December, asking whether the time had not now arrived to bring the period of the postwar purges to an end and to unite Frenchmen once again.[28] At the same time the newspaper *La Croix* maintained its position that true anti-communism came from helping workers to attain higher standards of living, since communism thrived on social injustice. Following the Italian election of April 1948, the paper reminded the Italian Christian Democrats that so many Italians would not have voted Communist had not the Christian Democrats failed to pay enough attention to social problems.[29]

By the Spring of 1948 the Vatican was giving more and more support to the anti-communism of the RPF. The new conservatism in the Vatican was reflected in hostility to advanced scientific and intellectual views being espoused by French church leaders, most notably Monsignor de Solages, the rector of the Catholic Institute of Toulouse, and Cardinals Salièges and Liénart, whose views were attacked in an officially sanctioned article in the *Osservatore Romano* in March. It was perhaps fitting that Jacques Maritain resigned his ambassadorial post in June 1948 to accept a position at Princeton University; the climate at the Vatican was becoming less sympathetic to his personal outlook and values.

By June 1948 the Vatican had accepted its place at the side of the Americans in opposing the Communist bloc. In western Europe, the Vatican had shifted its support from the Catholic left to the anti-communist right. As the Vatican lined up with the Americans, the Soviet Union felt less hesitation in moving more directly to control the Catholic Church in eastern Europe.

16 Communist Consolidation and Catholic Division

While Communist parties had secured control in Albania, Yugoslavia, Romania, and Bulgaria immediately after the war, such was not the case in Poland, Hungary, and Czechoslovakia. The latter three countries had postwar governments drawn from the parties of the resistance coalition, including the Communists. It was only in 1947 and 1948 that the Communist parties were able to secure one-party control of the governments of these three countries: in Poland after the elections of January 1947, in Hungary after the elections of August 1947, and in Czechoslovakia after the coup d'état of February 1948. These takeovers coincided with the definition of sides in the Cold War through the Truman Doctrine in March 1947 and the founding of the Cominform in September. Given the threatening international situation of late 1947 and Moscow's renewed interest in east European developments, the pressure was on the east European Communist parties to consolidate their hold over their governments and people.

Since the Roman Catholic Church was an important independent institution in each of these three states, consolidation meant reaching some accommodation with the church, to prevent it from leading the people in opposition to the new regimes and to their reform programs. Since the war the church had been left at considerable liberty and had been shown respect and deference by the governments of these three countries. At the beginning of 1948 Monsignor Montini of the Vatican Secretariat of State weighed the condition of the church in those states of eastern Europe where it still had a degree of liberty and concluded that the church was best treated in Poland, and that the church in

Czechoslovakia was worse off than in Poland but better off than in Hungary.[1] Now the Communist parties and their allies expected the church to show its gratitude by providing them with support in their election campaigns. In some cases, the governments wanted Catholic parties or prominent Catholics to run for election as part of the government slate. The belief was that, if the church would endorse the government coalitions, then the people would willingly give these coalitions their electoral support.

The governments realized that the church had concerns about its future status which could be resolved in agreements between church and state in which guarantees could be given to the church about areas of interest, such as education and religious property. Some governments were willing to enter agreements and to offer concessions in order to secure the support of the church. They also sought to convey to church leaders that their best hope lay in a quick agreement with the current national government lest worse should befall them if the Russians should decide to intervene. In dealing with the Catholic Church, there was always the implied threat that, if the hierarchy and their Roman masters were unwilling to cooperate, the governments could be instrumental in the creation of national Catholic churches, divorced from Rome, based on those clergy and laity who were realistic enough to cooperate with the government.

During this period of consolidation, the church had to decide how to respond to Communist entreaties. There were Catholics in all countries who were willing to take the realistic approach of working with the government in hopes of protecting their interests. Many laymen and women believed in the need for serious social reform which was being offered by the Communists; as leaders of Catholic political parties, they were willing to collaborate as part of the government electoral slates. Some lower clergy, recognizing the attractiveness of reform in what had previously been traditional and hierarchic societies, were also willing to support the new governments. There were even bishops who saw the value of a short-term resolution of church-state differences in order to protect and preserve existing church privileges.

Against these Catholics was ranged the bulk of the bishops of eastern Europe whose position was fortified by the stance of the Vatican. The church did not approve of communism; so cooperation with these regimes, it was felt, would only assist them to impose their rule over the people. While east European governments might be reasonable as they sought church agreements, everyone knew that communists were atheists, who worked hand-in-glove with the rulers of the Kremlin and had little love or respect for the church. The attitude of most bishops was that the church should husband its resources and not commit itself to regimes whose tenure in office might be short in any case.

This was certainly the long-term view of the Holy See and the substance of its instructions to the bishops. The Catholics who had to be monitored in eastern Europe were those willing to cooperate with the Communist regimes. These Catholics had to be controlled, even to the extent of excommunication, if they moved too far from approved church practice. The Prague coup of February 1948 was a lesson to church leaders that the Communists, in spite of their talk of legal agreements, would act illegally and with force if that was how they could best get their own way.

THE RECOGNITION OF POLAND'S ODER-NEISSE FRONTIER

The situation in Poland was complicated by the unspoken distrust between the pope and the Polish hierarchy. When the Polish bishops, recognizing the strength of the church in Poland, wanted to negotiate with the government, they were restrained by the Vatican which expected Polish interests to be sacrificed in any German peace treaty. When it appeared in 1947 that there would be no German treaty and that Europe was to be divided between the superpowers, the Vatican suddenly opened negotiations with the Polish government without consulting the bishops. The Polish hierarchy eventually had to resort to a public demonstration through their pastoral letter of September 1947 in order to disrupt the negotiations and make the Vatican take note of their interests. As a result of this pastoral, bilateral negotiations between the Polish government and the Vatican were turned into trilateral talks between the Polish government, the Polish Church, and the Holy See.

The negotiations resumed in November 1947 and there was considerable optimism on both sides about the prospect of success. The only point of contention was over a Catholic request to expand their youth organizations but even this was not seen to be an insuperable difficulty and both church and government appeared to want an agreement when they adjourned the talks for Christmas.[2]

If the content of the negotiations within Poland gave cause for optimism, this was not the case in the international context. Aware of the growing rift between East and West, Polish government papers stressed that there was no ideological conflict between church and party in Poland and called for the cooperation of the church in Polish reconstruction. Yet growing antagonism between the Soviet Union and the western powers meant that negotiations such as this which were designed to bridge the ideological gap were unlikely to be favourably looked upon either in Moscow or in Washington.[3]

In December, Cardinal Hlond reviewed the negotiations with the pope, raising the question whether, in that uncertain winter, the church should enter an agreement which the Polish government obviously wanted, but which neither the government nor its Russian mentors might be prepared to honour. Given the seriousness of the international situation, the pope's assessment was that this was the time for the church and the Holy See to keep their hands free and not to rush into any hasty agreement with the Warsaw government.[4] In January, *Il Quotidiano* ran an "inspired" article which pointed out that while the Polish government was looking for an immediate settlement with the church, the latter was looking for evidence of long-term respect for the family and the institutions of the church. An agreement between church and state would only become possible once the government ceased its ideological war against the Church. Consequently, where the practical matter of the youth associations had originally been the main difficulty in the negotiations, Hlond returned from Rome placing new emphasis on the ideological differences between church and state. The bishops did, nevertheless, send a letter to the government indicating that they were prepared to resume talks over the youth associations. The intention was not to end discussions, but to spin them out and await the course of events.[5]

If some Polish bishops were disappointed because Vatican interference had prevented the conclusion of negotiations, they, along with many Polish Catholics, were mystified and annoyed by the difficult position in which they were placed in March 1948 by Pius XII himself. The reluctance of the pope to give serious consideration to Polish issues in their own right and his propensity to understand Poland only in its relationship to the international context was infuriating to Polish bishops and clergy. To the pope, Poland was important either because it demonstrated the extended power of the Soviet Union or because it gave evidence of the harsh Allied treatment of Germany; it was rarely important for its own sake.

On 1 March 1948 the pope sent an open letter to the German bishops, in which he deplored the condition of German refugees from the East,

since they were forcibly expelled from their homes in the Eastern Territories without any compensation and sent into occupied Germany ... We believe that We know what has taken place during the years of war in the spacious territories between the Vistula and the Volga. Was it, however, permissible, by way of reprisal, to drive 12 million people from hearth and home and to bring them to a state of miserable poverty? ... And were the measures which have been taken politically wise, and economically justifiable, when one thinks of what the German people needs in order to live and further what is required to ensure prosperity for the whole of Europe?

Not only was the pope again speaking out on behalf of the Germans, but he was also questioning the wisdom of the Oder-Niesse frontier and the legitimacy of the transfer of German territory to Poland.

This letter had not been intended for publication but had been leaked to the German press, possibly by a member of the German hierarchy who wanted to demonstrate how strongly the pope shared the views of the German bishops. The result was a major crisis in the relationship between the Vatican and the Polish hierarchy, especially when the government and press of Poland used the letter to demonstrate that the pope was still an unreconstructed Nazi sympathizer and that the Catholic Church would always look after German interests before those of Poland. The fact that Vatican officials first denied the existence of the letter and then confirmed that it had been written indicates the high degree of embarrassment that the publication of the pope's letter occasioned officials of the Holy See.[6]

The reaction of the Polish government and press to this letter was extreme. The press called on the episcopate to repudiate the pope's statement and to indicate that the church stood by the Oder-Niesse frontier and the Polish Western Territories. The press pointed out that the voice of the pope had never been heard when the Nazis killed and expelled Poles, not even at the end of the war when Poles and Czechs expelled Germans; they argued that the pope was only speaking out now at the behest of the United States as an instrument of American imperialism. The government took every opportunity to capitalize on the wave of Polish nationalism in reaction to the pope's letter. It knew that the hierarchy was constrained from defending their loyalty to Poland and also that the letter had created a great deal of dissatisfaction among the lower clergy "by fanning a latent hostility towards the Vatican and the fervent patriotism which is the inheritance of all Poles, priests as well as laymen." The Polish press attacked the church for its intervention in the 1948 Italian election campaign, pointing out that the church was not only anti-Polish, but it was also anti-democratic by seeking to interfere with the legitimate expression of Italian popular opinion.

The anti-Vatican press campaign continued into May, depicting the Vatican as pro-German, pro-American, and anti-Polish. The hierarchy finally replied to the government charges in *Tygodnik Warszawski* on 30 May. The editorial stressed that the patriotism of the Polish clergy was unquestionable and that, because the Polish government had not sought to improve relations with the Vatican since the war, it should not be surprised if the pope was more favourable to Germany. The editorial claimed that the pope had not called for a revision of the Oder-Niesse frontier, but had expressed sympathy for the uprooted Germans, as he had expressed sympathy for the Poles during the war. The Italian ambassador considered this a weak reply to the government charges.[7]

It was not, in fact, until 20 June that the Polish episcopate offered an appropriate public response to the pope's letter and to the Polish press campaign. The delay was due to the necessity for Hlond to clear his reply with the pope and Vatican officials and, in securing their approval, Hlond forced the Vatican to a public recognition of the Oder-Neisse Line. On 20 June a pastoral was read in all the churches of the Western Territories, formally recognizing "all former German territory in Polish hands as definitely Polish: The argument that the Church supports the idea of the revision of the Polish boundaries has no foundation. It is the intention of the Church not to permit Poland to be diminished by Peace Treaties, but to compel these Treaties to respect the independence of Poland, to guarantee its safety and to bestow the reward due to her for the bitter sufferings through which she has passed." These statements were endorsed by the pope. "No Pope," it said, "could desert Poland, because of her strategic position as a bastion of the Christian ethic against a tide of materialism flowing from the East."

The pastoral reversed Vatican policy of not recognizing the Oder-Niesse frontier prior to its legal confirmation by a peace conference. For this reason, the pope had refused to appoint bishops to the vacant sees in the Western Territories, and had left them in the charge of apostolic administrators. The pastoral was also significant because, to Catholics, it offered an adequate reply to the government's charges of the disloyalty of the church. It even went some direction to meeting Bierut's conditions of some months earlier that, before discussions between church and state could be resumed, the Polish cardinals must first state their views on Poland's claims to the Western Territories.[8] By the summer of 1948 church and state had once more established a basis for developing a working relationship. The possibility of doing so, however, was to be determined more and more by the polarization of the Cold War and by the operation of forces extraneous to the Polish situation.

A "BRIDGE BETWEEN TWO IDEOLOGIES" IN HUNGARY

The Hungarian peace treaty was signed on 10 February 1947, but Russian troops did not complete their withdrawal from Hungary until December of that year. As a result, the Communists and their Social Democratic allies sought to secure their position before the Red Army left Hungary. The first target of the Communists was the core of the governing coalition, the Smallholders' party, a party which had received strong Catholic support but whose leadership the Communists deliberately destroyed. The police were the responsibility of the Communist minister of the interior, and, as a result, a number of police investigations at the end of 1946 produced evidence that members of the Smallholders' party had been conspiring against the government and the Red Army. On 25 February 1947, barely two weeks after the signing of the peace treaty, Russian military authorities arrested the popular and effective general secretary of the Smallholders' party, Bela Kovacs, for "activities directed against the Red Army." He was never seen again. In May the Russians produced a "confession" from Kovacs that implicated the prime minister, Ferenc Nagy, and forced his resignation on 2 June in return for permission to take his child out of Hungary.[9] Nagy was replaced as prime minister by Lajos Dinnyés, a more compliant member of the Smallholders' party.

The failure of the government to follow up on its earlier initiative to open negotiations with the Vatican confirmed that Catholic influence was on the wane within the government. The Smallholders party took a radical shift to the left and became much more amenable to Communist direction. One aspect of this shift was the agreement reached in March 1947 between the leaders of the coalition parties in favour of the abolition of obligatory religious instruction in Hungarian schools. Yet strong church protests against this tampering with religious rights demonstrated the continuing influence of the church and forced the governing coalition to drop the issue for the remainder of the year.[10]

In July the Russians forced the Hungarian government to reject Marshall Plan aid and, on 24 July, President Tildy signed an electoral law providing for new elections and disfranchising those suspected of having "fascist" connections. Elections were scheduled for 31 August. The Catholic Church refrained from direct involvement in the campaign, the bishops only calling on Catholics to judge their candidates by whether they were faithful to God, their church, Hungary, and the freedom of man. Most parties sought Catholic support and even the Communists emphasized that they had no quarrel with the church.[11]

The election, which some observers judged to be relatively fair, was won by the governing coalition of Communists, Smallholders, Social Democrats and the National Peasant party, with the Communists replacing the Smallholders as the party with the largest number of seats. The election was not, however, a complete victory for the Communist strategy, as they only earned 22 percent of the popular vote. The striking outcome of this election was the shift of the Catholic vote away from the Smallholders', no doubt due to that party's willingness to abolish religious education. The Smallholders dropped from 57 percent of the popular vote in 1945 to 15 percent in 1947. Catholics had voted for two new parties, the Democratic People's party, led by István Barankovics, and the Hungarian Independence party, which won 16 and 14 percent of the popular vote respectively.

The rise of these two specifically Catholic parties represented an acceptance by some Catholics of the democratic republic and a willingness to participate in the electoral process. In spite of the ideological polarization in the rest of the world, it was felt that the church in Hungary could retain its role as a bridge between two ideologies. The Democratic People's party had presented itself to the electorate "on a definite Catholic programme" and had done extremely well in spite of its lack of funds and party organization. Diplomatic observers felt that it owed its success "in a large degree to the support of some of the Bishops and probably to very effective electioneering by at least some parish priests." The popularity of the party reflected the electoral strength of the Catholic Church and it could only be attacked if the Communists, by now completely in control of the government, were prepared to challenge the popular authority of the church.[12]

In spite of this demonstration of Catholic political strength, Cardinal Mindszenty took pains to dissociate the church from Barankovics's Democratic People's party. The primate told the British representative that there was no connection between the church and the party and that the church did not even "recognize the Party as standing for the Catholic way of life." Mindszenty claimed that the party had "illegitimately carried on a whispering campaign that it was backed by the Primate and bench of bishops." "The party," charged Mindszenty, "is pro-Soviet."[13] While political caution might have induced the primate to keep the church out of politics at this sensitive moment, the vitriol in his attack on Barankovics and his party suggest that his real opposition had to do with the fact that Barankovics accepted the republic and was willing to cooperate with the system created by the Communists.

If the new Catholic political parties had had a degree of electoral success, they were not to enjoy it for long. Immediately after the founding meeting of the Cominform in September, the Communists neutralized the new opposition parties and forced the exile of their leaders. In October, 106 of the 109 parliamentary representatives of the Democratic People's party and the Hungarian Independence party were arrested. While the Democratic People's party was barely able to survive, the Independence party was eliminated from the political arena.

Hungarian anti-communists thereafter looked to the Catholic Church as the sole remaining independent institution in the country. The challenge confronting Cardinal Mindszenty was the provision of appropriate leadership to his flock in this moment of great political danger. Mindszenty had two possible courses. He could rally all Catholics to the support of the church for a program of negotiation, compromise, and cooperation with the government to secure the church's desired objectives. In this way, Mindszenty could have worked with Bishop Banass, Barankovics, and the other Catholics who believed that the future lay in accepting the reality of the Hungarian political situation, however imperfect it might be. By following such a course, one British observer noted, "the Church could and might prove to be in the long run a most powerful, anti-Communist force in Hungary."

Alternatively, Mindszenty could hold firm to his principles, regardless of any opposition within the church and regardless of what the government might do to him and to the church. The latter course was the one preferred by the primate, who believed that there must be no compromise with evil and that church members as well as clergy and bishops must accept the authority and the guidance offered by their primate. Consequently, Mindszenty denounced those Catholics who advocated a cooperative ecclesiastical policy in the same fashion that he had dismissed Barankovics and his party for being pro-Soviet. Moreover, the primate held to this policy even though it created a significant split in the Hungarian church and weakened that church's long-run effectiveness.

The question to be considered is why Mindszenty chose this particular course. The diplomatic records confirm that Mindszenty shared the views of Pius XII on the correct way to deal with the threat of communism and that the Hungarian primate acted secure in the knowledge that he had the backing of the Holy See. Mindszenty knew that the compromisers within the church would get no support if they appealed to Rome. Early in 1948 the cardinal was informed of the pope's delegation to him of the power to excommunicate. Once apprised of this decision, Mindszenty acted secure in the knowledge that he was able to deal with any Catholics who dissented from his point of view.[14]

The Hungarian government had been rebuffed by the Catholic Church at every turn. Their support of the church prior to the 1947 election had not facilitated the opening of negotiations nor had emissaries sent to the Vatican fared much better. The Hungarian ambassador to Italy had been a personal friend of Eugenio Pacelli when they had both served in Munich, but had been refused when he sought a personal audience with the pope. Matyas Rakosi, the leader of the Communist party, believed that it might be possible to develop negotiations by separating the clergy and the liberal Catholics from the primate. If the government could not use the primate as a route for negotiations with Rome, it would see if Mindszenty's Catholic opponents had their own channels to the Vatican.

At the beginning of January 1948 the government announced that it was prepared to open diplomatic relations with the Holy See "provided that the Church recognized the Hungarian Republic." This deliberately played on the division within the church which had become apparent on the eve of the celebration of the centenary of the 1848 revolution in December 1947, when Mindszenty had denounced the Hungarian revolutionaries and patriots who had attacked the Habsburg Empire in 1848 as having been "irresponsible." His speech had drawn criticism from the newspaper of the Democratic People's party which supported the initiative for relations with the Vatican and attacked the primate for his callous suggestion that persons holding democratic principles were irresponsible. Barankovics had written that the state had not treated the church badly.[15]

Given Mindszenty's difficult personality, Rakosi calculated that the only enduring church-state negotiations would be those with the Vatican,[16] yet the Vatican also questioned the legitimacy of the Hungarian republic and was no more open to negotiations. In the spring of 1948 the Holy See accepted the crown of St Stephen in trust for the Hungarian people. This crown "symbolized the bonds between the Apostolic [Habsburg] King and his people, and the integrity of the domains which he established." It had been removed from Hungary at the end of the war and turned over to the Americans. The American State Department had refused the request of the Hungarian government for the return of the crown and sent it instead to the Vatican. The fact that the Vatican was prepared to receive the crown from the Americans and to hold it in trust for the Hungarian people was a clear indication that the Holy See did not recognize the legitimacy of the Hungarian republic.[17]

The flaw in the negotiating strategy of the Communists was that, while the offer of negotiations with the Vatican might divide Hungarian Catholics, only Mindszenty had the ear of the Vatican. Early in

April 1948 the archbishop of Győr, a colleague of Bishop Banass and an opponent of Mindszenty, travelled to Rome to try to reach some agreement for the government around the obstinacy of the primate. There is no record of the outcome of the visit, but by that time the Vatican was letting it be known that there could be no agreement with Hungary so long as the attacks on Cardinal Mindszenty continued. The Vatican had full confidence in the cardinal and admired his strength of character. Montini observed "admiringly" – and perhaps somewhat sarcastically – to the British ambassador that the cardinal "was quite remarkably authoritarian."[18]

Matters came to a head in May 1948 when talks for a new party of fusion between the Communists and their Social Democrat allies resulted in a draft program, under which it was agreed that the new party would introduce a uniform system of state education, requiring the nationalization of Catholic schools. When the minister of public instruction, Gyula Ortutay, announced the planned program at a press conference on 15 May, he held out an olive branch to the church by indicating that a committee, with representatives of the bishops, would coordinate outstanding problems between church and state associated with this legislation.

Mindszenty had been expecting this challenge for some time and, on the following day, issued a pastoral letter calling on Catholics to defend their rights in Hungary. This pastoral was designed to indicate to the dissenters who had not accepted his methods that they should get into line. Catholic unity was essential in this campaign and Mindszenty drew attention to a priest, the curate of Bakenykut, whom he had excommunicated because he had accepted a job in Ortutay's ministry. "Just as political parties excluded disloyal members, and governments expatriated traitors," wrote the primate, "so if a Christian were unfaithful to his faith and the Mother Church, he had to be admonished and if need be punished." A major problem within the church lay with the lower clergy, especially those who had organized their congregations to vote for the Democratic People's party. The lower clergy had much power and respect with their congregations and many of them favoured cooperation with the government. Mindszenty sought to prevent a split between the higher and lower clergy with his threat of excommunication. His pastoral letter was designed "to rouse the lower clergy and to prepare the way for their mobilization in the coming struggle." The British minister understood that Mindszenty's primacy was secure with the higher clergy "so long as he enjoys the confidence of the Vatican and nobody suggests that he does not do this abundantly."[19]

The fusion of the Communist and Social Democratic parties into the Hungarian Workers' party on 16 June turned Hungary into a one-party state. On that same day, the School Nationalization bill was presented to Parliament. Two days before, Mindszenty had issued a statement in which he had threatened Catholic members of the government with excommunication for "sharing in action aimed at attempting to limit the external and internal rights of the Church." The education bill was passed on 16 June. The Catholic protest was not without effect, however, for as soon as the bill became law, discussions were started by the government with a view to mitigating the effects of the law by excluding some schools from nationalization.[20]

THE CHURCH AND THE CZECHOSLOVAK COUP OF 1948

Prime Minister Gottwald of Czechoslovakia favoured a highly centralized state government and, unlike President Beneš, had little sympathy for Slovak autonomy. Gottwald saw little need to conciliate the Catholic Church, believing that weakening the church would also weaken Slovak nationalism. Accordingly, in the fall of 1947 his government made plans to eliminate confessional schools in favour of a unified secular school system and to expropriate ecclesiastical property in a land reform. New land reform legislation was approved on 21 January 1948 and a commission was immediately set up to decide which lands were to be expropriated and redistributed. Ambassador Maixner was recalled from the Holy See at the end of 1947 and the government made no move to replace him.

Archbishop Beran and the hierarchy were distressed by these developments and turned to Beneš for support only to be advised that he was a constitutional president who had to be guided by the decisions of his elected government. Beran was annoyed that the Catholic People's party, some of whose members belonged to the government, had been so ineffective in preventing the expropriation of church lands and, on 23 January 1948, he "vigorously berated the Party leaders for inactivity which he termed dereliction of duty."[21]

With the establishment of the Cominform in September 1947, the Soviet Union had put pressure on Gottwald to end the period of coalition government in favour of outright Communist control. In February 1948 Gottwald and his Communists seized control of the Czechoslovak government and Beneš resigned as president. Yet, instead of harsher restrictions being imposed on the church, the Prague coup resulted in an improved relationship between the church and the Czechoslovak government. Immediately after the Communist takeover, Dr Alexej Cepicka, the new minister of justice, visited Beran and assured him that "nothing shall occur to mar the good relations of the

Church to the State." The government also advised Catholics that the policy regarding religious education would not be altered and that compensation would be provided for any expropriated church lands.[22] In return, the Czechoslovak bishops pledged to make every effort to see that both the clergy and Catholic organizations "remain outside the sphere of politics and party-politics."[23]

Yet the new government had scheduled elections for 30 May in order to confirm the results of the coup and wanted members of the clergy to join the government slate for the election to encourage church members to vote for the government. Gottwald even named a Catholic priest, Father Josef Plojhar, the new leader of the Catholic People's party, to the cabinet as minister of health.

The campaign of the Gottwald government was relatively successful, much to the disgust of Laurence Steinhardt, the American ambassador, who commented on 23 April that "the Catholic clergy has certainly not distinguished itself by taking any stand (united or individually) against the totalitarian regime which has persecuted thousands of individuals and groups known to be anti-Communist." He said that the opportunistic statements of Plojhar and "even negative attitude of certain Czech bishops, are particularly revolting to large numbers of Catholics in Czechoslovakia, especially to People's Party members who have looked upon the church as a bulwark against Communists. The role of the Catholic Church in Italy as a militant anti-Communist force could hardly be repeated in Czechoslovakia under present conditions. The Communist Party's apparently friendly attitude toward religion in Czechoslovakia ... will facilitate the collaboration of many priests."[24]

Beran maintained reservations about this sudden Communist sympathy for religious sensibilities and was adamantly opposed to clerical participation in the government. On 21 April he wrote a private letter to the priests in his diocese, asking them "not to accept seats in parliament or posts in the government or in any political party, or to join action committees or the religious commissions attached to them." A few weeks later the hierarchy issued a public declaration prohibiting priests from active political involvement.

The major issue in church-state discussions in May was the question of whether the names of priests could be placed on the government list for the election. Cepicka had first asked Beran to permit the names of four priests to appear on the government slate, but the archbishop had flatly refused. When the list was published, the names of the priests were on it. After a protest by the chargé d'affaires of the internunciature, the names of all the priests except that of Father Plojhar were removed. Cepicka thereupon requested Beran to make an exception in Plojhar's case.[25]

On 21 May, having obtained permission from Rome, Beran wrote directly to Father Plojhar telling him that he did not have the arch-bishop's permission to run and threatening that "in the event of your not withdrawing your candidature, you would be *ipso facto* suspended as a Catholic priest."[26] Father Plojhar stood his ground and let his name stand in the elections. The result was his suspension from the priesthood on 15 June and a Vatican-inspired article in Rome's *Il Quo-tidiano* which attacked him for insubordination. Beran believed it essential to keep discipline within the church in the face of attempts by the communist government to divide the church camp.

17 The Religious Cold War: The Communist Offensive

The 1948 Italian election campaign represented the high point of cooperation between the Holy See and the American government in the early Cold War. Neither before nor after that event were the goals and interests of the Vatican and Washington in such close alignment. In fact, the close cooperation of the spring of 1948 is often taken by some as clear evidence of the way in which the American government and the Catholic Church worked hand-in-glove as allies during the Cold War[1]. Such, however, was far from the case, since the United States and the Holy See had had different goals in 1947 when the two sides in the Cold War were given their distinctive structures. While Washington and the Vatican worked together to keep Communists from power in Italy in 1948, by that date eastern Europe was entirely under the control of the Communists and, while the United States sought to contain communism behind the "iron curtain," the Vatican had to deal with the reality of life within the Communist bloc where the church was daily faced with increasing persecution.

With all the governments of eastern Europe controlled by the Communist party, there was little that the United States could do short of war to alter the situation in that part of the world after 1948. Yet by the summer of 1948 the Roman Catholic Church was still a relatively independent and influential institution in the most important satellite nations of Hungary, Czechoslovakia, and Poland. Catholics had to try to protect and defend the church in those countries with no help from the United States and slight assistance from the Vatican.

The Communist takeover in Czechoslovakia in February 1948 increased international tensions and led to the creation of the defence pact of the Western European Union in March and the opening of the Berlin blockade in May. One dimension of this increased tension was Stalin's growing concern about control within eastern Europe and, in particular, about Tito's independent stance and rejection of his tutelage in Yugoslavia. The growing tension between Moscow and Belgrade in the spring of 1948 culminated in the expulsion of Tito and the Yugoslav Communist party from the Cominform.

The conflict with Tito led Moscow to require the Communist governments of eastern Europe to purge their ranks of those members who were prepared to put the national interest ahead of the interests of world communism as defined by Stalin. Beginning in the summer of 1948, there followed an extensive series of purge trials and executions of leading communists throughout eastern Europe. Local communists were assisted in the collection of evidence, the organization of their cases and the mounting of show trials by NKVD agents from the Soviet Union. The public purges of leading east European communists represented only the tip of the iceberg; thousands of lesser officials in the state and party also lost their jobs and often their lives because of their perceived political unreliability.

The purges were initially a response to the challenge of Titoism, but they were also an aspect of the forced capitalization and industrialization which was imposed on eastern Europe at the same time. The purges of government and party officials were accompanied by a purge across the broader society, taking in representatives of business, labour, education, and culture, and having the general effect of terrorizing the population at a time of drastic social and economic change. The convulsions within the Soviet bloc following the expulsion of Tito from the Cominform were designed to enhance the control of Moscow within the bloc at a time when Mao Zedong was on the verge of winning a victory in China, a victory which Mao, like Tito, was expected to win with minimal assistance from the Soviet Union.[2]

The Roman Catholic Church in eastern Europe quickly became one of the targets of this drive for Soviet control. Its involvement as an active player in the Italian election of April 1948 had shown that the church was prepared to "subvert democracy" to achieve its political ends in countries with large Catholic populations. The result was that, by the summer of 1948, Moscow had decided it was time to curtail the independence of the Catholics.

This campaign was complex and subtle. By 1948 the Communists realized that the Catholic Church had deep roots in many countries and that it would be extremely difficult to eradicate the institutional structure of the church or its influence with the faithful. The new campaign sought, instead, to reduce the institutional independence of the church and to bring it under state control. The Orthodox Church had been controlled in this way in the Soviet Union, Romania, and Bulgaria and it had become a useful instrument of state policy. It was now time to bring the Catholic Church and any remaining Protestant churches into line. The coordination of this move took place at the meeting of the Cominform in Karlovy Vary in February 1948, at which time a directive was issued to the Communist governments for the nationalization of the Catholic Church.

The issue became one of finding ways to link the churches to the state in such a way that the churches could use their influence with their parishioners to explain how communism, by its profession of a belief in peace and social justice, was really carrying out the Christian mission. As part of their program of secularization, the Communists sought to remove the Catholic Church from education and other social services, which were to be provided and controlled by the state. They also sought to make the church dependent on the state by the confiscation of church property and the direct payment of clergy salaries. In order to control the Catholic Church in particular, it would be necessary to drive a wedge between the clergy and the church hierarchy, as well as between the laity and the hierarchy. It would also be necessary to prevent the church hierarchy from communication with Rome. In some countries, the ultimate goal of the government was the creation of national Catholic churches, independent of Rome and fully dependent on the local Communist government. This was an attempt to parallel the Orthodox relationship inside the Communist states.

Once the Communist parties had established their control in eastern Europe, they expected church leaders to recognize that communism was the power in the land and that the continued welfare and existence of the churches depended on the willingness of the church leadership – both clergy and laity – to cooperate with the national governments. It was through the collaboration of church leaders with the governments that the Communists saw their best hope of controlling religion. For this reason, they used both the carrot and the stick to win over the church leadership. Since many Catholics – bishops, clergy and laity – were prepared to consider the advantages of collaboration that was being offered, the struggle within the church in eastern Europe was between those who were prepared to compromise with the governments, even against the wishes of Rome, and those who believed that no accommodation should be made with these regimes unless Rome sanctioned it.

The religious cold war which developed after the summer of 1948 was a struggle for the loyalty of the Catholic clergy and laity behind the Iron Curtain. The contending parties were the Vatican and the Moscow leadership of the Cominform. Catholics throughout eastern Europe were called upon to decide whether they would collaborate with their local governments in order to preserve the functioning of their church or whether they would stand on principle and resist all government initiatives even though the main casualty might be the institution of the church itself. Both the Cominform and the Vatican were prepared to generalize this struggle into issues of principle in order to secure the loyalty of eastern Europe's Catholics.

The Roman Catholic Church after 1948 had to act alone in its confrontation with communism. Neither the United States nor the western allies were able or willing to assist it, committed as they were to the containment, rather than the rollback of communism. The outright persecution of the east European church after mid-1948 enhanced the stature of the pope and the east European hierarchy as they struggled alone against determined opponents. They were, however, operating from a position of weakness and, apart from encouraging the resistance of the faithful, had few weapons with which to fight.

The American government showed little sympathy for the plight of the church. While the United States was unable to assist the church behind the Iron Curtain, Tito's break with Moscow did not improve the position of the church in Yugoslavia in any way and Washington was reluctant to attempt to use a reduction of religious persecution as a condition for granting a loan to Tito in 1949. In fact, after 1948 the interests of Washington and the Vatican diverged markedly. Not only did they disagree over the treatment of Yugoslavia, but they also fell out over the recognition of the state of Israel and the Vatican campaign for the internationalization of Jerusalem and the Holy Places in 1948. When Myron Taylor finally resigned as the president's personal representative to the pope at the beginning of 1950, President Truman responded to pressure from the Protestant lobby by not naming a successor.

Yet while the American government showed scant sympathy for the plight and the interests of the church, details of religious persecution in eastern Europe were relayed to the American people by the media, with the result that persecuted figures such as Cardinal Mindszenty of Hungary became icons of the anti-communist struggle. Where

American Catholics and American church leaders appeared to exercise little influence with Washington politicians, they provided a ready audience for the charges of radicals such as Senator Joseph McCarthy who, in February 1950, claimed that it was communists and communist agents in high places in Washington who were preventing genuine assistance being given to the persecuted peoples of eastern Europe.

THE MOSCOW ORTHODOX CHURCH CONGRESS

The relationship of the Russian Orthodox Church with the Orthodox churches of Romania, Bulgaria, and Serbia had been difficult because these churches had valued their autonomy and had retained a loyalty to the Ecumenical Patriarch in Constantinople. As Stalin had assisted the Russian Orthodox to incorporate the Ukrainian Uniate Church and also Uniates from Poland and the Baltic States in 1946, so the Russian Orthodox Church, under the leadership of Patriarch Alexei, was prepared to complement Communist control of eastern Europe by establishing the dominance of the Russian church among the Orthodox churches.

In the summer of 1948 a pan-Orthodox Church congress was convened in Moscow in celebration of the five-hundredth anniversary of the establishment of the Russian patriarchate. In seeking to place Russia at the head of the Orthodox Church, Alexei had made earlier attempts to convene a world congress of the Orthodox Church, only to be reminded by church leaders of other countries that the Ecumenical Patriarch had the sole authority to summon such a meeting. Consequently, Alexei used the occasion of the anniversary celebrations to bring Orthodox leaders to Moscow in July 1948. This meeting "appear[ed] calculated to carry into effect the Soviet plan for the severance of the Romanian Church's ties with the West and the establishment of the primacy of the Patriarch of Moscow amongst the Patriarchs of the autocephalous churches of Eastern Europe."[3] Through this congress, the Russian churchmen and the Communists were setting a clear policy of isolation for the dependent churches and governments in the Balkans. Those present discussed relations with the Catholic Church and the Vatican and condemned Vatican warmongering. They decided against Orthodox membership in the World Council of Churches and they also discussed their relationship with the Anglican Church. While representatives of the Ecumenical Patriarch and the Greek Orthodox Church attended the religious services in Moscow, they did not participate in the meetings or agree with the conclusions. The patriarch also sent his representatives to the founding meeting of the World Council of Churches in Amsterdam in 1948.[4]

The Moscow Congress established Moscow as a significant religious centre and resulted in a much closer working relationship between the Romanian and Bulgarian churches and the Russian. For Romania, this was made possible by the election of Archbishop Justinian Marina as Orthodox patriarch of Romania on 24 May 1948. Patriarch Justinian, as he styled himself, was the favoured candidate of the Romanian Communists because of his willingness to cooperate with the political regime; the Communists had apparently packed the electoral synod to ensure his election. Justinian was elected in time to represent his church in Moscow and he immediately initiated a purge of the Romanian Church to remove those who objected to Communist domination.[5] Alexei had secured a close Romanian ally in Justinian.

Exarch Stephen of Bulgaria was open to Alexei's approaches, especially when the latter indicated a willingness to raise him to the status of patriarch, but at the same time Stephen retained good relations with Constantinople and with the Anglicans. On his return from Moscow, Stephen reiterated the Orthodox hostility to the warmongering activities of the papacy in spite of the fact that the Bulgarian Orthodox clergy had for years had excellent relations with Catholics.[6] On 12 September, however, following a meeting with the Bulgarian synod, Stephen resigned as exarch. It was suggested that the synod was not happy with Stephen receiving favours from Alexei rather than from Constantinople; it was also reported that the government were happy to see Stephen go since he had been promoting his own interests too heavily and, it was feared, could go into opposition.[7] Conceivably, Stephen may have been removed because he was not prepared to follow Moscow directives.

Attempts to develop closer relations between the Russian and the Serbian Orthodox churches foundered on the split between Stalin and Tito in June 1948, although Serb Patriarch Gavrilo, a strong anti-communist, had for some time been resisting pressure from Moscow to support Russian Orthodox attacks on the Vatican. In 1946 Bishop Sergei of the Russian Orthodox Church visited Belgrade to enlist the Serb Orthodox in the campaign against the Catholic Church. The Serbs politely declined, saying that this would force them to turn against some members of Tito's cabinet who were nominally Catholic and, in turn, had warned the regent of the nunciature, Bishop Hurley, "that all his movements and every activity of the Nunciature were being watched by the secret police."[8] When the Russian Orthodox tried to convince other Orthodox churches attending a Slav Congress in December 1946 to join the anti-Catholic campaign, the Serb Orthodox had once again refused.

PATRIARCH JUSTINIAN AND THE ROMANIAN CATHOLICS

The first criticisms of the Roman Catholic Church in Romania did not occur until October 1947, since that church had been relatively safe as long as the Communist government was working out its relationship with the Orthodox. Once the Orthodox Church had been neutralized under Justinian, however, the campaign could begin against the Catholics, especially against the Uniates. A new constitution for the Romanian People's Republic banning confessional schools had been approved in April 1948. The accompanying anti-Catholic press campaign cited particularly the anti-democratic intervention of the Vatican in the Italian election campaign.[9] Regent O'Hara protested that the new constitution violated the Romanian concordat's provision for separate Catholic schools, only to learn of the denunciation of the concordat by the government on 18 July 1948, on the argument that the concordat contradicted the provisions of the new constitution.[10]

On 5 August the government regulated the position and activities of the various religious "cults" in Romania. The British minister believed that this law was specifically aimed at establishing government control over Latin-rite Roman Catholics. The law required all cults to submit their charters to the government for recognition and, should such recognition be granted, they would then have their internal functioning and codes of conduct, as well as their finances and property holdings, reviewed and monitored by the state. Catholic contact with the Vatican had to have the approval of the Ministry of Cults and had to go through Foreign Ministry channels. The law also reduced the number of Catholic dioceses allowed in Romania to two for the Latin rite and two for the Uniates.[11]

On 15 May 1948 Archbishop Balan, the Orthodox metropolitan of Transylvania, had opened the campaign for the voluntary reunion of the Uniates with Orthodoxy when he said that "since the Romanians of Transylvania had long ago achieved their political independence of the Habsburgs ... it was high time for them to achieve their spiritual independence of the Papacy." He appealed to the Uniates "whom foreign interests led astray and divided from your mother, the Orthodox Church, to return home." This campaign worried the nunciature, for they did not feel that the Uniates had any "leaders of character willing to take responsibility" and didn't feel that the faithful alone would be long able to resist the full campaign of the government and Orthodox Church for this reunion.[12]

When this campaign for voluntary reunion failed, more direct methods were employed. The government removed four of the five Uniate bishops from office by ministerial decree and put pressure on the non-celibate Uniate clergy with threats against their wives and children. The Communists reminded those priests who had collaborated with the wartime Antonescu regime that they could be denounced on that ground if they did not cooperate. As a result of these tactics, four hundred and thirty Uniate clergy from Transylvania and the Banat, representing 25 percent of the Uniate Church, met at Cluj on 1 October, and voted unanimously to forswear their subservience to the pope and return to the Orthodox Church. On 3 October they travelled to Bucharest where they signed the document of reunion and celebrated a Te Deum in the cathedral.

Twenty-five percent was, however, a "poor harvest" for Justinian and, on 21 October, the two-hundred-and-fiftieth anniversary of the original schism of the Uniates from Orthodoxy, a mass meeting attended by the former Uniates was held in Alba Julia, the scene of the original schism, at which a resolution was passed, declaring on behalf of all Romanian Uniates:

That we break off for ever all ties with the Vatican and Papal Rome;

That we wholeheartedly join the Romanian Orthodox Church, whose teachings and canonical rules we shall follow;

That we shall submit, like good sons, to all the decisions taken by the Holy Synod of our Romanian Orthodox Church;

From now on all Romanians are and will remain for ever *united* in our just creed, *united* in devotedly serving our peiople and *united* in loyal observance of the innovatory rules of Our beloved Romanian People's Republic.

Justinian pronounced that the union of 1698 was annulled and that the Uniate Church officially ceased to exist. Government officials thereafter visited all members of the Uniate clergy to offer them the choice of swearing allegiance to the Orthodox Church or undergoing arrest and imprisonment. Arrests continued into the spring of 1949, with the two remaining Latin Catholic bishops being arrested in June because they had been unable to define a new constitution for the Catholic Church which was acceptable to the government.[13]

As regent of the nunciature, Bishop O'Hara was given no official notice of these actions and, while he protested against them, it was a futile gesture against a determined antagonist. O'Hara was himself harassed by the police. Vatican officials were stoic, feeling that the Communists were at last practising the persecution that the Vatican had expected for some time. Montini spoke of the Vatican's "policy of patience," whereby it allowed local churchmen to make the best response to these provocations that the local situations allowed.[14] The one action that the Vatican did take was to ensure that the American public was informed of this development by sending "an article on Religious Persecution in Rumania as well as a communication from the Secretariat of State of Vatican City on this subject" to the NCWC indicating that "it would be very useful if it could be found possible to print a translation of the article in its entirety."[15] By the end of June 1949, following the arrest of the Latin Catholic bishops, O'Hara was the sole remaining channel between the church in Romania and the Vatican and he very much feared for the continuation of his position.[16]

THE DESTRUCTION OF THE CATHOLIC CHURCH IN BULGARIA

Relations between the Bulgarian government and the Catholic Church were undisturbed until the summer of 1948. Before that, the government had been solicitous of the interests of the Catholics. Their properties had been exempted from the land reform program and Father Galloni continued to serve as the director of the Pro Oriente school while he was regent of the nunciature. Priests and nuns were treated with respect, Catholic schools continued to operate, and Catholic periodicals were published without hindrance.

The Catholics were tolerated because their small numbers posed no threat to the regime, because the government perceived the Catholics of the Latin rite of Pauline origins to be persecuted revolutionaries, because some cabinet ministers had been educated in Catholic schools, and because of the personal friendship between the regent and Georgi Dimitrov, the secretary of the Bulgarian Communist party. It was even suggested that Dimitrov's rivalry with Tito of Yugoslavia meant that Dimitrov practised religious toleration in order to contrast with Yugoslav persecution of the Catholics.[17] Relations between the Catholic Church and the government remained good until the summer of 1948.

The tone changed dramatically, however, following the Moscow pan-Orthodox Church Congress. In August the Bulgarian government introduced a decree to close foreign schools, many of which were Catholic, and Minister of Cults Iliev attacked Catholics through the government press. Relations between the Catholic Church and the

Bulgarian government deteriorated as the year progressed and an impossible tax was levied on Galloni's Pro Oriente school which the Vatican was unable to pay. Early in 1949 the press began to attack the Vatican as an agent of American imperialism and Galloni was refused a visa to return to Bulgaria.[18]

On 16 February 1949 a Law for Religious Sects, designed to nationalize the churches, was presented to the Bulgarian Grand National Assembly. Under this law, all sects were to have constitutions approved by the minister of foreign affairs, who was required to approve any initiative by any church. Foreign-based churches were not allowed to own property. The law was approved by the Assembly on 23 February and, at the same time, the apostolic delegation to Bulgaria was terminated by government decree. As a result of the new law the Orthodox Church effectively became a tool of state policy and the other churches were gradually closed down. The Italian government assisted the Italian and Bulgarian members of Pro Oriente to get out of Bulgaria. Foreign powers protested the Bulgarian treatment of the church and Catholic bishops in Bulgaria sought to develop a new church constitution for themselves.[19]

THE ARREST AND TRIAL OF
CARDINAL MINDSZENTY

The coincidence of moves against the Catholic Church in Romania, Bulgaria, and Hungary in the latter months of 1948 pointed to the fact that these strategies were being orchestrated in Moscow.[20] Certainly, in the case of Hungary, Cardinal Mindszenty had been constant in his opposition to the Hungarian government and its policies throughout 1948.

The nationalization of the confessional schools had been approved in the early summer and implemented in September. While Mindszenty led the opposition to this program and instructed priests not to teach in state schools, the government had sought some entente between church and state. The nationalization of the confessional schools had been followed by the collectivization of agriculture in July which had been mandated by Cominform pressure. The government feared that the unpopularity of their move against the church could be compounded by the agricultural collectivization should the church also oppose the latter program.[21]

Monsignor Csapik, the archbishop of Eger, paid his regular visit to Rome in September. The archbishop, who favoured a less intransigeant stance than Mindszenty and feared for the position of Catholic school teachers,[22] carried with him proposals from the Hungarian government for a compromise over the schools issue. The archbishop placed these proposals before Vatican officials as a way of circumventing Mindszenty's opposition. These officials, however, supported Mindszenty and opposed any settlement with the Hungarian government. In frustration, the Hungarian prime minister attacked Mindszenty in October as a leading counter-revolutionary and suggested that the government might soon have to act against him. Later in that month, the Cabinet Council issued a communiqué claiming that Mindszenty was breaking the laws and that he must be called to account. By the end of October the French ambassador was reporting that the press were writing that it was time "to finish with Mindszentyism" and that it appeared that the government was preparing some kind of trial which would enable them to remove him.[23]

By the time the Vatican offered to open discussions with the Budapest government in November, they were told that the prerequisite for the opening of talks was now the removal of Mindszenty from the primacy.[24] The British minister noted that the Communists had imposed harder and harsher rule on Hungary in recent months. While Rakosi was still in charge, new figures had been coming into political prominence who not only would not tolerate opposition, but were prepared to use the most brutal means to deal with it. All the churches were subservient to the state except for the Catholic which was being subjected to merciless public attacks. The minister suspected that the new desperation of the government arose because the Hungarians were being subjected to outside pressures.[25] Mindszenty anticipated his imminent arrest and sent a statement of his position out of the country in case it could not be published in Hungary. In the event, it was his private secretary, Dr Zakar, who was arrested first, on 20 November, and Mindszenty's statement was published at the end of November in the Vienna *Morning News*.

The Vatican expected Mindszenty's martyrdom. Certainly this was the position of Tardini in the Secretariat of State, who felt that Mindszenty had perhaps been too outspoken. Montini also thought that Mindszenty's strong stance had been counter-productive, especially over the school question. Tardini and Montini both stressed, however, that the Vatican would never disavow Mindszenty and his intransigent position.[26]

In early December a representative of the government met Mindszenty and apparently got the cardinal's agreement to make a statement recognizing the regime and accepting the recent social reforms, provided that the Bench of Bishops would agree. In spite of a conciliatory gesture by the Bench of Bishops on 16 December, no statement was forthcoming from Mindszenty. When asked about his earlier agreement to make such a statement, Mindszenty indicated that he had changed his mind.[27]

The Hungarian government hoped that the divisions within the Catholic hierarchy would facilitate reaching some kind of agreement with the church and permit them to sidestep the demands of Moscow for draconian action against Mindszenty. The Hungarian ambassador in Italy had been negotiating unsuccessfully with the Vatican to try to get them to recall Mindszenty. With no real possibility of negotiations, the Hungarian authorities were eventually left with no option but to comply with Moscow's wishes and to arrest Mindszenty on 27 December 1948.[28] The presence of Russian public prosecutor Andrei Vyshinsky in Budapest at the end of December was noted as evidence of Moscow's interest in this case.

The domestic reaction to Mindszenty's arrest was insignificant, indicating that the Catholic Church in Hungary was not as strong as the government may have thought. The government may not, however, have anticipated the extent of the foreign reaction, especially that of world Catholicism. The arrest of Mindszenty served to focus Catholic opinion on the new wave of persecution of the church behind the Iron Curtain and to involve Catholics directly in the issues of the Cold War. Seeking the strongest and the widest public support, the Vatican immediately asked Archbishop McNicholas, the chairman of the NCWC, to protest the arrest of Mindszenty "because of his defense of human rights and human freedom." Two days after the cardinal's arrest, McNicholas sent a formal protest to the Hungarian legation in Washington and a letter of sympathy to the pope. The president of the Canadian Catholic Congress asked Prime Minister St Laurent for a strong protest from the Canadian government.[29] Protests flowed into the Vatican from all over the world and were published as they arrived in the *Osservatore Romano*.

The official Vatican stance on the arrest of Mindszenty was to lodge a formal protest against the arrest of a member of the College of Cardinals, an "act of violence committed against a strenuous defender of the rights of the Church and of the human person, whose work for relief of his fellow countrymen during and after the war was well known."[30] The Vatican also excommunicated all those connected with the arrest of Mindszenty. It was important, above all, to preserve Catholic unity in Hungary. The Vatican feared that the removal of Mindszenty might open the rift in the church between conciliators and intransigents which could leave the Hungarian church at the mercy of the state. For this reason, Montini indicated that the Vatican was reluctant to throw oil on this fire and would encourage the bishops to work for an agreement with the state. At the beginning of the new year the pope sent a letter to the Hungarian bishops, offering condolences and calling on them to stand firm in defence of the church and their faith.[31]

Given the Catholic and the Vatican reaction, the question posed at the beginning of 1949 was whether the western powers would also protest the arrest of Mindszenty. Early indications were that neither the French nor the Italians would protest. The British believed that the Hungarian government already had their evidence against Mindszenty, so a protest would not be very helpful and could even be counter-productive.[32] The American government decided against lodging a protest and decided to wait and see whether U.S. Catholic opinion would demand that they take some action. The American indication was to let the Vatican "make the running."[33] Louis St Laurent told Cardinal McGuigan of Toronto that Canada was considering protesting the Mindszenty arrest as a violation of the peace treaty.[34] The Hungarian church hierarchy appreciated foreign reluctance to condemn the government action, since they felt that serious external criticism could effectively doom Mindszenty.[35]

Following the arrest of Mindszenty, the Hungarian government once again invited the bishops to take up the offer of negotiations. Even though there were reports that the bishops were divided over their response to this offer, by mid-January, to the great relief of the Vatican, they issued a statement that no negotiations would be possible with the government so long as Mindszenty remained in prison. Church-state relations had reached an impasse in the spring of 1949, and the church was now at the mercy of whatever policy the State wished to impose.[36]

Cardinal Mindszenty's show trial opened on 3 February. He was found guilty, and was sentenced to life imprisonment. International reaction to the sentence was outspoken and hostile. Reactions were noted from places as diverse as France, Panama, Belgium, and Brazil. In India a special mass was held in the Catholic churches throughout the country to protest religious persecution and, in Bombay, Mindszenty was held up as a "sublime example of Christian heroism."

A NEW PRIMATE FOR POLAND

On 22 October 1948 Cardinal Hlond, the primate of Poland, died. In response to friendly comments by President Bierut, the Polish bishops issued a conciliatory pastoral on 31 October, which asserted that the Vatican did not question the Polish frontiers and was sympathetic to the reorganization of the clergy in the western territories. Calling on Catholic parents to provide religious education for their children, the pastoral, at the same time, urged all Polish Catholics to work together to rebuild the Polish state.[37]

With the death of Hlond, the Polish church was leaderless. The government took advantage of this fact to initiate new attacks on the church in November, leading the hierarchy to urge Rome to fill the vacant primacy without delay. Diplomatic observers believed that these new attacks on the church were not made on the initiative of the Warsaw government, but that they were done on direct orders from Moscow.[38] In December the Polish Socialist and Communist parties were amalgamated at a conference, during which there was much public talk of the need to settle accounts with the church, leading to further speculation that the Polish government was under pressure from Moscow.[39] Under these circumstances, the Vatican made a quick decision; on 7 January 1949 it appointed the forty-seven-year-old Bishop Stefan Wyszynski as the new primate of Poland. This haste to shore up the church in Poland was a response to the general crisis in eastern Europe which had been brought to a head by the arrest of Cardinal Mindszenty.

The Vatican made this appointment on the suggestion of the Polish bishops; Wyszynski was an unknown quantity in Rome, although he had earlier been named by Cardinal Hlond as his spiritual successor.[40] The prominent features of Wyszynski were his youth and his energy; the Polish government was clearly hostile to such an appointment to lead the Polish church. Yet, with the death of Hlond, it was felt that the Polish church had lost their only bishop with an intransigeance similar to that of Cardinal Mindszenty and the appointment of Wyszynski replaced him with a young bishop with a clean record.[41] The new primate was enthroned on 2 February and promptly left Warsaw for a month's tour of the dioceses of Poland, during which time he avoided contact with all politicians and all representatives of foreign powers.

While Wyszynski was acquainting himself with the dioceses of Poland, the government argued that it was possible for a good communist to be, at the same time, a good Christian.[42] Talks resumed between Bishop Choromanski and Minister Wolski, and on 21 March, Wolski declared that the government were prepared to tolerate the church, as long as it remained in its own sphere and its clergy did not collaborate with groups opposing the government.

Wyszynski broke his silence on 3 April with a sermon attacking the Polish government and its imitation of the behaviour of the Soviet Union.[43] At Easter a pastoral of the Polish bishops responded to

Wolski's statement and called for support of religious education in the schools and the access of children to religious associations. In what was intended as a conciliatory gesture, the bishops assured the government that priests had been told to stay out of politics. New church-state negotiations were expected to follow when the church was given permission by the government to expand its membership on the negotiating commission from one (Bishop Choromanski) to three. In order to show good faith to the government, the primate and members of the hierarchy took great care not to discuss church-state relations with western diplomats in Warsaw. [44]

TOWARDS A NATIONAL CATHOLIC CHURCH IN CZECHOSLOVAKIA

Following the ecclesiastical suspension of Father Plojhar in June 1948, the government continued its attempts to attract the lower clergy to support the progressive goals of the regime, while at the same time restricting the activities of the church. By the end of the summer church control over religious education in the state schools had been restricted to one seminary and one boys' and one girls' school in each diocese. At the same time, the Catholic press had been either closed down or brought under tight censorship. A pastoral protesting these restrictions and other interference with the work of the church was read from all Catholic pulpits at the end of August. In spite of this pastoral, the state was reluctant to have an open breach and by November Beran was able to report that relations with the government were generally good.[45]

The original intention of the regime in Czechoslovakia had been to weaken the Catholic Church by splitting the lower clergy from the hierarchy, using Father Plojhar as an example of clerical cooperation. But the solidarity of the bulk of the clergy with their bishops under the astute leadership of Beran had negated this effort. In early 1949 the government, under Cominform orders to settle accounts, tried a different tack and introduced draft legislation to make the churches administratively subservient to the state. In this case, the government secured the agreement of the weaker Orthodox and Czechoslovak churches first and thereby isolated the Catholics. One bill was designed to make the clergy state employees and give the minister of education final say over the appointment of clergy and bishops. Another was designed to give privileges in the price of newsprint and foodstuffs only to cooperating churches.[46]

Negotiations resumed between the government and the Catholic Church in mid-February. In addition to Catholic acceptance of the new legislation, the government wanted a loyalty oath from the bishops and the lifting of Father Plojhar's suspension. They threatened retaliation against Catholic education and the creation of a Czechoslovak national church as a Catholic state church without ties to Rome if the Catholics would not comply. The Czech and Slovak bishops refused to negotiate under those conditions and, in the middle of May, the first concrete step towards the creation of a Czechoslovak national church occurred when the Ministry of Education published the first issue of *Catholic Clergy Gazette*, a government newsletter directed to the Catholic clergy.[47] At the end of that month Beran warned the clergy against the attempt to set up a new national church and threatened excommunication for any Catholics collaborating with the state in attacking the Catholic Church. In early June the authorities banned the publication of the primate's newsletter, *Acta Curiae*, and decreed that the *Catholic Clergy Gazette* was henceforth to be the only official publication for disseminating information to the clergy.[48]

On 11 June, Father Plojhar, assisted by the minister of education and a number of dissident priests, founded the National Committee of Catholic Action which declared itself to be loyal to the regime and opposed to western capitalism. Beran believed this to be the first step towards the creation of the national church. The National Committee immediately demanded that the hierarchy agree to continue negotiations with the government.[49] The bishops, in turn, issued a statement on 15 June, in which they denounced government claims that the church had not been willing to talk, excommunicated those responsible for creating and supporting the Committee on Catholic Action, and set out church conditions for the resumption of discussions with the state. One of these conditions called for ceasing the publication of the *Catholic Clergy Gazette*.[50]

A meeting of bishops at Beran's archepiscopal palace on 15 June was interrupted by the police who demanded the key to the archdiocesan archives and arrested Beran's secretary. The following day the palace was placed under police guard. At the same time, the police occupied the diocesan consistories of the other bishops of Czechoslovakia. On 18 June, from the pulpit of his cathedral, Beran attacked those who were betraying the church. But when he tried to read the bishops' pastoral letter the following day, he was heckled by members of the congregation. Pierson Dixon, the British minister in Prague, felt that the Czech government was under pressure to meet a Cominform deadline and that, because of Beran's resistance and reluctance to submit, the government had been forced to a direct and open confrontation between church and state.[51]

The Vatican were not surprised by this attack on the church in

Czechoslovakia. Montini felt that the attack on Beran only demonstrated how impossible it was for any churchman to deal with the Communists, since, unlike Cardinal Mindszenty, Beran had been completely accommodating and agreeable in his dealings with the government. Beran had, in fact, been an outspoken advocate of Catholic-Communist collaboration. A Canadian observer believed that the position of the church had been well managed by Beran, who was noted for his "moderation and democratic good sense." He was "no medieval prelate like Mindszenty."[52]

In order to support and defend the church in Czechoslovakia, the Holy Office issued a decree declaring that the Catholic Action movement promoted by the Czechoslovak government was schismatic "and that all those who associated themselves with it willingly were apostates and, *ipso facto*, excommunicated."[53] The government moves also prompted action by Slovak Catholics in defence of their church. At the end of June, it was reported that harsh measures taken against the church in Slovakia had been resisted by armed parishioners and had caused thirteen priests to be arrested and some towns to be placed under martial law. There were even rumours of Russian troop movements on the Slovak frontier. Verolino, the chargé d'affaires at the Prague nunciature, was harassed by the police when he went on a fact-finding tour of Slovakia at the end of June and his secretary was arrested in early July.[54]

The Czechoslovak government had intended to attract priests to join the Catholic Action movement and thereby to separate them from loyalty to Rome. By mid-July this initiative appeared to be a failure, since few priests had joined. The structure of Catholic Action was being installed throughout the country but the government felt that it needed more time to attract clergy and laity to this movement. Precipitous action could produce domestic and international reaction which would be counter-productive. In order to create a national church, the government needed real priests to support the movement. The Communist leaders of Czechoslovakia were alarmed by the determined resistance of Catholics and, as a result, secured Moscow's agreement to a temporary respite in the anti-church campaign.[55]

THE CHURCHES OF YUGOSLAVIA AND TITO'S BREAK WITH STALIN

In contrast with Romania, Bulgaria, Poland, Czechoslovakia, and Hungary, the Catholic Church had lost all semblance of independence in Yugoslavia by the end of 1947. The Tito regime had circumscribed the activity of the church in Croatia and the imprisonment of Stepinac had sapped the Catholics' will to resist. While the Slovenian clergy, which had not collaborated with the Axis during the war, was initially left alone, it too was attacked by the government in the summer and fall of 1947. In addition to this restriction and persecution, the Yugoslav government attempted to separate the lower clergy from the hierarchy and to win the former to support a national church. In January 1947 the president of the Croatian government called for the creation of a national Yugoslav Catholic Church which would be in accord with the fundamental aspirations of the people.[56]

By the spring of 1948 the Catholic Church existed on the suffrance of government and party in Yugoslavia. The churches were open for services, but too much enthusiastic support by the laity would put them in the bad books of the party. Religious education was non-existent, seminaries had been closed, religious had been prevented from living in convents and monasteries, hospitals and schools had been taken away from orders of nuns, the Catholic press had been suppressed, and the state promoted constant propaganda in favour of atheism. Regent Hurley protested constantly but his protests had little effect. By 1948, Hurley believed that his most valuable contribution, through his continued presence in Yugoslavia, was in providing moral support to the bishops in their dealings with the government.[57]

In June 1948 Yugoslavia entered a new phase of its history when it was expelled from the Cominform, and Tito was courted by the western powers in order to enhance the split between Belgrade and Moscow. Under these circumstances, Tito might have been expected to change his treatment of the churches in order to curry western favour. Such, however, was not the case since Tito continued his harsh treatment of the Catholic clergy and laity after his break with Moscow.

During the summer of 1948 Tito's press attacked the Vatican as being in league with world capitalism and the bishop of Mostar and other clergy were put on trial, as were a number of Croats who were charged with spying for the Vatican.[58] There was no respite in Yugoslav persecution of the Catholics at a time when western nations such as Canada were establishing diplomatic relations with Tito. In the late fall of 1948, in a gesture designed to placate his western supporters, Tito offered, in return for Croat political support, to release Archbishop Stepinac provided that he left Yugoslavia permanently. The discussions allegedly foundered on the reluctance of Stepinac to consider leaving the country, in spite of Tito's increasing pressure on the Catholics to induce them to come to terms.[59]

There was no improvement in the treatment of any of the churches in 1949. The arrest of the bishop of Mostar had meant that no Catholic bishops were left in Bosnia-Herzegovina. In March the first congress of the Union of Societies of Orthodox Priests of Yugoslavia was held. This organization, first established in 1947, had been formed for those priests willing to collaborate with the government. It sought to establish a labour-management model in the Orthodox Church and thereby to undermine the influence of the hierarchy.[60]

While the United States did an abrupt about-face in its relationship with Yugoslavia after June 1948, the Vatican realized that Yugoslavia had changed little as a result of the split with the Cominform and that "the split was inconsequential in terms of policy."[61] Immediately following Tito's expulsion from the Cominform, Pope Pius XII commented to the British ambassador to the Holy See that the split with Moscow was irrelevant since, even if Tito was at odds with Moscow, he was still a communist who persecuted the church and the church must not enter compromise agreements with such people.[62]

Through official channels, the Vatican sought to impress on the American government that the Tito regime was consistently violating religious liberties. Where in earlier years Bishop Hurley's reports from Belgrade had been read with interest by American officials, by 1948 and 1949 they became an embarrassment since the United States was determined to exploit the split between Tito and Stalin as part of their Cold War strategy and to ignore Vatican sensibilities in doing so. Historian Charles Gallagher claims that Tito's expulsion from the Soviet bloc in 1948 "represented a complete fracture of US-Vatican interests."[63]

Realizing that the State Department was less sympathetic to the Vatican position, in the summer of 1948 Hurley had circumvented the State Department by making an appeal directly to Myron Taylor. Taylor submitted Hurley's report, entitled "The Controversy between the Komonform [sic] and the Communist Party of Yugoslavia," to President Truman. In his report, Hurley warned that Tito was no less a communist because of his quarrel with Stalin and expressed a fear that, in order to drive a wedge between the two dictators, the United States might be willing to subsidize the Tito regime with outside aid, not realizing that this would have no effect whatsoever on the behaviour of the regime. Hurley was, however, too late with his warnings. In May 1949 the Yugoslavs asked directly for $25 million from the US Export-Import Bank in Washington. Hurley was outraged and wrote another report on Yugoslav religious persecution for President Truman, cataloguing the anti-Catholic measures of the Tito regime from 1947 to 1949. This Taylor delivered to Truman on 14 June but the United States still proceeded to grant the requested loan to Yugoslavia in September 1949.

Realizing that the American Catholic presence in Yugoslavia was of diminishing utility, in June 1949 the Vatican sent a Monsignor Sigismondi to Belgrade as the first Italian to be appointed since the war. One observer commented that the Vatican appeared to think that Italians might now be more useful than Americans in the Belgrade nunciature.[64]

18 The Religious Cold War: The Catholic Counter-Offensive

The situation in Yugoslavia demonstrated the extent to which the Vatican and the United States were increasingly out of sympathy with each other. Vatican concern about religious persecution in the Communist bloc was not eliciting much sympathy or support from American policy-makers. Nor did the United States see much value in bolstering the position of east European Catholics as leaders of opposition to the Communist regimes in the area. The Vatican realized that, in protecting east European Catholics, they were very much alone, in spite of the Cold War rhetoric of the Americans.

Ostensibly, from the American perspective, the Cold War was a program to contain communism and prevent its extension outside the area directly controlled by Moscow.[1] Tito's break with Stalin meant that the United States was prepared to incorporate Tito's regime into the anti-Moscow bloc. Contrasted with these strategic calculations, the Vatican remained in an ideological conflict with communism. Tito was no less anti-Catholic by being inside the American camp than he had been when he had been part of Stalin's bloc. It was apparent that the United States was not prepared to support the Catholic Church in resisting the encroachment of atheistic policies and practices on the Catholic community within the Communist bloc. Under these circumstances, the Cold War took on a different meaning for the Vatican and the Catholic Church than it did for the United States and the western entente. By the spring of 1949 the Vatican took the lead in defining new directions for the church in coping with the threats from the East. With the church under attack in a variety of locations in eastern

Europe, from Romania to Hungary, it was essential that Catholics be given direction in how best to respond to these attacks. The French ambassador to the Holy See noted that, in the spring of 1949, Pius XII was preparing the Holy See for a major struggle with communism in eastern Europe and for continued control within Italy.[2]

It was the arrest and conviction of Cardinal Mindszenty which prompted the pope into action. On 14 February 1949, in response to the life sentence imposed on the cardinal, Pius XII convened a special consistory of the College of Cardinals, "to unfold to you Our soul which is crushed with most bitter grief." In his allocution the pope denounced the treatment of Mindszenty as an attempt by the Communist authorities to disrupt the Catholic Church in Hungary. Pius asserted that the Holy See was prepared to live with any form of government and called on the Hungarian episcopate to stand united in strengthening the hope of the faithful.[3] A week later the pope made an eloquent public address to the people of Rome on the imprisonment of Mindszenty and on the persecution of the church in totalitarian and anti-religious states. "The condemnation inflicted on the banks of the Danube on a Cardinal of the Holy Roman Church," he said, "has raised on the banks of the Tiber a cry of indignation worthy of the eternal city. But the fact that a Government hostile to religion has struck this time at a Prince of the Church, venerated by the vast majority of his people, is no isolated case; it is one of the links in the long chain of persecutions which certain dictatorial States are carrying out against Christian life and doctrine." Totalitarian and anti-religious states, according to Pius, wanted weak and silent churches which stood for no principle whatsoever.

Can [the Pope] then be silent, when in a certain country men tear with violence or fraud from the centre of Christianity, from Rome, the Churches united to her, imprison all the Greek Catholic Bishops because they refuse to apostatize from their faith, persecute and arrest priests and faithful because they refuse to leave their true Mother Church?

Can the Pope be silent, when a minority regime removes from parents the right to educate their own children, in order to draw those children away from Christ?

Can the Pope be silent, when a State, exceeding the limits of its competence, arrogates to itself the power to suppress dioceses, to depose Bishops, to upset the organisation of the Church, and to reduce it below the minimum requirements for the effective cure of souls?

Can the Pope be silent, when men reach the point of punishing with imprisonment a priest guilty of having refused to violate the most sacred and involate of secrets, the secret of sacramental confession?[4]

A week later the pope talked proudly with a representative of the American Office to the Holy See of the positive reaction which he had received to this speech. "He said that time had come to speak out clearly and fearlessly and that he would continue to do so as it was now evident that there could be no compromise or modus vivendi between Christianity and Bolshevism." The pope took pains to point out that the "immense crowd who came to hear him speak was predominantly male.⁵ He called them 'soldiers prepared for the battle'." It was noted that "his entire tone and bearing was that of a militant leader who was prepared to engage the enemy at whatever cost."⁶

Coupled with this public militancy on the part of the pope was a new Vatican emphasis on the social doctrine of the church, designed to underline Catholic credentials for reforming society. In the spring of 1949 the Holy See sought to differentiate the Catholic position from that of both capitalism and communism. While Cardinal Suhard of Paris would issue a communiqué against the French Movement of Progressive Christians in early March, leading the *Osservatore Romano* to comment approvingly that good Catholics cannot affiliate or cooperate with communists, Vatican Radio in January had indicated that it was possible for Catholics to work with those socialists, like the British Labour party, which had departed from doctrinaire marxism and espoused principles of Christian social reform.⁷

The real restatement of the papal social position occurred in the late spring, in a series of articles in the *Osservatore Romano*. Social justice had been selected as the central theme of the 1950 Holy Year and the articles consisted of a reprinting of pastoral letters by various bishops, setting out the Catholic social position between the values of capitalism and those of communism:

Neither system met with the approval of the Church, which desired an economic system in which the majority could own property and the accumulation of wealth in the hands of a few would be prevented. The Church regarded private ownership as indispensable to freedom and the development of the human personality: it also encouraged the foundation of a family and increased diligence. But the Church desired also a fairer distribution of human wealth, and private property should not attain proportions harmful to the common good.

On 27 March the pope spoke in similar fashion to pottery workers from Civita Castellana. He said "that work was no doubt often not only toilsome but ill-remunerated. He had already done and would continue to do whatever he could not only to help those in need, but also to face with their responsibilities those who tried to shirk them."

He made a further statement on social and economic policy to an international Catholic employers' association in May, referring often to the 1931 encyclical *Quadragesimo Anno*, calling for cooperation in the workplace and praising the corporate approach to economic planning.[8]

The onset of the Holy Year provided the Holy See with several opportunities for reinforcing the Christian message at a time when it felt the need to have its voice heard above the din of international politics. One such preparation for the Holy Year was a series of lectures, which culminated on 27 May with the first major public address by Giovanni Battista Montini on the theme of Christian peace. The choice of Montini to give this speech was interpreted as a significant public gesture of papal confidence.

THE ORTHODOX CHURCH AND THE COLD WAR

In spite of its reluctance to assist the Catholic Church behind the Iron Curtain, the United States, working through Myron Taylor, brought the Cold War to the Orthodox Church in 1948 by organizing resistance to the growing power of the Russian Church within the Orthodox communion. The increasing influence of the Moscow patriarchy was also of concern to the Ecumenical Patriarch in Constantinople, to the Greek Orthodox Church, then participating in a civil war against Greek communists, and to the Vatican. The illness and subsequent weakness of Ecumenical Patriarch Maximos was a concern when Moscow was putting itself forward as the "Protector of the Mother Church."

Since this situation was working to the advantage of the Soviets in eastern Europe and the Middle East, it soon brought a response from Washington. On the eve of the founding meeting of the World Council of Churches in 1948, Truman expanded Myron Taylor's responsibility to include relationships with the heads of various religious denominations. The World Council of Churches refused to play a role in the Cold War, however, advising Taylor that there was "no iron curtain in religion," and keeping the door open for the eventual participation of the Russian Orthodox Church in its deliberations.

Instead, Taylor sought to replace the Ecumenical Patriarch Maximos with a candidate who would be more willing and able to resist the growing influence of Moscow. The candidate of the Americans and the Greeks was an American citizen, Archbishop Athenagoras, metropolitan of the Greek Orthodox Church in the United States. Taylor had met Athenagoras in the spring of 1948 and had sounded the Vatican about this possible change through Roncalli, the nuncio in Paris. On the advice of Roncalli, Taylor approached the Turkish government indirectly to ensure that they would overlook the problem of the candidate's American citizenship and, on 1 November 1948, Maximos having resigned, Athenagoras was elected Ecumenical Patriarch.

The election of Athenagoras threatened to bring the Cold War to the Orthodox Church, since he was clearly the American candidate and was even flown to Istanbul in the American presidential plane. Yet while his association with the United States enhanced his prestige, Athenagoras was not willing to play the American game, since he did not believe that Patriarch Alexei was a Soviet pawn but rather a sincere churchman attempting to cope in very difficult circumstances. As a consequence, Athenagoras held a positive attitude to Moscow and sought, where he could, to reach out to the Russian Orthodox Church in the interest of Orthodox unity.[9]

Because of his American connections, Athenagoras initially had little influence with the Orthodox churches under Soviet rule who had deliberately snubbed his installation as Patriarch in January 1949. Accordingly, he immediately let it be known through the Italian ambassador that he was interested in a closer working relationship with the Vatican, perhaps even working together for representation at the United Nations. At the same time, he professed his loyalty to Turkey and a desire for closer relations with Islam.[10]

The Vatican initially responded favourably to the prospect of coordinating resistance to the activities of the Moscow Patriarchate with Athenagoras. In early April 1949 Monsignor Cassulo, the apostolic delegate in Istanbul, had his first meeting with Athenagoras. They later agreed to meet secretly during their mutual summer holidays on the island of Prinkipo for serious conversations on the relationship between their two churches. The secrecy was necessary lest members of either church should be concerned about the conversations. Initial talks took place on 11 August; while the Holy See was interested in closer ties with the patriarch, it was, at the same time, cautious about where these talks might lead.[11] Yet the more Athenagoras learned of the expectations of his various followers, the less able he became to open a dialogue with the Vatican. Part of the difficulty lay in the fact that Rome was unprepared to recognize the validity of the Orthodox communion. At the beginning of the Holy Year the pope called on all separated brethren to return to the true church and, in his opposition to communism, proved himself unwilling to share moral leadership with the Ecumenical Patriarch.[12]

THE HOLY OFFICE DECREE

On 1 July 1949 the Holy Office published a decree indicating that members or supporters of the Communist party, or those who publish, read, write or disseminate printed materials in support of communist doctrine and practice, would be excommunicated. This decree represented a significant counter-offensive by the Holy See in the religious cold war with the Communist bloc.

Following the 1948 elections in Italy, it was felt that there should be a clarification of the relationship which should exist between Catholics and Communists. The Holy Office accordingly initiated a study to give guidance to clergy and laity on the position they should take when faced with the question of belonging to or supporting the Communist party. Where Italian politics had provided the reason for initiating the study, it was the increased pressure on Catholics in Czechoslovakia in the spring of 1949 which demonstrated the urgent need for a response to the question.[13] Realizing that the anti-communist west was unwilling and unable to help those Catholics who were under Communist rule, the Vatican had no alternative but to use weapons of its own to cope with Communist persecution by denying to the persecutors and their Catholic allies the prospects of eternal salvation.

Where the decree could be seen as a response to an immediate political situation in eastern Europe, it could also serve as a guide to Catholics in western Europe and the rest of the world in their confrontation with communism in their daily lives. For this reason, the Vatican saw the decree not as a response to an immediate political situation, but as a timeless statement of long-term principle, similar in its intent to the 1864 Syllabus of Errors, which outlined for the faithful the principal errors of contemporary civilization in the nineteenth century. According to Montini's conversation with Frankin Gowen of the American Office, the pope felt that matters had now reached the point where no compromise with communism was possible, even if it meant the possible rupture of diplomatic relations and even the persecution of Catholics.[14] The elimination of the ambiguities in the Catholic-communist relationship meant that a religious cold war had in effect been defined as a holy war against communist unrighteousness. The influence of Ottaviani and the Roman party could be seen behind the decree which effectively limited the potential political partners for the Italian Christian Democrats to parties of the centre and the right wing.

In spite of the long-term intent behind the decree, the Holy Office bungled the public release of the document, with the result that it was not received with the intended contextual explanation. Once it had been approved by the pope, the Holy Office gave the text to the printers for publication but the printers leaked the decree to the press well ahead of the expected time of release. Even the pope, it appears, learned of the decree's release from the media. The Secretariat of State was faced with exercising damage control, since the public had not been adequately prepared for this announcement.

Before long, the annoyance of the Secretariat of State was succeeded by astonishment at the impact of the decree and the kind of public support for this response to communist treatment of the church. Much of the positive support came from Protestant countries and much of the negative comment came, as expected, from the communists. Togliatti, the Italian Communist party leader, was extremely careful in his response, since many Italian communists were also practising Catholics. It was understood by the Secretariat of State that clear instructions for the implementation of the decree must now be sent to the clergy and that the religious prohibition of the decree must be accompanied by a more fully developed social doctrine.[15]

Where the restatement of Catholic social policy had been important in the spring of 1949, the Holy Office decree re-emphasized the need to cope with the attractiveness to many Catholics of communist social policy. Hence more emphasis was placed on Catholic social policy in the fall, notably when Pius XII addressed a delegation of twelve hundred members of the Christian Working Class Movement of Belgium on 11 September. The Holy See quite deliberately sought to position itself between the two sides in the Cold War as it approached the Holy Year of 1950. In his Christmas message of 23 December, on the eve of the opening of the Holy Year, the pope called for a religious renewal of the modern world and a return to the true faith, directing his remarks particularly towards those following materialistic ideologies.[16]

With this decree, the Holy See issued its challenge to the Communist rulers of eastern Europe and to those Catholics who were prepared to collaborate with the east European regimes. The religious cold war was now joined in earnest, since the Vatican had brandished its weapon of excommunication to challenge the strategies of the east European Communists for subverting Catholic communities which had been forced to live under communism. The specific conflicts and persecutions in eastern Europe and elsewhere had now been universalized into aspects of a holy war against unrighteousness.

Initial reactions to the decree ranged from strong official approval in Franco's Spain to silence from the Soviet press to outright hostility in the Italian left-wing press. Athenagoras gave his warm approval to the decree, but resisted pressure from the United States to issue a similar one.[17] At the same time, Romanian Patriarch Justinian attacked the decree as the worst mistake that the Vatican had made in years. The Mexican Communist party claimed that the decree was evidence of the Vatican connection to American imperialism.[18] Many Hungarian Catholics were worried by the decree which, they claimed, did not indicate an understanding of the east European situation and was too much influenced by Italian and American perspectives. They felt it particularly difficult at a time when the Hungarian government appeared to have abandoned the plan to create a separate Hungarian national church.[19] The Turkish press, as a result of the Holy Office decree, spoke about the need for Turkish rapprochement with the Vatican and with the Islamic world to create a strong front to resist the spread of communism.[20]

In Italy the Communists minimized the significance of the decree, while members of the anti-clerical left were reported to be confused. A British diplomat believed that the church would let individual priests resolve matters in their parishes and felt that the main effect of the decree would be on Italian women with their strong influence on family life. It was expected to have the greatest effect in the Italian south, less in the centre, and considerably less in the north, although it was felt that it might affect the consciences of some "bourgeois communists" there. In the long term, the British analyst believed that it could make Communist proselytization more difficult.[21]

AFTERMATH OF
THE HOLY OFFICE DECREE

While the Holy Office decree was a grand gesture to show the Vatican's determination to resist communism, it was ultimately an ill-judged move and counter-productive in its aim of sustaining church solidarity in the face of communism. At first, the decree gave the Vatican the initiative in its struggle with the regimes of eastern Europe and the rulers of the East were reported to have been alarmed enough to decrease their persecution of the church, and leading members of the Czechoslovak government travelled to Moscow in July to urge the necessity of a slower pace in the anti-Catholic campaign.[22]

In October the BBC quoted a *Civiltà Cattolica* report that a recent Cominform meeting had developed new tactics against the church in order to neutralize the impact of Holy Year. In November Cardinal Tisserant told the French ambassador to the Holy See that he felt the Soviets had changed their tactics on religion, based on their conviction that it is impossible to eradicate religious belief from a people and that religion could in fact prove to be a good vehicle for communist expansion if communism and Christianity could be equated. This appeared to have worked well in the Soviet Union once the Russian Orthodox hierarchy had come on side and the support of the Russian church had influenced the situation in Bulgaria and Romania. The difficulty for the Soviets lay in the Catholic satellites of Poland, Hungary, and Czechoslovakia, where Tisserant believed the strategy was to split the lower clergy from the bishops and from Rome through support of progressive Catholics. Moscow also hoped to sell the idea of the Soviet Union as a protector of Christianity.[23]

What soon became apparent was not a lessening of pressure on the church but a standardization of approach across eastern Europe, with legislation being introduced in many countries for the direct financial administration of the church by government departments. In most countries of eastern Europe in the winter of 1949–50, the Roman Catholic Church had been so limited and controlled that, without external assistance, it was powerless in the face of new moves to restrict its activities. The Holy Office decree gave little comfort and created considerable embarrassment for east European Catholics, since its message was to accept persecution with stoic determination and under no circumstances negotiate a modus vivendi with the regimes of the anti-Christ. Yet for those Catholics who understood the weakness of the church, such negotiation with local governments was the only option left to them if they were to preserve any vestige of Catholic independence. The Holy Office decree forced some east European churchmen to choose between loyalty to their church and loyalty to the Holy See.

Czechoslovakia

Within Czechoslovakia, priests and nuns were warned by the government that any priest who gave effect to the Holy Office decree would be prosecuted for treason. By early August it was reported that Archbishop Olomouc, who was subsequently placed under house arrest, had excommunicated a priest who had supported the National Committee of Catholic Action. It was also reported that another priest had been convicted in Prague of high treason for refusing the sacraments to a sick woman who had admitted to being a communist. Neither the church nor the government wished to push this situation to an open break, however.[24]

In September the government took a different approach when it introduced a bill in the National Assembly to assume financial control of the church. Approved on 14 October, this legislation created a State Office for Church Affairs to administer all church property and to pay all expenses, including salaries, of the church.[25] The bishops had little choice but to advise their clergy to take the required oath of loyalty to the government and accept the new salaries; only the bishops would refuse them. While this prevented a split between clergy and hierarchy, the new laws considerably strengthened the state and weakened the position of the bishops. On 17 November the bishops advised the government that they could not obey the new legislation and asked that it be amended to recognize the responsibility of the bishops for the administration of the Church.[26] This refusal to obey the new laws did not elicit any response from the state which, by the end of 1949, was distracted by new purge trials and by plans for the collectivization of agriculture, as insisted upon by Moscow. From his observation post in Rome, Tardini was encouraged by the resistance of the Czech bishops and clergy and felt that Archbishop Beran's serenity contrasted well with the posture of Mindszenty. Some felt that Beran had learned a great deal from Mindszenty's mistakes.[27] During the third week in January 1950 the Czechoslovak clergy took the oath of allegiance to the state as they were ordered to do by their bishops.

Acceptance of state control over the church did not stop the hostility of the state towards the church. In mid-March 1950 Verolino, the Vatican chargé d'affaires, was ordered to leave Czechoslovakia and the government refused to approve visas for his designated successors. At the beginning of April the chargé d'affaires and the chancellor were withdrawn from the Czechoslovak legation to the Holy See, with the result that diplomatic relations between the Czechoslovak government and the Holy See effectively stopped, even though they were never officially broken off.[28]

While dealing with the institutional Catholic Church, the state found itself also involved with the spiritual and social aspects of church life. On 11 December 1949 nineteen parishioners in the church of Cihost claimed to have seen the cross in the church move during the mass. This alleged "Miracle of Cihost" was treated cautiously by church authorities. It attracted such popular interest, however, that the government eventually felt that it had to turn the church over to priests who were supporters of the government and had, consequently, been excommunicated, who set about to prove that the miracle had been fabricated.[29]

While the spiritual enthusiasm associated with this alleged miracle embarrassed the Communist government, it did try to align itself closely with the social goals of the churches by promoting what one British diplomat referred to as the "insidious fiction" of equating the goals of socialism with the goals of Christianity. The government-sponsored Catholic Action movement promoted this view, as did many of the non-Catholic churches, notably the Czechoslovak church. The Roman Catholic Church found itself isolated in the face of this ideological offensive, designed to confuse the opponents of communism by making them forget the fundamental antagonism of marxism-leninism to religion.[30]

Romania

Following the Holy Office decree, the Romanian government closed fifteen Catholic religious orders and put an end to ongoing negotiations between church and state. By the fall of 1949 the Catholic Church in Romania was devastated. The Uniate Church had been brutally dissolved, Latin-rite priests had been put on salaries, and plans were being made for the creation of a national Catholic Church. All six Uniate bishops and both Latin-rite bishops had been put in prison and not been heard from since.[31] Given the weakness of the Catholic Church in Romania, the remaining priests were showing themselves ever more willing to reach accommodation with the government. Yet in May 1950 the Holy Office excommunicated those Latin-rite priests in Romania who were trying "to entice the Catholic clergy and the faithful from their due allegiance to their legitimate Bishops and, in particular, to the Roman Pontiff."[32]

Romanian authorities ignored the existence of the papal representative in Bucharest. When Regent O'Hara protested the arrest of two bishops in July 1949, his note was returned unopened. While O'Hara continued in office, he believed that he was only kept there to witness the demise of the Catholic Church.[33] In June 1950 the government decided to close the nunciature. O'Hara was accused of spying and of plotting the overthrow of the Romanian Communist regime, and was expelled from Romania. On papal orders, before leaving the country, he secretly consecrated six new bishops as a means of sustaining the Romanian hierarchy underground. He returned to the United States as archbishop bishop of Savannah-Atlanta, being honoured by the pope with the personal title of archbishop in "recognition of the valued services rendered to the Church under such difficult circumstances and at such great personal sacrifice."[34]

Poland

In contrast to the other east European churches, the church in Poland was influential enough that it could still conduct effective negotiations even though to do so was in clear violation of Vatican orders. The Polish hierarchy deliberately said nothing about the Holy Office decree and Primate Wyszynski let it be known that he did not intend to make much of it. Nevertheless, the bishops were attacked, along with the Vatican, for what was perceived to be unwarranted interference in Polish affairs. The Council of Ministers issued a decree on 10 August to protect freedom of religion in Poland in response to the threat to this freedom posed by the Holy Office decree.[35]

The decree was only one of a number of issues which came between church and state in the summer of 1949. On 3 July an old woman saw tears on a portrait of the Virgin Mary in Lublin cathedral and another woman was cured of blindness. This "miracle of Lublin" generated much popular enthusiasm and brought such great crowds of believers to Lublin that the government was moved to close the cathedral to visitors. Although the church had not officially validated this alleged miracle, the harsh action of the government worsened church-state relations.[36]

Another crisis was occasioned by the 17 July address by the pope to the residents of Berlin. In this broadcast, Pius XII offered much praise for the Christian way of life of the Berlin Catholics, leading one British diplomat to comment that the speech showed the pope's affinity for Germany and the Germans, since there was no suggestion that they might have brought their recent calamities upon themselves. The pope's speech was reported by the Polish press as an anti-Polish gesture designed to foster moves to revise the German-Polish frontier.[37]

With the creation of the Federal Republic of Germany in May 1949, an Italian diplomat speculated that one of the first embassies that the Germans would seek to open would be at the Holy See, where they could be expected to raise the question of the German-Polish frontier and the Polish western territories.[38] In fact, it was the Vatican that moved unilaterally to grant diplomatic recognition to the German Federal Republic when the pope named Monsignor Muench as regent of the nunciature in Bonn in October. The pope had acted without the expected diplomatic reciprocity from the Bonn government and in violation, according to the French, of the statute of German occupation. The Lublin "miracle" and the pope's speech were held to have reopened the conflict between church and state in Poland.

Nevertheless, the government authorized the resumption of talks between Wolski and Bishop Choromanski in July, in order, it was suggested, to prevent the church from informing Poles of the decree.[39] The pope's gesture of sending an open letter to the Polish bishops on the tenth anniversary of the German invasion of Poland on 1 September served to counteract his 1948 letter to the German bishops. The letter went some way towards smoothing relations, praising the suffering of the Polish church and calling on the church to stand firm against other persecutions.[40]

Negotiations between church and state continued throughout the latter half of 1949. The longer the negotiations dragged on, the more potential there was for divisions to appear in the church. Some progressive Catholic intellectuals, particularly those around the publications *Slowo Powszechny* and *Dzis I Jutro*, wanted to see a socialist Catholic state survive, and wanted the church to be accommodating to the regime in order to reach a firm church-state accord. At the same time, the Vatican reminded the Polish bishops that Communists never keep their agreements. By December, Cardinal Sapieha was discouraged with the unsatisfactory state of the negotiations, since nothing the hierarchy appeared willing to do would satisfy the government.[41]

In January 1950 the government claimed to find evidence of financial mismanagement in the clerical administration of the Catholic welfare agency *Caritas*, and took over the direct administration of the agency. When it convened a series of meetings of clergy to explain the reasons for the takeover, some priests spoke favourably of the government action. At a national conference at Warsaw in January 1950 attended by fifteen hundred members of the clergy, many criticized the "bad shepherds" who had administered *Caritas*. While the hierarchy protested the takeover and admonished those priests who had attended the government-sponsored meetings, it was noted that the participating priests represented a significant number of younger clergy who were obviously looking for some way to resolve the differences between church and state.[42]

Some observers, including Cardinal Sapieha, interpreted this move as part of a government strategy to create a national Catholic Church in Poland. Government control of *Caritas* was seen as the equivalent of the move by the Czechoslovak government to create a state-directed Catholic Action movement. These new institutions could eventually form the basis for national Catholic Churches. In early March 1950 the government announced the takeover of larger church estates and indicated that the revenues from some of these lands would be used for a fund to support deserving priests in their social programs.

Given this evidence of government aggression against the Catholic Church, observers were stunned by the announcement on 14 April that agreement had been reached in the negotiations between state and church carried out by Minister Wolski and Bishop Choromanski and that an agreement had been signed by government and church representatives. In this agreement, the church supported the social and political goals of the state, including the permanence of the so-called recovered territories in western Poland, in return for control over religious education and freedom of public worship.[43] The advantages to the government included the acceptance by the Church of the status quo in Poland, the fact that the agreement would have a calming effect on public opinion, and the fact that the agreement could be seen as proof that religion was not being oppressed in Poland. It was seen to be an appropriate agreement for a nation where the population was overwhelmingly Roman Catholic.[44]

The church was aware of strategies being used by Communist governments in eastern Europe to divide clergy and bishops and to separate the Roman Catholic Church from Rome. The hierarchy was also aware of a growing body of Catholic opinion that favoured accommodation with the state and might forsake the hierarchy and their allegiance to Rome if that were the only way that some accommodation could be achieved. The Polish hierarchy, with the exception of Cardinal Sapieha, were in agreement with signing the accord to ensure domestic peace in Poland. Sapieha deliberately left for Rome before the accord was signed and thereby facilitated the conclusion of negotiations.[45]

Since the appointment of Wyszynski as primate at the beginning of 1949, leading members of the Polish hierarchy had deliberately avoided contact with western diplomats in Warsaw. This continued to be the case after the signing of the church-state agreement. It became apparent that the Polish hierarchy had also kept their distance from the Vatican and had used their own judgment in concluding the agreement with the Polish government, recognizing that it was in direct violation of the 1949 Holy Office decree.

The Vatican was not pleased that this agreement had been concluded without its prior approval, especially since the agreement was out of line with the positions taken by the Polish hierarchy earlier in the year over the *Caritas* affair. Tardini told the British minister to the Holy See that the agreement was "simply disastrous." Not only should it have been referred to the Holy See for approval before it was signed, but the Vatican did not like being committed to support of the Oder-Neisse frontier. The Polish hierarchy had, in fact, played into the hands of the Communist authorities by separating themselves from Rome over this issue. The agreement was felt to set a bad precedent for the church in Hungary and Czechoslovakia. Indeed, shortly after the signing of the agreement, members of the Hungarian government urged the Hungarian church to be similarly accommodating. The Polish church had left the Vatican the choice of either disavowing the Polish hierarchy or accepting the agreement. The Secretariat of State chose the latter course and retained a stony public silence.[46]

Hungary

In a fashion comparable to the situation in Czechoslovakia and Romania, the church in Hungary had been totally defeated by the government. Many Hungarian Catholics thought that the Holy Office decree did not apply well to the situation in eastern Europe and, while the government press attacked the decree, neither the clergy nor the Hungarian Bench of Bishops were willing to make any reference to it.[47] Since the arrest of Cardinal Mindszenty, the Hungarian church had been quiet and docile and was unwilling to create any further trouble for itself with the government. In December 1949 the Bench of Bishops authorized the priests to take a modified oath of allegiance to the state; the bishops themselves would only take this oath with the authorization of the Vatican. Following the Polish church-state agreement, Archbishop Joszef Grösz, acting as primate during the imprisonment of Mindszenty, sought and obtained a similar agreement with the Hungarian government on 15 August 1950. This agreement, unlike that concluded in Poland, secured fewer advantages for the church and gave more to the state, to the chagrin of the Vatican.[48]

THE END OF THE TAYLOR MISSION

The Yugoslav situation and the more independent stance of the Vatican had repercussions on relations between Washington and the Holy See. Fearing war between East and West as a result of the Berlin blockade in the fall and winter of 1948–9, the Vatican sought to give the impression of neutrality in order to be available to play a mediating role between Moscow and Washington. On 19 October 1948 Pius XII received a visit from George Marshall, the American secretary of state. Vatican officials worried that Marshall's visit might suggest to the Communists that the Holy See was an active participant in the Anglo-American camp. The Americans, on the other hand, wanted the Marshall visit to give exactly that impression of the pope as a close ally of the United States in the Cold War.[49]

The differing views of the Marshall visit were symptomatic of a growing rift between the Vatican and the United States. In contrast to the Cold War division of Europe, Pius XII continued to speak warmly of European Union as he did in an address to the International Congress on European Union on 12 November 1948. The pope claimed to have favoured European Union as the solution to Europe's problems since the war, provided that it had a solid moral base and was made by people with good moral values.[50] The support for European Union reflected the views of Montini, who was most interested in the integration of Italy with the rest of Europe; the alternative position of military preparedness and active Italian participation in the North Atlantic Treaty Organization (NATO) was espoused more in 1949 by Tardini within the Secretariat of State.[51] The re-election of Truman and the prospective Communist victory in China allayed Vatican fears of imminent war by the end of 1948, since it believed that the Soviet Union had had its attention diverted into Asia.[52]

While American media and the American Catholic community reacted with shock and horror to the arrest and imprisonment of Mindszenty, Vatican relations with the American government deteriorated in 1949. One thorny issue arose out of relations with the new state of Israel, which had been created with American support in May 1948. The foundation of this Jewish state created difficulties for the other residents of Palestine, many of whom were Roman Catholic. On 24 October 1948 the pope issued the encyclical *In Multiplicibus,* calling for the preservation of accessibility to Jerusalem and the Holy Places and for the maintenance of peace in Palestine. The Vatican had consulted the British and French about the encyclical, timed to influence the United Nations debate on the future of Israel, but not the Americans. Shortly after, two Israeli representatives visited Rome for secret talks about defining the religious rights of the Catholic communities in Israel. The talks were cordial, but the Israelis did not meet any senior Vatican officials. By 1949 the Secretariat of State was making diplomatic recognition of Israel dependent on the internationalization of Jerusalem and the Holy Places.[53]

While Wladimir d'Ormesson, the French ambassador to the Holy See, proposed to the pope that he should encourage American Catholics to lobby for the internationalization of Jerusalem and the Holy Places, the pope preferred to work privately through Cardinal Spellman's channels to the American government. Following a meeting with Israeli President Chaim Weizmann and Foreign Minister Abba Eban, Spellman reported to Truman that, rather than accepting the November 1947 United Nations plan for internationalization, the Israelis were proposing a plan of their own. Truman indicated that the United States supported internationalization, but felt that complete internationalization would be very expensive and preferred nominal UN supervision of Israeli and Jordanian administration of Jerusalem and the Holy Places, as Weizmann and Eban were proposing. Spellman objected strongly to this position, since he did not believe that a joint Israel-Jordan administration would provide the guarantees of international accessibility to Jerusalem at all.[54] With this stand-off between Washington and Rome over Israel, on 13 August 1949 the Vatican nailed its standard to the mast by declaring publicly that it sought the international administration of Jerusalem, paid for by the faithful and by volunteer labour, and that no other arrangement would be acceptable. Where the State Department hoped that the Vatican could support the recommendation of the Palestine Conciliation Commission on internationalization, the annual meeting of the American Catholic hierarchy in November 1949 criticized the report of that commission and called for the complete internationalization of Jerusalem under the United Nations.[55]

Given this deteriorating relationship, what was the status and role of the personal representative of the American president to the pope? By 1949 Myron Taylor had held that position for ten years. He was getting old and rarely visited Rome. A Canadian report in March suggested that the Vatican office was not serving the United States particularly well. Yet, in spite of growing Protestant opposition, the State Department had no intention of closing the office.[56] In late May Taylor flew to Rome, with the American press speculating that he was making his trip to give orders to the pope, especially over the recognition of Israel. This prompted a strong reaction and an article critical of Taylor in the 5 June edition of *Quotidiano*. The article indicated that the Secretariat of State and the pope were growing tired of the cavalier attitude of the United States and of Taylor and that this was symptomatic of the growing independence of the Holy See in the international field. After Taylor had held his meetings with the pope, he flew to Istanbul for a meeting with Patriarch Athenagoras. This meeting was undertaken on Taylor's own initiative in an attempt to create an anti-Soviet religious front, which he had first proposed to the World Council of Churches in Amsterdam. Montini suggested that the visit to the patriarch could do Athenagoras more harm than good, as he would then be seen by many as being too close to the Americans.[57]

Montini was not impressed by Taylor's showy style and Vatican officials, including the pope, were embarrassed by a dinner party given by Taylor at Rome's Hotel Excelsior at which he indiscriminately mixed "Quirinal and Vatican; Catholics, Orthodox and Protestants; and questions both sacred and profane." It was felt that Taylor had served a useful purpose during the war and in the immediate postwar period, but with the stabilization of Italy his role and that of his office had changed. The Vatican believed it was now time for the United States to send a regular diplomatic representative to the Holy See as other countries did. These criticisms were indicators that, by mid-1949, the Vatican believed that it no longer had the same need of American patronage as before.[58]

Cardinal Spellman visited Rome in September 1949 to review Vatican-American relations with the pope. Spellman's concern was that the Truman administration was increasingly under the influence of Protestant anti-Catholicism as well as the Jewish and Zionist lobby, which resulted in less sympathy being shown to Catholic positions and policies. The cardinal carried a message from Myron Taylor to the pope suggesting that Vatican recognition of the state of Israel would help to secure the internationalization of Jerusalem. The Vatican, however, continued with its own quest for the internationalization of Jerusalem and the Holy Places by asking Catholics in all countries to raise money for the Pontifical Commission for Palestine which was providing aid to Arab refugees. In seeking Arab support for its position on Jerusalem, the Vatican was opposed to any compromise plan. Into 1950, it insisted that the United Nations resolution on Palestine should be fully implemented.[59]

Taylor arrived in Rome in early December 1949 for what the Vatican expected to be his last visit as the president's personal representative. Ostensibly, he was in Rome for the inauguration of the Holy Year but, in reality, he was there to tell the pope of his resignation. With Taylor's resignation, Franklin Gowen, his assistant, closed the American office at the Vatican and returned to Washington "for consultations," not returning until late June 1950.

The Vatican was not sorry to see the end of the Taylor mission, since in the latter years Taylor was perpetually absent from Rome. The Secretariat of State did, however, want to see American representation continue at the Vatican, preferably in a less idiosyncratic fashion. Tardini thought that Vatican dissatisfaction with the mission may have been the reason for Taylor's resignation. Both Vatican officials and diplomats accredited to the Holy See felt the timing of the resignation and the closing of the American office at the beginning of Holy Year, with Rome full of American pilgrims, represented a deliberate insult to the Vatican. It also came at an unfortunate time, with the Vatican attempting to use the Holy Year as a means of challenging communism.[60]

The resignation of Taylor had been handled by President Truman, not by the State Department, but officials of the latter, who felt that Taylor had been too old to do anything useful in later years, nevertheless wanted to see the position continue. Taylor's resignation opened the question of who, if anyone, should be named to replace him. American Protestants immediately opened a public campaign against the continuation of the office; in response, the State Department encouraged representatives of the Latin American countries and of Italy to make representations in favour of continuing American diplomatic representation at the Vatican.[61]

THE DIFFICULTIES OF THE HOLY YEAR

The Vatican had hoped to use the celebration of the 1950 Holy Year as a way of consolidating its position as the moral arbiter of the world in the context of the Cold War. This was an opportunity to exalt the power and the glory of the living church by inviting the faithful to visit Rome to participate in the spectacles and assemblies of that year, culminating in November with the proclamation of the dogma of the corporeal assumption of the Virgin Mary into heaven. This proclamation represented the only public manifestation of the doctrine of papal infallibility since the 1870 Vatican Council. According to Peter Hebblethwaite, Montini's biographer, "the Church in 1950 had a papal spectacular, the first in the era of the mass media ... It dramatized the unity of the Church after the last and most terrible 'European civil war' ... It was a marvellous display of the Church triumphant."[62]

Yet the weakness of the Vatican in the international context was made apparent during the first half of that year. The resignation of Myron Taylor and the question of the continuation of the American mission indicated that the United States was much divided over the value of its ties with the Holy See. The Polish church-state agreement of April and the Hungarian agreement of August 1950 demonstrated that the Holy See was not able to even give direction to members of its own church on the position to take in its dealings with the Communists. In the rest of eastern Europe, the Catholic Church, where it existed at all, was under the iron grip of Communist regimes.

The Holy Year had been devoted to "activity on behalf of peace"[63] yet, even in terms of moral leadership, the Vatican found itself outmaneuvred by the Communists in 1950. The Stockholm peace conference of March 1950 had been organized by the Communists in reaction to President Truman's January authorization of American production of the hydrogen bomb, and resulted in the Stockholm Appeal against the use of nuclear weapons. It was intended that this appeal should be signed by all people of goodwill and presented to the nuclear powers with a plea for international peace. As part of their peace offensive of 1950, Communists promoted the Stockholm Appeal and, in eastern Europe, church leaders were expected to attend peace demonstrations and to sign the appeal. When the leaders of the Polish church resisted this pressure, they were accused of violating the church-state agreement until they finally capitulated and signed at the end of June.[64] The Vatican and the Catholic Church had difficulty deciding how best to respond to this obvious Communist propaganda without, in turn, being accused of being warmongers. The *Osservatore Romano* was a case in point, descending at first into squabbling with the Italian Communist press about which was the more peace-loving. When the French cardinals and archbishops issued their statement on the Stockholm Appeal in June, quoting extensively from the peace statements of Pius XII, the *Osservatore* changed its tack to charge the Soviet Union with being largely responsible for the outbreak of the Second World War. Eventually the pope, a month after the outbreak of the Korean War, issued a special encyclical on world peace, not opposing atomic weapons as the Stockholm Appeal wanted but calling for peace in men's hearts. The Vatican was having difficulty choosing between different moral claims.

For the Roman Catholic Church, the outlook was bleak as pope, bishops, clergy, and laity stood alone in the Holy Year of 1950 against the continuing challenge of communism.

Epilogue

The reign of Pope Pius XII began on the eve of the Second World War – a time when he feared that the imminent war would lead to the destabilization of Europe and culminate in the victory of militant atheism. When his services as a mediator were unsought during the war, he tried to galvanize his church to resist the extension of Soviet influence in Europe. At the end of the war Pius XII called for conciliatory peace settlements for Germany and Italy in order to reconstitute Christian Europe. The influence of the Soviet Union, coupled with the discovery of Holocaust atrocities, militated against such settlements. With a political vacuum in Europe, the United States and the Soviet Union divided the continent and by 1947 the Catholic Church was one of the few remaining pan-European institutions. When the church was pressed by the Communist governments of the East to accept subservience to the state, it found that even its American friends offered little help. As a result, the church was forced to use its own weapon of excommunication in a futile attempt to prevent capitulation by its clergy and laity.

By 1950 the Cold War was well established in Europe, with military and political structures such as the Cominform, NATO, and the German Federal Republic which served to institionalize the division of Europe between the power blocs. The outbreak of war in Korea in June 1950 and the commitment of American troops in support of the South Korean government translated the Cold War from Europe to Asia and turned it into a global confrontation. The first half of the decade of the 1950s represented the classic depth of the Cold War as Stalinist repression confronted McCarthy-induced American hysteria.

Until Stalin's death in March 1953, "eastern Europe lived through monstrous terror,"[1] with the Roman Catholic Church being one of the victims of that terror. The east European churches were leaderless for much of that time, with Cardinal Mindszenty in prison in Hungary and Archbishop Beran under house arrest in Czechoslovakia. The church-state agreements signed in Poland and Hungary in 1950 did not protect Archbishop Grosz from a thirteen-year prison sentence in 1951 or Cardinal Wyczynski from imprisonment without trial in 1953. Many east European priests and bishops were executed and others were imprisoned. Nevertheless, churches remained open for worship under Communist rule, with the expectation that the church would give active and enthusiastic support to the various peace initiatives and peace congresses sponsored by the Soviet Union. The peace movement, effective in all east European countries except Poland, served as a vehicle whereby the regimes could encourage loyal clergy and turn them against their bishops and against Rome. A number of clergy, designated "patriotic priests," cooperated with the regimes in fashioning national Catholic churches independent of Rome.[2]

Stalin's death in 1953 was followed by even harsher repression as the new Soviet leadership sought to cope with revolt in East Germany and the internal power struggle in the Soviet Union. When Nikita Khrushchev emerged as the dominant figure in the Soviet government, he marked the new direction of the Soviet Union by his secret speech to the Twentieth Congress of the Communist party in February 1956, denouncing Stalin and his legacy to the party. The deStalinization program of 1956 did not long remain secret and prompted restlessness within the satellite states of eastern Europe.

This restlessness manifested itself in Poland in 1956 with a rebellion of the intelligentsia, criticism of the Russians, and demands for Polish independence. The revolt came into the open in June with demands for the return of the purged Wladyslaw Gomulka as party secretary and calls for the release of Cardinal Wyczynski from prison. The restoration of Gomulka as party secretary on 21 October and the release of Wyczynski on 28 October averted revolution in Poland and resulted in a restoration of some freedoms for the church, including the end of government control over ecclesiastical appointments. The cardinal signed a new church-state agreement, again against the wishes of the Vatican, in December 1956. When Wyczynski finally visited Rome in April 1957 to collect his cardinal's hat, Pius XII demonstrated his displeasure by keeping him waiting for three days before granting him an audience.

The Polish restlessness was a prelude to the revolution which broke out in Hungary late in October and culminated in the Soviet invasion of Hungary in November. Archbishop Grosz had been released from prison in May and during the summer Hungarians had demanded the release of Mindszenty. The charges against the cardinal were annulled and he was freed from prison on 30 October, only to be forced to seek sanctuary in the American embassy when Soviet troops marched into Budapest.

While the events of 1956 did not bring immediate change to eastern Europe, they did represent the beginning of new freedoms for the peoples of that area. The church found that it had greater autonomy, that restrictions on its press and its operations were gradually lifted, and that, in some countries, a more critical openness came to exist.

In the United States, Joseph McCarthy, the junior senator from Wisconsin, had warned in February 1950 of the large number of communists who had infiltrated the government and influential institutions of the United States.[3] The resulting investigations by McCarthy in his search for the enemy within were reported with sympathy in the Catholic press which contributed to the anti-communist hysteria of the period. The investigations were also supported by some influential Catholic leaders, including Cardinal Spellman, dubbed the "chaplain of the Cold War." Spellman publicly endorsed Senator McCarthy at a communion breakfast for the New York Police Department in the spring of 1953 and, even after McCarthy's disgrace and death, Spellman never repudiated him, continuing to celebrate a McCarthy Mass at St Patrick's Cathedral every year on the anniversary of his death.[4]

Myron Taylor was never replaced as American representative and the link was not restored between the United States government and the Vatican during the 1950s. In 1951 Truman announced his intention to appoint General Mark Clark as his personal representative to the Vatican, only to find that a majority in Congress, encouraged by the Protestant lobby, refused to approve a budget for the position. The position was allowed to lapse and it was not until 1984 that regular diplomatic relations were finally established through Ronald Reagan's appointment of William Wilson as the first American ambassador to the Holy See.[5]

Within the Vatican, Cardinal Ottaviani at the Holy Office had been distressed by the various theological experiments which had taken place in France under the protection of the archbishop of Paris, Cardinal Suhard, and centring on the Dominican Order. The most famous of these experiments was that of the worker-priests that had emerged from the experience of the French clergy during the war. By 1948 Ottaviani and Cardinal Ruffini of Palermo had proposed to Pius XII the calling of a church council to discuss and, presumably, to condemn these new initiatives. While a preparatory commission was established, a council was never called, and the condemnation instead took the form of the major papal encyclical of the Holy Year, *Humani Generis*, issued on 12 August 1950. According to Peter Hebblethwaite, "*Humani Generis* was a catch-all net designed by the political and theological right-wing to entangle anyone linked, however tenuously, with *la nouvelle théologie* developed by the French Dominicans and Jesuits."[6] *Humani Generis*, coupled with the proclamation of the Assumption of the Virgin later in the Holy Year, set the stamp on a new anti-modernist campaign within the church in the last years of Pius XII. Conformity was expected in theology as well as ideology and the French experiment with worker-priests was terminated by the Holy Office in September 1954.

The pressure for conformity signalled a resurgence of the Roman party within the Curia. By 1952 both the Roman Party and Luigi Gedda of the civic committees were concerned that de Gasperi was making too many concessions to the left wing. The Jesuits tried to convince the neo-fascist Movimento Sociale Italiano (MSI) to develop a more Christian patina to impress the Vatican and, at the same time, they looked for some right-wing alternative to de Gasperi. In April 1952 Pius XII, ever fearful of the left, put pressure on de Gasperi to have the Christian Democrats enter a coalition municipal government in Rome with the MSI. On principle, de Gasperi refused to succumb to pressure for partnership with either the neo-fascists or the monarchists. As a result he earned the enmity of Pius XII with whom de Gasperi was never reconciled before his death in 1954.[7]

Within the Vatican, the *bête noire* of the Roman party, the friend of Maritain and the French, and the mentor of de Gasperi and the Christian Democrats was Giovanni Battista Montini. Maritain and the French, who looked to Montini to defend the worker priests, never understood that he was helpless when it came to dealing with the conservatism of Ottaviani and the Holy Office. On the death of Cardinal Schuster in 1954, the archepiscopal see of Milan fell vacant. On 1 November 1954 Pius XII named Montini to that position, thus removing him as a player from curial politics, and leaving the Vatican in the control of Ottaviani and the Roman party.

Pius XII was diagnosed with cancer in 1954. As a result of his illness, he became more isolated and withdrawn within the Vatican. Most influential at this time was his German housekeeper, Sister Pasqualina, who severely restricted access to the pontiff. As a result of the pope's partial withdrawal from the governance of the church in his last years, power within the church was exercised by Ottaviani and his colleagues.[8]

By the mid-1950s Italy was at the beginning of a massive social transformation, with population shifting from the countryside to the cities and the beginnings of industrial growth and consumerism. Some of the leaders of the Christian Democrats recognized that these new times warranted new politics and started to speak of the need for an "opening to the left" through an electoral alliance with the Italian Socialist party. The Vatican, on the other hand, blinkered by the rigidity of its fight against communism, was oblivious to the changes taking place in Italian and European society. Led by Ottaviani, the Vatican refused to approve any gesture toward a centre-left political alliance and sought to control the directions taken by the Christian Democrats.[9]

Only Montini, according to Andrea Riccardi, recognized the importance of leaving politics to the laity and allowing the church to concern itself with the pastoral and religious dimension of life.[10] Resistance to the "opening to the left" continued in the Vatican well past the death of Pius XII in October 1958, and it was left to his successor, Pope John XXIII, to remove Vatican resistance to a Socialist–Christian Democrat coalition in Italy. The advent of John XXIII, the calling of a Vatican Council, and the provision for *aggiornamento* – daylight – in the Roman Catholic Church ushered in a new phase in the life of that venerable institution. The first phase of the Cold War had ended and, as the pope received Alexis Adzhubei, Nikita Khrushchev's son-in-law, at the Vatican in 1963, a new and more flexible phase was about to begin.

Notes

ABBREVIATIONS

ADSS   *Actes et Documents du Saint Siège*
ASMAE   Papers of the Ministero degli Affari Esteri, Foreign Ministry
        Archives, Rome
FO   Papers of the British Foreign Office, Public Record Office,
        London
NAC   National Archives of Canada, Ottawa
NARA   National Archives and Research Administration, Washington, DC
NCWC   Archives of the National Catholic Welfare Conference,
        Washington, DC
Q d'O   Papers of the Ministère des Affaires Étrangères, Archives of the
        Quai d'Orsay, Paris

NOTES

Introduction

1 The role of Pope John Paul II in ending the Cold War is discussed in
  Bernstein and Politi, *His Holiness*.
2 In this connection, see Friedlander, *Pius XII and the Third Reich*; Falconi,
  The Silence of Pius XII; Morley, *Vatican Diplomacy and the Jews*, as well
  as O'Carroll, *Pius XII*, and Blet, *Pio XII e la Seconda Guerra Mondiale*.
3 Riccardi, *Partito Romano*; *Pio XII*; and *Le Chiese di Pio XII*.
4 Di Nolfo, *Vaticano e Stati Uniti*.

5 Stehle, *Eastern Politics of the Vatican*; Riccardi, *Vaticano e Mosca*.
6 Hebblethwaite, *John XXIII* and *Paul VI*.
7 Luxmoore and Babiuch, *The Vatican and the Red Flag*.
8 Phayer, *Catholic Church and the Holocaust*.

Chapter One

1 This is discussed in Stehle, *Eastern Politics of the Vatican*.
2 Roman Solchanyk and Ivan Hvat, "The Catholic Church in the Soviet Union", in Ramet, *Catholicism and Politics in Communist Societies*, 49–57.
3 "*Caritate Christi*," in McLaughlin, *Church and the Reconstruction of the Modern World*, 280–95; this encyclical is discussed in Kent, *The Pope and the Duce*, 127–9.
4 "*Mit Brennender Sorge*," in McLaughlin, *Church and the Reconstruction of the Modern World*, 336–63.
5 "*Divini Redemptoris*," quoted in ibid., 366–401.
6 On the contrast between Pius XI and Pius XII, see Kent, "A Tale of Two Popes"; also see Friedlander, *Pius XII and the Third Reich*.
7 Falconi, *Popes of the Twentieth Century*, 250.
8 Later Pope Paul VI (1963–78)
9 O'Carroll, *Pius XII*, 13, 69.
10 Cornwell, *Hitler's Pope*, 336.

Chapter Two

1 Greek Catholic churches, sometimes referred to as Uniate or Eastern Rite churches, accepted the primacy of the pope while practising an Orthodox liturgy.
2 Peter Hebblethwaite, "The End of the Vatican's *Ostpolitik*," in Kent and Pollard, eds. *Papal Diplomacy in the Modern Age*, 253–61; Bernstein and Politi, *His Holiness*.
3 See especially Cornwell, *Hitler's Pope*, 105–56, which draws heavily on the memoirs of German Chancellor Heinrich Brüning.
4 Ibid., 105–78; Phayer, *Catholic Church and the Holocaust*, 67–81.
5 Conway, *Nazi Persecution of the Churches*, especially chapters 9–11.
6 O'Carroll, *Pius XII*, 84, 114–15, 170.
7 Foreign Office Research Department, "Some Facts about the Present Situation of the Roman Catholic Church in Germany," 11 March 1947, FO, C5312/477/18.
8 The best study of FUCI is Wolff, *Between Pope and Duce*. The most recent biography of Montini is Hebblethwaite, *Paul VI*.
9 Malcolm (Rome) to Eden, 8 March 1945, FO, ZM1564/3/22.

10   Maritain (Holy See) to Bidault, 7 May 1945, Q d'o, z Europe 1944–49, Italie 52.
11   Riccardi, *Partito Romano*, 3–54. Riccardi makes the point that the Roman party was active in the internal politics of the Vatican until 1963 when Montini was elected pope.
12   *Time*, 24 July 1944.
13   Malcolm (Rome) to Hoyer Millar, 1 February 1945, FO, ZM1000/1000/57.
14   *New York Times*, 15 July 1944.
15   As reported in the *Washington Star*, 23 July 1944.
16   Telegram from Osborne (Holy See), 26 July 1944, FO, R11724/1681/57.
17   Malcolm (Rome) to Eden, 8 March 1945, FO, ZM1564/3/22; Osborne (Holy See) to Eden, 4 January 1945, FO, ZM391/237/57.
18   Osborne (Holy See) to Eden, 15 March 1945, FO, ZM1722/38/57; Taylor (Holy See) to secretary of state, 22 March 1945, NARA, Myron C. Taylor Papers, 9/800.
19   Osborne (Holy See) to Eden, 24 April 1945, FO, ZM2836/2836/57; telegram from Taylor (Holy See), 11 May 1945, NARA, Taylor Papers, RG59/box 8/800.
20   Osborne (Holy See) to Eden, 16 May 1945, FO, ZM2862/2836/57.
21   Foreign Office Research Department, "The Vatican and the Successor States," 1 January 1945, FO, R3392/3392/57 (1944).
22   Mindszenty, *Memoirs,* 23; Tardini to Cicognani (Washington), 27 October 1944, *ADSS*, vol. XI, no. 405, 593.
23   Gascoigne (Budapest) to Eden, 30 April 1945, FO, ZM2927/1600/57.
24   Toma and Volgyes, *Politics in Hungary*, 4; Mindszenty, *Memoirs*, 31.
25   Telegram from Osborne (Holy See), 31 March 1945, FO, ZM2011/1600/57.

Chapter Three

1   Karel Skalicky, "The Vicissitudes of the Catholic Church in Czechoslovakia, 1918 to 1988," in Stone and Strouhal, *Czechoslovakia*, 297–324; Sutherland, *Dr Jozef Tiso and Modern Slovakia*, 18–28.
2   Sutherland, *Dr Jozef Tiso and Modern Slovakia*, 88–90; Jörg K. Hoensch, "The Slovak Republic, 1939–1945," in Mamatey and Luza, *History of the Czechoslovak Republic*, 271–95.
3   General background to church-state relations in Rizzo to Foreign Ministry, 31 August 1944, ASMAE, busta 74, Santa Sede 5 – Cecoslovakia (1945); Foreign Office Research Department Paper, "The Vatican and the Successor States," 1 January 1945, FO, R3392/3392/57/144; annual report from the Holy See for 1944, FO, ZM2608/2608/57.
4   Kersten, *Establishment of Communist Rule in Poland*, 213–14.
5   Szajkowski, *Next to God*, 1.

6   On Polish-Vatican relations, see Pease, "Poland and the Holy See."

7   Foreign Office Research Department, "The Vatican and Poland," 19 April 1944, FO, R6746/3392/57; Riccardi, *Vaticano e Mosca*, 97; Phayer, *Catholic Church and the Holocaust*, 20–30.

8   Notes of the Secretariat of State, 12 June 1944, *ADSS*, vol. XI, 390–1.

9   Coutouvidis and Reynolds, *Poland*, chapter 6.

10 Foreign Office Research Department, "The Vatican and France," 29 April 1944, in FO, R19580/3392/57 of 20 November 1944; Duff Cooper (Paris) to Bevin, 31 May 1946, FO, Z5142/21/17.

11 Duquesne, *Catholiques français sous l'occupation*, 273–310, 348.

12 De Gaulle, *Memoirs*, 263–5.

13 See *ADSS*, vol. XI, 422, n. 5; Delle Piane (Leopoldville) to Maglione, 3 July 1944, ibid., no. 274, 435; Valeri (Vichy) to Maglione, 10 July 1944, ibid., no. 290, 450.

14 Rizzo (Holy See) to Foreign Ministry, 13 August 1944, ASMAE, busta 71, Santa Sede 5 – Francia.

15 Guérin to Chauvel, 23 August 1944, Q d'O, z Europe 1944–49.

16 Guérin to Chauvel, 27 August 1944, ibid., 2; notes of the Secretariat of State, 26 August 1944, *ADSS*, vol. XI, no. 336, 512–3.

17 Guérin to Chauvel, 6 and 9 September 1944; notes of Montini, 9 September 1944, *ADSS*, vol. XI, no. 346, 532–4; Guérin to Bidault, 22 September 1944.

18 Note pour le Ministre, 19 September 1944, Q d'O, z Europe 1944–49.

19 Telegram to Guérin, 3 October 1944, ibid.

20 Duquesne, *Catholiques français sous l'occupation*, 414–9.

21 Cooney, *American Pope*, 188.

22 Guérin to Bidault, 17 October 1944, Q d'O, z Europe 1944–49; telegram from Guérin, 23 October 1944, ibid.

23 Traditionally, the papal nuncio served as the dean of the diplomatic corps in any capital which had relations with the Holy See. One of the duties of this largely ceremonial role was to present official greetings to the head of state on behalf of the diplomatic corps accredited to that country.

24 Valeri (Paris) to Tardini, 25 October 1944, *ADSS*, vol. XI, no. 402, 586–7.

25 Telegrams from Guérin, 27 October, 3 November 1944, Q d'O, z Europe 1944–49.

26 Tardini to Godfrey (London), 1 November 1944, *ADSS*, vol. XI, no. 412, 599; Godfrey to Massigli, 7 November 1944, Q d'O, z Europe 1944–49.

27 Research Report, 22 and 26 November 1944, Q d'O, z Europe 1944–49.

28 Valeri (Paris) to Tardini, 12 December 1944, *ADSS*, vol. XI, no. 464, 644–5.

29 Osborne (Holy See) to Bevin, 22 February 1946, "Annual Report from the Holy See for 1945," FO, ZM868/868/57; Peter Hebblethwaite suggests that the Vatican was also prompted into action by the fact that, if a new

nuncio were not able to present the official new year's greetings to de Gaulle, that task would fall to the next in seniority, the Soviet ambassador to France. See Hebblethwaite, *John XXIII*, 200.

30 Dunaway, *Jacques Maritain*, 13–26.

31 Telegram from Bidault to Washington, 19 January 1945, Q d'O, Z Europe 1944–49.

32 Roncalli (Paris) to Tardini, 13 January 1945, *ADSS*, vol. XI, no. 489, 676; John Pollard, "Italy," in Buchanan and Conway, *Political Catholicism in Europe*, 95; Casula, *Domenico Tardini*, 253–6; Hebblethwaite explains that Tardini's opposition was based on Maritain's recent tour of Latin America, when he created much controversy by lecturing on human rights. Hebblethwaite, *John XXIII*, 207.

33 Tardini to Roncalli (Paris), 18 January 1945; Roncalli (Paris) to Tardini, 29 January 1945, *ADSS*, vol. XI, no. 491, 679, and no. 497, 686–7.

34 Guérin to Bidault, 19 February 1945, Q d'O, Z Europe 1944–49.

35 Guérin to Bidault, 22 September 1944, ibid.

Chapter Four

1 Prifti, *Socialist Albania since 1944*, 157–60.

2 Ibid., 9–21; Nicolas C. Pano, "Albania," in Rakowska-Harmstone, ed., *Communism in Eastern Europe*, 213–17.

3 British Military Mission Albania, "Brief Memorandum on the Catholic Church in Albania," 11 January 1946, FO, R2278/2278/90; Report for the Naval General Staff, 22 January 1946, ASMAE, busta l, Santa Sede 4/5.

4 Phayer, *Catholic Church and the Holocaust*, 47.

5 Alexander, *Triple Myth*, chapters 6–8; O'Carroll, *Pius XII*, 142–4.

6 Foreign Office Research Department, "The Vatican and the Successor States," 1 January 1945, FO, R3392/3392/57 (1944); Alexander, *Church and State in Yugoslavia*, 7–52.

7 Notes of Tardini, 17 May 1941, and notes of Montini, 18 May 1941, *ADSS*, vol. 4, document nos. 351, 352, 356, 358, 493, 495, 498, 500; Foreign Ministry to Zagreb, 11 June 1943, ASMAE, busta 65, Santa Sede 5 – Croazia.

8 Alexander, *Triple Myth*, 66–7; notes of Tardini, 13 June 1941, *ADSS*, vol. 4, doc. no. 400, 547.

9 Foreign Ministry to Zagreb, 28 July 1941, ASMAE, busta 59, Santa Sede 5 – Croazia (1942).

10 Woodford D. McClellan, "Postwar Political Evolution," in Vucinich, *Contemporary Yugoslavia*, 125.

11 Reports of Yugoslav Massacres, 8 May 1945, Q d'O, Z Europe 1944–49, Yougoslavie 34, 2–12.

12 Foreign Ministry to Army High Command, 6 October 1944, ASMAE, busta 71, Santa Sede 36.
13 Osborne to Bevin, 22 February 1946, "Annual Report for 1945," FO, ZM868/868/57.
14 Foreign Office Research Department, "The Vatican and the Successor States," 1 January 1945, R3392/3392/57 (1944), and Sarell (Bucharest) to Attlee, 29 March 1947, FO, R4480/299/37; Memorandum on Political and Religious Situation in Romania (prepared by the Holy See), 13 July 1946, NARA, State Department, 121. 866A/9–146.
15 Jelavich, *History of the Balkans*, 250–5, 287–92; Walter M. Bacon, Jr, "Romania," in Rakowska-Harmstone, ed., *Communism in Eastern Europe*, 162–85; Janice Brown, "The Catholic Church in Romania," in Ramet, *Catholicism and Politics in Communist Societies*, 207–31.
16 Jelavich, *History of the Balkans*, 255–61; Patrick Moore, "Bulgaria," in Rakowska-Harmstone, ed., *Communism in Eastern Europe*, 186–212.
17 "Activities of the Anglican Church in the Orthodox World," 17 April 1944, NCWC, box 10, Communism: Russia: 1944–45.
18 Foreign Ministry to Holy See, 16 July 1945, ASMAE, busta 74, Santa Sede 5 – URSS.
19 Bennett (Sofia) to Bevin, 8 April 1947, FO, R5102/41/7.
20 There is no mention of Bulgaria being one of the countries with which the Vatican had difficulty maintaining diplomatic contact after the war, even though it was occupied by Soviet troops. See Foreign Minister to President of the Council, 28 May 1945, ASMAE, busta 2, Santa Sede 12 (1946), and Holy See to Foreign Minister, 19 July 1945, ASMAE, busta 74, Santa Sede 12 PG.

Chapter Five

1 Fogarty, *Vatican and the American Hierarchy*, 306–12.
2 Stehle, *Eastern Politics of the Vatican*, 212; Fogarty, *Vatican and the American Hierarchy*, 269–78.
3 Flynn, *Roosevelt and Romanism*, 189.
4 Bullitt, "The World from Rome."
5 Earl Boyea, "National Catholic Welfare Conference," 413–15; Ready to Archbishop Mooney, 17 April 1944, NCWC, box 8, Communism: General 1943–45.
6 Memorandum from the Union of Slovenian Parishes of America, 11 September 1944, NCWC, 9, Communism: Jugoslavia: 1944–46; telegram to Mooney from Kaszubowski and Skoniecki, November 1944, NCWC, 10, Communism: Poland: 1939–44.
7 In deference to Vatican objections, the name of the NCWC was changed

from National Catholic Welfare Council to National Catholic Welfare Conference. See Morris, *American Catholic,* 135.

8 Flynn, *Roosevelt and Romanism,* 3–6; Morris, *American Catholic,* 135.

9 Cicognani (Washington) to Tardini, 19 November 1944, ADSS, vol. XI, no. 438, 626; Hoppenot (Washington) to Foreign Ministry, 25 November 1944, Q d'O, B – Amérique 1944–52, EU 97.

10 *Catholic Action,* May 1945.

11 Boyea, "National Catholic Welfare Conference," 424.

12 Osborne (Holy See) to Eden, 18 April 1945, FO, U3158/396/70; Cicognani (Washington) to Tardini, 15 April 1945, ADSS, vol. XI, no. 541, 734–5.

13 Memorandum by Robert Graham, SJ, "Soviet Policy and Tactics in Europe," 5 December 1944, NCWC, box 8, Communism General: 1943–45.

14 Ambrose, *Nixon,* 144.

15 Confidential Questionnaires on Communism, 1945, NCWC, box 8, Communism: Cronin.

16 Distribution List, 17 April 1945, NCWC, box 8, Communism: Cronin.

17 Memorandum by Graham, "Soviet Policy and Tactics in Europe," 5 December 1944, NCWC, box 8, Communism: General 1943–45.

18 "Tentative Confidential Report on Communism" by Rev. John F. Cronin SS, April 1945, NCWC, box 8, Communism: Cronin.

19 Fogarty, *Vatican and the American Hierarchy,* chapter 10.

20 Cooney, *American Pope,* 154–95; Fogarty,*Vatican and the American Hierarchy,* 268.

21 In Murphy, *La Popessa,* which is based on the recollections of Sister Pasqualina, Pius XII's housekeeper and secretary, it is pointed out that Spellman was the only senior churchman that the pope was willing to receive socially and informally.

22 Morris, *American Catholic,* 148.

23 Fogarty, *Vatican and the American Hierarchy,* 259–66.

24 Guerin (Holy See) to Bidault, 3 November 1944, Q d'O, B – Amérique 1944–52, Etats-Unis 200.

25 Cooney, *American Pope,* 189–91; Fogarty, *Vatican and the American Hierarchy,* 306–12; Foreign Ministry to President of the Council, 26 April 1945, ASMAE, busta 74, Santa Sede 5 – USA.

26 Fogarty, *Vatican and the American Hierarchy,* 257.

27 Cooney, *American Pope,* 221; Fogarty, *Vatican and the American Hierarchy,* 341; One manifestation of popular Catholic concern about the threat of communism in the United States was to be found in the popularity of Marian devotions in the late 1940s and early 1950s, especially when the Virgin Mary herself was reputedly giving warnings against the communists. See Kselman and Avella, "Marian Piety and the Cold War."

Chapter Six

1 Bohdan R. Bociurkiw, "The Suppression of the Ukrainian Greek Catholic Church in Postwar Soviet Union and Poland," in Dunn, *Religion and Nationalism in Eastern Europe,* 98; see also Markus, *Religion and Nationalism in Soviet Ukraine.*

2 Stehle, *Eastern Politics of the Vatican,* 220.

3 Potichnyj, "Pacification of Ukraine."

4 Riccardi, *Vaticano e Mosca,* 11–26.

5 For general background on the Russian Orthodox Church, see Wilgress (Moscow) to Canadian Department of External Affairs, 8 February 1945, in FO, N4534/744/38 of 20 April 1945; Peterson to Attlee, 18 November 1946, FO, N15147/54/38; Quaroni (Moscow) to Foreign Ministry, 25 May 1945, ASMAE, busta 74, Santa Sede 5 – URSS; Memorandum on Religious Situation in Russia, 31 July 1946, NARA, State Department, 121. 866A/ 9–146.

6 Peterson to Attlee, 18 November 1946, FO, N15147/54/38.

7 See, for example, telegram from Clark Kerr (Moscow), 10 February 1944, FO, R2205/1561/57.

8 "Sunday Observer," 16 April 1944, in FO, R6208/1681/57; see also Fletcher, "The Soviet Bible Belt."

9 Riccardi, *Vaticano e Mosca,* 18–26.

10 Quaroni (Moscow) to Foreign Ministry, 25 May 1945, ASMAE, busta 74, Santa Sede 5 – URSS.

11 Wilgress (Moscow) to the Canadian Minister of External Affairs, 8 February 1945, in FO, N4534/744/38 of 20 April 1945.

12 Bociurkiw, "The Suppression," 99; Dunn, *Religion and Nationalism in Eastern Europe,* 129–41; Potichnyj, "Pacification of Ukraine."

13 ASMAE, Foreign Ministry to Ankara, 18 April 1946, busta 2, Santa Sede 5 – URSS.

14 Telegram from Watson (Moscow), 2 February 1945, FO, ZM789/38/57.

15 Chancery (Moscow) to Southern Department, 1 May 1945, FO, ZM2978/36/57.

16 Foreign Ministry to President of the Council, 21 February 1945, ASMAE, busta 71, Santa Sede 5 – URSS (1944).

Chapter Seven

1 Stehle, *Eastern Politics of the Vatican,* 201–6.

2 Pius XII to Roosevelt, 7 January 1940, di Nolfo, *Vaticano e Stati Uniti,* 100.

3 Flynn, *Roosevelt and Romanism,* 118; Falconi, *Popes of the Twentieth Century,* 253.

4 Flynn, *Roosevelt and Romanism*, 189.

5 Dunn, *Catholic Church and the Soviet Government*, 83–105; Stehle, *Eastern Politics of the Vatican*, 220–4.

6 "Summi Pontificatus," Ihm, *Papal Encyclicals*, 5–22.

7 Conway, "Pope Pius XII and the Myron Taylor Mission"; Italo Garzia, "Pope Pius XII, Italy and the Second World War," in Kent and Pollard, *Papal Diplomacy in the Modern Age*, 121–36.

8 Taylor to Pius XII, 28 November 1944, ADSS, vol. XI, no. 446, 631–2; Pius XII to Taylor, 12 December 1944, ADSS, vol. XI, no. 463, 642–4.

9 Osborne (Holy See) to Eden, 4 April 1945, "Annual Report from the Holy See for 1944," FO, ZM2608/2608/57.

10 The pope told de Gaulle in June 1944 of his worry about the fate waiting for the German people. "'Those wretched people!' he said several times. 'How they will suffer!'" See de Gaulle, *Memoirs*, 263–5. This argument is also made in a memorandum on "Soviet Policy and Tactics in Europe" prepared by Robert Graham for the Social Action Department of the National Catholic Welfare Council, 5 December 1944, NCWC, 1919–55, box 8, Communism: General: 1943/45.

11 Godfrey (London) to Maglione, 1 February 1944, ADSS, vol. XI, 106-8.

12 Flynn, *Roosevelt and Romanism*, 202–3, 217–18.

13 Tittmann (Holy See) to Pius XII, 5 February 1944, ADSS, vol. XI, no. 29, 125–6.

14 Maglione to Cicognani (Washington), 27 February 1944, and Maglione to Godfrey (London), 9 March 1944, ADSS, vol. XI, 164-5, 195.

15 Godfrey (London) to Maglione, 21 August 1944, ibid., 501–2.

16 Griffin to Clancy, 27 March 1945, ibid., 723–4; British Catholic support for Poland is discussed in Sword, "Cardinal and the Commissars."

17 Maglione to Cicognani (Washington), 16 February 1944, ADSS, vol. XI, no. 40, 139–40; notes of Montini, 1 April 1944, ibid., No. 143, 261.

18 Donahoe, " Dictator and the Priest"; Dunn, *Catholic Church and the Soviet Government*, 117–28; Stehle, *Eastern Politics of the Vatican*, 225–32; Flynn, *Roosevelt and Romanism*, 220; Rizzo (Holy See) to Foreign Ministry, 8 July 1944, ASMAE, busta 71, Santa Sede 5 – URSS.

19 Notes of the Secretariat of State, 12 June 1944, ADSS, vol. XI, no. 236, 390–1.

20 Maglione to Cicognani (Washington), 15 July 1944, ibid., no. 298, 464.

21 Myron Taylor to Pius XII, 12 July 1944, ibid., no. 292, 453–6.

22 Notes of Tardini, 12 July 1944, Secretariat of State to Myron Taylor, 13 July 1944; notes of Tardini, 14 July 1944, ibid., nos. 293, 296, 297, 456–8, 460–3.

23 Rizzo (Holy See) to Foreign Ministry, 28 July 1944, ASMAE, busta 71, Santa Sede 5 – Polonia.

24 Taylor to Pius XII, 18 October 1944, *ADSS*, vol. XI, no. 395, 577–9; Cicognani (Washington) to Tardini, 6 December 1944, ibid., 640–1; Tardini to Cicognani (Washington), 15 December 1944, ibid., 649.

25 Telegram from Halifax (Washington), 14 March 1945, FO, AN950/6/45.

26 Memorandum of Conversation, 26 February 1945, NARA, State Department Papers, 861. 404/ 3-1445; telegram from Bourdeillette (Holy See), 30 March 1945, Q d'O, Z Europe 1944–49, URSS 25.

27 These speculations are contained in a letter from Bronowska, a Polish informant inside the Vatican, to Mikolajczyk of the Polish government-in-exile in London, 1 April 1945, in FO, ZM2463/1600/57 of 26 April 1945.

28 Tardini to Myron Taylor, 13 July 1944, NARA, State Department, 121. 866A/9-146; telegram from Osborne (Holy See), 28 March 1945, FO, ZM1927/36/57.

29 Minute, 24 August 1944, and Foreign Ministry to Holy See, 21 February 1945, ASMAE, busta 74, Santa Sede 5 – USA.

30 Notes of Monsignor Carroll, 3 July 1944, *ADSS*, vol. XI, no. 271, 428–30; it was noted by officials of the National Catholic Welfare Conference that towards the end of the war a continuous flow of appeals emanated from the Vatican to secure assistance for Italy from the American bishops and the American church, and that the Vatican asked for similar support for no other country. See Boyea, "National Catholic Welfare Conference," 177–9.

31 Guido Gonella, director of the Christian Democrat paper *Politica Estera,* and known as a mouthpiece of Pius XII, outlined this view as it applied to both Germany and Italy in an article at the beginning of 1945. Guérin to Bidault, 2 January 1945, Q d'O, Z Europe 1944–49, Saint Siège 8.

32 Stehle, *Eastern Politics of the Vatican,* 244–50, 250–6, 262.

Chapter Eight

1 Falconi, *Popes of the Twentieth Century,* 272.

2 Each year on 2 June, it was the custom of Pius XII to deliver a major allocution in reply to those cardinals who brought him congratulations on the occasion of the day in honour of St Eugene, after whom the pope, as Eugenio Pacelli, had been named. The allocution of 2 June enjoyed a status equal to the pope's annual Christmas message as an opportunity for major papal pronouncements.

3 Osborne (Holy See) to Eden, 4 June 1945, FO, ZM3216/38/57; Conway, *Nazi Persecution of the Churches,* 326; Falconi, *Popes of the Twentieth Century,* 252.

4 Osborne (Holy See) to Churchill, 11 June 1945, FO, ZM3623/36/57;

telegram from Osborne, 10 August 1945, ibid., ZM4263/4237/57;
Osborne to Bevin, 20 August 1945, ibid., ZM4651/4237/57

5 Leigh-Smith (Holy See) to Bevin, 14 September 1945, FO, ZM4954/38/57;
Osborne (Holy See) to Bevin, 26 December 1945, ibid., ZM77/8/57.

6 Osborne (Holy See) to Bevin, 22 February 1946, "Annual Report from
the Holy See for 1945," ibid., ZM868/868/57.

7 Osborne (Holy See) to Eden, 28 May 1945, ibid., ZM3083/237/57.

8 Rizzo (Holy See) to Prunas, l August 1945, ASMAE, busta l, Santa Sede
4/5 (1946); minute, 11 July 1945, Q d'O, Z Europe 1944–49, Saint Siège
8; Tarchiani (Washington) to de Gasperi, l September 1945, ASMAE, busta
74, Santa Sede 5 – USA.

9 Prunas to Rizzo (Holy See), 13 August 1945, ASMAE, busta l, Santa Sede
4/5 (1946); Rizzo (Holy See) to Prunas, 22 August 1945, busta l, Santa
Sede 4/5 (1946); Leigh-Smith (Holy See) to Bevin, 14 September 1945,
FO, ZM4954/38/57.

10 The Italians feared that the Allies would turn part of Venezia Giulia,
including the city of Trieste, over to the Yugoslavs.

11 De Gasperi to Tarchiani (Washington), 16 November 1945, ASMAE, busta
l, Santa Sede 4/5 (1946).

12 Catholic Action, 18 November 1945, "Between War and Peace"; Boyea,
"National Catholic Welfare Conference," 79–80.

13 Osborne (Holy See) to Churchill, 14 June 1945, FO, ZM3536/36/57.

14 Tittmann (Holy See) to Secretary of State, 7 August 1945, NARA, State
Department, 866A.001/ 8–745; Osborne (Holy See) to Bevin, 30 October
1945, FO, ZM5584/38/57.

15 Maritain (Holy See) to Bidault, 14 December 1945, Q d'O, Z Europe
1944–49, Italie 52; Riccardi, Partito Romano, 65–78.

16 Maritain (Holy See) to Bidault, 2 November 1945, ibid., Saint Siège 5;
minute by Pollet, 25 November 1945, ibid., Saint Siège 8.

17 Falconi contends that the pope looked on the United States as a source of
"defence and preservation for Europe, which to him was the one true
cradle of civilization and the natural meeting-point of Christianity with
Greco-Roman culture." The pope had no real interest in American culture or values by themselves and was never moved by pro-Americanism
as an end in itself, according to Falconi. See Popes of the Twentieth Century, 270–1.

18 Osborne (Holy See) to Churchill, 25 June 1945, FO, ZM3626/389/57.

19 Tittmann (Holy See) to Byrnes, 25 July 1945, NARA, State Department,
866A. 00/ 7–2545.

20 Telegram from Osborne (Holy See), 20 June 1945, FO, ZM3389/389/57;
Osborne (Holy See) to Churchill, 25 June 1945, ibid., ZM3626/389/57.

21 Telegram from Tittmann (Holy See), 5 July 1945, NARA, State Department, 866A. 404/ 7–545.

22 Leigh-Hunt (Holy See) to Bevin, 30 September 1945, FO,
    ZM5147/389/57; and Cooney, *American Pope*, 189–91.
23 O'Carroll, *Pius XII*, 169; Stehle, *Eastern Politics of the Vatican*, 211;
    Pius XII is reputed to have said this on 5 November 1944. See Hebbleth-
    waite, *Paul VI*, 198.
24 Tittmann (Holy See) to Byrnes, 19 July 1945, NARA, State Department,
    866A. 404/ 7–1445.
25 Tittmann (Holy See) to Byrnes, 17 September 1945, ibid., 866A. 4611/
    9–1745.
26 Osborne (Holy See) to Churchill, 29 June 1945, FO, ZM3769/38/57;
    Osborne (Holy See) to Bevin, 31 August 1945, ibid., ZM4764/4237/57;
    Leigh-Smith (Holy See) to Bevin, 14 September 1945, ibid.,
    ZM4954/38/57.
27 Notes by Taylor, 16 August 1945, Di Nolfo, *Vaticano e Stati Uniti*,
    466–7.
28 Tiernan to Truman, 6 November 1945, NARA, State Department, 711.
    66A/ 11–1745; Truman to Byrnes, 17 November 1945, Di Nolfo, *Vati-
    cano e Stati Uniti*, 473.
29 Jan Gross, "War as Revolution," in Naimark and Gibianskii, *Establish-
    ment of Communist Regimes in Eastern Europe*, 17–40.
30 In this respect, the east European church leaders were in a similar situa-
    tion to east European Communist leaders who were also caught between
    following orders from Moscow and making decisions which were adapt-
    ed to their circumstances. See Inessa Iazhborovskaia, translated by Anna
    M. Cienciala, "The Gomulka Alternative: The Untravelled Road," in
    Naimark and Gibianskii, *Establishment of Communist Regimes in East-
    ern Europe*, 123–37.
31 Stehle, *Eastern Politics of the Vatican*, 246.
32 Osborne (Holy See) to Bevin, 26 October 1946, FO, N14076/53/38.
33 Chadwick, *Christian Church in the Cold War*, 53; Riccardi, *Vaticano e
    Mosca*, 40–9.
34 On the suppression of the Uniates, see Bociurkiw, "The Suppression,"
    Ukrainian Churches under Soviet Rule, and *Ukrainian Greek Catholic
    Church and the Soviet State*; Conquest, *Religion in the USSR*; Chadwick,
    Christian Church in the Cold War; Foreign Ministry to Ankara, 18 April
    1946, ASMAE, busta 2, Santa Sede 5 – URSS; telegram from Roberts
    (Moscow), 18 March 1946, FO, N3965/53/388.
35 Perowne (Holy See) to Bevin, 6 May 1948, FO, N5798/906/59; Vardys,
    Catholic Church, Dissent and Nationality, 46–79; Vittorio Vignieri,
    "Soviet Policy toward Religion in Lithuania: The Case of Roman
    Catholicism," in Vardys, *Lithuania under the Soviets*, 215–22.
36 Report on the Religious Situation in Latvia, 30 April 1945, FO,

ZM2510/1600/57; Church of England Council on Foreign Relations, October 1946, ibid., N15864/22/59.

37 Dunn, *Catholic Church and the Soviet Government,* 129–41.

Chapter Nine

1 British Military Mission Albania, "Brief Memorandum on the Catholic Church in Albania," 11 January 1946, FO, R2278/2278/90.
2 Prifti, 150–1.
3 Foreign Ministry to Holy See, 18 and 24 October 1945, ASMAE, busta 74, Santa Sede 5 – Albania.
4 Gjini to Hoxha, 8 January 1946, in FO, R2278/2278/90 of 11 January 1946; Research Department Note, 5 February 1946, Q d'o, Z Europe 1944–49, Albanie 8.
5 Telegram from Broad (Caserta), 24 February 1946, FO, R2947/470/90.
6 Memorandum by Archbishop Nigris, 8 May 1946, FO, R7841/470/90; Foreign Ministry to Holy See, 11 May, 20 August 1946, ASMAE, busta 1, Santa Sede 4/5.
7 Chancery (Holy See) to Foreign Office, 24 February 1947, FO, R2807/698/90, and Perowne (Holy See) to Bevin, 14 May 1948, ibid., R6018/1002/90.
8 This is a point of view expressed in British Military Mission Albania, "Brief Memorandum on the Catholic Church in Albania," 11 January 1946, FO, R2278/2278/90.
9 Telegram from Osborne (Holy See) to Broad (Caserta), 16 February 1946, FO, R2558/470/90, and telegram from Broad, 24 February 1946, ibid., R2948/470/90; notes from Vatican, 2 and 15 March 1946, ibid., R4310 and R5116/470/90
10 Roncalli to Bidault, 24 February 1948, and Bidault to Roncalli, 5 March 1948, Q d'o, Z Europe 1944-49, Albanie 8
11 Pedro Ramet, "The Catholic Church in Yugoslavia, 1945–1989," Pedro Ramet, ed., *Catholicism and Politics in Communist Societies,* 184–5; Alexander, *Church and State,* 57–9; Rizzo to Foreign Ministry, 7 June 1945, Foreign Ministry to Holy See, ll June 1945, Rizzo to Foreign Ministry, 5 July 1945, ASMAE, busta 74, Santa Sede 5 – Jugoslavia; note de renseignement, 5 July 1945, Q d'o, Z Europe 1944–1949, Yugoslavia 34; telegram from Stevenson, 1 February 1946, FO, R1737/68/92, Osborne to Bevin, 22 February 1946, ibid., ZM868/868/57.
12 As quoted in Annual Report for 1945, in Osborne to Bevin, 22 February 1946, FO, ZM868/868/57.
13 Alexander, *Church and State,* 69–73.

14 Reply by Marshal Tito, 25 October 1945, Q d'O, Z Europe 1944–49, Yougoslavie 34; Payart (Belgrade) to Bidault, 30 October 1945, ibid.

15 Stepinac to Tito, 24 November 1945, FO, R917/68/92 (1946).

16 Godfrey (London) to Maglione, 31 July 1944, *ADSS*, vol. XI, no. 308, 479–81; notes of Tardini, 4 July 1944, ibid., doc. 276, 436–7.

17 Reported by Osborne to Bevin, 22 February 1946, in "Annual Report for 1945," FO, ZM868/868/57.

18 Circular to Clergy by Stepinac, 17 December 1945, ibid., R1171/68/92 (1946).

19 Telegrams from Stevenson, 31 January and 1 February 1946, FO, R1755 and R2995/68/92; R1737/68/92.

20 Memorandum on Political and Religious Situation in Romania, 13 July 1946, State Department, 121. 866A/ 9–146; Sarell (Bucharest) to Attlee, 29 March 1947, FO, R4480/299/37.

21 Holman (Bucharest) to Bevin, 22 June 1948, FO, R7680/898/37.

22 Memorandum on Political and Religious Situation in Romania, 13 July 1946, State Department, 121. 866A/ 9–146.

23 Holy See to Foreign Ministry, 27 May 1946, ASMAE, busta 2, Santa Sede 5 – Romania.

24 Foreign Ministry to Holy See, 5 April 1947, ibid., busta 6, Santa Sede 5 – Romania.

25 Sofia to Foreign Ministry, 26 January 1946, ibid., busta 2, Santa Sede 12; Paris (Sofia) to Bidault, 1 March 1947, Q d'O, Z Europe 1944–49, Bulgarie 15.

26 Sofia to Foreign Ministry, 24 July 1947, ASMAE, busta 5, Santa Sede 5 – Bulgaria; Foreign Ministry to Holy See, 16 July 1945, ibid., busta 74, Santa Sede 5 – URSS.

Chapter Ten

1 Kovrig, *Communism in Hungary,* 160–2, and "Hungary" in Rakowska-Harmstone, ed., *Communism in Eastern Europe*, 87.

2 Mindszenty, *Memoirs*, 18; Foreign Office Research Department, Biography of Mindszenty, 9 November 1945, FO, R19879/9778/21; Stehle, *Eastern Politics of the Vatican*, 257.

3 Mindszenty, *Memoirs*, 36.

4 *Hungarian Courier*, 8 October 1945, in FO, R18115/9778/21 of 16 October 1945.

5 Gascoigne (Budapest) to Bevin, 9 October 1945, ibid., R17900/9778/21.

6 Foreign Office Research Department, Biography of Mindszenty, 9 November 1945, ibid., R19879/9778/21.

7 Gascoigne (Budapest) to Howard, 13 September 1945, ibid.,

R16071/9778/21; letter from Mindszenty, 14 September 1945, in ibid., R18115/9778/21 of 16 October 1945.

8   Kovrig, *Communism in Hungary,* 180–3.
9   Mindszenty, *Memoirs,* 43–4; Gascoigne (Budapest) to Bevin, 14 November 1945, FO, R20197/9778/21.
10 Gascoigne (Budapest) to Bevin, 14 November 1945, FO, R20197/9778/21; telegram from Carse (Budapest), 26 November 1945, ibid., R19962/9778/21.
11 Mindszenty, *Memoirs,* 44–9.
12 Gascoigne (Budapest) to Bevin, 7 January 1946, FO, R856/256/21.
13 Nagy to Mindszenty, 26 July 1946, in Helm (Budapest) to Foreign Office, 30 July 1946, ibid., R11506/436/21; telegram from Carse (Budapest), 25 February 1946, ibid., R3020/436/21.
14 Osborne (Holy See) to Bevin, 9 March 1946, ibid., R4516/436/21. After the war Hungary had maintained a legation to the Holy See, headed by a Monsignor Luttor, who had been appointed by Admiral Horthy's government. While Luttor had nothing to do, the Holy See had continued to recognize him until such time as the new provisional government of Hungary should decide to appoint a replacement or to close down the legation (Holy See to Foreign Ministry, 19 July 1945, ASMAE, busta 74, Santa Sede 12 PG).
15 Mindszenty, *Memoirs,* 69.
16 Osborne (Holy See) to Foreign Office, 27 February 1946, FO, R4090/436/21.
17 Mindszenty to Gyöngyösi, 22 July 1946, in Helm (Budapest) to Foreign Office, 30 July 1946, ibid., R11506/436/21; Nagy to Mindszenty, 26 July 1946, in ibid.
18 Foreign Ministry to the Holy See, 12 October 1946, A, busta 2, Santa Sede 5 – Ungheria; Foreign Ministry to London, 13 January 1947, ibid.
19 Osborne (Holy See) to Foreign Office, 22 August 1946, FO, R12761/436/21.
20 Telegram from Parsons (Holy See), 19 August 1947, NARA, State Department, 866A.00/8–1947.
21 Inessa Iazhborovskaia, "The Gomulka Alternative: The Untravelled Road," in Naimark and Gibianskii, eds., *Establishment of Communist Regimes in Eastern Europe,* 123–37.
22 Coutouvidis and Reynolds, *Poland,* 223.
23 Telegram from Clark Kerr, 6 April 1945, FO, ZM1600/1600/57; Wheeler-Bennett to Ross, 26 April 1945, ibid., ZM2463/1600/57.
24 Warsaw to the Foreign Ministry, 19 July 1946, ASMAE, busta 2, Santa Sede 5 – Polonia.
25 Coutouvidis and Reynolds, *Poland,* 224–5.
26 Telegram from Osborne, 25 August 1945, FO, N11882/6/55.
27 Telegram from Cavendish-Bentinck, 31 August 1945, ibid., N11388/23/55.

28 Telegrams from Cavendish-Bentinck, 30 August and 5 September 1945, ibid., N11759 and N11773/6/55.

29 Telegrams from Cavendish-Bentinck, 15 September 1945, ibid., N12317/23/55.

30 Telegram from Cavendish-Bentinck, 21 September 1945, ibid., N12616/23/55.

31 Warsaw to the Foreign Ministry, 30 November 1945, ASMAE, busta 2, Santa Sede 5 – Polonia (1946).

32 Telegram from Leigh-Smith (Holy See), 26 September 1945, FO, N12943/23/55; telegram from Maritain (Holy See), 20 September 1945, Q d'O, z Europe 1944–49/ Pologne 52, 8–9.

33 Garreau (Warsaw) to Bidault, 26 March 1946, Q d'O, z Europe 1944–49, Pologne 52, 69–70.

34 Warsaw to the Foreign Ministry, 16 January, 14 February 1946, ASMAE, busta 2, Santa Sede 5 – Polonia.

35 British Ambassador in Warsaw to Osborne, 23 January 1946, FO, N1373/125/55.

36 See Coutouvidis and Reynolds, *Poland*, chapters 8 and 9.

37 *The Times* (London), 13 July 1946.

38 Telegram from Osborne (Holy See), 25 April 1946, FO, N5686/125/55; telegram from Cavendish-Bentinck, 10 May 1946, ibid., N6198/125/55.

39 Warsaw to Foreign Ministry, 5 April 1946, ASMAE, busta 2, Santa Sede 5 – Polonia; on Piasecki, see Blit, *Eastern Pretender*.

40 In the winter of 1945–6, the Polish communists followed Soviet direction in building a police state and in creating the Urzad Bezpieczenstwa (UB), a secret police force modelled on the Soviet NKVD, which was designed to combat the underground opposition. For the atmosphere of this Polish police state after the war, see Lane, *I Saw Poland Betrayed*; see also John Micgiel, "'Bandits and Reactionaries': The Suppression of the Opposition in Poland, 1944–1946," in Naimark and Gibianskii, eds., *Establishment of Communist Regimes in Eastern Europe*, 93–110.

41 Telegram from Cavendish-Bentinck, 1 June 1946, FO, N7247/125/55; Garreau (Warsaw) to Bidault, 19 June 1946, Q d'O, z Europe 1944–49, Pologne 52, 93–4.

42 Telegram from Russell, 13 July 1946, FO, N9185/34/55.

43 *New York Times*, 4 July 1946; Coutouvidis and Reynolds, *Poland*, 251–5.

44 *New York Times*, 5 July 1946

45 Bonnet (Washington) to Bidault, 29 July 1946, Q d'O, z Europe 1944–49, Pologne 52, 128–31; note, 24 December 1945, ibid., 378; Garreau (Warsaw) to Bidault, 26 March 1946, ibid., 69–70.

46 See Kersten, *Establishment of Communist Rule in Poland*, 211–20; Lane, *I Saw Poland Betrayed*, 246–51.

47 Pro-memoria on the Political-Religious Situation in Poland, 11 October 1946, NARA, State Department, 121.866A/10–2346.

48 Kersten, *Establishment of Communist Rule in Poland,* 215; report, 15 July 1946, NARA, Myron Taylor Papers, 34/800.

49 Lane, *I Saw Poland Betrayed,* 246–51; Warsaw to Foreign Ministry, 19 July 1946, ASMAE, busta 2, Santa Sede 5 – Polonia.

50 Leigh-Smith to Bevin, 23 July 1946, FO, N9868/6757/55; Warsaw to Foreign Ministry, 23 July 1946, ASMAE, busta 2, Santa Sede 5 – Polonia.

51 Cavendish-Bentinck to Hankey, 14 September 1946, FO, N12208/1381/55.

Chapter Eleven

1 Radomir Luza, "Czechoslovakia between Democracy and Communism, 1945–1948," in Mamatey and Luza, *History of the Czechoslovak Republic,* 387–415.

2 Billy to Carroll, 8 October 1945, NCWC, 8/Communism: Czechoslovakia 45–8; Memorandum on the Political-Religious Situation in Czechoslovakia, 1 August 1946, Department of State, National Archives, Washington, 121.866A/9–146.

3 Guidotti to Foreign Ministry, 12 October 1945, ASMAE, busta 74, Santa Sede 5 – Cecoslovakia; Guidotti to Foreign Ministry, 12 December 1945, ibid., busta 2, Santa Sede 5 – Cecoslovakia.

4 Paris to Foreign Ministry, 21 June 1945, ibid., busta 74, Santa Sede 5 – Francia; note from the Office of Southern Europe, 29 November 1945, Q d'O, z Europe 1944–49, Saint Siège 11; Hebblethwaite, *John XXIII,* 210.

5 Note pour le Cabinet, 8 December 1946, Q d'O, z Europe 1944–49, Saint Siège 11.

6 Maritain (Holy See) to Bidault, 5 February 1947, ibid., Saint Siège 7.

7 Foreign Ministry to Maritain, 24 November 1945, ibid.; note from the Office of Southern Europe, 29 November 1945, ibid., Saint Siège 11.

8 Maritain(Holy See) to Bidault, 1 December 1945, ibid., Saint Siège 7; telegram from Maritain (Holy See), 23 December 1945, ibid.

9 Duff Cooper (Paris) to Bevin, 31 May 1946, FO, Z5142/21/17.

10 Minute, 11 July 1945, Q d'O, z Europe 1944–49, Saint Siège 8.

11 Duquesne, *Les catholiques français,* 81–5.

12 *La Croix,* 18 May and 13 June 1945.

13 Ibid., 27 November, 18 December 1945, 8 January, 27 February 1946.

14 Osborne (Holy See) to Bevin, 19 April 1946, FO, ZM1347/8/57.

15 Duff Cooper (Paris) to Bevin, 31 May 1946, ibid., Z5142/21/17.

16 Rioux, *The Fourth Republic,* 102.

17 Maritain (Holy See) to Bidault, 23 March 1946, Q d'O, z Europe 1944–49, Italie 52.

18 Quoted by Osborne (Holy See) to Bevin, 24 and 27 April 1946, FO, ZM1385/8/57 and ZM1469, 1994/8/57.
19 Ibid.
20 Telegram from Osborne, 26 March 1946, ibid., UR2624/974/851; Osborne to Bevin, 11 April 1946, ibid., UR3570/974/851; Foreign Ministry to Holy See, 20 April 1946, ASMAE, busta l, Santa Sede 4/5.
21 Telegram from Osborne (Holy See), 12 June 1946, FO, ZM2107/8/57.

Chapter Twelve

1 Foreign Office Research Department, "Some Facts about the Present Situation of the Roman Catholic Church in Germany," 11 March 1947, FO, C5312/477/18.
2 Ibid.
3 Foreign Office Research Department paper, "Germany: The Guilt Controversy in the German Evangelical Church and Elsewhere," 14 May 1946, ibid., C5454/251/18.
4 Foreign Office Research Department, "Some Facts about the Present Situation of the Roman Catholic Church in Germany," 11 March 1947, FO, C5312/477/18; German bishops and the question of war guilt is discussed in Frank M. Buscher and Michael Phayer, "German Catholic Bishops and the Holocaust, 1940–1952," *German Studies Review* 11, no. 3 (1988), 463–85 and in Phayer, *Catholic Church and the Holocaust*, chapter 7.
5 On these arguments, see Religious Affairs Branch to Foreign Office Research Department, 16 April 1947, FO, C6210/477/18.
6 Special Report on Conference of RC Bishops of the British Zone," 30 January 1946, ibid., C2332/251/18.
7 Osborne (Holy See) to Bevin, 23 February 1946, FO, C5089/251/18; Monthly Technical Report from the Religious Affairs Branch, 18 April 1946, ibid., C4637/251/18.
8 *The Times*, 26 June 1946.
9 Translation of the Easter Pastoral of the R.C. Bishops of Western Germany, 21 April 1946, FO, C5208/251/18.
10 Minute by Pollet, 12–18 November 1945, and Maritain (Holy See) to Bidault, 26 November 1945, Q d'O, z Europe 1944–49, Saint Siège 8.
11 Allied Control Authority Coordinating Committee, Policy Recommendations on Religious Affairs, 15 April 1946, FO, C4627/251/18.
12 Minutes of the Allied Religious Affairs Committee, 25 September 1947, ibid., C13097/13097/180.
13 Telegram from Osborne (Holy See), 8 March 1946, ibid., C2831/251/8; Maritain (Holy See) to Bidault, 16 March 1946, Q d'O, z Europe 1944–49, Saint Siège 2.
14 Telegram from Strang (Berlin), 22 March 1946, FO, C3331/251/18; telegram from Osborne (Holy See), 9 May 1946, ibid., C5178/251/18

and 6 June 1946, ibid., C6572/251/18; Maritain (Holy See) to Bidault, 10 May 1946, Q d'O, Z Europe 1944–49, Saint Siège 8.

15 Minute, 18 December 1947, Q d'O, Z Europe 1944–49, Saint Siège 2; G.M. Weber, "Aloisius Joseph Muench," *New Catholic Encyclopedia*, vol. X 1967, 63–4.

16 Foreign Office Research Department, "Policy Towards Religion in the Soviet Zone," 27 November 1947, FO, C15365/114/18; in 1951 Muench was named apostolic nuncio to the Federal Republic of Germany.

17 Minute, 18 December 1947, Q d'O, Z Europe 1944–49, Saint Siège 2; Foreign Ministry to Washington, 25 February 1947, ASMAE, busta 6, Santa Sede 12 – Germania.

18 Minute, 18 December 1947, Q d'O, Z Europe 1944–49, Saint Siège 2.

19 Maritain (Holy See) to Bidault, 5 March 1947, ibid.

20 Press Digest, 10 October 1946, FO, C12525/251/18, and Osborne (Holy See) to Bevin, Annual Report from the Holy See for 1946, 29 January 1947, ibid., C1498/1498/57.

21 Maritain (Holy See) to Bidault, 12 October 1945, Q d'O, Z Europe 1944–49, Saint Siège 8; minute on meeting of Eisenhower and Clark with Pius XII, 17 September 1945, US State Department, National Archives of the United States.

22 Foreign Ministry to Washington, 25 February 1947, ASMAE, busta 6, Santa Sede 12 – Germania; Cronin to Carroll, 6 November 1947, NCWC, box 8, Communism: General 1947–49.

23 "Special Report on Conference of RC Bishops of the British Zone," 30 January 1946, FO, C2332/251/18; Foreign Office Research Department, 9 May 1946, ibid., C5208/251/18.

24 Frankfort to Foreign Ministry, 12 February 1948, ASMAE, busta 12, Santa Sede 5 – Germania (1949).

25 Murphy to Taylor, 2 July 1946, Taylor Papers, NARA 13/800.

26 Leigh-Smith (Holy See) to Bevin, 23 July 1946, FO, N9868/6757/55, and 29 July 1946, ibid., N10099/6957/55.

27 Memorandum on Religious Situation in Germany, 20 August 1946, State Department, 121. 866A/ 9–146.

28 Steele (German Control Commission) to Dean, 8 July 1946, FO, C7846/251/18; Frankfort to Foreign Ministry, 12 February 1948, ASMAE, busta 12, Santa Sede 5 – Germania.

29 Galloway (Baden-Baden) to Bevin, 30 June 1947, FO, C9181/173/18; Frankfort to Foreign Ministry, 12 February 1948, ASMAE, busta 12, Santa Sede 5 – Germania (1949).

30 Galloway (Baden-Baden) to Bevin, 28 June 1947, FO, C9180/173/18.

31 Maritain (Holy See) to Bidault, 10 May 1946, Q d'O, Z Europe 1944–49, Saint Siège 8.

32 Frankfort to Foreign Ministry, 12 February 1948, ASMAE, busta 12, Santa Sede 5 – Germania (1949).

33 Diana (Holy See) to Foreign Ministry, 27 September 1946, ibid., busta 5, Santa Sede 5 – Germania; Foreign Office Research Department, "The Churches in the Soviet Zone," 1 October 1946, FO, C12210/251/18, and "Policy towards Religion in the Soviet Zone," 27 November 1947, ibid., C15365/114/188.

Chapter Thirteen

1 Osborne (Holy See) to Bevin, 30 July 1945, FO, ZM4305/36/57.
2 *Catholic Action*, 18 November 1945, "Between War and Peace"; Foreign Ministry to Holy See, 4 and 18 January 1946, ASMAE, busta 1, Santa Sede 4/5.
3 Osborne (Holy See) to Bevin, 26 December 1945, FO, ZM77/8/57 (1946).
4 Ibid., 22 February 1946, ZM766/8/57.
5 Bonnet (Washington) to Bidault, 4 March 1946, Q d'O, B – Amérique 1944–52, EU 97; telegram from Halifax (Washington), 25 February 1946, FO, AN548/1/45.
6 Annual Report for 1945 for the Holy See, Osborne (Holy See) to Bevin, 22 February 1946, FO, ZM868/868/57; Maritain (Holy See) to Bidault, 4 March 1946, Q d'O, Z Europe 1944–49, Saint Siège 7.
7 Telegram from Halifax (Washington), 25 February 1946, FO, AN548/1/45.
8 Ibid., 4 January 1946, AN35/1/45; telegram from Gowen (Holy See), 21 January 1946, NARA, State Department, 866A. 404/ 1–2146; *Le Monde*, 24–25 February 1946.
9 Osborne (Holy See) to Bevin, 28 February 1946, FO, ZM839 and ZM867/65/57.
10 Maritain (Holy See) to Bidault, 26 October 1945, Q d'O, Z Europe 1944–49, Saint Siège 2, 120–2; Payart (Belgrade) to Bidault, 30 October 1945, ibid., Europe 1944–49, Yougoslavie 34.
11 Cicognani to Tanner, 2 March 1946, NCWC, box 9, Communism: Yugoslavia: 1944–46.
12 Cicognani to Carroll, 13, 18, 20 April, 7 June and 14 August 1946, ibid.
13 Tanner to Cicognani, 11 April 1946; Carroll to Cicognani, 29 May 1946, ibid.
14 Excerpt from the *Congressional Record* for the 79th Congress, speech of Hon. John W. McCormack in the House of Representatives, 27 July 1946, in ibid.
15 Great Britain had been supportive of the Yugoslav Partisans during the war and was expected to support Tito's point of view. In February 1946, when talking to the British minister to the Holy See, Monsignor Tardini of the Secretariat of State, while anxious about Stepinac's situation in

Zagreb, did not ask for any action from the British. Moreover, the Anglican Church had traditionally supported the Serb Orthodox Church
against Catholic proselytism and this connection was being renewed by
the Anglicans in the spring of 1946. On 24 May 1946 Dr Parsons, the
bishop of Hereford, arrived in Belgrade on a mission from the archbishop
of Canterbury to renew friendly relations with the Serb Orthodox hierarchy. Great Britain had also shown little inclination to help Catholics in
Albania when they were being imprisoned and executed by the Communists there. Telegram from Osborne, 7 February 1946, FO, R1990/68/92;
telegram from Hateau (Belgrade), 26 May 1946, Q d'O, Z Europe
1944–1949, Yougoslavie 34; see also Kirby, *Church, State and Propaganda*, 148–9.

16 Patterson to Tittmann, 12 October 1945, NARA, Taylor Papers, box 36,
Vatican Matters; telegram from Tittmann, 28 March 1946, NARA, State
Department, 866A.4611/3–2846.

17 Taylor to Truman, 25 June 1946, Truman to Taylor, 19 July 1946, in Di
Nolfo, *Vaticano e Stati Uniti*, 497–503.

18 Memorandum on Political and Religious Situation in Yugoslavia, 1
August 1946, NARA, State Department, 121.866A/9–146.

19 Diana (Holy See) to Foreign Ministry, 4 April 1946, and minute by Con-
sol Oberto Fabriani (Zagreb), 5 April 1946, ASMAE, busta 2, Santa Sede 5
– Jugoslavia; Foreign Ministry to Moscow, 18 June 1946, ibid.

20 Foreign Office Research Department, "Archbishop Stepinac," 25 September 1946, FO, R14440/68/92.

21 Payart (Belgrade) to Bidault, 21 September 1946, Q d'O, Z Europe
1944–49, Yougoslavie 34.

22 Telegram from Clutton (Belgrade), 3 August 1946, FO, R11823/68/92;
Payart (Belgrade) to Bidault, 31 July 1946, Q d'O, Z Europe 1944–49,
Yougoslavie 34.

23 Peake (Belgrade) to Bevin, 27 August 1946, FO, R13083/5/92; Payart
(Belgrade) to Bidault, 31 July 1946, Q d'O, Z Europe 1944–49,
Yougoslavie 34.

24 Peake (Belgrade) to Bevin, 14 October 1946, FO, R15803/68/92.

25 Peake (Belgrade) to Bevin, 31 August 1946, FO, R12996/5/92.

26 Telegram from Peake (Belgrade), 18 September 1946, FO, R13906/68/92;
telegram from Payart (Belgrade), 19 September 1946, Q d'O, Z Europe
1944–1949, Yugoslavia 34; for the description of the trial, see Alexander,
Triple Myth, 143–81.

27 Peake (Belgrade) to Bevin, 14 October 1946, FO, R15803/68/92.

28 Payart (Belgrade) to Bidault, 17 October 1946, Q d'O, Z Europe
1944–49, Yougoslavie 35; Alexander, *Church and State*, 120.

29 Foreign Ministry to Holy See, 20 April 1946, ASMAE, busta 1, Santa Sede
4/5.

30 Foreign Ministry to Holy See, 1 and 22 June 1946, and Diana (Holy See) to Foreign Ministry, 11 June 1946, ibid. 4/5.

31 Diana to Foreign Ministry, 3 July 1946, ibid.

32 Diana (Holy See) to Affari Esteri, 5 and 13 July 1946, ibid., Santa Sede 4/2.

33 Wheeler-Bennett and Nicholls, *Semblance of Peace*, 432–6.

34 Bourdeillette (Holy See) to Bidault, 22 August 1946, Q d'O, Z Europe 1944–49, Saint Siège 11.

35 Tittmann to Byrnes, 14 March 1946, NARA, Taylor Papers, 34/800.1.

36 Truman to Taylor, 19 and 20 April 1946, Di Nolfo, *Vaticano e Stati Uniti*, 478–9; telegram from Taylor (Holy See), 7 May 1946, NARA, State Department, 866A. 4611/ 5–746.

37 Osborne (Holy See) to Hoyer Millar, 10 May 1946, FO, ZM1620/65/57; Maritain (Holy See) to Bidault, 17 May 1946, Q d'O, Z Europe 1944–49, Saint Siège 3.

38 Taylor to Pius XII, 24 July 1946, Di Nolfo, *Vaticano e Stati Uniti*, 504–5.

39 Taylor (Holy See) to Truman, 11 June 1946, ibid., 493–4; Taylor to Truman, 16 August 1946, NARA, State Department, 121. 866A/ 9–146; telegram from Inverchapel (Washington), 4 September 1946, FO, AN2716/15/45.

40 Telegram from Inverchapel (Washington), 26 November 1946, FO, AN3621/15/45; telegram from Taylor (Holy See), 3 December 1946, NARA, State Department, 865. 00/ 12–346.

41 Telegram from Osborne (Holy See), 20 September 1946, FO, R14131/68/92

42 Hurley to Carroll, 27 December 1946, NCWC, box 9, Communism: Jugoslavia: 1946–48; Brietenbeck to Carroll, 4 January 1947, ibid.

43 Cardinal Griffin to Bevin, 25 September 1946, FO, R14389/68/92; *The Tablet*, 28 September 1946.

44 Press release, 29 September 1946, NCWC, box 9, Communism: Jugoslavia: Stepinac: 1946–48.

45 Randall to Editors, 4 October 1946, ibid.

46 McNicholas to Truman, after 13 October 1946; telegram from Manning, 16 October 1946; and press release, 11 January 1947, NCWC, ibid.

47 Pro-memoria, 16 October 1946; Carroll to McNicholas, 27 November 1946, ibid.; and McNicholas to Carroll, 6 December 1946, ibid.

48 Acheson to Wagner, 4 March 1947, ibid., Stepinac: 1946–48; Bonnet (Washington) to Bidault, 17 October 1946, Q d'O, Z Europe 1944–49, Yougoslavie 35.

49 Memo to Pearson, 13 November 1946; memo for St Laurent, December 19, 1946; memo to Pearson, 12 February 1947, NAC, Department of External Affairs [84–85/019] 289/9203–40 (2).

50 Balay (Italy) to Foreign Ministry, l7 October 1946, Q d'O, Z Europe 1944–49, Yugoslavia 35.
51 *La Croix*, 12 October 1946.
52 Telegram from Osborne, 25 April 1946, FO, N5630/5630/12; Foreign Ministry to Prague, 10 May 1946, ASMAE, busta 2, Santa Sede 5 – Cecoslovakia; Foreign Ministry to London, 14 June 1946, ibid.; Memorandum on the Political-Religious Situation in Czechoslovakia, 1 August 1946, NARA, State Department, 121.866A/9–146.
53 Foreign Ministry to Prague, 27 August 1946, ASMAE, busta 2, Santa Sede 5 – Cecoslovakia; Bourdeillette (Holy See) to Bidault, 27 August 1946, Q d'O, Z Europe 1944–49/ Saint Siège 3, 27–30.
54 Foreign Ministry to Prague, 24 December 1946, Tacoli to Foreign Ministry, 6 March 1947, and Foreign Ministry to Moscow, 26 March 1947, busta 5, Santa Sede 5 – Cecoslovakia; Rhodes, *Vatican in the Age of the Cold War*, 116.
55 Osborne to Bevin, Annual Report on the Holy See, 1946, 29 January 1947, FO, Z1498/1498/57.
56 Sutherland, *Dr. Josef Tiso and Modern Slovakia*, 96.
57 Telegram from Tittmann, 3 November 1945, NARA, Department of State, National Archives, 860F.00/11–345.
58 Krasula to Carroll, March 1946, NCWC Archives, 8/Communism: Czechoslovakia 1945–8; Billy to Carroll, 8 October 1945, ibid.
59 Carroll to Kenney, 28 October 1946, and Report on the Trial of Dr. Tiso, October/November 1946, ibid.
60 Article by Kushner, November 1946, Krasula to Carroll, 25 November 1946, ibid.
61 Cicognani to Carroll, 5 December 1946, and Carroll to American Bishops, 9 December 1946; Stritch to Carroll, 11 December 1946, ibid.
62 Cicognani to Carroll, 17 April 1947; Stritch to Carroll, 7 May 1947, ibid.

Chapter Fourteen

1 Osborne (Holy See) to Bevin, 21 February, 7 March 1947, FO, Z2152 and Z2785/201/57; Maritain (Holy See) to Bidault, 25 February 1947, Q d'O, Z Europe 1944–49, Saint Siège 5.
2 Maritain (Holy See) to Bidault, 2 April 1947, Q d'O, Z Europe 1944–49, Italie 52.
3 Notes by Carroll on his conversation with Byrnes, 11 October 1946, NCWC, box 8, Communism: General 1946.
4 Bishops' Statement on "Man and the Peace," 15 November 1946, *Catholic Action*, December 1946.
5 Maritain (Holy See) to Bidault, 5 June 1947, Q d'O, Z Europe 1944–49,

Saint Siège 6; Gowen (Holy See) to Marshall, 5 June 1947, NARA, State Department, 866A. 001/ 6–547.

6 Bourdeillette (Holy See) to Bidault, 29 August 1947, Q d'O, Z Europe 1944–49, Pologne 53, 83–6.

7 Maritain (Holy See) to Bidault, 27 June 1947, ibid., Saint Siège 9; *New York Herald Tribune*, 22 June 1947.

8 Bidault to Maritain (Holy See), 14 August 1947, Q d'O, Z Europe 1944–49, Pologne 53, 78–82.

9 Maritain (Holy See) to Bidault, 10 and 24 July 1947, ibid., Saint Siège 9.

10 Memorandum by Acheson, 17 February 1947, NARA, State Department, 121. 866A/2–1747.

11 Osborne (Holy See) to Wilson-Young, 10 April 1947, FO, AN1431/96/45.

12 Taylor to Pius XII, 11 April 1947, Di Nolfo, *Vaticano e Stati Uniti*, 521–2.

13 Marshall to Acheson, 15 May 1947, NARA, State Department, 121. 866A/5–1547.

14 *La Croix*, 14, 24, and 28 November, 11 December 1946.

15 Ibid., 30–31 March, 27–28 April, and 5 June 1947.

16 See Coutouvidis and Reynolds, *Poland,* chapter 10.

17 Cavendish-Bentinck to Attlee, 26 November 1946, FO, N15375/1381/55; consul in Cracow to Bidault, 9 and 14 August 1946, Q d'O, Z Europe 1944–49, Pologne 52, 141–2, 149.

18 Soardi to Foreign Ministry, 30 December 1946, ASMAE, busta 2, Santa Sede 5 – Polonia; Cavendish-Bentinck to Hankey, 7 January 1947, FO, N556/556/55; Foreign Ministry to the Holy See, 22 February 1947, ASMAE, busta 6, Santa Sede 5 – Polonia.

19 Foreign Ministry to the Embassy to the Holy See, 18 December 1946, ASMAE, busta 2, Santa Sede 5 – Polonia; telegram from de Beausse (Warsaw), 3 January 1947; Garreau (Warsaw) to Blum, 7 January 1947, Q d'O, Z Europe 1944–49, Pologne 53, 2–5.

20 Cavendish-Bentinck to Attlee, 26 November 1946, FO, N15375/1381/55; Foreign Ministry to the Holy See, 18 December 1946, ASMAE, busta 2, Santa Sede 5 – Polonia; telegram from Maritain (Holy See), 26 February 1947, Q d'O, Z Europe 1944–49, Pologne 53, 20–1; telegram from de Beausse (Warsaw), 3 April 1947, ibid., 31.

21 Maritain (Holy See) to Bidault, 5 March 1947, ibid., 22–7; Diana to Foreign Ministry, 18 April 1947, ASMAE, busta 6, Santa Sede 5 – Polonia.

22 Bidault to Maritain (Holy See), 14 August 1947, Q d'O, Z Europe 1944–49, Pologne 53, 78–82.

23 Bourdeillette (Holy See) to Bidault, 29 August 1947, ibid., 83–6.

24 Donini to Foreign Ministry, 2 June 1947, ASMAE, busta 6, Santa Sede 5 – Polonia; Foreign Ministry to Moscow, 7 June 1947, ibid.

25 Jalenques (Warsaw) to Bidault, 26 July 1947, Q d'O, Z Europe 1944–49, Pologne 53, 128–9; note, 28 July 1947, ibid., Saint Siège 9.

26 Broad to Bevin, 10 October 1947, FO, N12037/556/55.
27 Donini to Foreign Ministry, 14 October 1947, ASMAE, busta 6, Santa
   Sede 5 – Polonia.
28 Gainer to Bevin, 12 December 1947, FO, N14472/556/55.

Chapter Fifteen

1 Hassett to Marshall, 4 August 1947, NARA, State Department, 121. 866A/
   8-447; Bonnet (Washington) to Bidault, 19 August 1947, Q d'O, Z
   Europe 1944–49, Saint Siège 9.
2 Telegram from Taylor (Holy See), 27 August 1947, NARA, State Department, 866A. 4611/ 8-2747.
3 Parsons (Holy See) to Marshall, 17 October 1947, ibid., 711. 66A/
   10-1747.
4 Maritain (Holy See) to Bidault, 23 October 1947, Q d'O, Z Europe
   1944–49, Saint Siège 9.
5 Parsons (Holy See) to Marshall, 13 November 1947, NARA, State Department, 033. 1100/ 11-1347.
6 *Osservatore Romano*, 24–25 November 1947.
7 Minute, 7 January 1948, Q d'O, Z Europe 1944–49, Saint Siège 9.
8 Perowne (Holy See) to Bevin, 2 April 1948, FO, Z2869/ 2869/57.
9 Maritain (Holy See) to Bidault, 4 June 1947, Q d'O, Z Europe 1944–49,
   Italie 52; minute by Hoyer Millar, 6 May 1947, FO, Z4561/4561/57.
10 Parsons (Holy See) to Secretary of State, 2 March 1948, NARA, State
   Department, 865.00/3–248; ibid., 27 October 1947, NARA, Taylor Papers,
   17/800; Perowne (Holy See) to Bevin, 8 December 1947, FO,
   Z10856/32/22.
11 Telegram from Parsons (Holy See), 22 November 1947, NARA, State
   Department, 866A.001/ 11-2247; Parsons to Secretary of State, 2 March
   1948, ibid., 865.00/3–248.
12 Perowne (Holy See) to Bevin, 8 December 1947, FO, Z10856/32/22.
13 Telegram from Dunn (Rome), 25 February 1948, NARA, State Department, 865.404/ 2–2548.
14 Parsons (Holy See) to Secretary of State, 2 March 1948, ibid., 865.000/
   3–248.
15 Parsons (Holy See) to Secretary of State, 15 January 1948, ibid.,
   866A.404/ 1–1548.
16 Riccardi, *Partito Romano*, 45–54, 95–110.
17 Turgeon (Dublin) to Minister of External Affairs, 12 April 1948, NAC,
   Department of External Affairs, [84-85/019] 192/7453–40; Dunn (Rome)
   to Secretary of State, 17 May 1948, NARA, State Department, 865.00/
   5–1748.
18 McNicholas to Carroll, 16 February 1948, and Carroll to McNicholas, 1

March 1948, NCWC, box 9, Communism: Italy; Carroll to Cicognani, 28 April 1948, ibid.

19 Emmet to Carroll, 15 March 1948, and Carroll to Cicognani, 2 April 1948; and Cicognani to Carroll, 5 April, 8 May 1948, ibid.

20 Telegram from Parsons (Holy See), 2 March 1948, ibid., 865.00/ 3–248.

21 Parsons (Holy See) to Secretary of State, 30 March 1948, ibid., 866A.001/ 3–3048; Perowne (Holy See) to Bevin, 31 March 1948, FO, Z2868/133/57.

22 Maritain (Holy See) to Bidault, 2 April 1948, Q d'O, Z Europe 1944–49, Saint Siège 9.

23 On 4 March 1948 an official communiqué in the *Osservatore Romano* informed the public that the priest Edward Prettner-Cippico, a former official in the archives of the Secretariat of State, had been suspended when found guilty of abuse of his position and, following the results of a commission of inquiry, had been defrocked. The Vatican thought it wiser to "come clean" before the scandal was picked up by its political opponents, although even here it provided political ammunition for left-wing cartoonists and campaign gimmicks, as little red strips of paper with the words "E Cippico?" which were attached to Christian Democrat and left-wing posters alike. At the same time, information about another dismissed prelate, one Monsignor Guidetti, the secretary of the Commission of Cardinals for the Administration of the Property of the Holy See, also came to light. In both cases, the Vatican acted before the scandals broke, but the developing news was received by the public with great amusement. It was the dignity, more than the integrity of the Vatican that suffered from these incidents.

24 Dunn (Rome) to Secretary of State, 17 May 1948, NARA, State Department, 865.00/ 5-1748; Bourdeillette (Holy See) to Bidault, 30 April 1948, Q d'O, Z Europe 1944–49, Saint Siège 9.

25 Riccardi, *Partito Romano*, 103–10.

26 Minute, 22 June 1948, Q d'O, Z Europe 1944–49, Saint Siège 10.

27 Rioux, *Fourth Republic*, 128.

28 Foreign Ministry to Prime Minister, 20 January 1948, ASMAE, busta 9, Santa Sede 5 – Francia.

29 *La Croix*, 28–29 December 1947, 25–26 April 1948.

Chapter Sixteen

1 Perowne (Holy See) to Bevin, 26 January 1948, FO, N1145/304/12.

2 Warsaw to Foreign Ministry, 7, 14 December 1947, ASMAE, busta 10, Santa Sede 5 – Polonia (1948); Perowne to Warner, 8 December 1947, FO, N14534/556/55.

3 Warsaw to Foreign Ministry, 24 December 1947, ASMAE, busta 10, Santa

Sede 5 – Polonia (1948); Gainer to Bevin, 12 December 1947, FO, N14472/556/55.

4 Telegram from Gainer, 19 December 1947, FO, N14637/5050/55; Foreign Ministry to Holy See, 5 January 1948, ASMAE, busta 10, Santa Sede 5 – Polonia; Perowne to Hankey, 12 January 1948, FO, N664/356/55.

5 Gainer to Bevin, 20 February 1948, FO, N2080/356/55; Foreign Ministry to the Holy See, 23 February 1948, ASMAE, busta 10, Santa Sede 5 – Polonia; Szudy to Swanstrom, 25 February 1948, NCWC, 10/Communism; Poland: 45–50.

6 Perowne (Holy See) to Bevin, 19 April 1948, FO, Z3555/3111/57, and 4 May 1948, ibid., Z4168/4168/57.

7 Crocker to the Secretary of State, 1 June 1948, NARA, Myron Taylor Papers, 21/800; Warsaw to Foreign Ministry, 10 June 1948, ASMAE, busta 10, Santa Sede 5 – Polonia.

8 Gainer to Bevin, 23 June 1948, FO, N7466/356/55.

9 Váli, *Rift and Revolt in Hungary*, 31.

10 Kovrig, *Communism in Hungary*, 205–10; Mindszenty, *Memoirs*, 69–71.

11 Foreign Ministry to Budapest, 13 August 1947, ASMAE, busta 6, Santa Sede 5 – Ungheria; Chancery (Budapest) to Foreign Office, 22 October 1947, FO, R14370/11/21.

12 Helm (Budapest) to Wallinger, 29 December 1947, FO, R250/250/21 (l948). Political developments in Hungary in 1947 are outlined in Helm (Budapest) to Attlee, 3 January 1948, FO, R607/53/21; the August elections are reported in Helm (Budapest) to Bevin, 2 September 1947, ibid., R12258/11/21.

13 Telegram from Walsh (Budapest), 6 September 1947, FO, R12277/11/21.

14 Perowne (Holy See) to Wallinger, 5 December 1947, FO, R16478/11/21; Helm (Budapest) to Wallinger, 29 December 1947, R250/250/21.

15 Foreign Ministry to Holy See, 16 January, 9 March 1948, ASMAE, busta 10, Santa Sede 5 – Ungheria.

16 Summary of article in *Il Quotidiano* of 22 January 1948, entitled "Hungary and the Holy See," FO, R1422/250/21; Kovrig, *Communism in Hungary*, 225.

17 Coe (London) to Marshall, 8 March 1948, NARA, State Department, 740.00119 EW/ 3–848.

18 Helm (Budapest) to Wallinger, 8 and 13 April 1948, FO, R4630/53/21 and R4957/250/21; Perowne (Holy See) to Wallinger, 22 April 1948, ibid., R5237/250/21.

19 Helm (Budapest) to Bevin, 19 May 1948, ibid., R6278/250/21.

20 Perowne (Holy See) to Bevin, 21 June 1948, ibid., R7519/250/21; Helm (Budapest) to Wallinger, 7 July 1948, ibid., R8351/53/21.

21 Bruins to Secretary of State, 27 January 1948, NARA, State Department, 860F.404/1–2748.

22 Steinhardt to Secretary of State, 13 April 1948, ibid., 4–1348; Soragna to Foreign Ministry, 23 March 1948, ASMAE, busta 9, Santa Sede 5 – Cecoslovakia.

23 Czechoslovak Bishops to Cepicka, 4 March 1948, FO, N6520/5904/12; Prague to Foreign Ministry, 26 March 1948, Q d'O, z Europe 1944–49, Tchécoslovaquie 47, 116–21.

24 Telegram from Steinhardt, 23 April 1948, NARA, State Department, 860F.404/4–2348.

25 Prague to Foreign Ministry, 4 and 15 May 1948, ASMAE, busta 9, Santa Sede 5 – Cecoslovakia.

26 Beran to Plojhar, 21 May 1948, in Dixon to Hankey, 17 June 1948, FO, N7146/5904/12.

Chapter Seventeen

1 See, for example, Kirby, *Church, State and Propaganda*, 160.

2 Crampton, *Eastern Europe in the Twentieth Century*, 255–74.

3 Holman (Bucharest) to Bevin, 22 June 1948, FO, R7680/898/37.

4 Chataigneau (Moscow) to Schumann, 28 July 1948, Q d'O, z Europe 1944–49, URSS 27, 105–13; Riccardi, *Vaticano e Mosca*, 59–69.

5 Holman (Bucharest) to Bevin, 22 June 1948, FO, R7680/898/37.

6 Paris (Sofia) to Schumann, 17 August 1948, Q d'O, z Europe 1944–49, Bulgarie 15, 74–7.

7 Foreign Ministry to Holy See, 11 November 1948, ASMAE, busta 10, Santa Sede 5 – URSS.

8 Note of the Foreign Ministry, 5 January 1946, and Payart (Belgrade) to Bidault, 17 April 1946, Q d'O, z Europe 1944–49, Yougoslavie 34; Kirby, *Church, State and Propaganda*, 148–9.

9 Excerpts from the Romanian press, 17 April 1948, ASMAE, busta 10, Santa Sede 5 – Romania; Foreign Ministry to Washington, 22 July 1948, ibid.

10 Bucharest to Foreign Ministry, 7 May, 19 July, 1948, ibid.; telegram from Holman (Bucharest), 19 July 1948, FO, R8514/898/37.

11 Foreign Ministry to Holy See, 25 September 1948, ASMAE, busta 10, Santa Sede 5 – Romania; Holman (Bucharest) to Bevin, 19 August 1948, FO, R10107/898/37.

12 Holman (Bucharest) to Bevin, 25 June 1948, FO, R7931/898/37.

13 Holman (Bucharest) to Bevin, 26 October 1948, ibid., R12283/898/37; Perowne (HS) to Bevin, 4 February 1949, ibid., R1429/1782/37; Bucharest to Foreign Minister, 27 June 1949, ASMAE, busta 13, Santa Sede 5 – Romania.

14 Somers Cocks (Holy See) to Wallinger, 27 July 1948, FO, R8928/898/37; Foreign Ministry to Holy See, 6 September 1948, ASMAE, busta 10, Santa Sede 5 – Romania.

15 Cicognani to Carroll, 3 November 1948, NCWC, box 10, Communism: Romania.

16 Telegram from Roberts (Bucharest), 30 June 1949, FO, R6389/1782/37.

17 Sofia to Foreign Ministry, 23 June 1947, ASMAE, busta 5, Santa Sede 5 – Bulgaria; Paris (Sofia) to Bidault, 25 February 1947, Q d'O, Z Europe 1944–49, Bulgarie 15, 38–45.

18 Telegram from O'Donoghue (Sofia), 16 December 1948, NARA, State Department, 766A.74/ 12–1648; Paris (Sofia) to Foreign Minister, 4 February 1949, Q d'O, Z Europe 1944–49, Bulgarie 15; Foreign Ministry to Holy See, 4 February 1949, ASMAE, busta 12, Santa Sede 5 – Bulgaria.

19 Tisserant to Foreign Minister, 6 April 1949, ASMAE, busta 12, Santa Sede 5 – Bulgaria; article by A. Mirolubov, 30 April 1949, FO, R4887/1783/7.

20 Telegram from Baelen (Warsaw), 31 December 1948, Q d'O, Z Europe 1944–49, Pologne 54.

21 Gauquié (Budapest) to Bidault, 14 July 1948, ibid., Hongrie 18, 67+ to 69+.

22 Minute, 6 December 1948, ASMAE, busta 10, Santa Sede 5 – Ungheria.

23 Telegrams from Young (Budapest), 12 October 1948, FO, R11609 and R11613/250/21, and 23 October 1948, R12022/250/21; Gauquié (Budapest) to Foreign Minister, 30 October 1948, Q d'O, Z Europe 1944–49, Hongrie 18, 101+ to 104; Foreign Ministry to Holy See, 12 November 1948, ASMAE, busta 10, Santa Sede 5 – Ungheria.

24 Telegram from Helm (Budapest), 30 December 1948, FO, R14534/250/21.

25 Helm (Budapest) to McNeil, 20 November 1948, FO, R13434/53/21.

26 Perowne (Holy See) to Wallinger, 24 November 1948, FO, R13430/250/21; D'Ormesson (Holy See) to Schuman, 26 November 1948, Q d'O, Z Europe 1944–49, Pologne 54; minute, 6 December 1948, ASMAE, busta 10, Santa Sede 5 – Ungheria.

27 Minute by Helm (Budapest), 22 January 1949, ibid., R1260/1781/21.

28 Telegram from Helm (Budapest), 18 December 1948, FO, R14241/250/21; minute by Helm (Budapest), 22 January 1949, ibid., R1260/1781/21.

29 Tanner to Carroll, 28 December 1948, McNicholas to Sik, 29 December 1948, and McNicholas to Montini, 29 December 1948, NCWC, 8/ Hungary: Mindszenty: 46–9; telegram from McGuigan (Toronto) to St Laurent, December 27, 1948, and telegram from Vachon (Ottawa) to St Laurent, NAC, St Laurent 53/ H–35–M.

30 As reported in telegram from Perowne (Holy See), 31 December 1948, FO, R144/1781/21 (1949).

31 Telegram from d'Ormesson (Holy See), 7 January 1949, Q d'O, Z Europe 1944–49, Hongrie 18; Pius XII to the Hungarian Episcopate, 2 January 1949, FO, R1731/1781/21.

32 Désy (Rome) to Pearson, 31 December 1948, NAC, St Laurent 52/ H–35–M; memorandum for External Affairs, January 3, 1949, ibid.

33 Telegram from Franks (Washington), 3 January 1949, FO, R65/1781/21.

34 St Laurent to McGuigan, 5 January 1949, NAC, St Laurent 53, H–35–M; Foreign Office to Budapest, 31 December 1948, FO, R14412/250/21.

35 Minute by Helm (Budapest), 22 January 1949, FO, R1260/1781/21.

36 Hall to Tanner, 13 January 1949, NCWC, 8/ Communism: Hungary: Mindszenty: 46–9; telegram from d'Ormesson (Holy See), 14 January 1949, Q d'O, Z Europe 1944–49, Hongrie 18; minute by Smith (Budapest), 11 April 1949, FO, R4186/1781/21.

37 Foreign Ministry to Holy See, 29 November 1948, ASMAE, busta 10, Santa Sede 5 – Polonia.

38 Baelen (Warsaw) to Schuman, 24 November 1948, Q d'O, Z Europe 1944–49, Pologne 54; Foreign Ministry to Holy See, 17 December 1948, ASMAE, busta 10, Santa Sede 5 – Polonia.

39 Warsaw to Foreign Minister, 30 December 1948, ibid., busta 13; telegram from Baelen (Warsaw), 31 December 1948, Q d'O, Z Europe 1944–49, Pologne 54.

40 Stehle, *Eastern Politics of the Vatican,* 275–6.

41 Baelen (Warsaw) to Schuman, 12 January 1949, Q d'O, Z Europe 1944–49, Pologne 54; Foreign Ministry to Minister of the Interior, 26 January 1949, ASMAE, busta 13, Santa Sede 5 – Polonia; Gainer (Warsaw) to Bevin, 16 March 1949, FO, N2748/1781/55.

42 Baelen (Warsaw) to Schuman, 3 and 18 February 1949, Europe 1944–49, Pologne 54; Kirkwood (Warsaw) to Pearson, 23 February 1949, NAC, Department of External Affairs [84–85/019] 335/9845–40.

43 Gainer (Warsaw) to Bevin, 5 April 1949, FO, N3340/1781/55; Warsaw to Foreign Ministry, 6 April 1949, ASMAE, busta 13, Santa Sede 5 – Polonia.

44 Baelen (Warsaw) to Foreign Ministry, 20 April 1949, Q d'O, Z Europe 1944–49, Pologne 54; Warsaw to Foreign Ministry, 28 April 1949, ASMAE, busta 13, Santa Sede 5 – Polonia; Gainer (Warsaw) to Bevin, 24 June 1949, FO, N5776/1781/55.

45 Rumbold (Prague) to Bevin, 3 September 1948, FO, N9745/5904/12; Prague to Foreign Minister, 30 August 1948, ASMAE, busta 9, Santa Sede 5 – Cecoslovacchia; D'Ormesson (Holy See) to Schuman, 18 November 1948, Q d'O, Z Europe 1944–49, Tchécoslovakie 47, 177–9; Vanni (Prague) to Foreign Minister, 9 December 1948, ASMAE, busta 9, Santa Sede 5 – Cecoslovacchia.

46 Dixon (Prague) to Bevin, 18 January 1949, FO, N638/1781/12; Foreign Ministry to Minister of the Interior, 10 March 1949, ASMAE, busta 12, Santa Sede 5 – Cecoslovacchia.

47 BBC Report, 25 April 1949, FO, N3759/1781/12; Prague to Foreign Minister, 15 May 1949, ASMAE, busta 17, Santa Sede 5 – Cecoslovacchia (1950); Penfield (Prague) to Secretary of State, 6 June 1949, NARA, State Department, 860F.404/6–649.

48 Macdonnell to Pearson, 1 June 1949, NAC, Department of External

Affairs [84–85/ 019] 384/10927–40; Penfield (Prague) to Secretary of State, 6 June 1949, NARA, State Department, 860F.404/6–649.

49 Macdonnell to Pearson, 14 June 1949, NAC, Department of External Affairs [84–85/019] 384/10927–40.

50 Statement by the Czech Bishops, 15 June 1949, reported in ibid.

51 Telegram from Dixon (Prague), 20 June 1949, FO, N5547/1781/12; Dixon to Bevin, 20 June 1949, ibid.

52 Telegram from d'Ormesson, 17 June 1949, Q d'O, Z Europe 1944–49, Tchécoslovaquie 47; telegram from Bruce (Paris), 27 June 1949, NARA, State Department, 860F. 404/ 6–2749; Macdonnell to MacDermot, 28 July 1949, NAC, Department of External Affairs [84–85/019] 384/10927–40.

53 Somers Cocks (Holy See) to Bevin, 22 June 1949, FO, N5661/1781/12.

54 Foreign Ministry to London, 26 July 1949, ASMAE, busta 17, Santa Sede 5 – Cecoslovacchia; telegram from Jacobs (Prague), 2 July 1949, NARA, State Department, 860F. 404/7–249.

55 MacDermot to Macdonnell, 11 July 1949, NAC, Department of External Affairs [84-85/019] 384/10927–40.

56 Payart (Belgrade) to Bidault, 8 February 1947, 5 January 1948, Q d'O, Z Europe 1944–49, Yougoslavie 35, 36.

57 Payart (Belgrade) to Bidault, 28 April 1948, ibid.

58 Foreign Ministry to Holy See, 12 July 1948, ASMAE, busta 10, Santa Sede 5 – Jugoslavia; Vaillancourt (Belgrade) to St Laurent, 23 July 1948, NAC, St Laurent 18/100–1–5; Foreign Ministry to Minister of the Interior, 11 September 1948, ASMAE, busta 10, Santa Sede 5 – Jugoslavia.

59 Rhodes, *Vatican in the Age of the Cold War*, 138.

60 Peake (Belgrade) to Bevin, 25 January 1949, FO, R1252/1782/92; Vaillancourt (Belgrade) to Pearson, 21 March 1949, NAC, Department of External Affairs [84 – 85/019] 205/7805–40.

61 Gallagher, "Accommodation and Abandonment."

62 Perowne (Holy See) to Kirkpatrick, 1 July 1948, FO, Z5512/133/57.

63 Gallagher, "Accommodation and Abandonment."

64 Belgrade to Foreign Minister, 21 June 1949, ASMAE, busta 13, Santa Sede 5 – Jugoslavia.

Chapter Eighteen

1 Sarah-Jane Corke contends that the American commitment to containment was less than coherent during this period and that American policy was occasionally marked by conflicting and contradictory strategic visions. Corke, "The War of the Potomac."

2 D'Ormesson (Holy See) to Schumann, 14 February 1949, Q d'O, Z Europe 1944–49, Saint Siège 10, 170–203.

3 Text of Papal Allocution, 14 February 1949, FO, R2000/1786/21; *Eastern Politics*, Stehle, 270.

4 Speech by Pius XII, 20 February 1949, FO, Z2057/1024/57.

5 The gender of the crowd was important to the pope since it was normally women who were the most active and evident members of the church.

6 Telegram from Dunn (Holy See), 28 February 1949, NARA, State Department, 866A.001/2–2849.

7 Transcript from Vatican Radio, 5 January 1949, FO, Z2789/1052/57.

8 Perowne (Holy See) to Bevin, 28 April, 1 June 1949, ibid., Z3407/1731/57; d'Ormesson (Holy See) to Schuman, 11 May 1949, Q d'O, Z Europe 1944–49, Saint Siège 6.

9 Riccardi, *Vaticano e Mosca*, 79–85.

10 Foreign Ministry to Holy See, 24 February, 18 March, and 14 April 1949, ASMAE, busta 12, Santa Sede 4.

11 Ibid., 3 September 1949.

12 Prunas (Ankara) to Foreign Ministry, 17 April 1950, ASMAE, busta 19, Santa Sede 5 – Turchia.

13 Telegram from Perowne (Holy See), 20 July 1949, FO, Z5051/1027/57.

14 Telegram from Gowen (Holy See), 15 July 1949, NARA, State Department, 800.404/7–1549.

15 D'Ormesson (Holy See) to Schuman, 22 July 1949, Q d'O, EU – Europe 1949–55, Saint Siège 14.

16 Somers Cocks (Holy See) to Bevin, 15 September 1949, FO, Z6124/1731/57; Perowne (Holy See) to Attlee, 30 December 1949, FO, WV1782/1/1950.

17 Telegram from Wadsworth (Ankara), 5 August 1949, NARA, State Department, 800.404/8–549; Foreign Ministry to Holy See, 22 September 1949, ASMAE, busta 13, Santa Sede 5 –Turchia.

18 Foreign Ministry to Holy See, 26 September 1949, ASMAE, busta 12, Santa Sede 4; Barrett (Mexico City) to Secretary of State, 8 August 1949, NARA, State Department, 800.404/8–849.

19 Telegram from Gauquié (Budapest), 22 July 1949, Q d'O, EU – Europe 1949–55, Saint Siège 14.

20 Istanbul to Foreign Ministry, 20 July 1949, ASMAE, busta 13, Santa Sede 5 – Turchia.

21 Mallet (Rome) to Attlee, 29 July 1949, FO, Z5365/1027/57.

22 Prague to Foreign Ministry, 15 July 1949, ASMAE, busta 17, Santa Sede 5 – Cecoslovacchia (1950).

23 D'Ormesson (Holy See) to Schuman, 11 November 1949, Q d'O, EU – Europe 1949–55, Pologne 40; Chataigneau (Moscow) to Schuman, 21 January 1950, ibid., URSS 39.

24 Prague to Foreign Ministry, 12 September 1949, ASMAE, busta 17, Santa Sede 5 – Cecoslovacchia (1950); telegram from Malcolm (Prague), 4 August 1949, FO, N7097/1781/12.

25 Macdonnell (Prague) to Pearson, 5 August, 21 September 1949, NAC, Department of External Affairs [84–85/019] 384/10927–40; Prague to Foreign Ministry, 3 October 1949, ASMAE, busta 17, Santa Sede 5 – Cecoslovacchia (1950); Dixon (Prague) to Bevin, 19 October 1949, FO, N9124/1781/12.

26 Czechoslovak Bishops to Government, 17 November 1949, translation in FO, N10712/1781/12.

27 Perowne (Holy See) to Rumbold, 8 August 1949, FO, N7282/1781/12; Somers Cocks (Holy See) to Bevin, 24 August 1949, ibid., N7706/1781/12.

28 Telegram from Dixon (Prague), 16 March 1950, ibid.; telegram from Perowne (Holy See), 4 April 1950, ibid./ 24; d'Ormesson (Holy See) to Schuman, 6 May 1950, Q d'O, EU – Europe 1949–55, Saint Siège 4.

29 Telegram from Perowne (Holy See), 5 April 1950, FO, NC1781/25.

30 Malcolm (Prague) to Younger, 16 June 1950, ibid./ 42.

31 Toffin (Bucharest) to Schuman, 13 October 1949, Q d'O, EU – Europe 1949–55, Roumanie 42; d'Ormesson (Holy See) to Schuman, 25 October 1949, ibid.

32 Holy Office Decree, 2 May 1950, FO, RR1783/1.

33 Memo by May (Bucharest), 25 May 1950, FO, RR1783/2.

34 Stehle, *Eastern Politics of the Vatican,* 264; Montini to O'Hara, 21 July 1950, Archives of the Diocese of Savannah, GA, O'Hara Papers.

35 Winch (Warsaw) to Hankey, 5 August 1949, FO, N7222/1781/55; Pofilet (Warsaw) to Foreign Ministry, 10 August 1949, Q d'O, EU – Europe 1949–55, Pologne 40.

36 Kirkwood (Warsaw) to Pearson, 14 July 1949, NAC, Department of External Affairs, [84–85/019] 335/9845–40; telegram from Gainer (Warsaw), 15 July 1949, FO, N6403/1781/55.

37 Perowne (Holy See) to Bevin, 20 July 1949, FO, Z5077/10318/57; telegram from Gainer (Warsaw), 20 July 1949, ibid., N6595/1781/55.

38 Foreign Ministry to the Holy See, 26 July 1949, ASMAE, busta 13, Santa Sede 5 – Polonia.

39 Kirkwood (Warsaw) to Pearson, 29 July 1949, NAC, Department of External Affairs [84–85/019] 335, 9845–40; Foreign Ministry to London, 6 August 1949, ASMAE, busta 13, Santa Sede 5 – Polonia; Gainer (Warsaw) to Attlee, 3 August 1949, FO, N7148/1781/55.

40 Somers Cocks to Bevin, 6 September 1949, FO, N8083/1781/55; Gowen (Holy See) to Secretary of State, 8 September 1949, NARA, State Department, 866A.001/9–849.

41 Telegram from Baelen (Warsaw), 25 and 31 October 1949, Q d'O, EU – Europe 1949–55, Pologne 40; Gainer (Warsaw) to Bevin, 28 October 1949, FO, N9405/1781/55; telegram from Hall (Warsaw), 16 December 1949, NARA, Myron Taylor Papers, 26/350.

42 Chancery (Warsaw) to Foreign Office, 24 February 1950, FO, NP1781/4;

Kirkwood (Warsaw) to Pearson, 1 February 1950, NAC, Department of External Affairs, [84–85/019] 335/9845–40; Baelen (Warsaw) to Foreign Ministry, 2 February 1950, Q d'O, EU – Europe 1949–55, Pologne 40.

43 Church-State Agreement in Poland, 14 April 1950, NAC, Department of External Affairs [84–85/150] 147/9845–40; BBC report, 15 April 1950, FO, NP1781/10.

44 Winch (Warsaw) to Harrison, 21 April 1950, FO, NP1781/14.

45 Telegram from Perowne (Holy See), 17 April 1950, ibid./9; d'Ormesson (Holy See) to Schuman, 19 April 1950, Q d'O, EU – Europe 1949–55, Pologne 40; Perowne (Holy See) to Bevin, 14 June 1950, FO, NP1781/30.

46 D'Ormesson (Holy See) to Schuman, 19, 21 April 1950, Q d'O, EU – Europe 1949–55, Pologne 40; Winch (Warsaw) to Harrison, 21 April 1950, FO, NP1781/ 14; telegram from Perowne (Holy See), 24 April, 1 May 1950, ibid./ 15, 19; Perowne (Holy See) to Bevin, 14 June 1950, ibid./ 30.

47 Telegram from Gauquié (Budapest), 22 July 1949, Q d'O, EU – Europe 1949–55, Saint Siège 14; Wallinger (Budapest) to Attlee, 26 July 1949, FO, R7368/1787/21.

48 Stehle, *Eastern Politics of the Vatican,* 280–2.

49 Foreign Ministry to Washington, 27 November 1948, ASMAE, busta 10, Santa Sede 5 – Stati Uniti; Perowne (Holy See) to Kirkpatrick, 15 October 1948, FO, Z8502/4233/57; d'Ormesson (Holy See) to Schuman, 20, 21 October 1948, Q d'O, Z Europe 1944–49, Saint Siège 10.

50 Perowne (Holy See) to Bevin, 17 November 1948, FO, Z9464/133/57.

51 Soragna (Holy See) to Foreign Ministry, 20 February 1949, ASMAE, busta 12, Santa Sede 5 – General.

52 *Journal de Genève,* 29 November 1948, ibid., busta 9, Santa Sede 5 – Italia.

53 Soragna (Holy See) to Foreign Ministry, 1 November 1948, ibid., busta 10, Santa Sede 5 – Palestine; Gowen (Holy See) to Secretary of State, 2 November 1948, NARA, Myron Taylor Papers, 20/322; Foreign Ministry to Ankara, 2 April 1949, ASMAE, busta 13, Santa Sede 5 – Palestine.

54 Spellman to Truman, 29 April 1949, NARA, State Department, 867N.01/5–449; Truman to Spellman, 9 May, 22 June 1949, ibid., 1349; Spellman to Truman, 13 July 1949, ibid.

55 Gowen to Secretary of State, 13 August 1949, NARA, Myron Taylor Papers, 26/322; memo to the Secretary of State, 20 October 1949, ibid., State Department, 121.866A/10–2049; statement by United States Bishops, 16–18 November 1949, NCWC, *Catholic Action.*

56 Wrong (Washington) to Pearson, 24 March 1949, NAC, Department of External Affairs, [86–87/159] 33/7951–40.

57 Telegram from d'Ormesson (Holy See), 24 June 1949, Q d'O, Z Europe 1944–49, Saint Siège 10.

58 d'Ormesson (Holy See) to Schuman, 7 July 1949, ibid., Europe 1949–55, Saint Siège 4.

59 Foreign Ministry to Holy See, 1 February 1950, ASMAE, busta 18, Santa Sede 5 – Palestina; Foreign Ministry to Ankara, 6 February, 22 June 1950, ibid.

60 d'Ormesson (Holy See) to Schuman, 20, 25 January 1950, Q d'O, EU – Europe 1949–55, Saint Siège 4; Perowne (Holy See) to Hoyer Millar (Washington), 20 March 1950, FO, WV1901/13.

61 Hoyer Millar (Washington) to Perowne (Holy See), 10 February 1950, FO, WV1901/6; d'Ormesson (Holy See) to Schuman, 25 January 1950, Q d'O, EU – Europe 1949-55, Saint Siège 4; *U.S. News and World Report*, 10 February 1950, FO, WV1901/7; Perowne (Holy See) to Hoyer Millar (Washington), 20 March 1950, ibid., 13; Tarchiani (Washington) to Foreign Ministry, 12 April 1950, ASMAE, busta 19, Santa Sede 5 – Stati Uniti.

62 Hebblethwaite, *Paul VI*, 228–9.

63 Halecki and Murray, *Pius XII*, 226–8.

64 Chancery (Prague) to Foreign Office, 28 June 1950, FO, NC1781/44; d'Ormesson to Schuman, 30 June 1950, Q d'O, EU – Europe 1949–55, Saint Siège 14; memorandum by May (Bucharest), 25 May 1950, FO, RR1783/2.

Epilogue

1 Crampton, *Eastern Europe in the Twentieth Century*, 265.

2 Riccardi, *Vaticano e Mosca*, 87–94.

3 Father John Cronin had made an identical speech to a communion breakfast in Arlington, Virginia, in March 1946, based on his report for the American bishops. But in the climate of the times, the media had not taken him seriously. See *Washington Post*, 11 and 13 March 1946; *Washington Times Herald*, 11 March 1946; and *Chicago Tribune*, 12 March 1946.

4 Whitfield, *Culture of the Cold War*, chapter 4.

5 Rhodes, *Vatican in the Age of the Cold War*, 187; Gerald P. Fogarty, "The United States and the Vatican, 1939–1984," in Kent and Pollard, *Papal Diplomacy in the Modern Age*, 221–43.

6 Hebblethwaite, *Paul VI*, 235

7 Riccardi, *Partito Romano*, 143–9; Luxmoore and Babuich, *The Vatican and the Red Flag*, 98–9; Hebblethwaite, *Paul VI*, 230.

8 Falconi, *Popes of the Twentieth Century*, 289–95; Luxmoore and Babuich, *The Vatican and the Red Flag*, 99.

9 Pietro Scoppola, "Chiesa e società negli anni della modernizzazione," and Andrea Riccardi, "Chiesa di Pio XII o Chiese italiane?", in Riccardi, *Le Chiese di Pio XII*.

10 Riccardi, *Partito Romano*, 225–39.

Bibliography

PRIMARY SOURCES

MANUSCRIPT COLLECTIONS

Myron Taylor Papers, National Archives of the United States, Washington, DC.
Papers of the Archdiocese of Westminster, Archives of the Archdiocese, London.
Papers of the British Foreign Office, Public Record Office, London.
Papers of the Canadian Conference of Catholic Bishops, Archives of the Conference, Ottawa.
Papers of the Department of External Affairs, National Archives of Canada, Ottawa.
Papers of the Diocese of Savannah, Archives of the Diocese, Savannah, Georgia.
Papers of the Diocese of St Augustine, Archives of the Diocese, Jacksonville, Florida.
Papers of the Ministère des Affaires Étrangères, Archives of the Foreign Ministry, Paris
Papers of the Ministero degli Affari Esteri, Archives of the Foreign Ministry, Rome
Papers of the National Catholic Welfare Conference, Archives of the United States Catholic Conference, Washington, DC.
Papers of the United States Department of State, National Archives and Records Administration, Washington, DC.

PUBLISHED COLLECTIONS

Blet, Pierre, Robert A. Graham, Angelo Martini and Burkhart Schneider, eds. *Actes et Documents du Saint Siège Relatifs a la Seconde Guerre Mondiale.* 11 volumes in 12, Vatican City 1965–81.

Di Nolfo, Ennio. *Vaticano e Stati Uniti, 1939–1952: Dalle carte di Myron C. Taylor.* Milan: Franco Angeli Editore 1978.

Ihm, Claudia Carlen, ed. *The Papal Encyclicals, 1939–1958.* Raleigh: McGrath Publishing Company 1981.

McLaughlin, Terence P., ed. *The Church and the Reconstruction of the Modern World: The Social Encyclicals of Pope Pius XI.* New York: Image Books 1957.

SECONDARY SOURCES

Alexander, Stella. *Church and State in Yugoslavia since 1945.* Cambridge: Cambridge University Press 1979.

– *The Triple Myth: A Life of Archbishop Alojzije Stepinac.* New York: Columbia University Press 1987.

Ambrose, Stephen. *Nixon: The Education of a Politician, 1913–1962.* New York: Simon and Schuster 1987.

Auty, Phyllis. *Tito: A Biography.* New York: McGraw-Hill 1970.

Bader, William B. *Austria Between East and West, 1945–1955.* Stanford, CA: Stanford University Press 1966.

Balfour, Neil, and Sally Mackay. *Paul of Yugoslavia: Britain's Maligned Friend.* London: Hamish Hamilton 1980.

Beeman, William O. "Anthropology and the Myths of American Foreign Policy," in Walter Goldschmidt, ed. *Anthropology and Public Policy: A Dialogue.* American Anthropological Association 1986.

Benes, Eduard. *Memoirs of Dr Eduard Benes: From Munich to New War and New Victory.* Westport CT: Greenwood Press 1954.

Bernstein, Carl, and Marco Politi. *His Holiness: John Paul II and the Hidden History of Our Time.* New York: Doubleday 1996.

Bethell, Nicholas. *Gomulka: His Poland, His Communism.* New York: Holt, Rinehart and Winston 1969.

Biddiscombe, Perry. "Prodding the Russian Bear: Pro-German Resistance in Romania, 1944–5." *European History Quarterly* 23 (1993): 193–232.

Blet, Pierre. *Pio XII e la Seconda Guerra Mondiale negli Archivi Vaticani.* Milan: Edizioni San Paolo 1999.

Blit, Lucjan. *The Eastern Pretender: Boleslaw Piasecki: His Life and Times.* London: Hutchinson 1965.

Bociurkiw, Bohdan R. *Ukrainian Churches under Soviet Rule: Two Case Studies.* Cambridge, MA: Harvard University Ukrainian Studies Fund 1984.

– *The Ukrainian Greek Catholic Church and the Soviet State (1939–1950).* Edmonton: Canadian Institute of Ukrainian Studies Press 1996.

Boyea, Earl. "The National Catholic Welfare Conference: An Experience in Episcopal Leadership, 1935–1945." Doctoral dissertation, the Catholic University of America 1987.

Buchanan, Tom, and Martin Conway, eds. *Political Catholicism in Europe, 1918–1965.* Oxford: Clarendon Press 1996.

Bullitt, William C. "The World from Rome: The Eternal City fears a struggle between Christianity and Communism." *Life,* 4 September 1944.

Buscher, Frank M., and Michael Phayer. "German Catholic Bishops and the Holocaust, 1940 - 1952." *German Studies Review* 11, no. 3 (1988): 463–85.

Casula, Carlo Felice. *Domenico Tardini (1888–1961): L'azione della Santa Sede nella crisi fra le due grande guerre.* Rome: Edizioni Studium 1988.

Chadwick, Owen. *Britain and the Vatican during the Second World War.* Cambridge: Cambridge University Press 1986.

– *The Christian Church in the Cold War.* London: Allen Lane 1992.

Chenaux, Philippe. *Une Europe Vaticane? Entre le Plan Marshall et les Traités de Rome.* Brussels: Editions Ciaco 1990.

Conquest, Robert, ed. *Religion in the USSR.* London: Bodley Head 1968.

Conway, John S. *The Nazi Persecution of the Churches, 1933–45.* Toronto: Ryerson Press 1968.

– "Myron C. Taylor's Mission to the Vatican, 1940–1950." *Church History* 44, no. 1 (March 1975): 85–99.

– "Pope Pius XII and the Myron Taylor Mission: The Vatican and American War-Time Diplomacy." Paper presented to the conference, "FDR, the Vatican and the Roman Catholic Church in America, 1933–1945," Hyde Park, NY, 9 October 1998.

Cooney, John. *The American Pope: The Life and Times of Francis Cardinal Spellman.* New York: Dell 1984.

Coppa, Frank J. *The Modern Papacy since 1789.* New York: Longman 1998.

Corke, Sarah-Jane. "The War of the Potomac: Covert Operations, Eastern Europe and the Policy Process Dilemma, 1945–1953." Doctoral thesis, University of New Brunswick 2000.

Cornwell, John. *Hitler's Pope: The Secret History of Pius XII.* London: Viking 1999.

Coutouvidis, John, and Jaime Reynolds. *Poland, 1939–1947.* New York: Holmes and Meier 1986.

Crampton, R.J. *Eastern Europe in the Twentieth Century.* London: Routledge 1994.

Dalloz, Jacques. *Georges Bidault: Biographie Politique.* Paris: l'Harmattan 1993.

De Gaulle, Charles. *War Memoirs;* Vol. II, "Unity: 1942–1944," translated by Richard Howard. New York: Simon and Schuster 1959.

Dedijer, Vladimir. *The Yugoslav Auschwitz and the Vatican*. Buffalo: Prometheus 1992.

Delzell, Charles F., ed. *The Papacy and Totalitarianism between the Two World Wars*. New York: John Wiley & Sons 1974.

Deutscher, Isaac. *Stalin: A Political Biography*. London: Oxford University Press 1949.

Djilas, Aleksa. *The Contested Country: Yugoslav Unity and Communist Revolution, 1919-1953*. Cambridge, MA: Harvard University Press 1991.

Doering, Bernard E. *Jacques Maritain and the French Catholic Intellectuals*. Notre Dame: University of Notre Dame Press 1983.

Donahoe, Brother Bernard. "The Dictator and the Priest: Stalin's Meeting with Father Stanislas Orlemanski." *Prologue* (Summer 1990): 169–83.

Dragnich, Alex N. *Serbs and Croats: The Struggle in Yugoslavia*. New York: Harcourt Brace Jovanovich 1992.

– *The First Yugoslavia: Search for a Viable Political System*. Stanford, CA: Hoover Institution Press 1983.

Duce, Alessandro. *Pio XII e la Polonia (1939–1945)*. Rome: Edizioni Studium 1997.

Dunaway, John M. *Jacques Maritain*. Boston: Twayne Publishers 1978.

Dunn, Dennis J., ed. *Religion and Nationalism in Eastern Europe and the Soviet Union*. Boulder, CO: Lynne Rienner Publishers 1987.

– *The Catholic Church and the Soviet Government, 1939–1949*. New York: Columbia University Press 1977.

Duquesne, Jacques. *Les catholiques français sous l'occupation*, revised edition. Paris: Bernard Grasset 1986.

Durand, Jean-Dominique. *L'Eglise Catholique dans la Crise de l'Italie (1943–1948)*. Rome: Ecole française de Rome.

Eksteins, Modris. *Walking since Daybreak: A Story of Eastern Europe, World War II, and the Heart of our Century*. Toronto: Key Porter Books 1999.

Falconi, Carlo. *The Popes in the Twentieth Century: From Pius X to John XXIII*, translated by Muriel Grindrod. London: Weidenfeld and Nicolson 1967.

Fletcher, William C. "The Soviet Bible Belt: World War II's Effects on Religion." in Susan J. Linz, ed. *The Impact of World War II on the Soviet Union*. Totowa, NJ: Rowman and Allanheld 1985: 91–106.

Flynn, George Q. *Roosevelt and Romanism: Catholics and American Diplomacy, 1937–1945*. Westport, CT: Greenwood Press 1976.

Fogarty, Gerald P. *The Vatican and the American Hierarchy*. Stuttgart: Anton Hiersemann 1982.

Friedländer, Saul. *Pius XII and the Third Reich: A Documentation*, translated from the French and German by Charles Fullman. New York: Alfred. A. Knopf 1966.

Gaddis, John Lewis. *The United States and the Origins of the Cold War, 1941-1947*. New York: Columbia University Press 1972.

Gallagher, Charles R. "Accommodation and Abandonment: The Vatican, the U.S. Department of State and Tito's Yugoslavia." Paper presented to the Society for Historians of American Foreign Relations, Washington, DC 1997.

– Patriot Bishop: "The Public Career of Archbishop Joseph P. Hurley, 1937–1967." Doctoral dissertation, Marquette University 1998.

Garzia, Italo. *Pio XII e l'Italia nella Seconda Guerra Mondiale*. Brescia: Editrice Morcelliana 1988.

Gedda, Luigi. *18 aprile 1948: Memorie inedite dell'artefice della sconfitta del Fronte Popolare*. Milan: Arnoldo Mondadori 1998.

Gee, Christopher. "American-Italian Relations: 1956–1963." MA thesis, University of New Brunswick 1999.

Geertz, Clifford. *The Interpretation of Cultures: Selected Essays*. New York: Basic Books 1973.

Ginsborg, Paul. *A History of Contemporary Italy: Society and Politics, 1943–1988*. London: Penguin Books 1990.

Graham, Robert A. *The Pope and Poland in World War Two*. London: Veritas Foundation, n.d. [1968 or 1969].

– *The Vatican and Communism during World War II: What Really Happened?* San Francisco: Ignatius Press 1996.

Halecki, Oscar, and James F. Murray, Jr. *Pius XII: Eugenio Pacelli, Pope of Peace*. New York: Lion Library Editions 1951.

Harper, John L. *American Visions of Europe: FDR, Kennan, Acheson*. Cambridge: Cambridge University Press 1994.

Hebblethwaite, Peter. *Paul VI: The First Modern Pope*. New York: The Paulist Press 1993.

– *Pope John XXIII: Shepherd of the Modern World*. Garden City, NY: Image Books 1987.

Hitchcock, William I. *France Restored: Cold War Diplomacy and the Quest for Leadership in Europe, 1944–1954*. Chapel Hill: University of North Carolina Press 1998.

Hoptner, J.B. *Yugoslavia in Crisis, 1934–1941*. New York: Columbia University Press 1962.

Hvat, Ivan. *The Catacomb Ukrainian Catholic Church and Pope John Paul II*. Cambridge, MA: Harvard University Ukrainian Studies Fund 1984.

Jasper, Ronald. *Arthur Cayley Headlam: Life and Letters of a Bishop*. London: Faith Press 1960.

Jelavich, Barbara. *History of the Balkans*, Vol. 2, "Twentieth Century." Cambridge: Cambridge University Press 1983.

Kent, Peter C. *The Pope and the Duce: The International Impact of the Lateran Agreements*. London: Macmillan 1981.

– "The Vatican and the Spanish Civil War." *European History Quarterly* (1986): 441–64.

- "A Tale of Two Popes: Pius XI, Pius XII and the Rome-Berlin Axis." *Journal of Contemporary History* 23 (1988): 589–608.
- "The 'Proffered Gift': The Vatican and the Abortive Yugoslav Concordat of 1935–1937," in Richard Richardson and Glyn Stone, eds. *Decisions in Diplomacy: Studies in Twentieth-Century International History.* London: Routledge Press 1995.
- and John F. Pollard, eds. *Papal Diplomacy in the Modern Age.* Westport, CT: Praeger 1994.

Keogh, Dermot. *Ireland and the Vatican: The Politics and Diplomacy of Church-State Relations, 1922–1960.* Cork: Cork University Press 1995.

Kersten, Krystyna. *The Establishment of Communist Rule in Poland, 1943–1948.* Berkeley: University of California Press 1991.

Kirby, Dianne. *Church, State and Propaganda. The Archbishop of York and International Relations: A Political Study of Cyril Forster Garbett, 1942–1955.* Hull: University of Hull Press 1999.

Kovrig, Bennett. *Hungarian Peoples' Republic.* Baltimore: Johns Hopkins University Press 1970.
- *The Myth of Liberation: East-Central Europe in US Diplomacy and Politics since 1941.* Baltimore: Johns Hopkins University Press 1973.
- *Communism in Hungary: From Kun to Kádár.* Stanford, CA: Hoover Institution Press 1979.

Kreutz, Andrej. *Vatican Policy in the Palestinian-Israeli Conflict: The Struggle for the Holy Land.* New York, Greenwood Press 1990.

Kselman, Thomas A., and Steven Avella. "Marian Piety and the Cold War in the United States." *Catholic Historical Review* 72, no. 3 (1986): 403–24.

Lane, Arthur Bliss. *I Saw Poland Betrayed.* Indianapolis: Bobbs-Merrill 1948.

Leffler, Melvyn P. *A Preponderance of Power: National Security, the Truman Administration, and the Cold War.* Stanford, CA: Stanford University Press 1992.

Lewy, Guenther. *The Catholic Church and Nazi Germany.* New York: McGraw-Hill 1965.

Luxmoore, Jonathan, and Jolanta Babiuch. *The Vatican and the Red Flag: The Struggle for the Soul of Eastern Europe.* London: Geoffrey Chapman 1999.

Maass, Walter B. *Country without a Name: Austria under Nazi Rule, 1938–1945.* New York: Frederick Ungar, 1979.

Magister, Sandro. *La politica vaticana e l'Italia, 1943–1978.* Rome: Editori Riuniti 1979.

Mamatey, Victor S., and Radomir Luza. *A History of the Czechoslovak Republic, 1918–1948.* Princeton, NJ: Princeton University Press 1973.

Markus, Vasyl. *Religion and Nationalism in Soviet Ukraine after 1945.* Cambridge, MA: Harvard University Ukrainian Studies Fund 1985.

Martin, David. *Ally Betrayed: The Uncensored Story of Tito and Mihailovich.* New York: Prentice-Hall 1946.

Miller, James Edward. *The United States and Italy, 1940–1950: The Politics and Diplomacy of Stabilization.* Chapel Hill: University of North Carolina Press 1986.

Mindszenty, Cardinal Jozsef. *Memoirs,* translated by Richard and Clara Winston. New York: Macmillan 1974.

Miscamble, Wilson D. "Catholics and American Foreign Policy from McKinley to McCarthy: A Historiographical Survey." *Diplomatic History* 4, no. 3 (Summer 1980): 223–40.

Monticone, Ronald C. *The Catholic Church in Communist Poland, 1945–1985: Forty Years of Church-State Relations.* Boulder, CO: East European Monographs 1986.

Morris, Charles R. *American Catholic: The Saints and Sinners Who Built America's Most Powerful Church.* New York: Vintage Books 1997.

Murphy, Paul I. with R. René Arlington. *La Popessa.* Warner Books 1983.

Myant, M.R. *Socialism and Democracy in Czechoslovakia, 1945-1948.* Cambridge: Cambridge University Press 1981.

Naimark, Norman, and Leonid Gibianskii, eds. *The Establishment of Communist Regimes in Eastern Europe, 1944–1949.* Boulder, CO: Westview Press 1997.

New Catholic Encyclopedia, Volume X, 1967.

O'Carroll, Michael, C.S.Sp. *Pius XII: Greatness Dishonoured.* Dublin: Laetare Press 1980.

Pease, Neal. "Poland and the Holy See, 1918–1939." *Slavic Review* 50, no. 3 (Fall 1991): 521–30.

Phayer, Michael. *The Catholic Church and the Holocaust, 1930–1945.* Bloomington: Indiana University Press 2000.

Pollard, John F. *The Unknown Pope: Benedict XV (1914–1922) and the Pursuit of Peace.* London: Geoffrey Chapman 1999.

Polonsky, Anthony, and Boleslaw Drukier. *The Beginnings of Communist Rule in Poland.* London: Routledge and Kegan Paul 1980.

Potichnyj, Peter J. "Pacification of Ukraine: Soviet Counterinsurgency, 1944–1956." Paper delivered to the Conference on Russian Counterinsurgency, Centre for Conflict Studies, University of New Brunswick 1987.

Prifti, Peter R. *Socialist Albania since 1944: Domestic and Foreign Developments.* Cambridge, MA: MIT Press 1978.

Quartararo, Rosaria. *Italia e Stati Uniti: Gli anni difficili (1945–1952).* Naples: Edizioni Scientifiche Italiane 1986.

Rakowska-Harmstone, Teresa, ed. *Communism in Eastern Europe,* 2nd ed. Bloomington, IN: Indiana University Press 1984.

Ramet, Pedro, ed. *Catholicism and Politics in Communist Societies.* Durham, NC: Duke University Press 1990.

Ramet, Sabrina Petra. *Balkan Babel: Politics, Culture, and Religion in Yugoslavia.* Boulder, CO: Westview 1992.

Rhodes, Anthony. *The Vatican in the Age of the Dictators, 1922–45*. London: Hodder & Stoughton 1973.
- *The Vatican in the Age of the Cold War, 1945–1980*. Norwich: Michael Russell 1992.
Riccardi, Andrea. *Il "Partito Romano" nel secondo dopoguerra (1945–1954)*. Brescia: Morcelliana 1983.
- ed. *Le Chiese di Pio XII*. Bari: Editori Laterza 1986.
- *Il Potere del Papa: da Pio XII a Paolo VI*. Bari: Editori Laterza 1988.
- *Il Vaticano e Mosca, 1940–1990*. Bari: Editori Laterza 1993.
- (ed.), *Pio XII*. Bari: Editori Laterza 1984.
Rioux, Jean-Pierre. *The Fourth Republic, 1944-1958*. Cambridge: Cambridge University Press 1987.
Ristic, Dragisa N. *Yugoslavia's Revolution of 1941*. London: Pennsylvania State University Press 1966.
Rossi, Joseph Samuel, SJ. "American Catholics and the Formation of the United Nations." Doctoral dissertation, Catholic University of America 1989.
Sadkovich, James J. *Italian Support for Croatian Separatism, 1927-1937*. New York: Garland 1987.
Sherry, Michael S. "War and Weapons: The New Cultural History." *Diplomatic History* 14, no. 3 (Summer 1990): 433–46.
Staar, Richard F. *The Communist Regimes in Eastern Europe*. Stanford, CA: Stanford University Press 1971.
Stehle, Hansjakob. *Eastern Politics of the Vatican, 1917–1979*, translated by Sandra Smith. Athens, OH: Ohio University Press 1981.
Stehlin, Stewart A. *Weimar and the Vatican: German-Vatican Diplomatic Relations in the Interwar Years*. Princeton, NJ: Princeton University Press 1983.
Stone, Norman, and Eduard Strouhal. *Czechoslovakia: Crossroads and Crises, 1918–88*. New York: St. Martin's Press 1989.
Strassberg, Barbara. "Changes in Religious Culture in Post War II Poland." *Sociological Analysis* 48, no. 4 (1988): 342–354.
Sutherland, Anthony X. *Dr Josef Tiso and Modern Slovakia*. Cleveland, OH: First Catholic Slovak Union 1978.
Sword, Keith R. "The Cardinal and the Commissars: Views of the English Catholic Primate on the Communist Takeover in Poland, 1944–47." *The Polish Review*, 31, no. 1 (1986): 49–59.
Szajkowski, Bogdan. *Next to God ... Poland: Politics and Religion in Contemporary Poland*. London: Frances Pinter 1983.
Taborsky, Edward. *President Edvard Beneš: Between East and West, 1938–1948*. Stanford, CA: Hoover Institution Press 1981.
Tasso, Antonio. *Italia e Çroazia*. Macerata: San Giuseppe 1967.
Toma, Peter A. and Ivan Volgyes. *Politics in Hungary*. San Francisco: W.H. Freeman and Co. 1977.

Tomasevich, Jozo. *The Chetniks*. Stanford, CA: Stanford University Press 1975.

Váli, Ferenc A. *Rift and Revolt in Hungary: Nationalism versus Communism*. Cambridge, MA: Harvard University Press 1961.

Vardys, V. Stanley, ed. *Lithuania under the Soviets: Portrait of a Nation, 1940–65*. New York: Praeger 1965.

– *The Catholic Church, Dissent and Nationality in Soviet Lithuania*. Boulder, CO: East European Monographs 1978.

Vucinich, Wayne S., ed. *Contemporary Yugoslavia: Twenty Years of Socialist Experiment*. Berkeley: University of California Press 1969.

Webb, Leicester C. *Church and State in Italy, 1947–1957*. Melbourne: Melbourne University Press 1958.

Weigel, George. *The Final Revolution: The Resistance Church and the Collapse of Communism*. New York: Oxford University Press 1992.

Wheeler-Bennett, Sir John, and Anthony Nicholls. *The Semblance of Peace: The Political Settlement after the Second World War*. London: Macmillan 1972.

Whitfield, Stephen J. *The Culture of the Cold War*. Baltimore: Johns Hopkins University Press 1991.

Whitnah, Donald R., and Edgar L. Erickson. *The American Occupation of Austria: Planning and Early Years*. Westport, CT: Greenwood Press 1985.

Wiggers, Richard D. "Competing Bureaucracies: The Selection of Bishop Aloisius Muench as Apostolic Visitator to Germany, 1945–1947." Manuscript, Georgetown University 1996.

Wills, Garry. *Nixon Agonistes: The Crisis of the Self-Made Man*. Boston: Houghton Mifflin 1969.

Wilson, Duncan. *Tito's Yugoslavia*. Cambridge: Cambridge University Press 1979.

Wolff, Richard J. *Between Pope and Duce: Catholic Students in Fascist Italy*. New York: Peter Lang 1990.

Wolff, Robert Lee. *The Balkans in Our Time*. Cambridge, MA: Harvard University Press 1974.

Zahn, Gordon C. *German Catholics and Hitler's Wars: A Study in Social Control*. New York: E. P. Dutton & Co. 1969.

Zuccotti, Susan. *Under His Very Windows: The Vatican and the Holocaust in Italy*. New Haven: Yale University Press 2000.

THE PRESS

Catholic Action
La Croix
Le Monde
New York Herald Tribune
New York Times

Osservatore Romano
The Tablet
Time
The Times (London)
Washington Star

Index

Hungarian Workers' party, 213

Hungary, 21, 23, 31–2, 60, 98, 112–20, 131, 166, 193, 203–4, 209–14, 238, 244–5, 250, 258; aftermath of the Holy Office decree, 251; arrest and trial of Mindszenty, 226–9; Catholic division over republic, 118–19; centenary of 1848 revolution, 212; church as remaining independent institution, 211, 217; church-state agreement, 251, 255, 258; Communist control in, 209, 213–14; creation of republic, 116–17; education reforms, 213–14; elections of August 1947, 209–10; elections of 1945, 115; fusion of Communists and Social Democrats, 213; government appeal to clergy, 119; land reform in, 32; peace treaty, 209; relations with the Holy See, 115–16, 119–20, 209, 212–13; revolution of 1956, 258–9

Hurley, Bishop Joseph P., 95, 162, 169, 222, 234–5; appointment to Yugoslavia, 159

hydrogen bomb, 255

Iliev, Minister of Cults, 225

India, 229

In Multiplicibus (1948), 252

International Congress on European Union, 251

Ireland, 172, 198

Islam, 45, 241, 244

Israel, 220, 252–4

Istrian peninsula, 104, 164

Italian peace treaty, 182

Italian Red Cross, 168

Italian Working Women, convention, 91

Italy, 22–3, 26–31, 60, 63, 73, 75, 77, 81, 83–4, 88, 90–3, 97, 103–5, 134, 157–8, 163, 169, 180–1, 185, 226, 236, 238, 241, 243, 248, 252–3, 257; and arrest of Mindszenty, 229; Catholic mobilization, 194–6; election of June 1946, 135–7; election of April 1948, 5, 191, 196–202, 207, 215, 217–18, 242; peace treaty, 155, 156, 160, 164–7; republican constitution, 165, 177–9, 195–6; social transformation, 260–1; and Stepinac trial, 172

Janosi, Professor Joseph, 119

Jasnagora Monastery, 121

Jerusalem, 220, 252–4

Jesuits, 260

Jewish Codex, 35

Jews, 25, 32, 48, 61–2, 127–8, 175

John XXIII: see Roncalli, Angelo

John Paul II, Pope (Karol Wojtyla), 3, 6, 8, 9, 23

Jordan, 252

Justinian Marina, Archbishop, 244; election of, 222; attack on Catholic Church, 223–5

Kaas, Monsignor Ludwig, 142

Kaller, Bishop Maximilian, 152

Karpov, G.G., 69, 71

Kaspar, Cardinal Karel, 173

Katyn Forest massacre, 78

Kennedy, John Fitzgerald, 66

Khrushchev, Nikita, 68, 258, 261

Kielce pogrom, 127–8

Korean War, 256–7

Kostelnyk, Dr Gabriel, 99

Kovacs, Bela, 209

Krek, Ambassador, 171

Labour party (Great Britain), 239

Lackovic, Father Stephen, 171

La Croix, 134, 172–3, 202; and the division of Europe, 185; and domestic politics, 183–4

Lane, Bliss, 128

Lateran Agreements, 26–7, 83, 92, 158, 165, 177–8

Latin America, 167, 172, 254

Latin-rite Catholics, 36, 50–2, 67–8, 99–100, 223–5, 247; of Pauline origin, 52, 225

Latvia, 68, 100

Lavitrano, Cardinal, 31

Law for Religious Sects (Bulgaria), 226

Legitimism, 31, 113

lend-lease, 56, 75

Leningrad, 12

Leo XIII, Pope (Gioacchino Pecci), 188

Liénart, Cardinal, 134, 202

Life magazine, 56

Lithuania, 68, 100

Lombardi, Father Riccardo, 196–7, 200–1

Luxmoore, Jonathan, 8

Maglione, Cardinal Luigi, 25, 28, 42, 65, 79–80

Maisky, Ivan, 80

Maixner, M., 173, 214

Maliq Bey Bushati, 46

Malone, Senator George W., 192

Mao Zedong, 218

Marcone, Abbot Ramiro, 49